Chico & Rita

Javier Mariscal and Fernando Trueba

SELF
MADE
HERO

CHICO & RITA
A graphic novel by Javier Mariscal and Fernando Trueba
© FERNANDO TRUEBA PRODUCCIONES CINEMATOGRÁFICAS
S.A., ESTUDIO MARISCAL S.A., MAGIC LIGHT PICTURES
(CHICO & RITA) IOM LIMITED 2010

This graphic novel is based on the original movie script
"Chico & Rita" by Fernando Trueba and Ignacio Martinez de Pisón

Adaptation: Marcello Quintanilha
Artwork: Carlos Arroyo, Alberto Guitián, Jose Carlos Jiménez,
Joan Masip, Bojan Pantelic, Esteve Puig
Colour Direction: Nuri Puig
Colour: Blanca Cumellas, Sole Garzón, Eva López, Mercè Mora,
Elena Nájar, Eila Rigau, Anna Rönsch, Montse Sanz
Graphic Assistance: Réka Darvas, Fernanda Palazuelos
Lettering: Josema Urós
Layout Designer: Cristina Rakosnik

First published in English in 2011
by SelfMadeHero
A division of Metro Media Ltd
5 Upper Wimpole Street
London W1G 6BP
www.selfmadehero.com

© 2011 SelfMadeHero

Translated from the Spanish edition by Howard Curtis
c/o Parkbench Publishing Services

Editorial Assistant and Lettering: Lizzie Kaye
Marketing Director: Doug Wallace
Publishing Director: Emma Hayley

A CIP record for this book is available from the British Library

ISBN: 978-1-906838-29-4

10 9 8 7 6 5 4 3 2 1

Printed and bound in China

Fernando Trueba PC Estudio Mariscal Magic Light Pictures CinemaNX Isle of Man Film
in association with Televisión Española SA Hanway Films Televisió de Catalunya SA
with the participation of MesFilms Televisió de Catalunya SA
with the participation of the Ministerio de Cultura -ICAA ICIC

Institut Català de les Indústries Culturals
with the support of ICO Instituto de Crédito Oficial ICF Institut Català de Finances
A film by Fernando Trueba and Javier Mariscal
Principal Music Bebo Valdés Line Producer Angélica Huete Head of Production Albert García Vila
Co-producer Andrew Fingret Associate Producer Antonio Resines

Executive Producers Steve Christian and Marc Samuelson
Produced by Santiago Errando, Cristina Huete, Martin Pope and Michael Rose
Written by Fernando Trueba and Ignacio Martinez de Pisón
Directed by Fernando Trueba, Javier Mariscal and Tono Errando

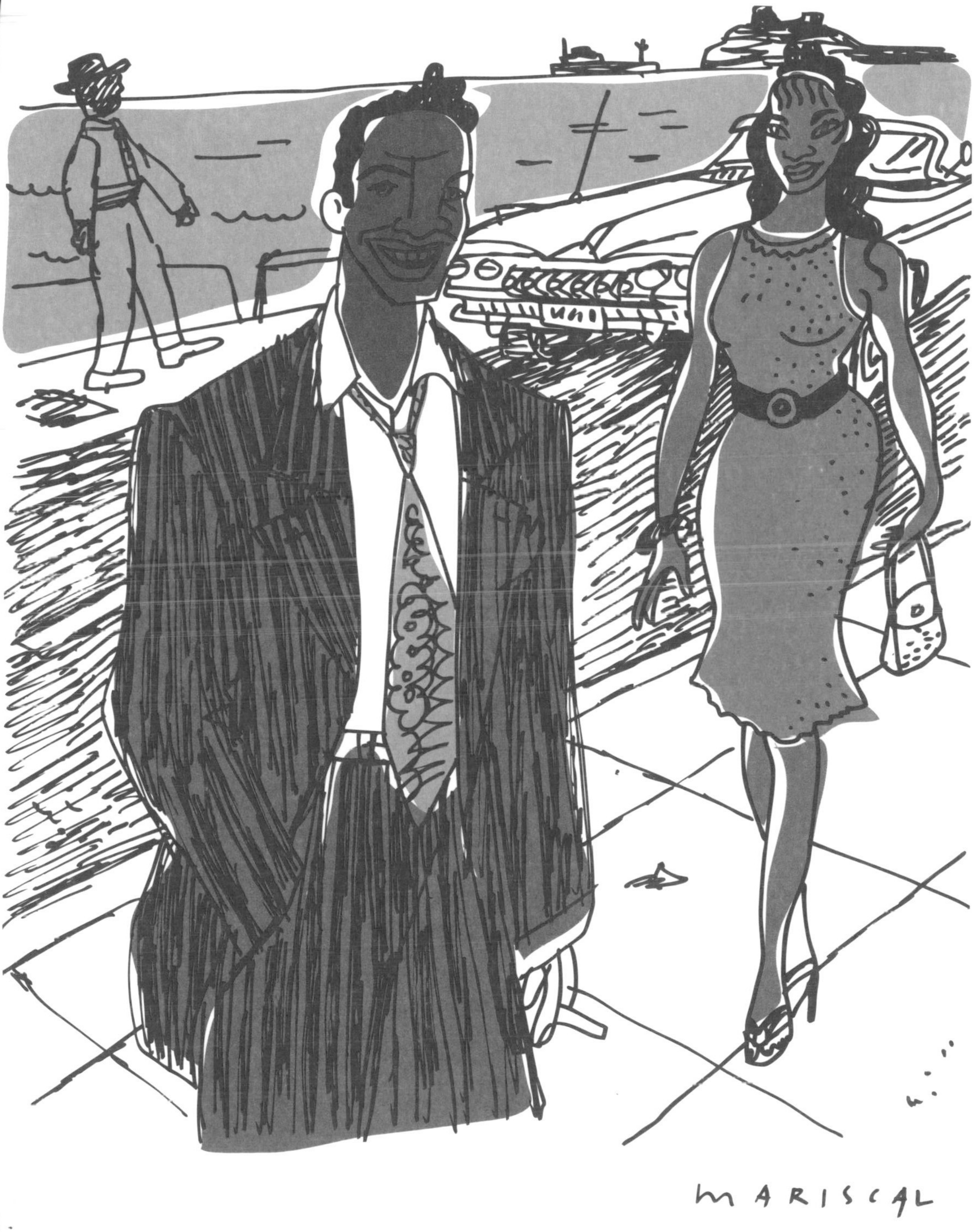
MARISCAL

Chico & Rita
Javier Mariscal for SelfMadeHero 2011

For Bebo

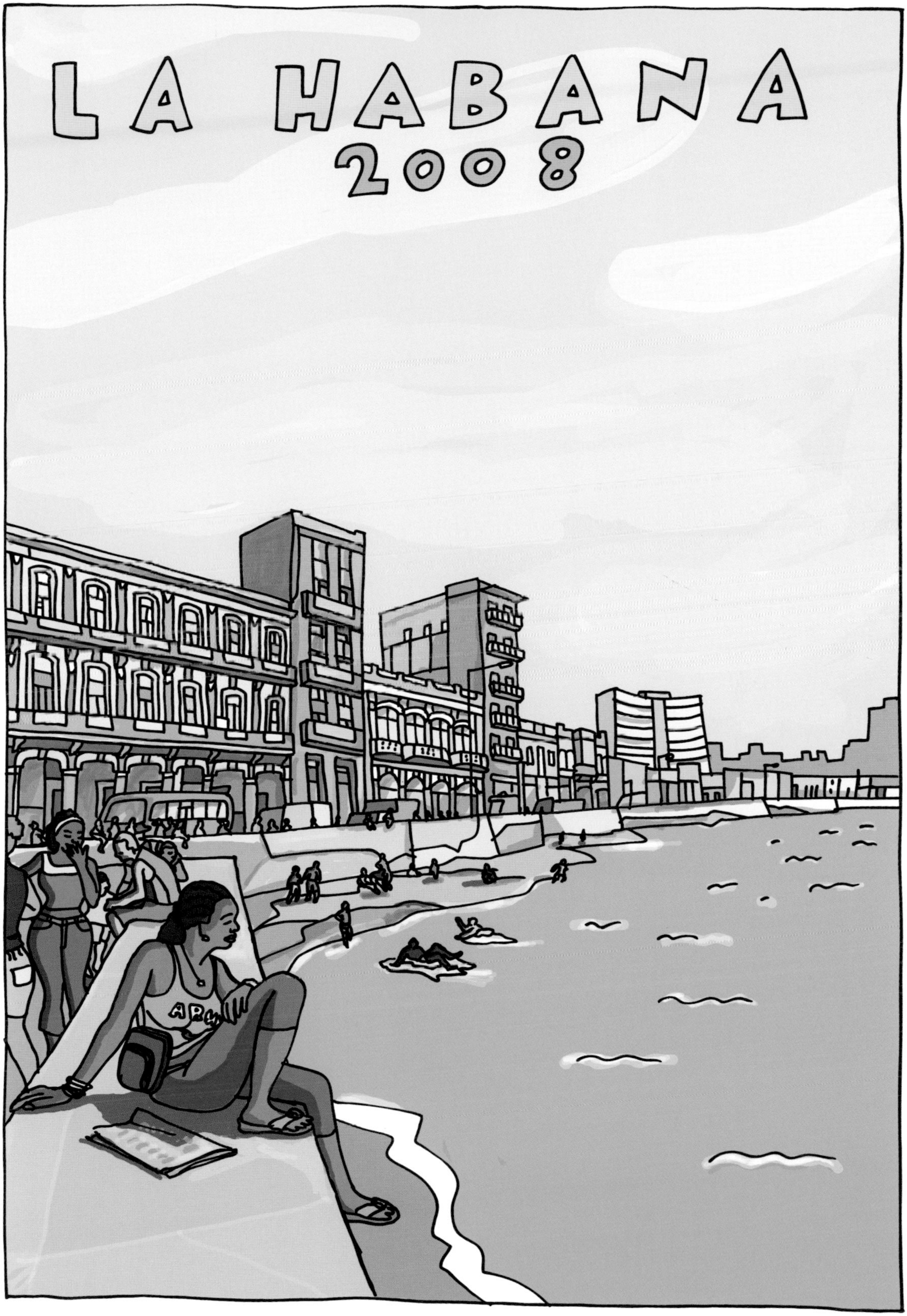
LA HABANA
2008

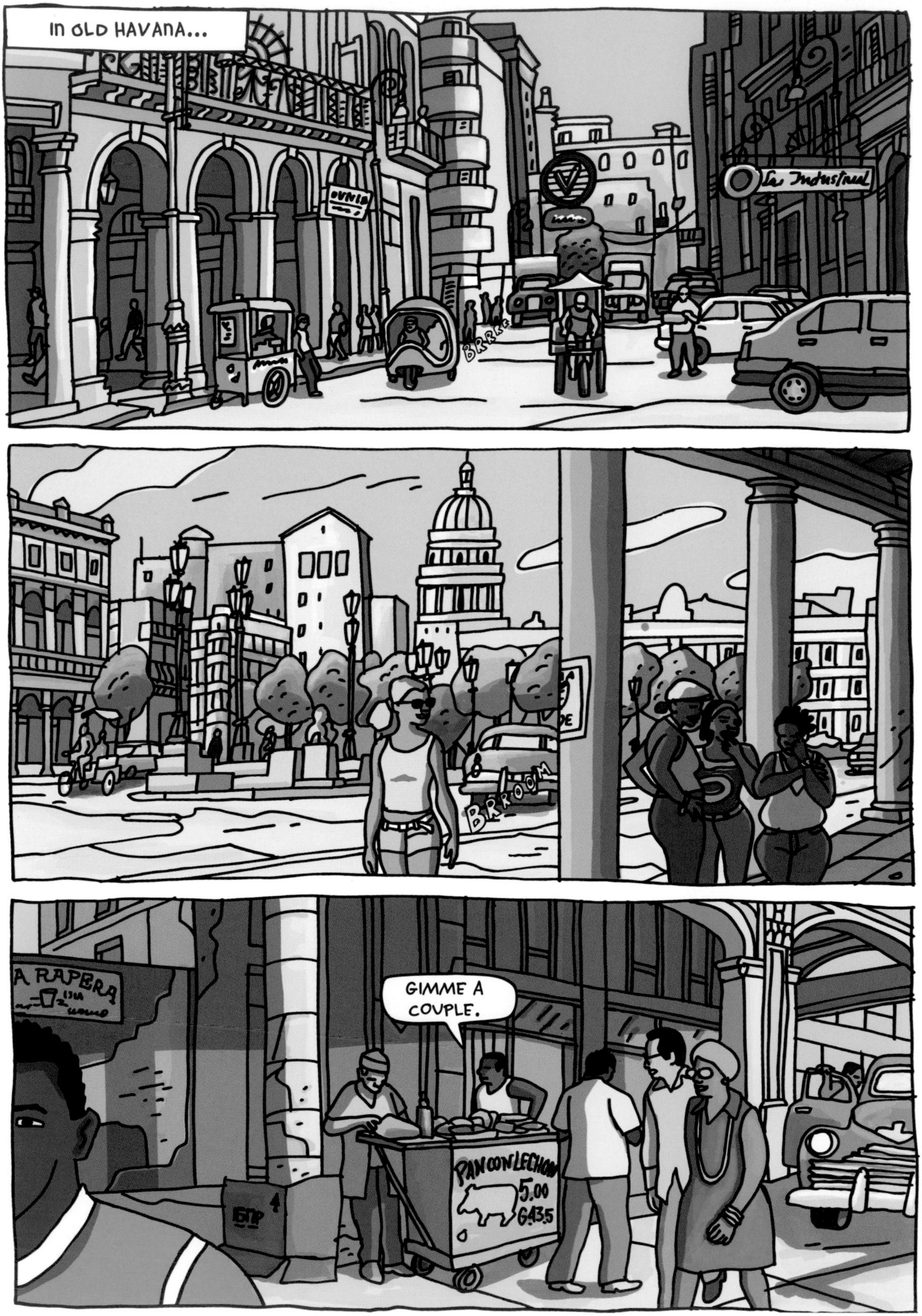
IN OLD HAVANA...
La Industrial
BRRRR
BRROOM
A RAPERA
GIMME A COUPLE.
PAN CON LECHON
5.00
G43.5

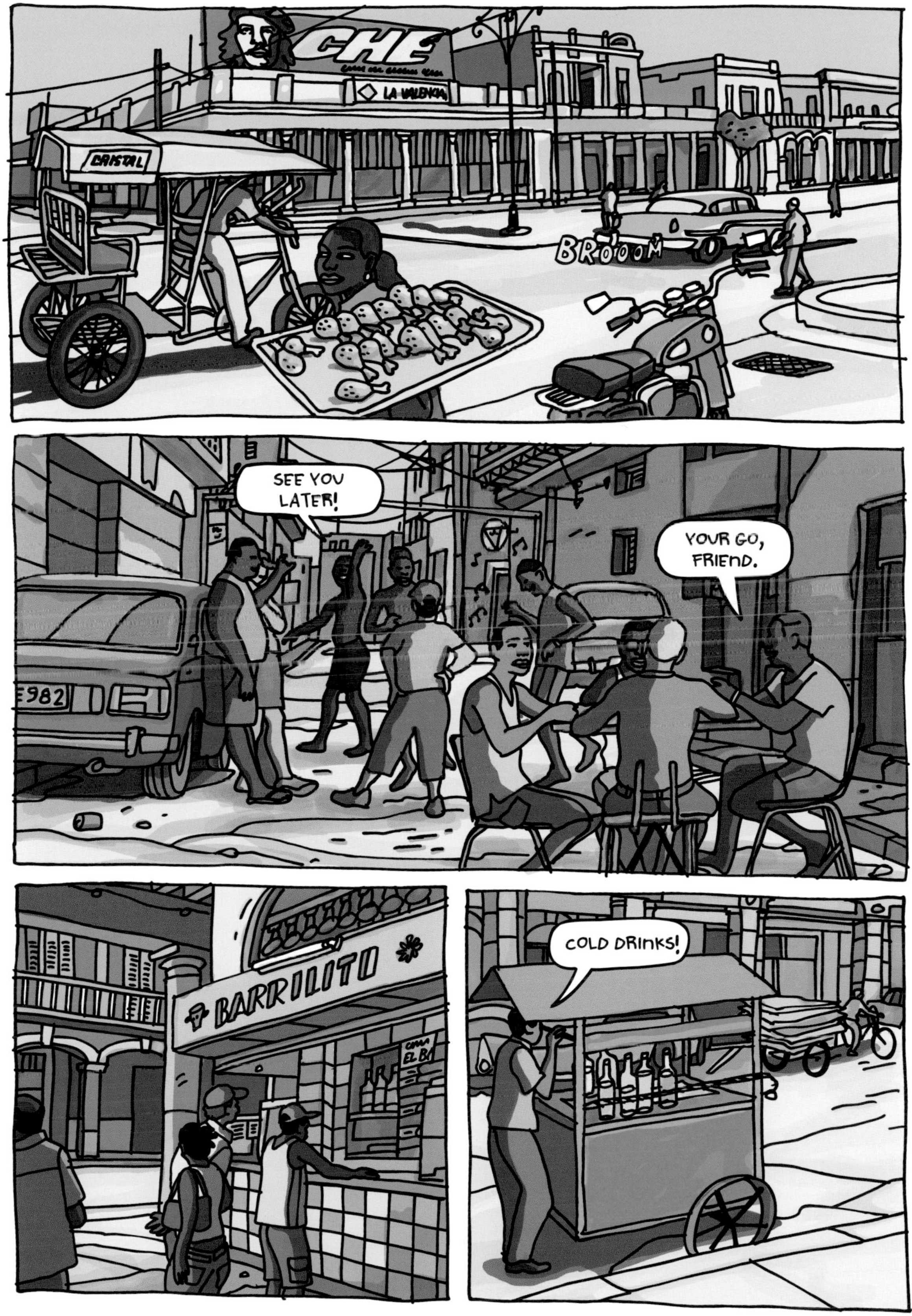
CHE
LA VALENCIA
CRISTAL
BROOOM
SEE YOU LATER!
YOUR GO, FRIEND.
E982
BARRILITO
COLD DRINKS!

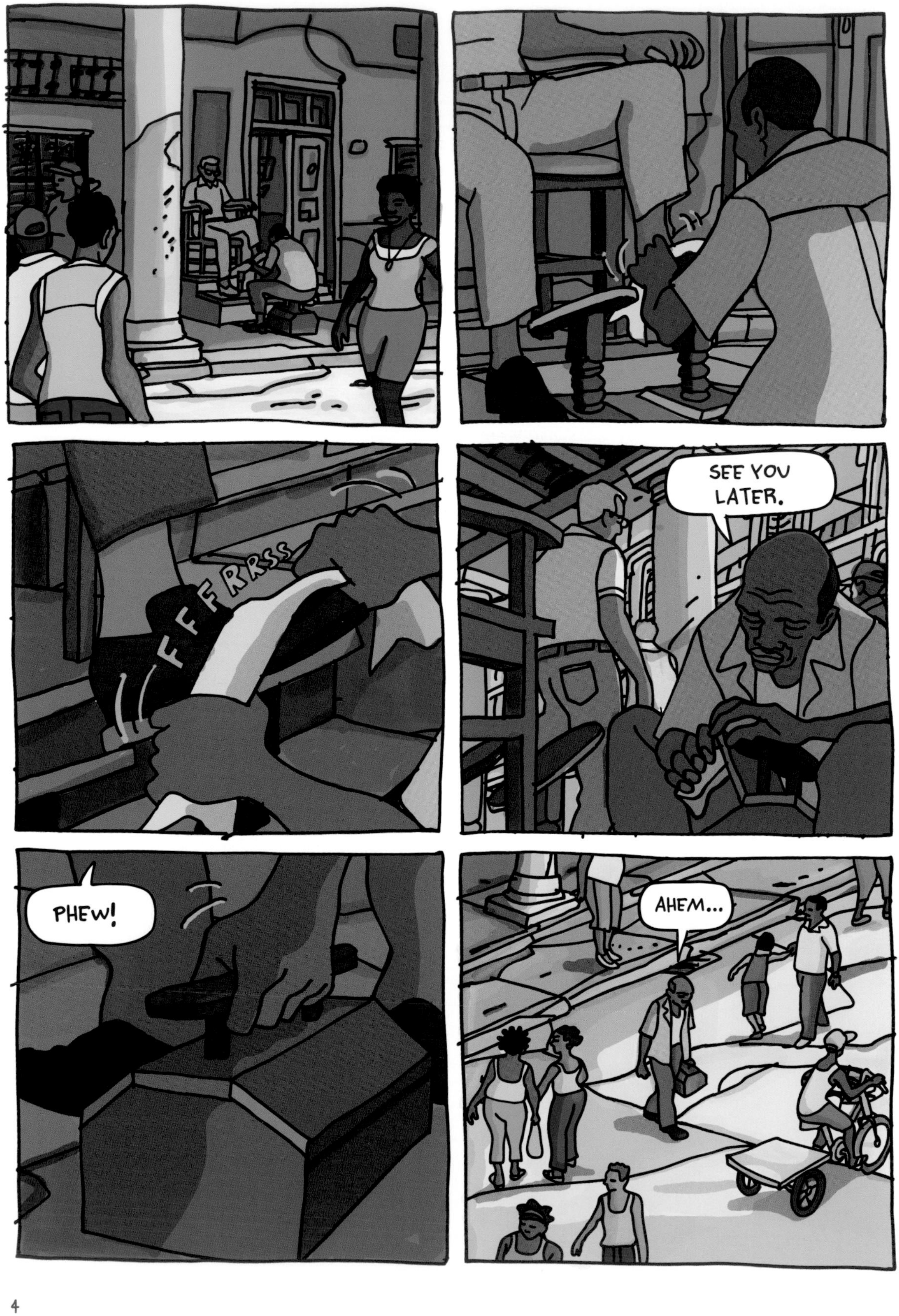
FFFRRSSS
SEE YOU LATER.
PHEW!
AHEM...

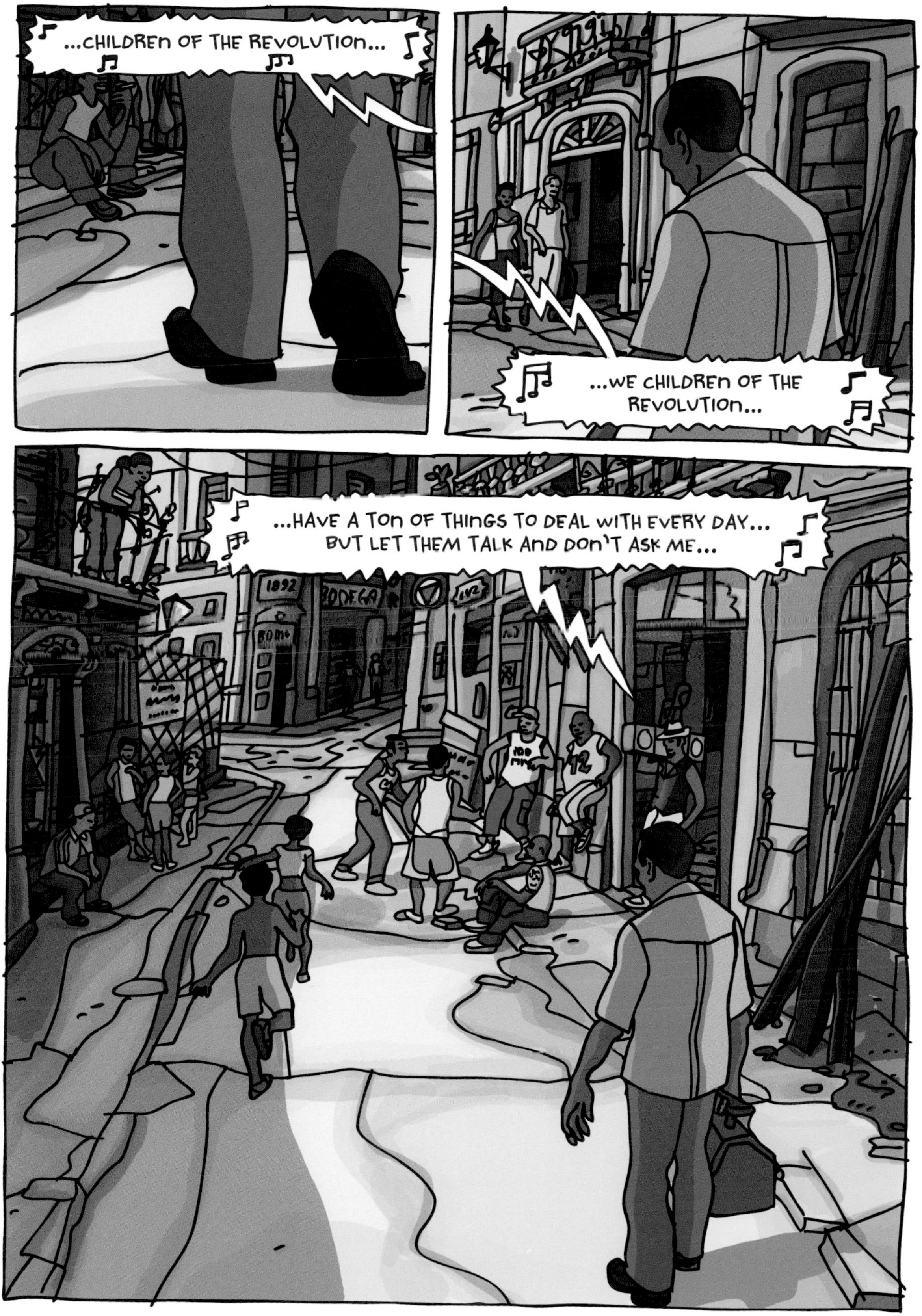
...CHILDREN OF THE REVOLUTION...
...WE CHILDREN OF THE REVOLUTION...
...HAVE A TON OF THINGS TO DEAL WITH EVERY DAY... BUT LET THEM TALK AND DON'T ASK ME...

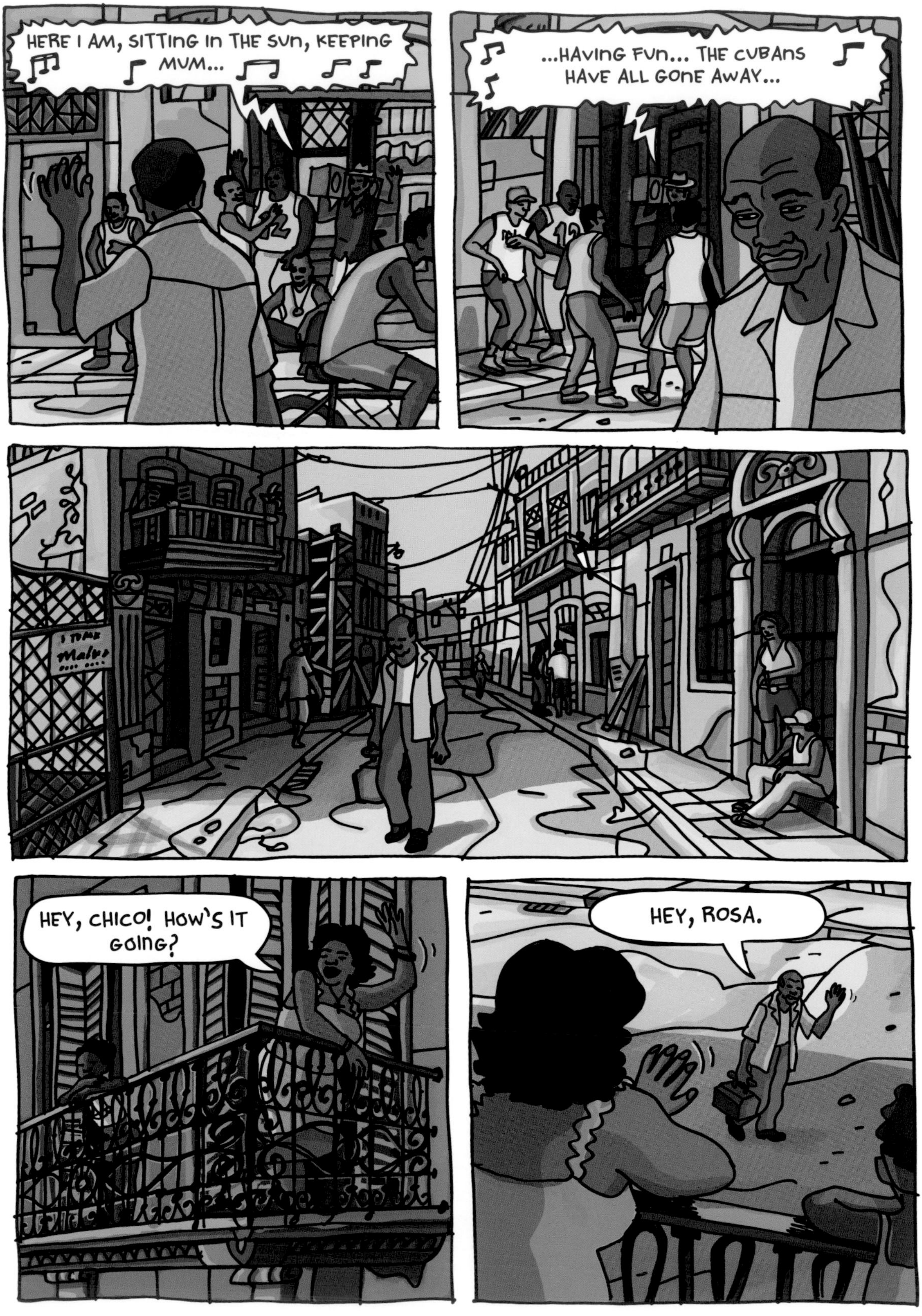
HERE I AM, SITTING IN THE SUN, KEEPING MUM...
...HAVING FUN... THE CUBANS HAVE ALL GONE AWAY...
HEY, CHICO! HOW'S IT GOING?
HEY, ROSA.

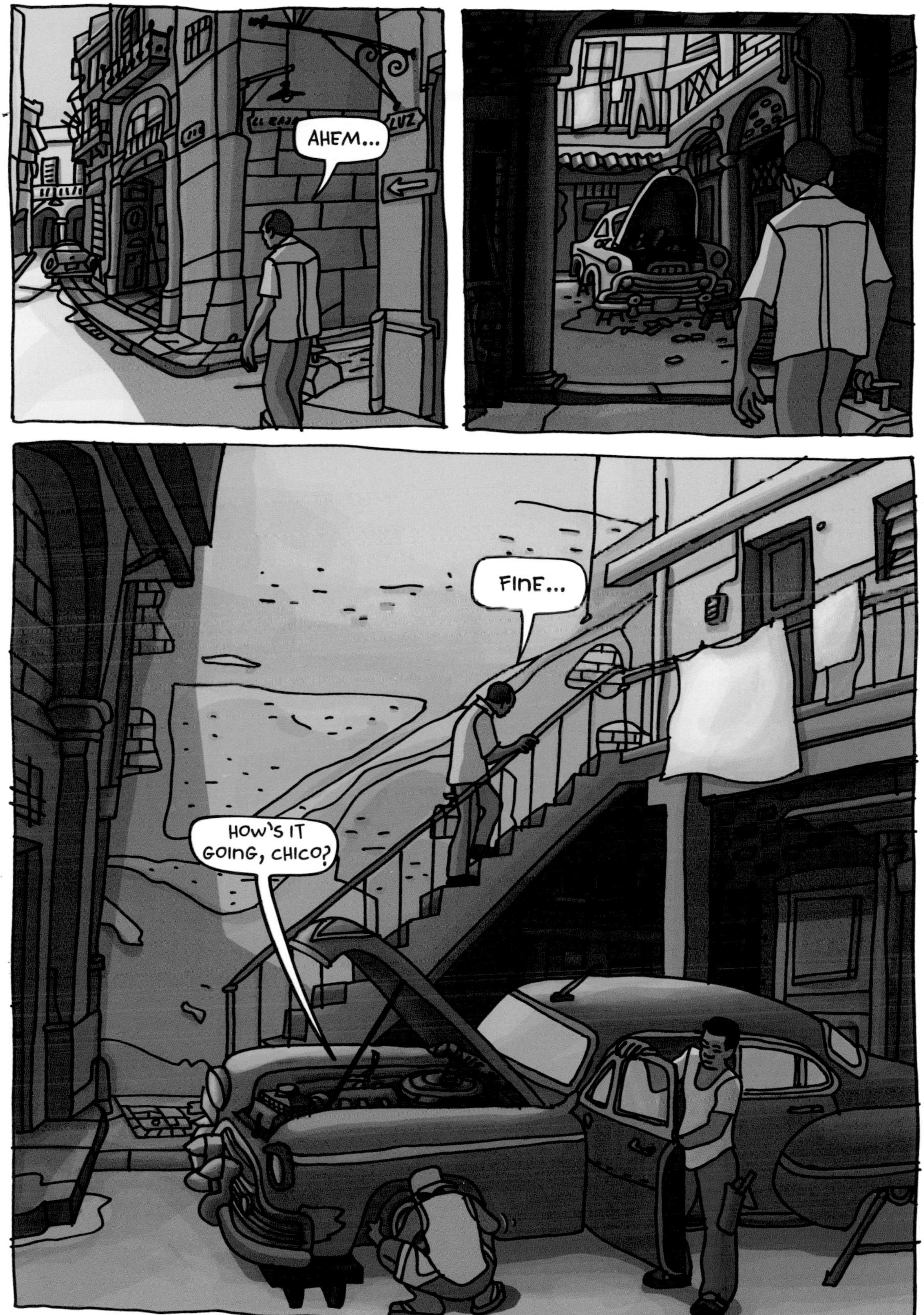
LUZ
AHEM...
HOW'S IT GOING, CHICO?
FINE...

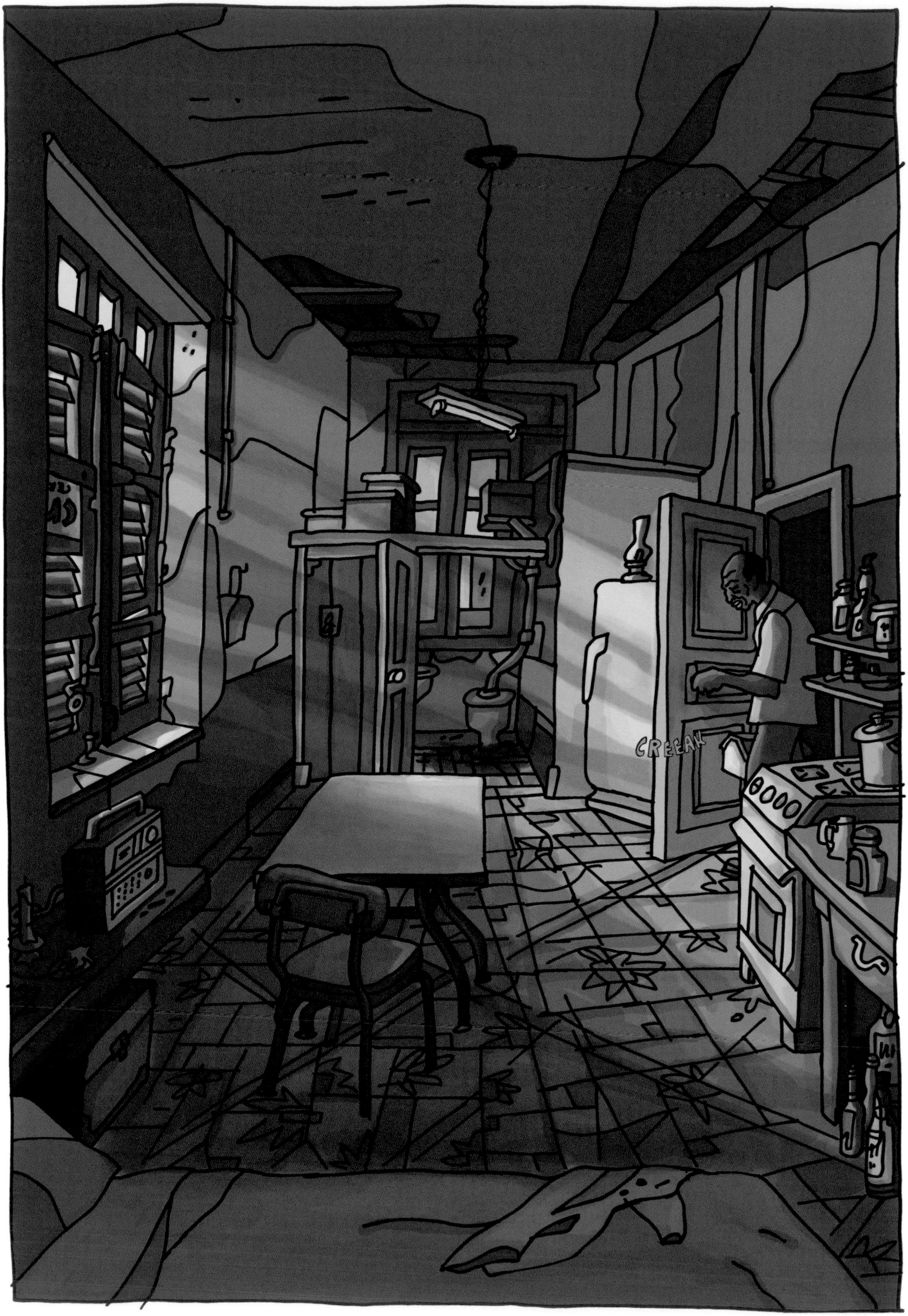
CREEAK

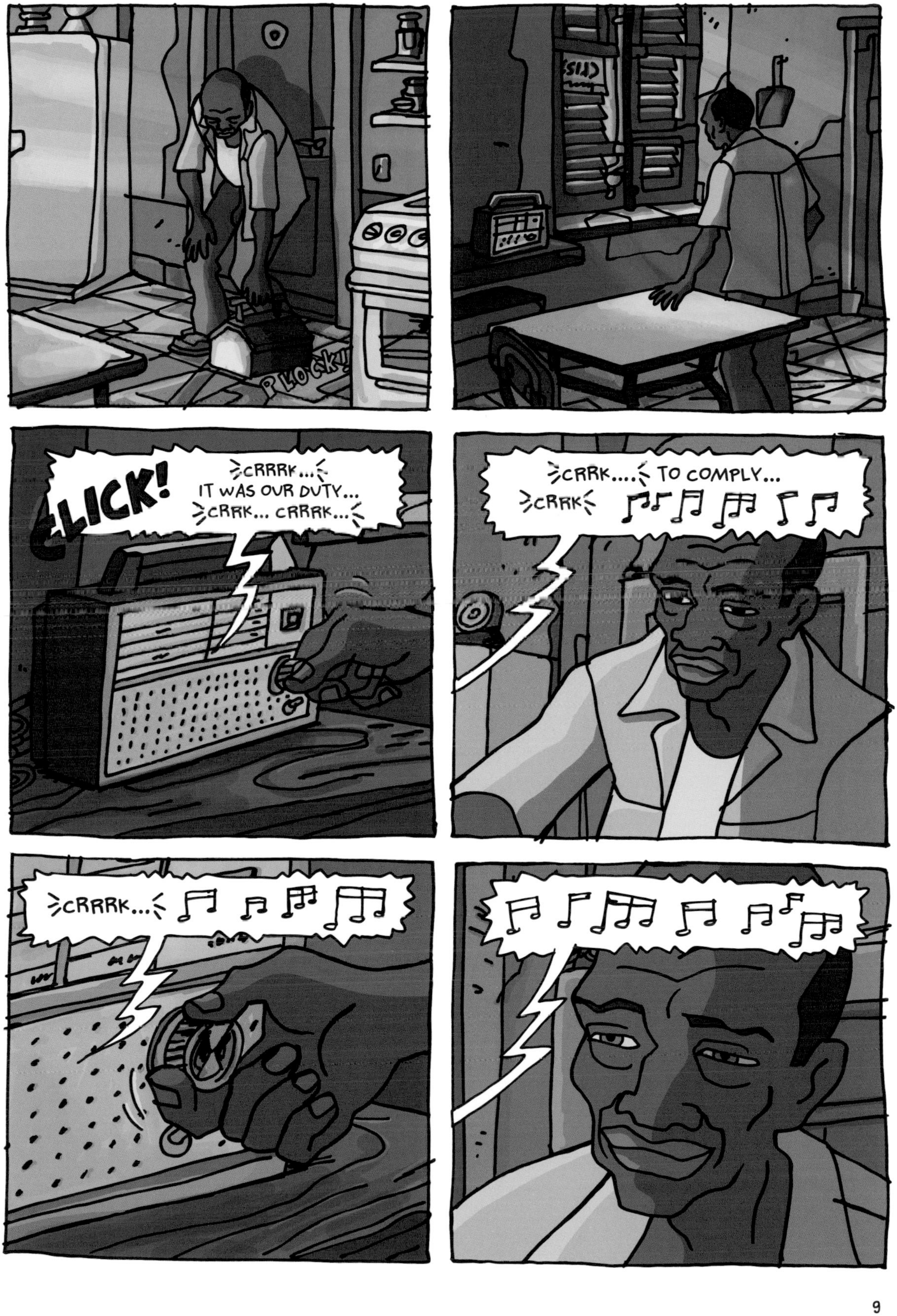
PLOCK!
CLICK!
CRRRK... IT WAS OUR DUTY... CRRK... CRRRK...
CRRK.... TO COMPLY... CRRK
CRRRK...

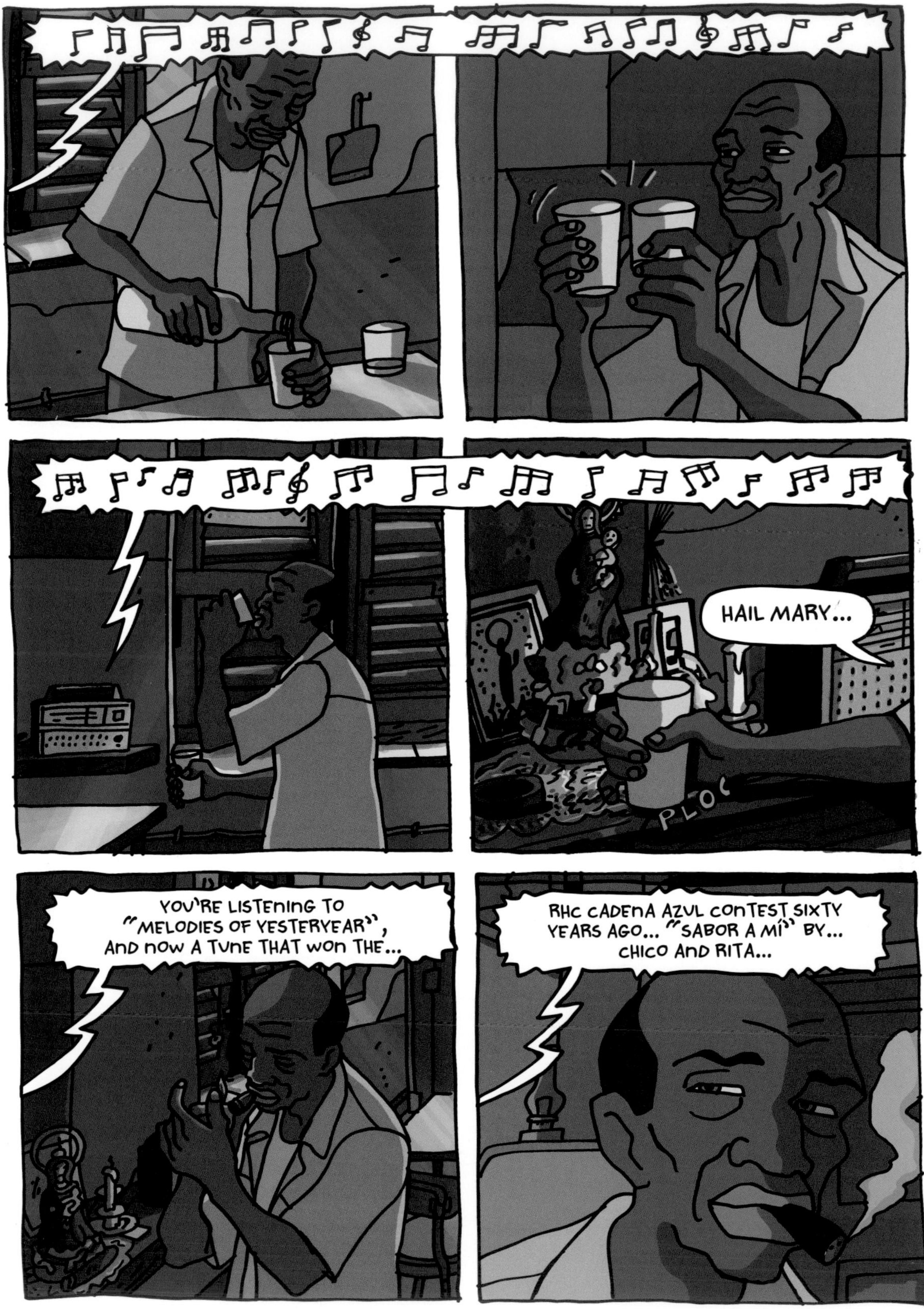
HAIL MARY...
PLOC
YOU'RE LISTENING TO "MELODIES OF YESTERYEAR", AND NOW A TUNE THAT WON THE...
RHC CADENA AZUL CONTEST SIXTY YEARS AGO... "SABOR A MÍ" BY... CHICO AND RITA...

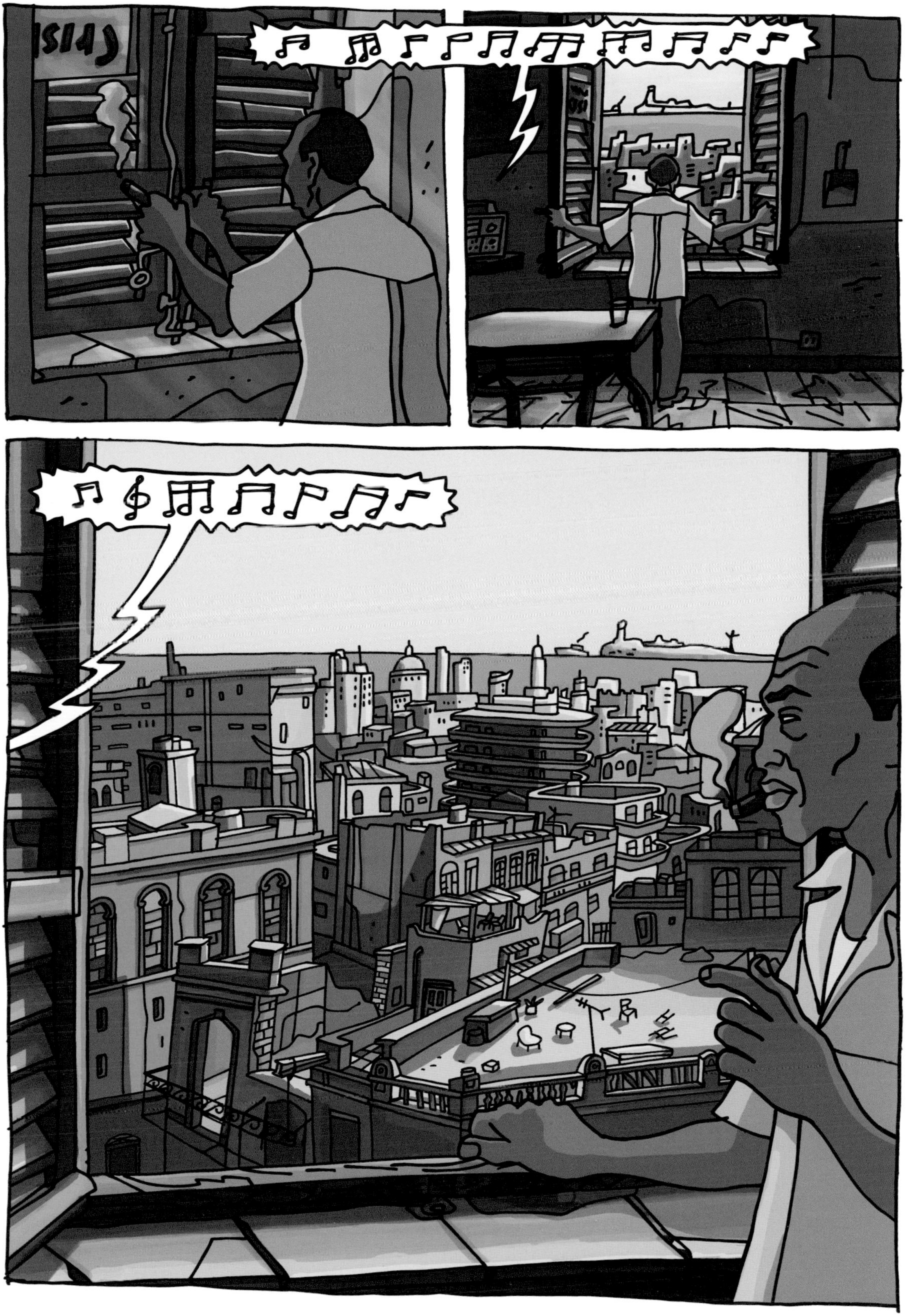

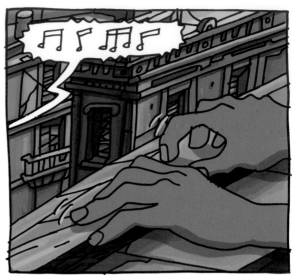

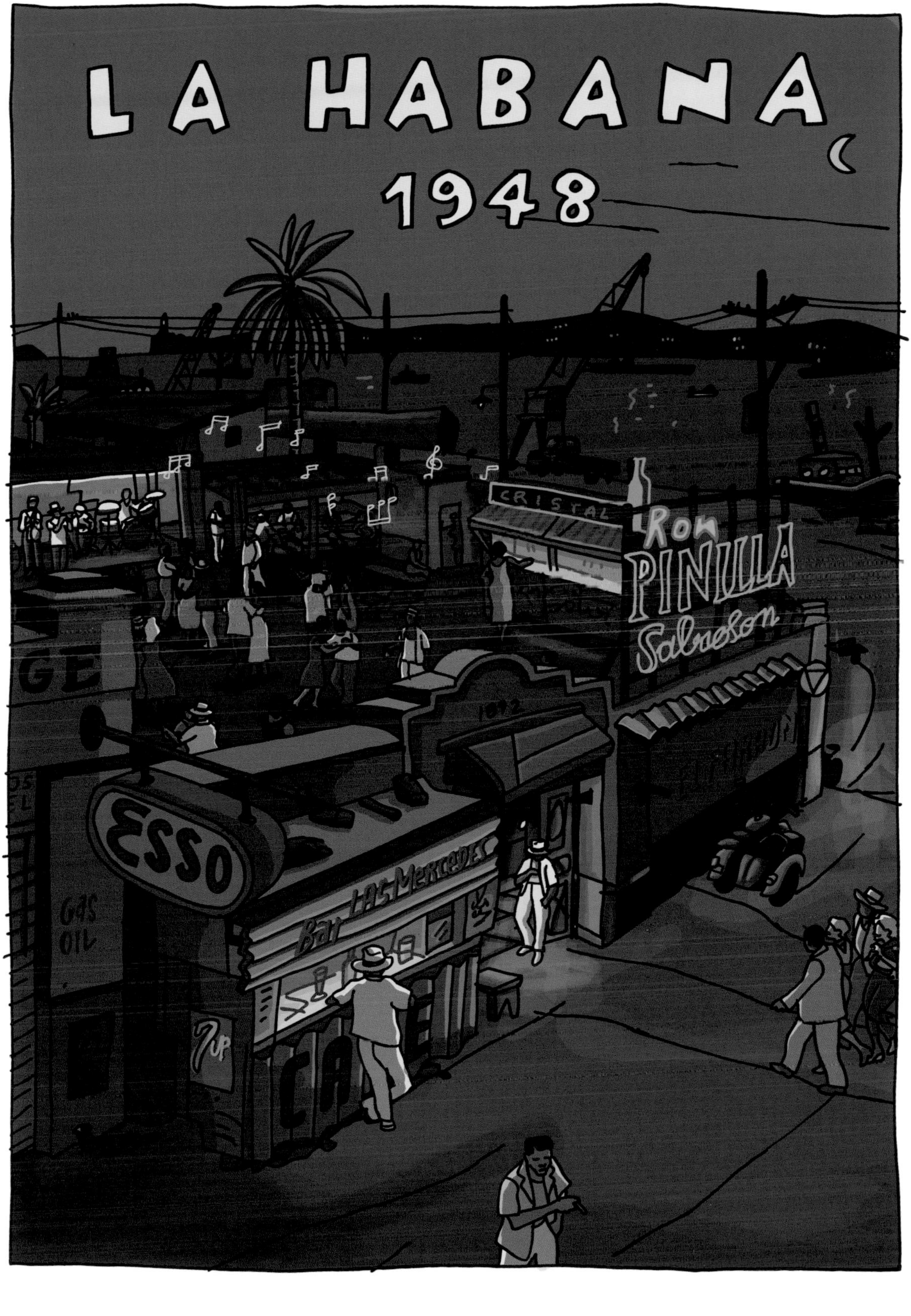
LA HABANA
1948
CRISTAL
Ron
PINILLA
Salvoson
ESSO
Bar LAS Mercedes
GAS
OIL
7up
1892

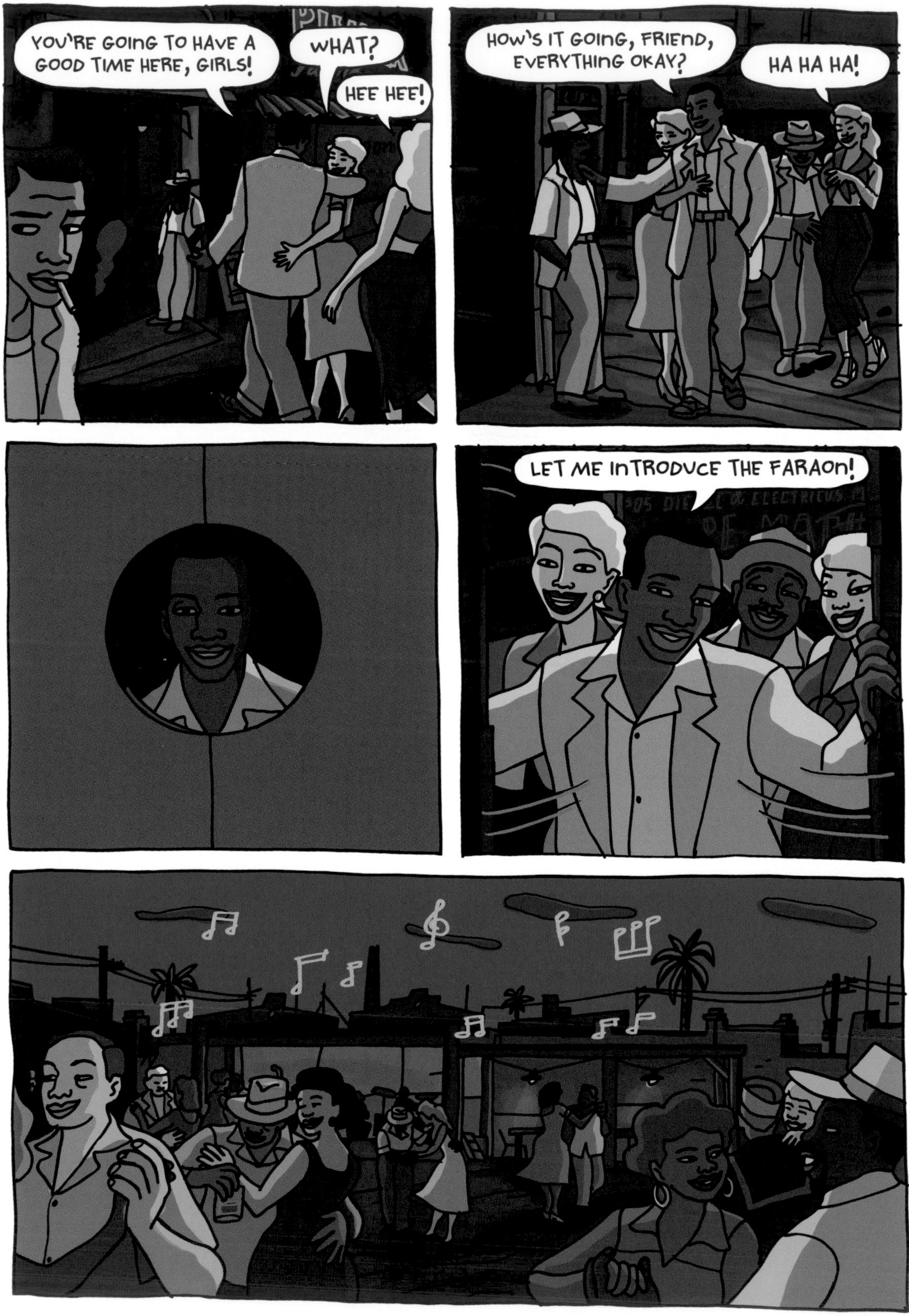
YOU'RE GOING TO HAVE A GOOD TIME HERE, GIRLS!
WHAT?
HEE HEE!
HOW'S IT GOING, FRIEND, EVERYTHING OKAY?
HA HA HA!
LET ME INTRODUCE THE FARAON!

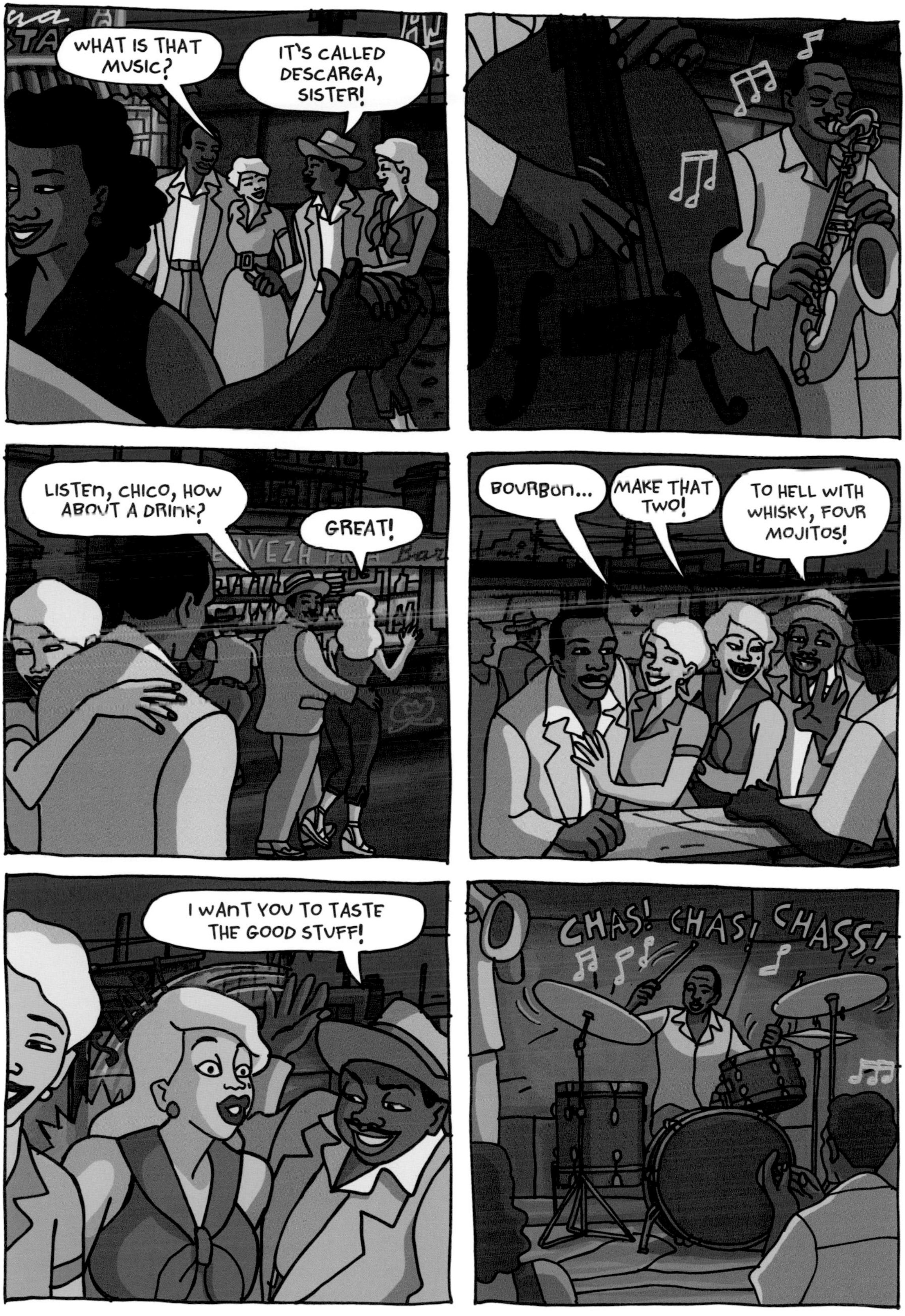
WHAT IS THAT MUSIC?
IT'S CALLED DESCARGA, SISTER!
LISTEN, CHICO, HOW ABOUT A DRINK?
GREAT!
BOURBON...
MAKE THAT TWO!
TO HELL WITH WHISKY, FOUR MOJITOS!
I WANT YOU TO TASTE THE GOOD STUFF!
CHAS! CHAS! CHASS!

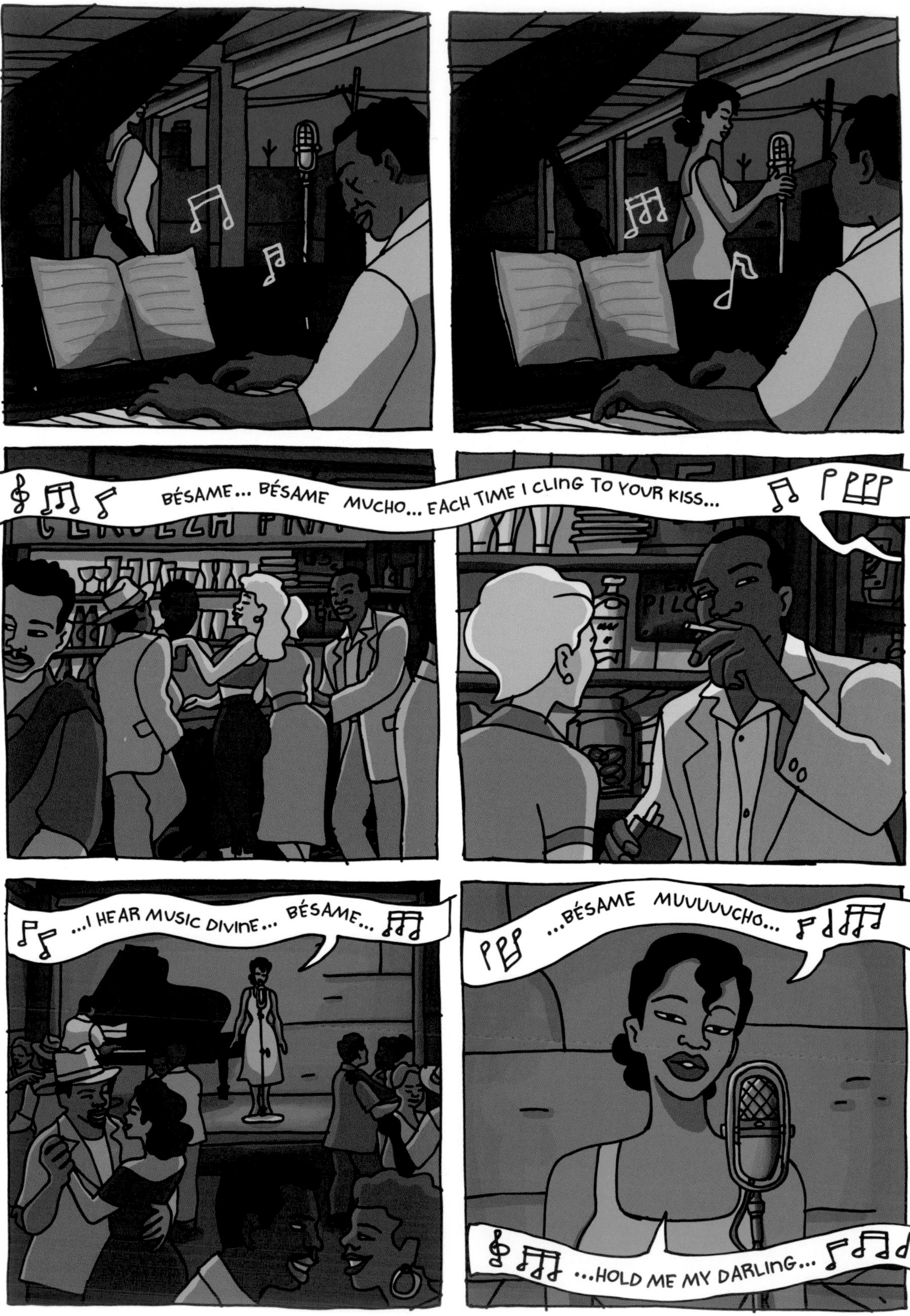
BÉSAME... BÉSAME MUCHO... EACH TIME I CLING TO YOUR KISS...
...I HEAR MUSIC DIVINE... BÉSAME...
...BÉSAME MUUUUUCHO...
...HOLD ME MY DARLING...

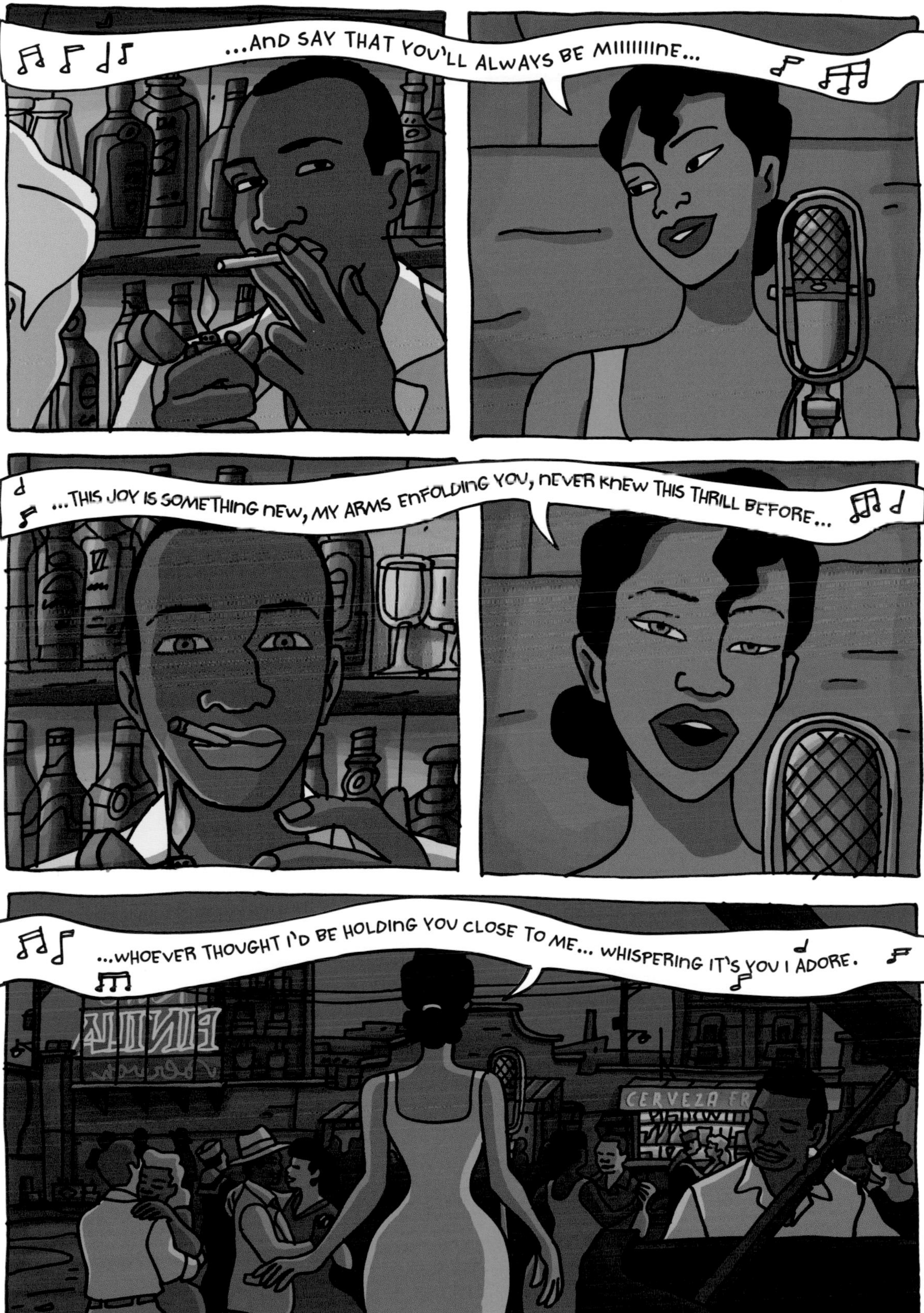
...AND SAY THAT YOU'LL ALWAYS BE MIIIIIIINE...
...THIS JOY IS SOMETHING NEW, MY ARMS ENFOLDING YOU, NEVER KNEW THIS THRILL BEFORE...
...WHOEVER THOUGHT I'D BE HOLDING YOU CLOSE TO ME... WHISPERING IT'S YOU I ADORE.
CERVEZA

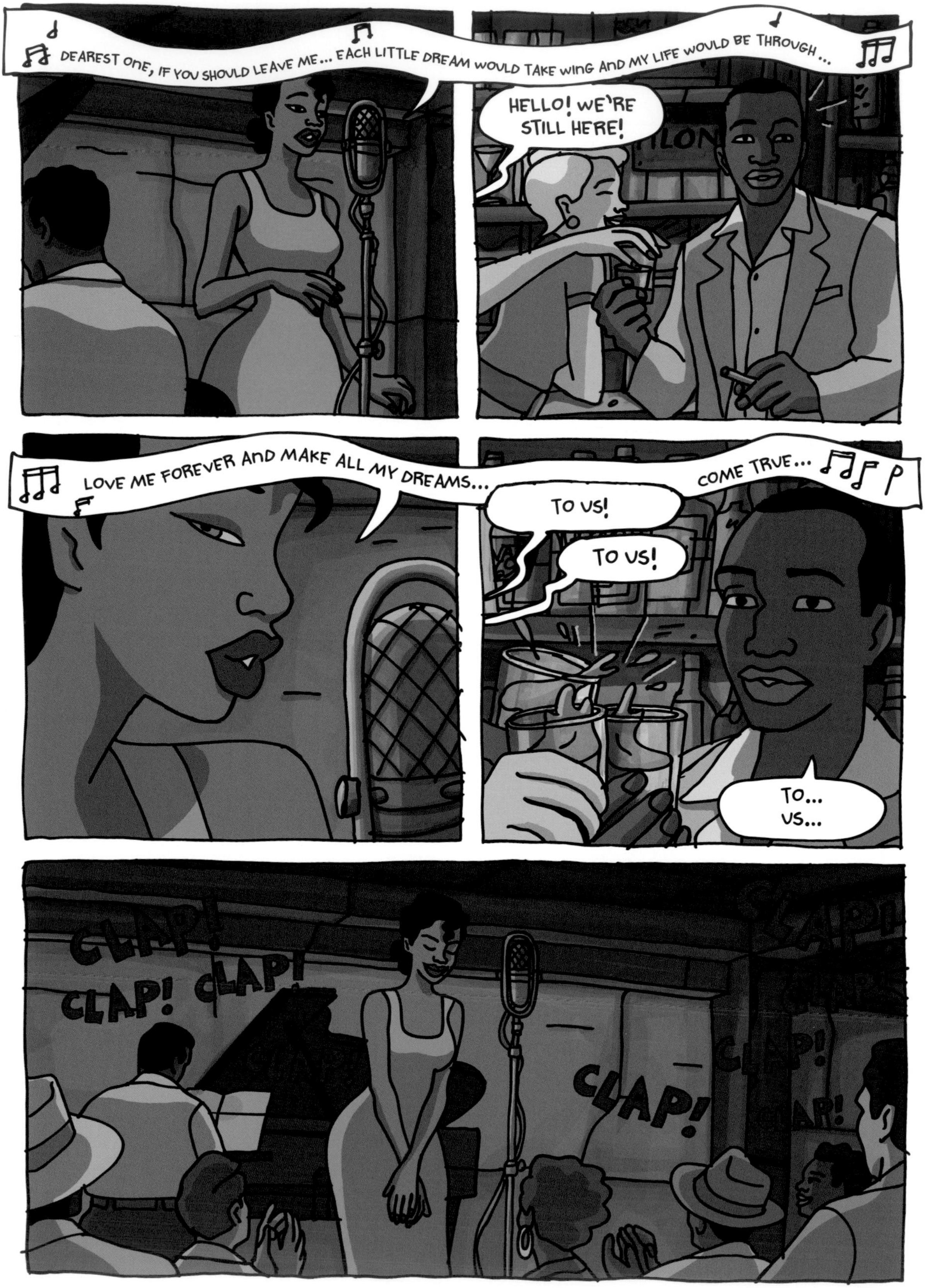
DEAREST ONE, IF YOU SHOULD LEAVE ME... EACH LITTLE DREAM WOULD TAKE WING AND MY LIFE WOULD BE THROUGH...
HELLO! WE'RE STILL HERE!
LOVE ME FOREVER AND MAKE ALL MY DREAMS...
COME TRUE...
TO US!
TO US!
TO... US...
CLAP!
CLAP! CLAP!
CLAP!
CLAP!
CLAP!

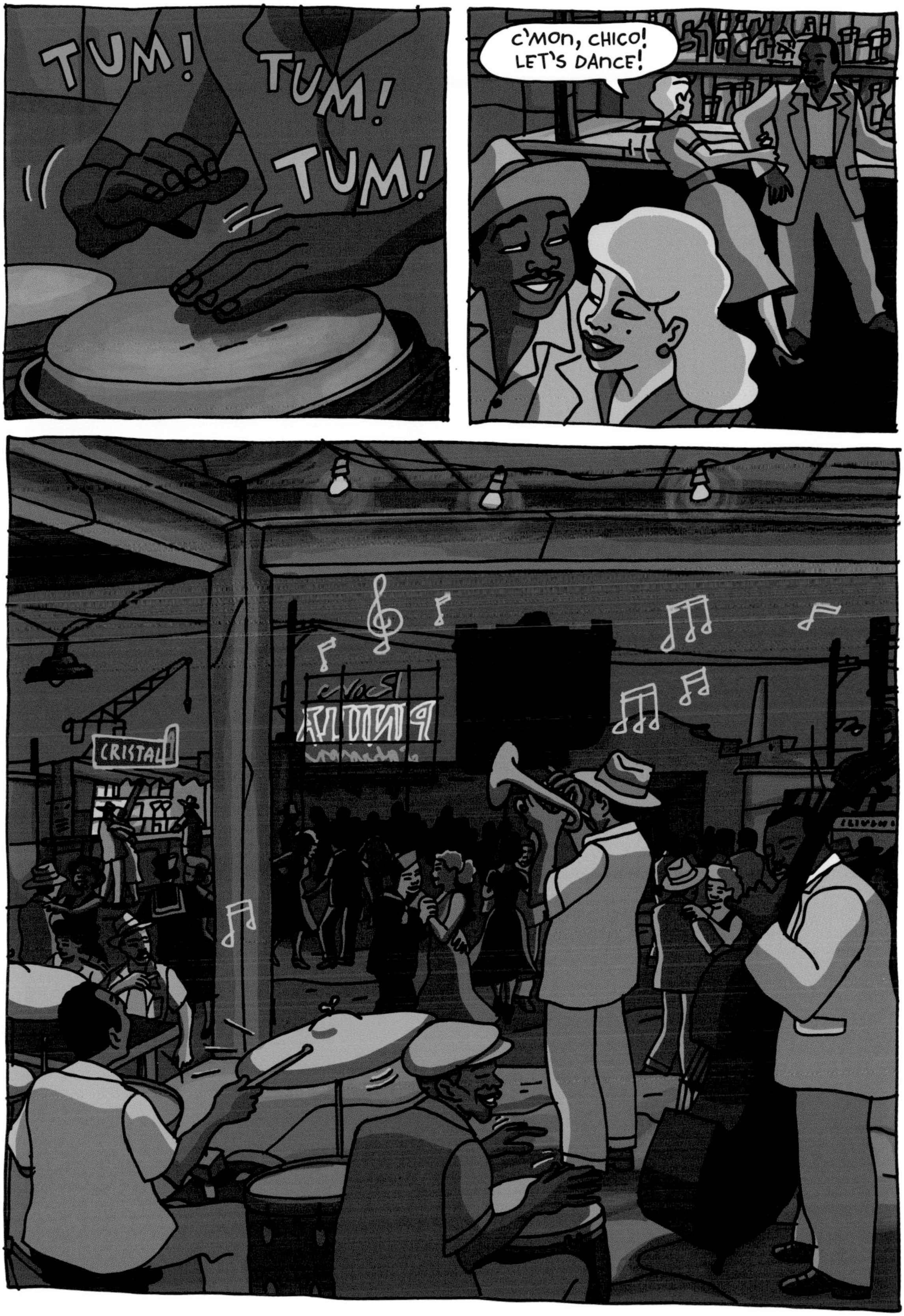
TUM!
TUM!
TUM!
C'MON, CHICO! LET'S DANCE!
CRISTAL

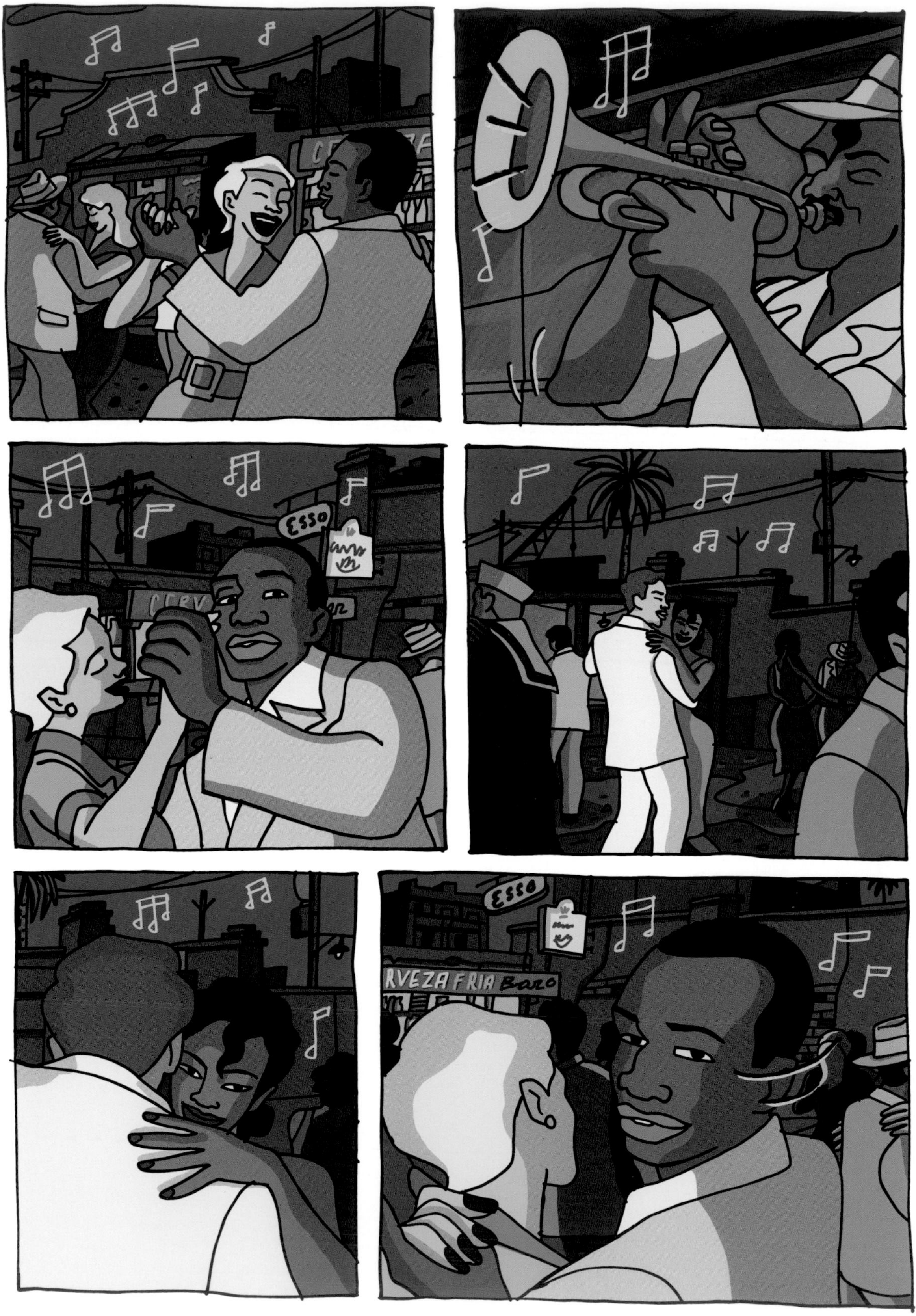
ESSO
ESSO
RVEZA FRIA

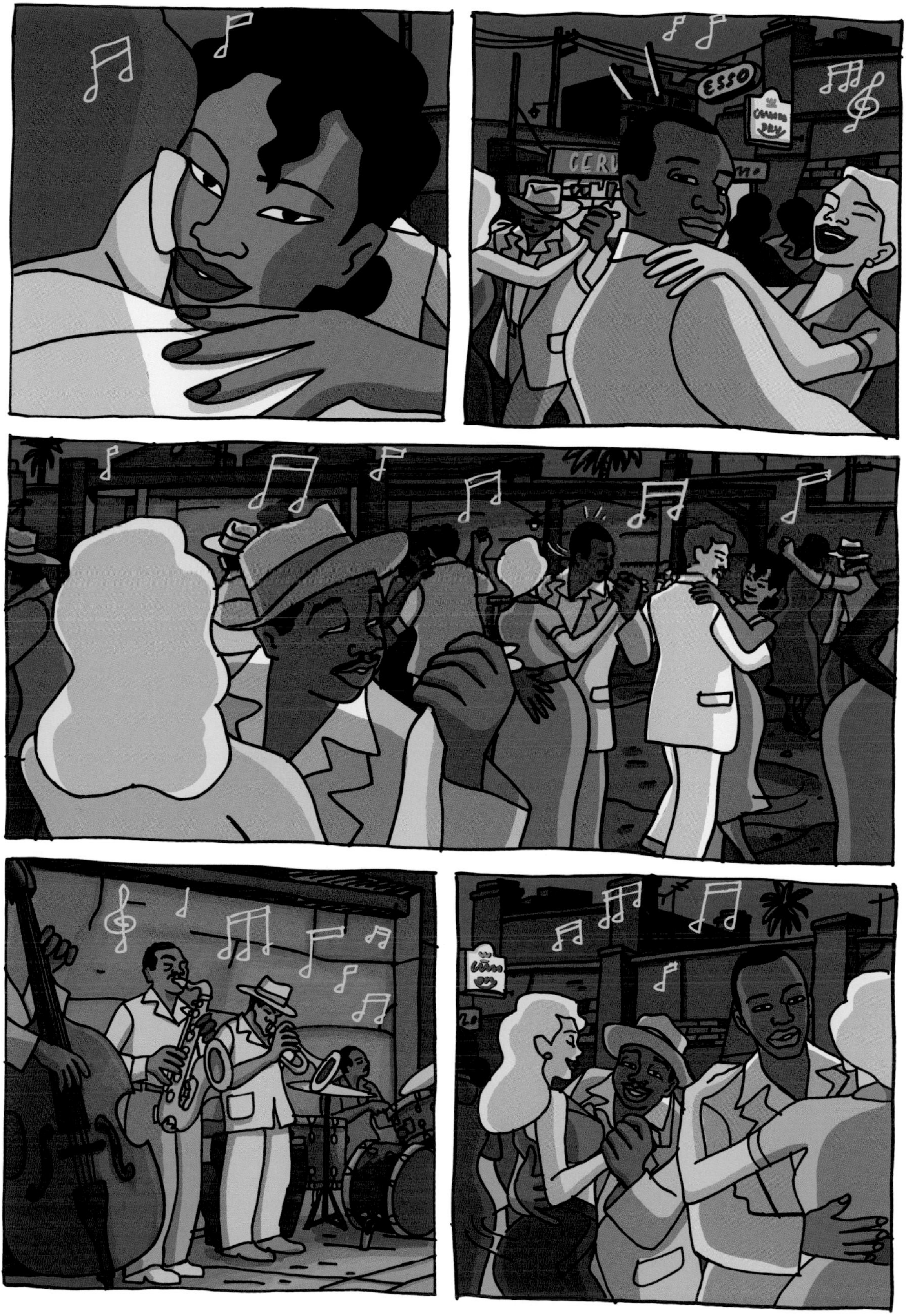
ESSO

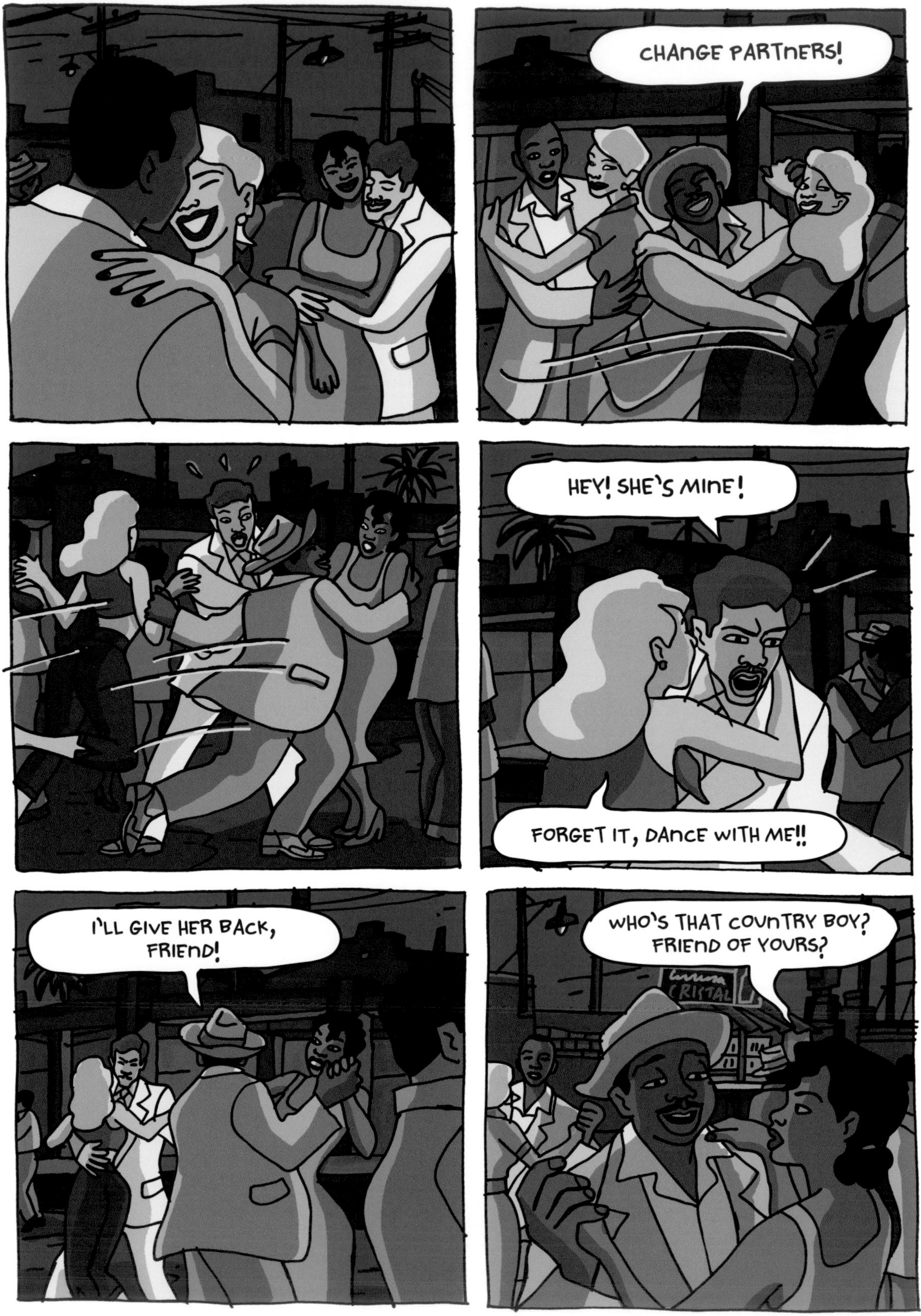
CHANGE PARTNERS!
HEY! SHE'S MINE!
FORGET IT, DANCE WITH ME!!
I'LL GIVE HER BACK, FRIEND!
WHO'S THAT COUNTRY BOY? FRIEND OF YOURS?

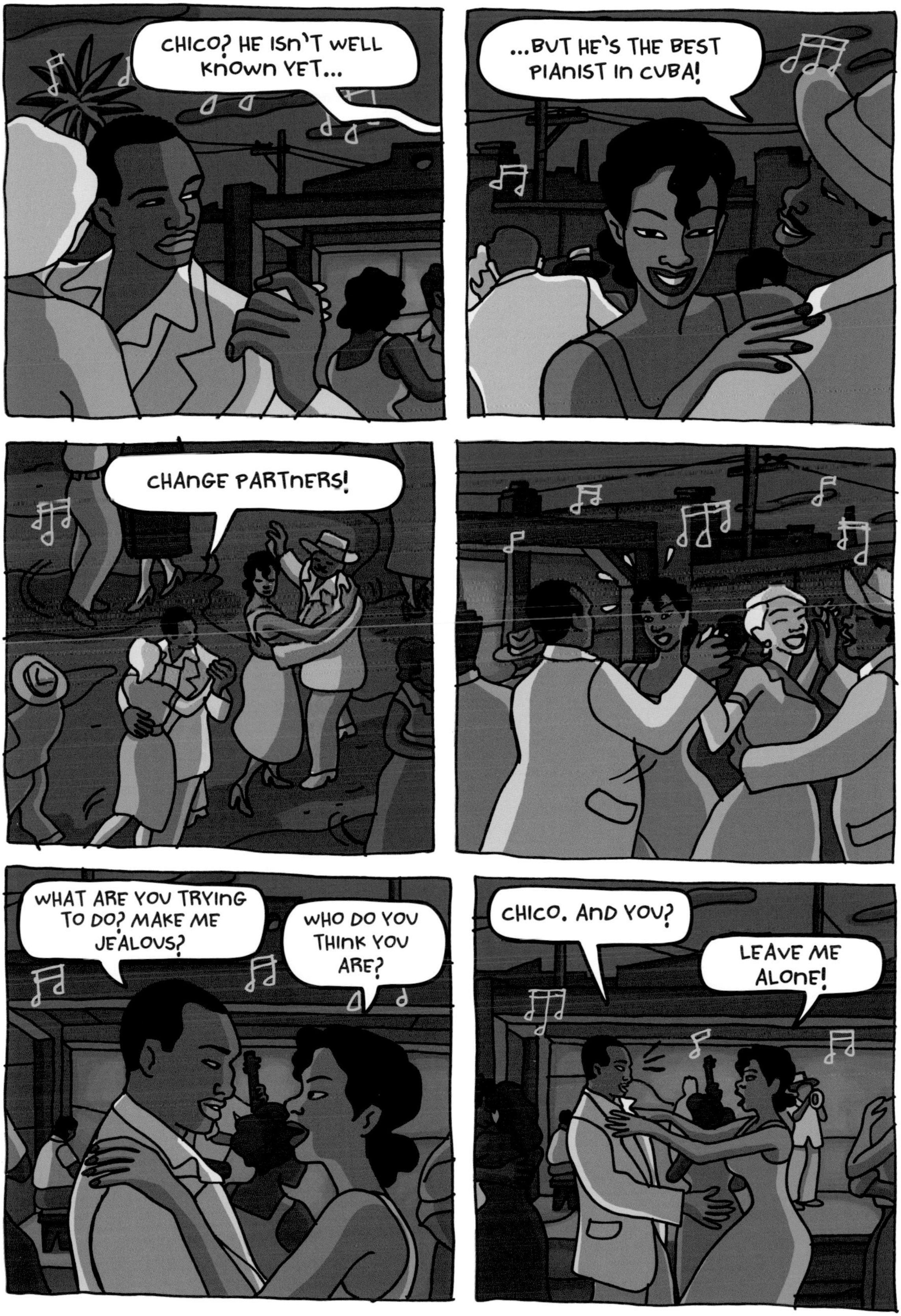
CHICO? HE ISN'T WELL KNOWN YET...
...BUT HE'S THE BEST PIANIST IN CUBA!
CHANGE PARTNERS!
WHAT ARE YOU TRYING TO DO? MAKE ME JEALOUS?
WHO DO YOU THINK YOU ARE?
CHICO. AND YOU?
LEAVE ME ALONE!

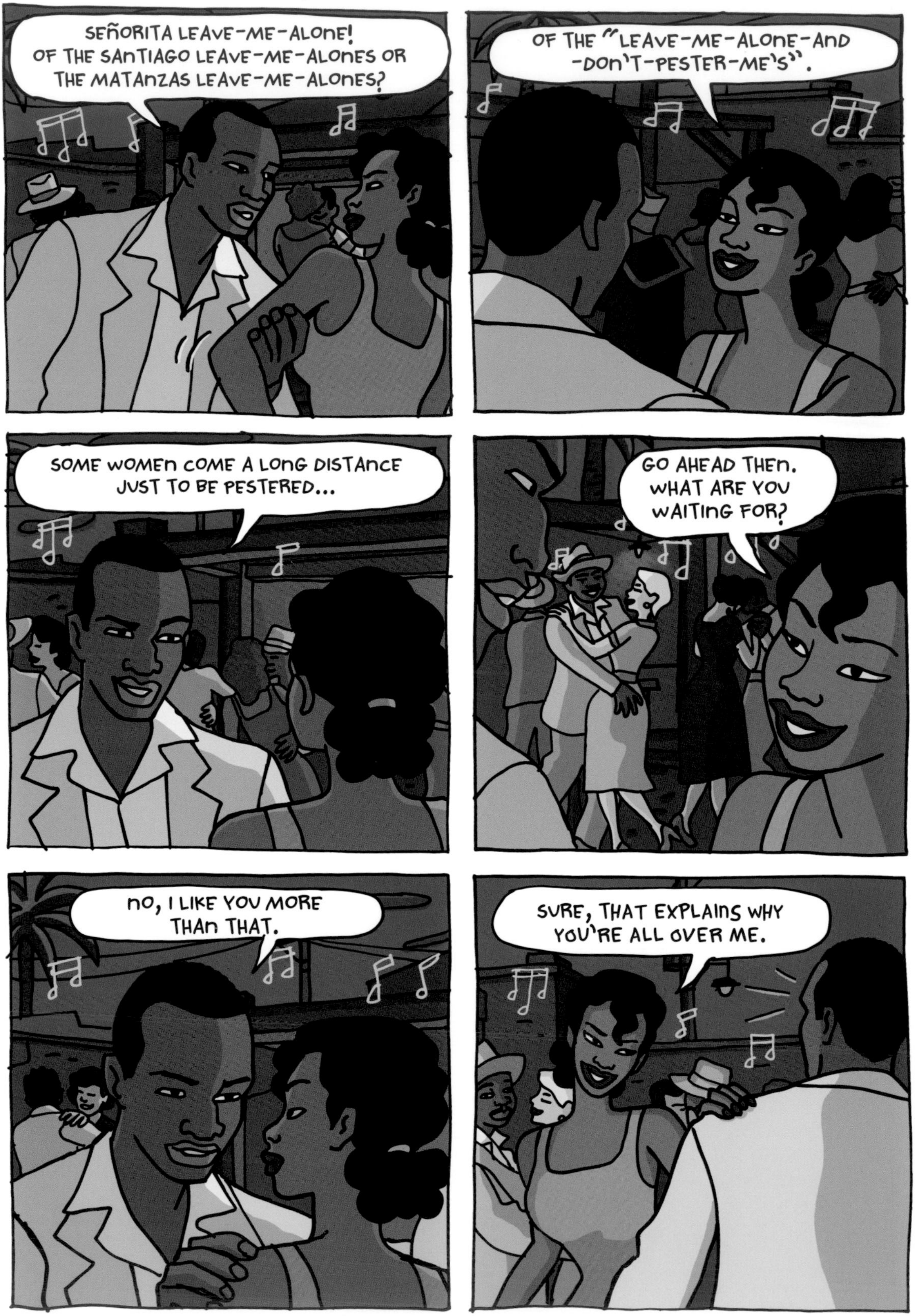
SEÑORITA LEAVE-ME-ALONE! OF THE SANTIAGO LEAVE-ME-ALONES OR THE MATANZAS LEAVE-ME-ALONES?
OF THE "LEAVE-ME-ALONE-AND-DON'T-PESTER-ME'S".
SOME WOMEN COME A LONG DISTANCE JUST TO BE PESTERED...
GO AHEAD THEN. WHAT ARE YOU WAITING FOR?
NO, I LIKE YOU MORE THAN THAT.
SURE, THAT EXPLAINS WHY YOU'RE ALL OVER ME.

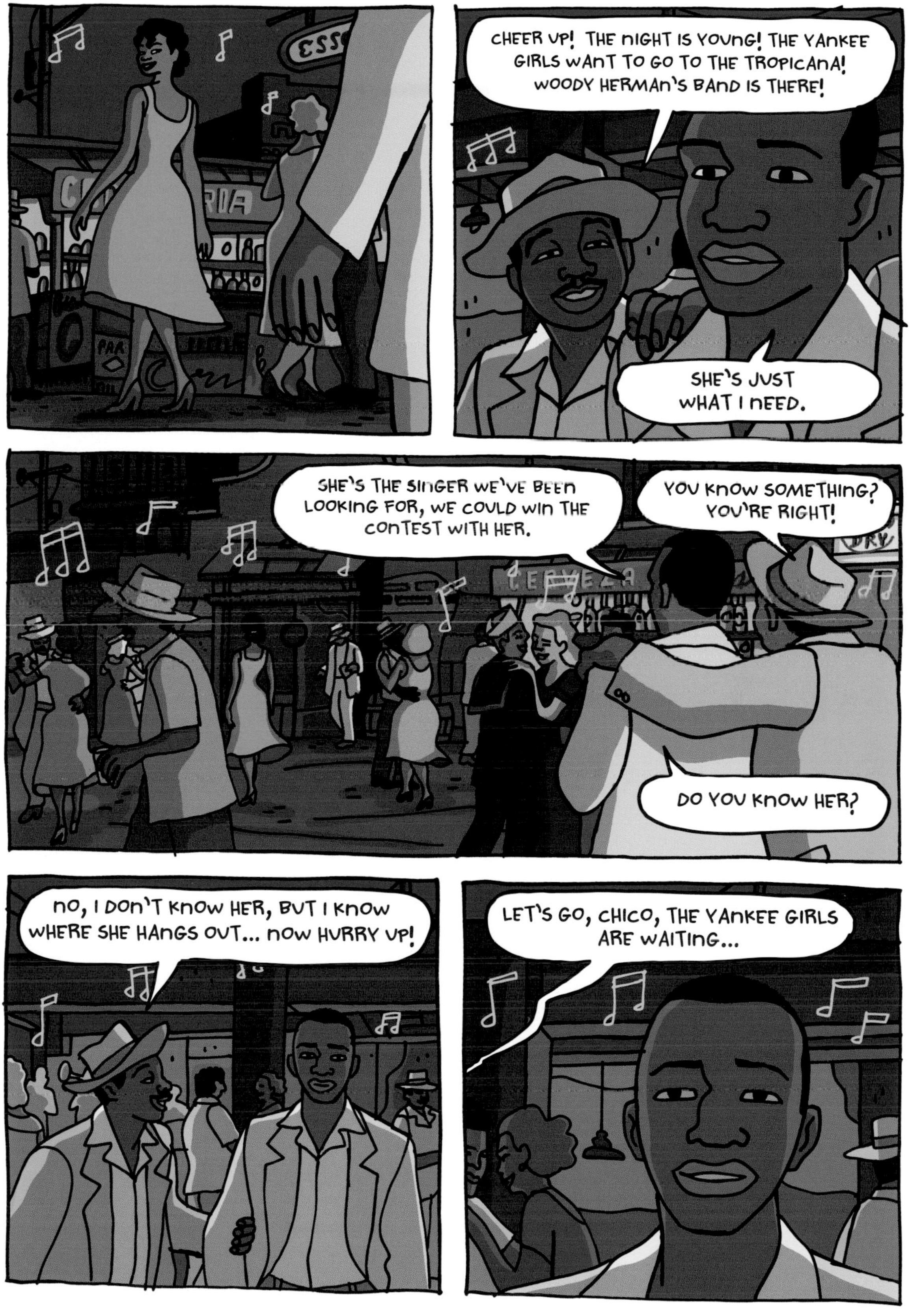
CHEER UP! THE NIGHT IS YOUNG! THE YANKEE GIRLS WANT TO GO TO THE TROPICANA! WOODY HERMAN'S BAND IS THERE!
SHE'S JUST WHAT I NEED.
SHE'S THE SINGER WE'VE BEEN LOOKING FOR, WE COULD WIN THE CONTEST WITH HER.
YOU KNOW SOMETHING? YOU'RE RIGHT!
CERVEZA
DO YOU KNOW HER?
NO, I DON'T KNOW HER, BUT I KNOW WHERE SHE HANGS OUT... NOW HURRY UP!
LET'S GO, CHICO, THE YANKEE GIRLS ARE WAITING...

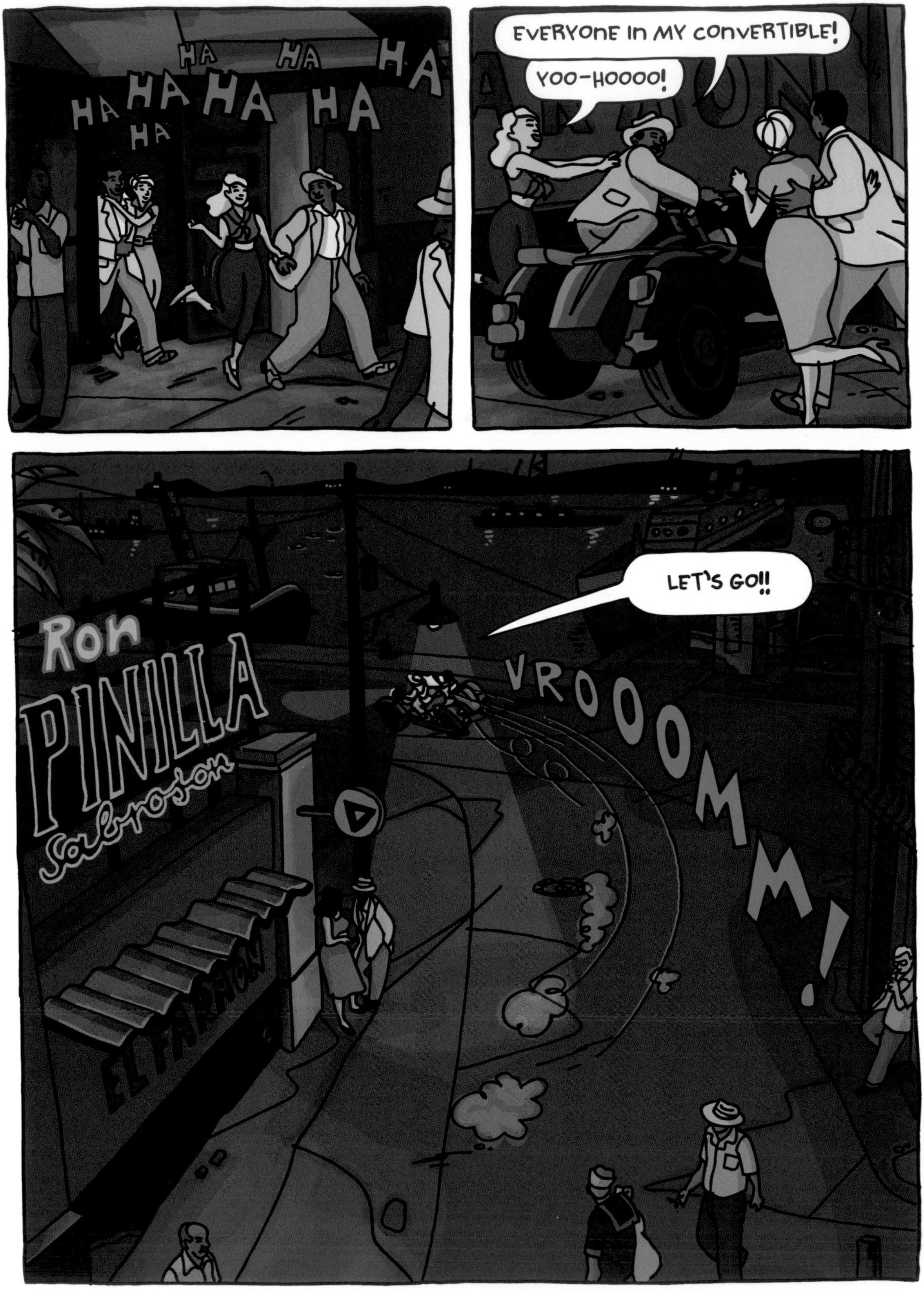
HA HA HA HA HA HA HA HA HA
EVERYONE IN MY CONVERTIBLE!
YOO-HOOOO!
LET'S GO!!
VROOOOMMM!
Ron
PINILLA
Sabroson
EL FARAON

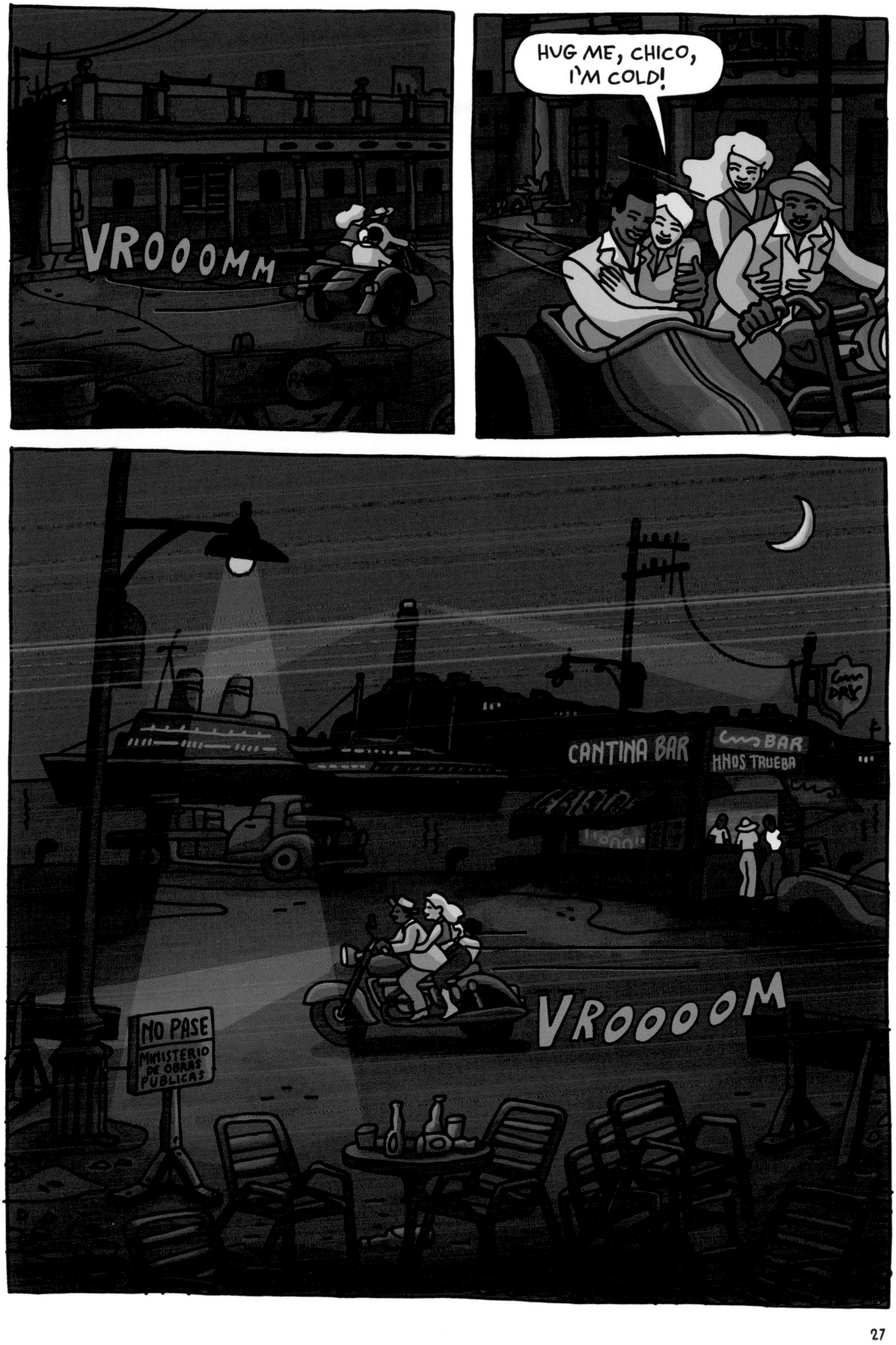
VROOOMM
HUG ME, CHICO, I'M COLD!
CANTINA BAR
BAR
HNOS TRUEBA
NO PASE
MINISTERIO DE OBRAS PUBLICAS
VROOOOM

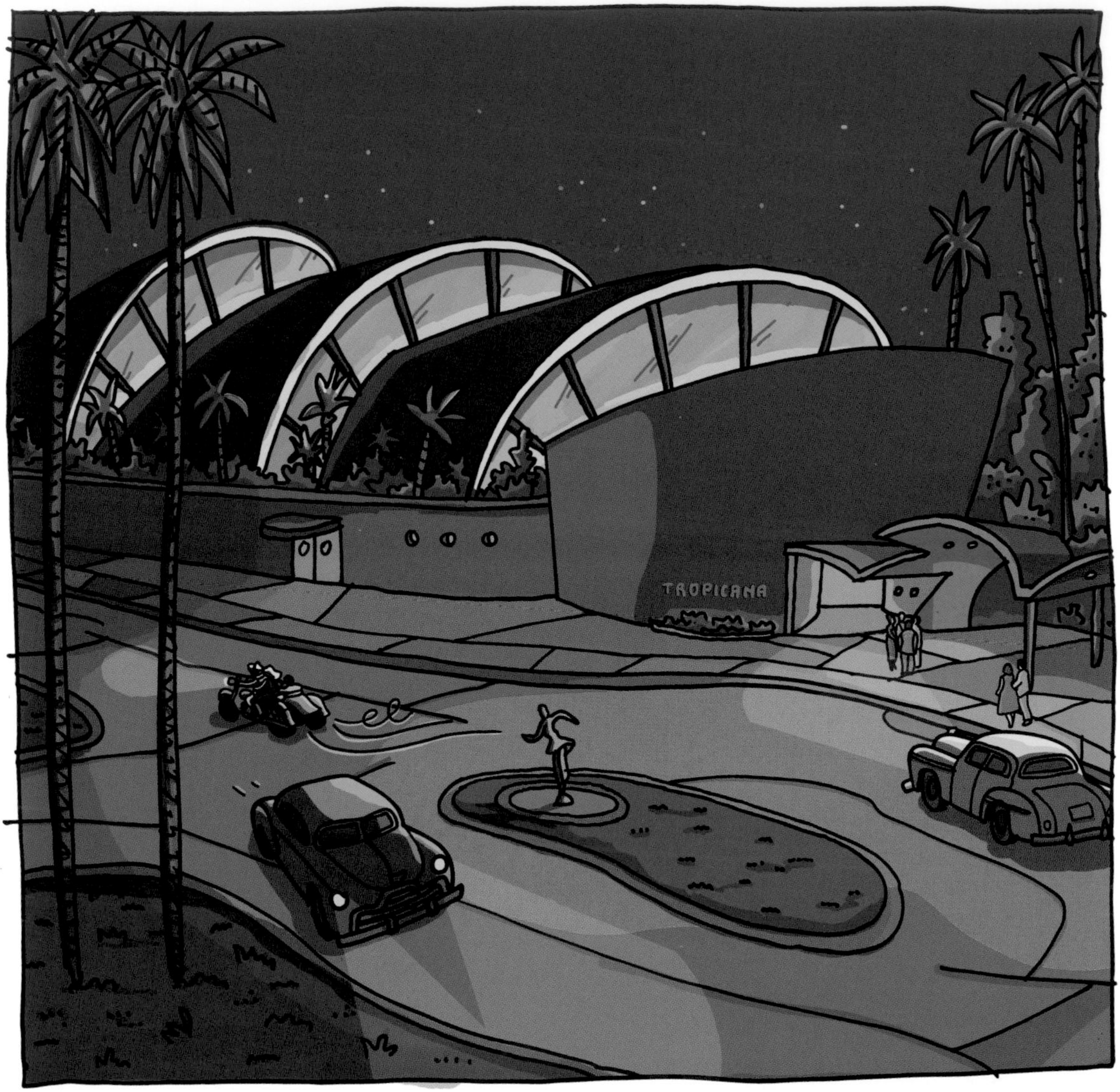
TROPICANA

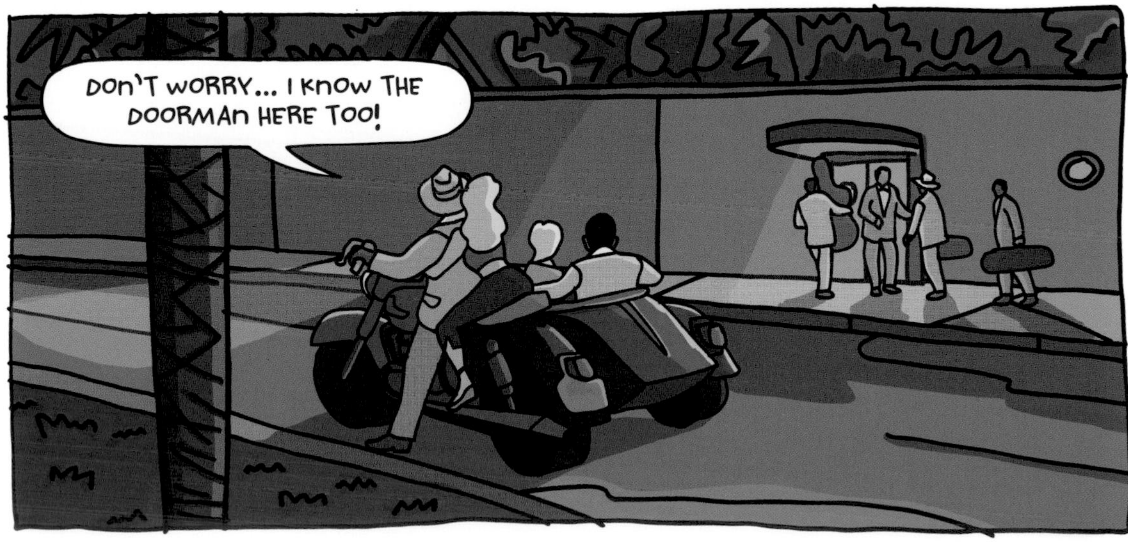
DON'T WORRY... I KNOW THE DOORMAN HERE TOO!

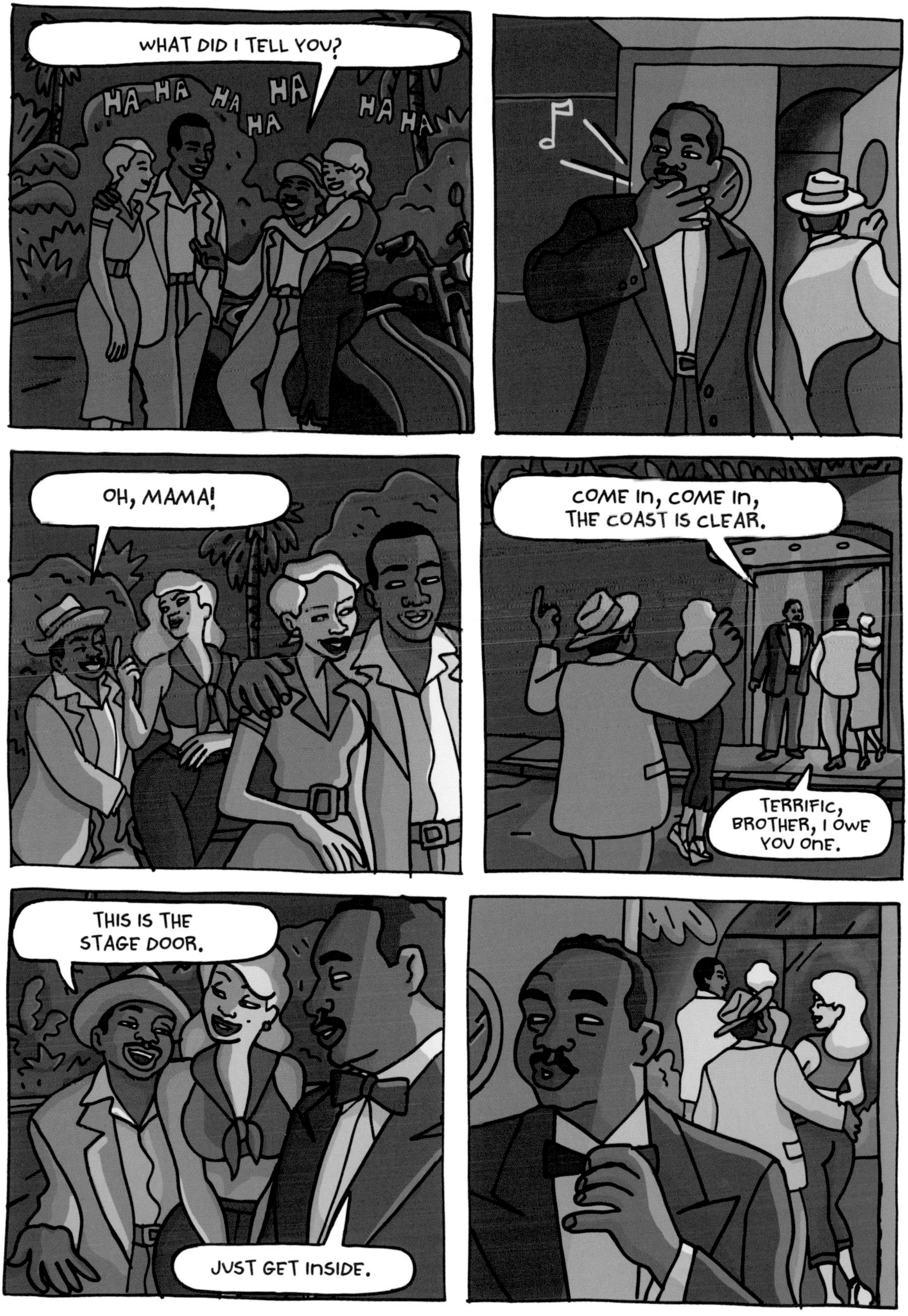
WHAT DID I TELL YOU?
HA HA HA HA HA HA HA
OH, MAMA!
COME IN, COME IN, THE COAST IS CLEAR.
TERRIFIC, BROTHER, I OWE YOU ONE.
THIS IS THE STAGE DOOR.
JUST GET INSIDE.

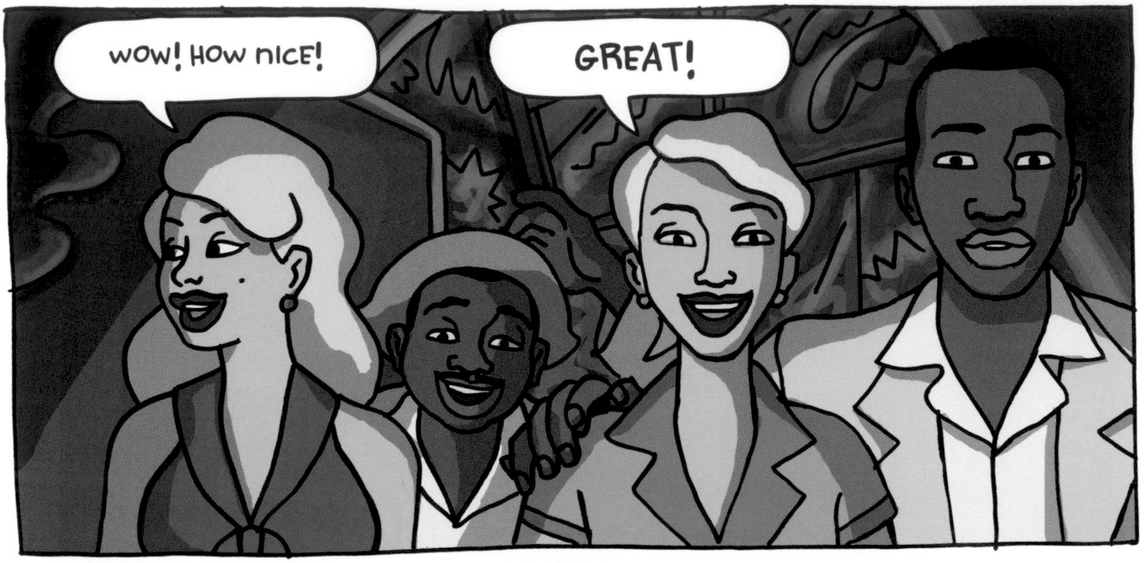
WOW! HOW NICE!
GREAT!

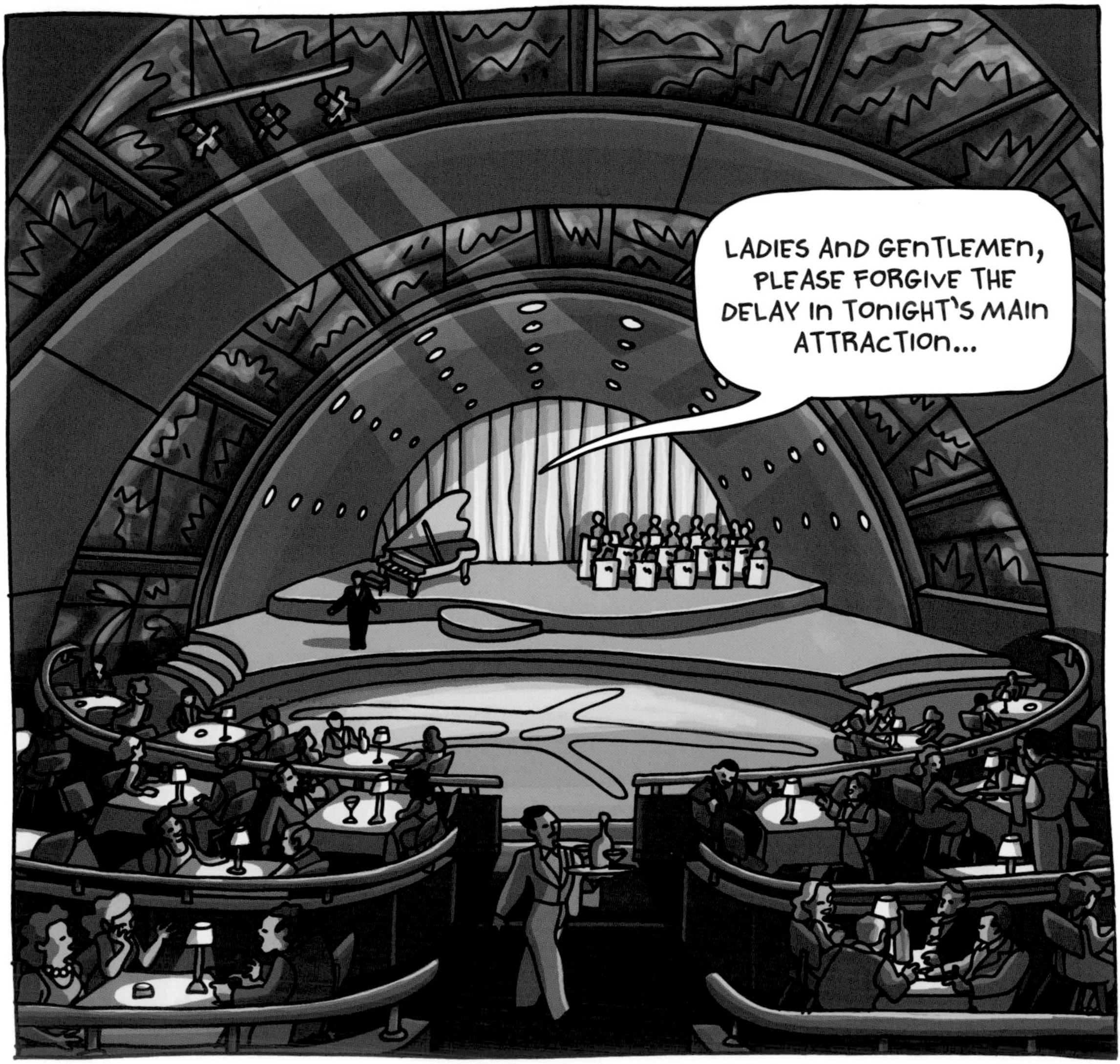
LADIES AND GENTLEMEN, PLEASE FORGIVE THE DELAY IN TONIGHT'S MAIN ATTRACTION...

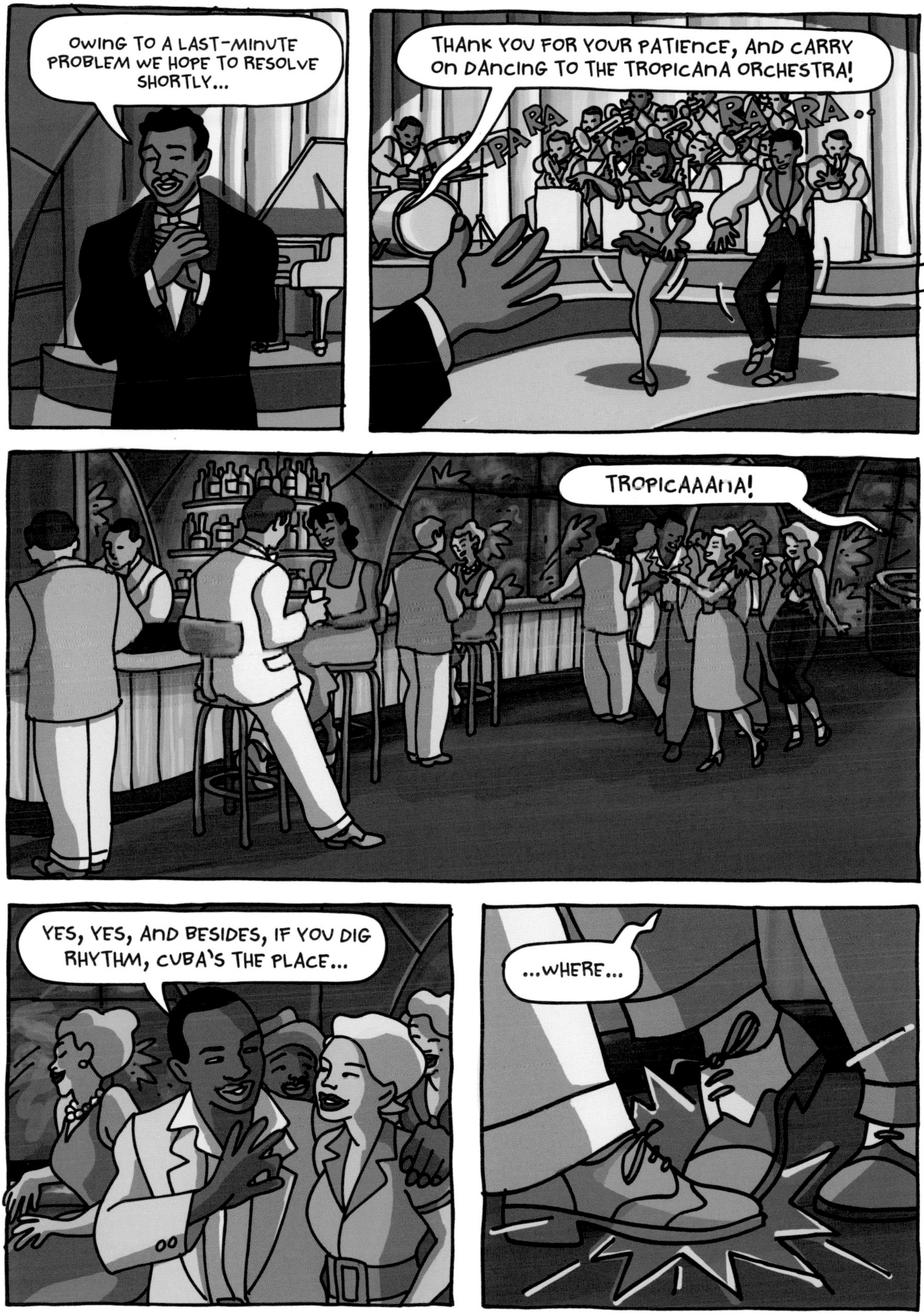
OWING TO A LAST-MINUTE PROBLEM WE HOPE TO RESOLVE SHORTLY...
THANK YOU FOR YOUR PATIENCE, AND CARRY ON DANCING TO THE TROPICANA ORCHESTRA!
PA RA RA RA..
TROPICAAAANA!
YES, YES, AND BESIDES, IF YOU DIG RHYTHM, CUBA'S THE PLACE...
...WHERE...

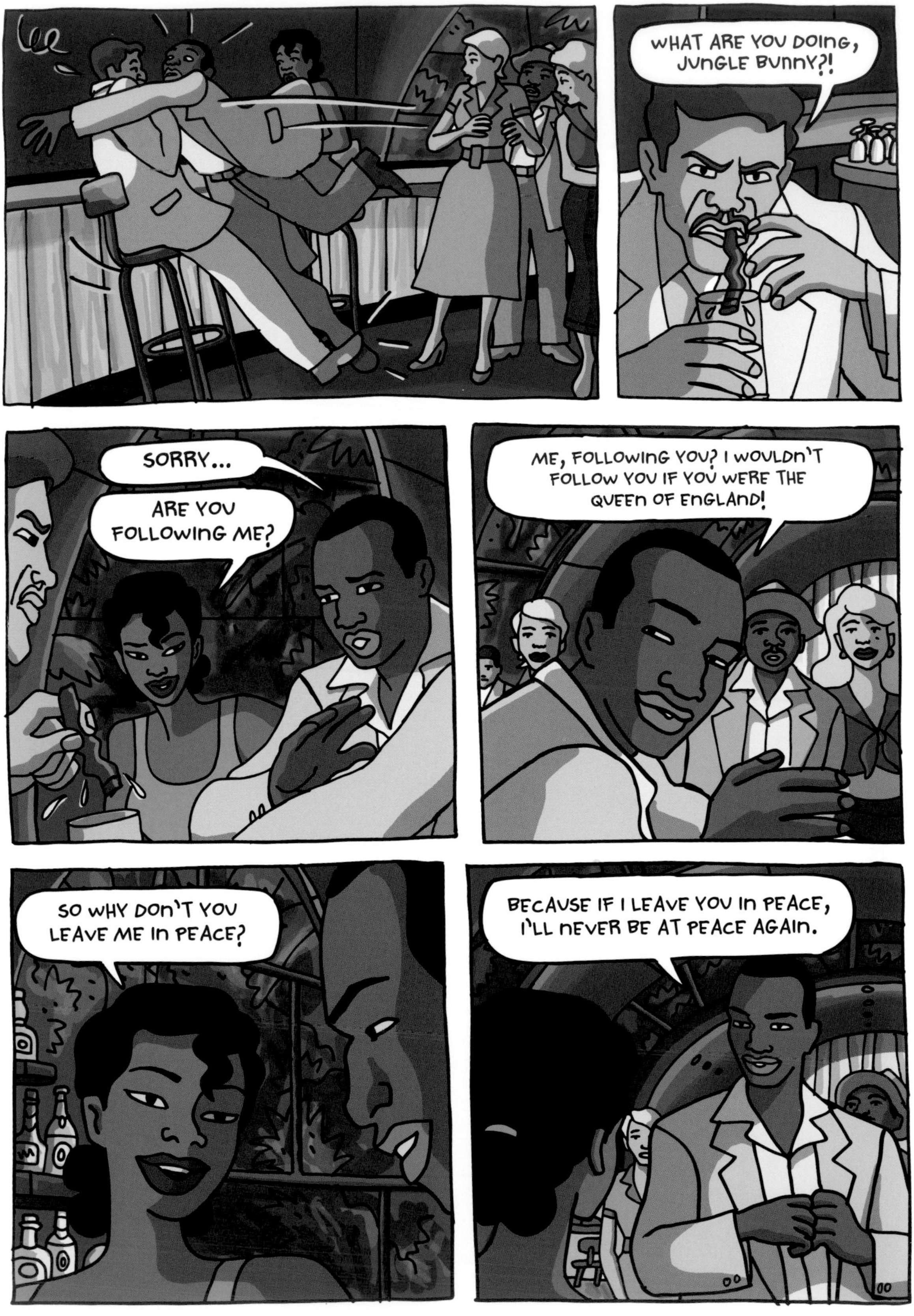
WHAT ARE YOU DOING, JUNGLE BUNNY?!
SORRY...
ARE YOU FOLLOWING ME?
ME, FOLLOWING YOU? I WOULDN'T FOLLOW YOU IF YOU WERE THE QUEEN OF ENGLAND!
SO WHY DON'T YOU LEAVE ME IN PEACE?
BECAUSE IF I LEAVE YOU IN PEACE, I'LL NEVER BE AT PEACE AGAIN.

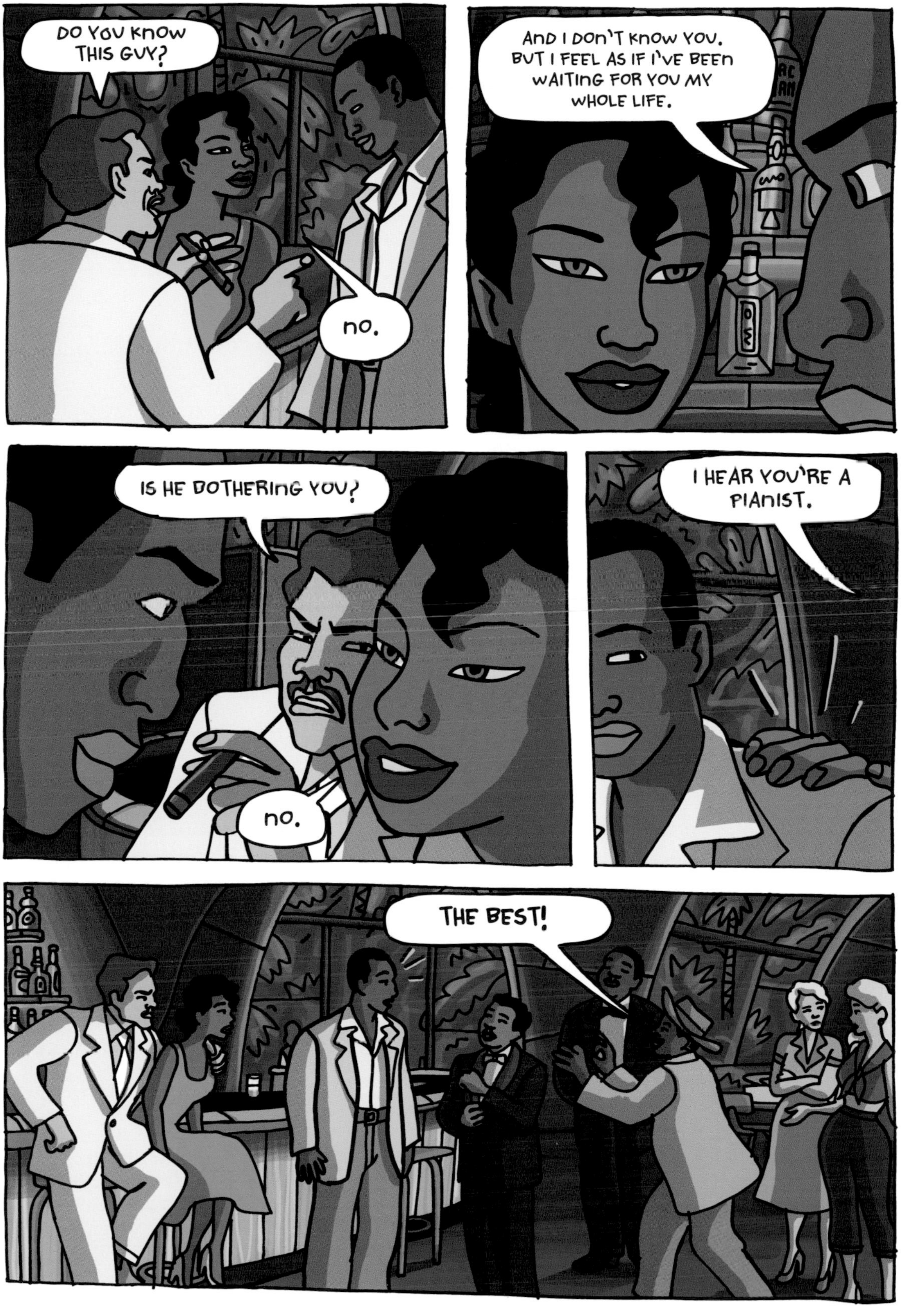
DO YOU KNOW THIS GUY?
no.
AND I DON'T KNOW YOU. BUT I FEEL AS IF I'VE BEEN WAITING FOR YOU MY WHOLE LIFE.
IS HE BOTHERING YOU?
no.
I HEAR YOU'RE A PIANIST.
THE BEST!

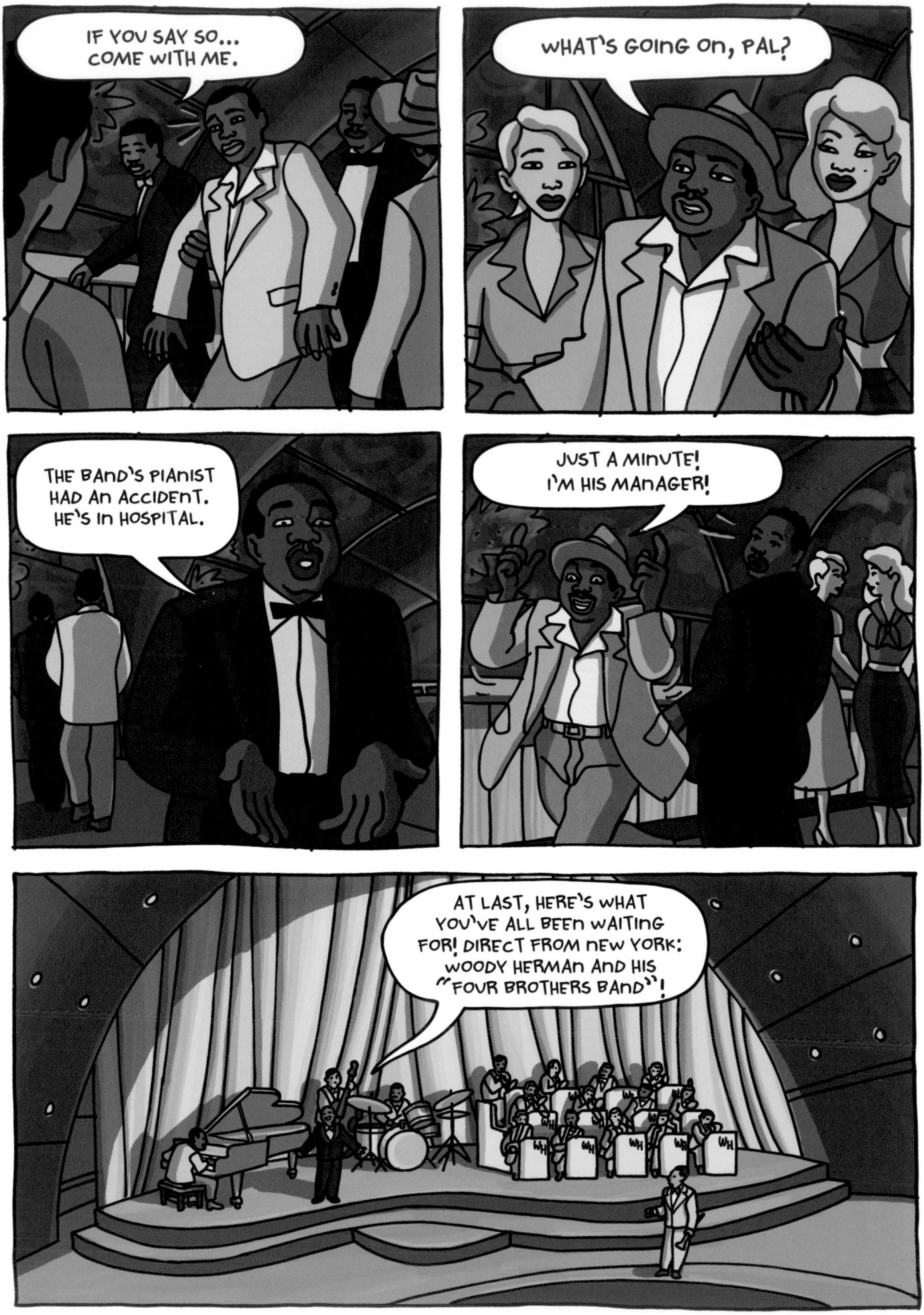

IF YOU SAY SO... COME WITH ME.
WHAT'S GOING ON, PAL?
THE BAND'S PIANIST HAD AN ACCIDENT. HE'S IN HOSPITAL.
JUST A MINUTE! I'M HIS MANAGER!
AT LAST, HERE'S WHAT YOU'VE ALL BEEN WAITING FOR! DIRECT FROM NEW YORK: WOODY HERMAN AND HIS "FOUR BROTHERS BAND"!

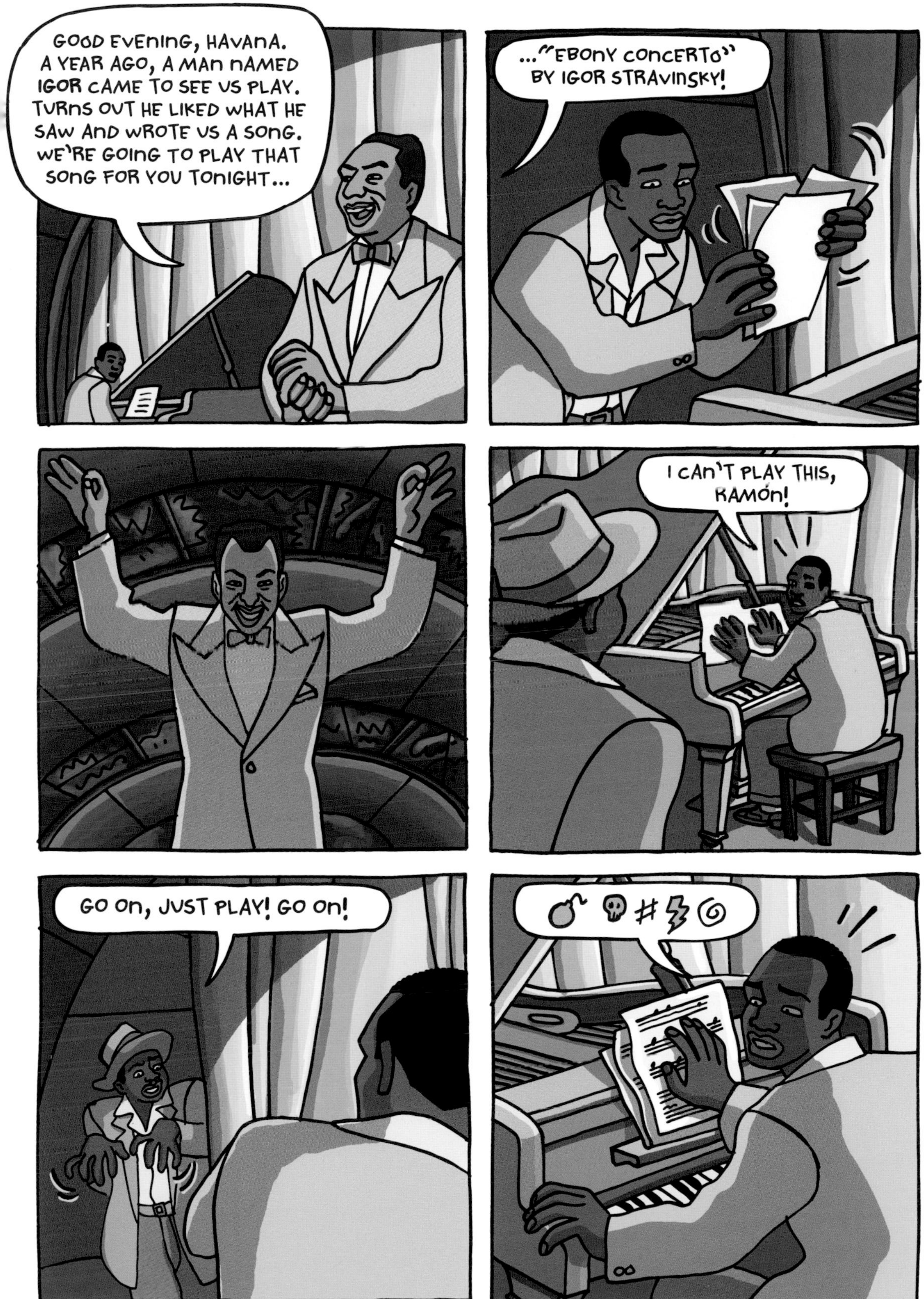
GOOD EVENING, HAVANA. A YEAR AGO, A MAN NAMED IGOR CAME TO SEE US PLAY. TURNS OUT HE LIKED WHAT HE SAW AND WROTE US A SONG. WE'RE GOING TO PLAY THAT SONG FOR YOU TONIGHT...
..."EBONY CONCERTO" BY IGOR STRAVINSKY!
I CAN'T PLAY THIS, RAMÓN!
GO ON, JUST PLAY! GO ON!
#

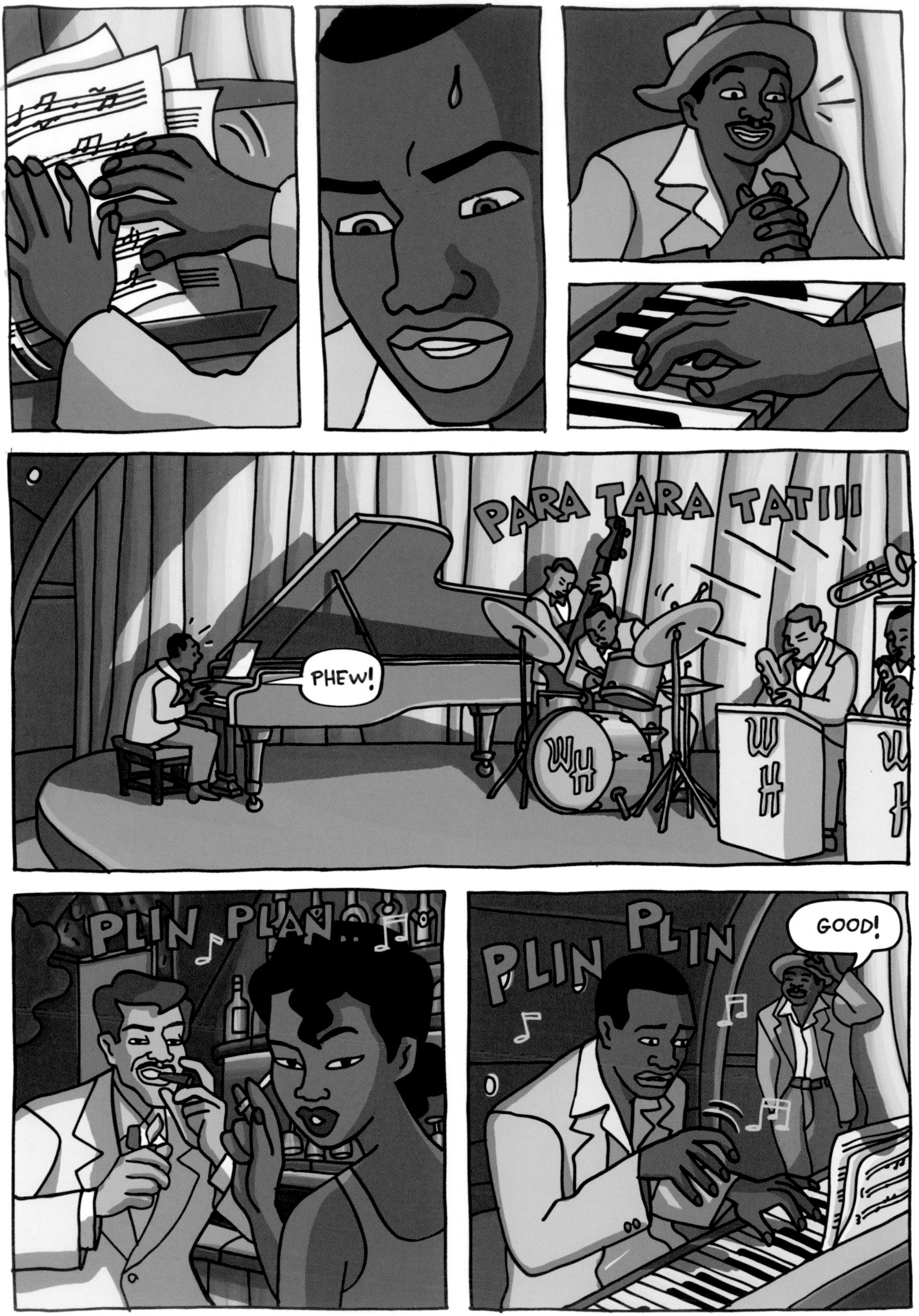
PARA TARA TATIII
PHEW!
PLIN PLAN..
PLIN PLIN
GOOD!

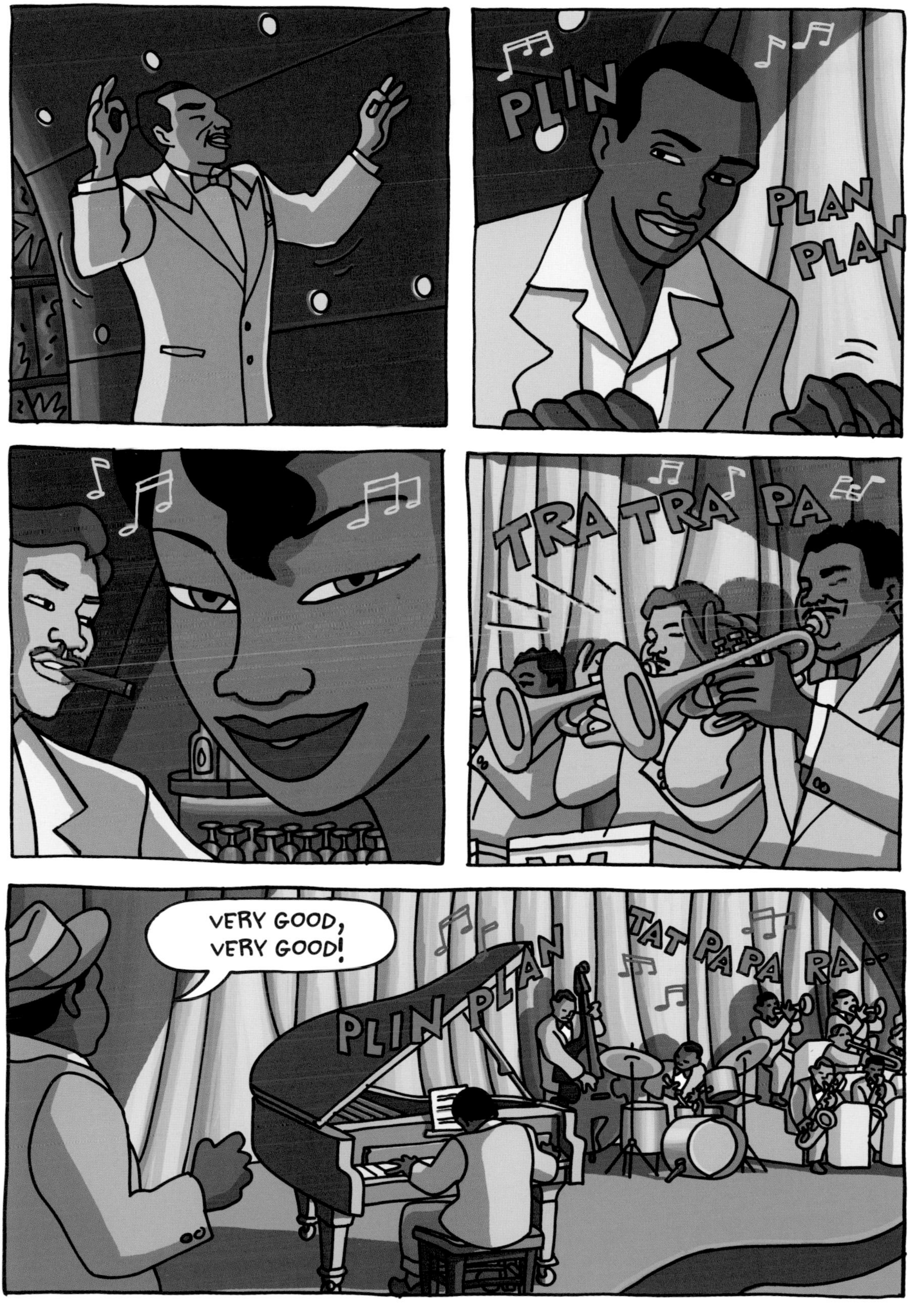
PLIN
PLAN
PLAN
TRA TRA PA
VERY GOOD, VERY GOOD!
PLIN PLAN
TAT PA PA RA-

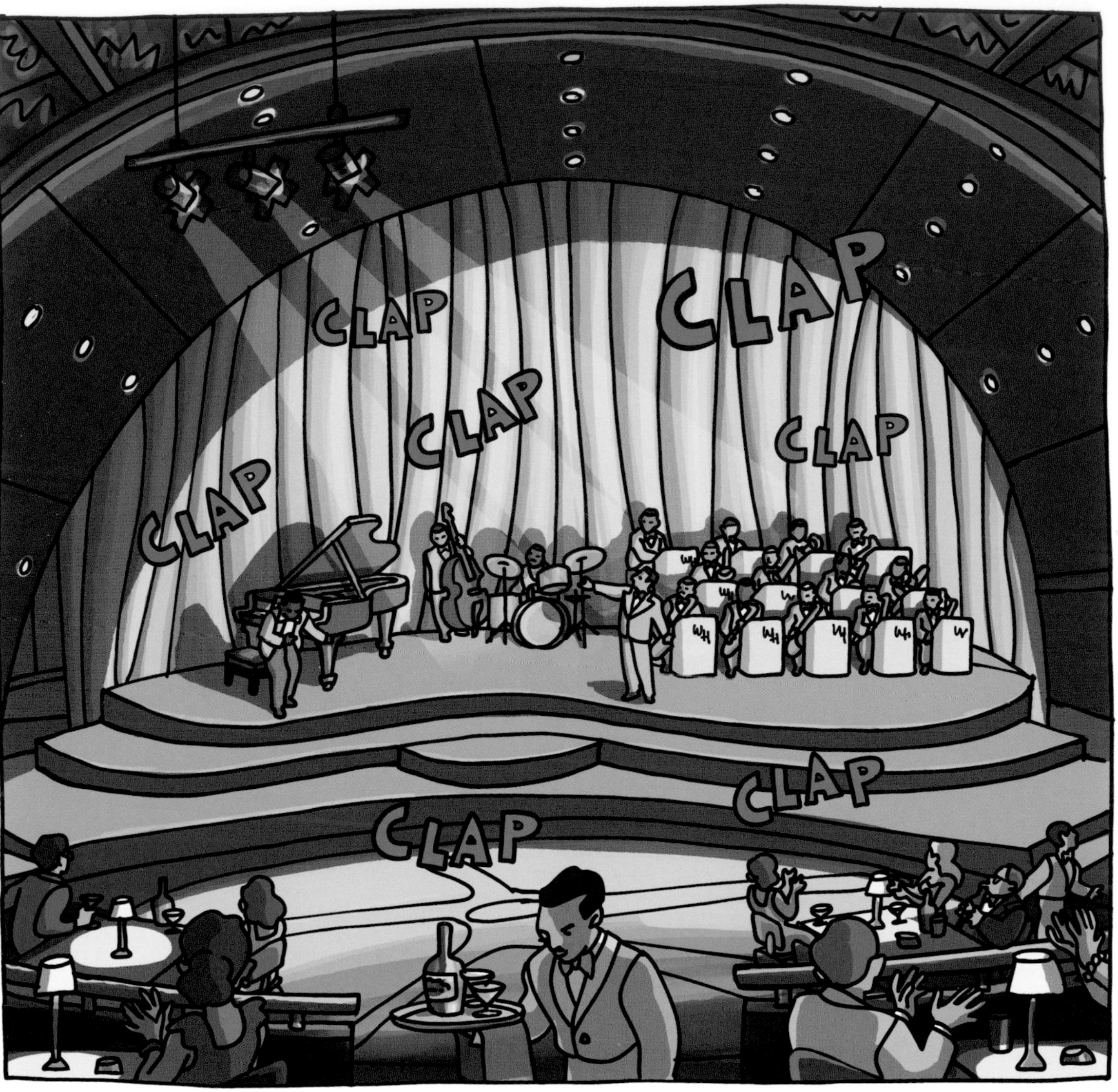
CLAP
CLAP
CLAP
CLAP
CLAP
CLAP
CLAP

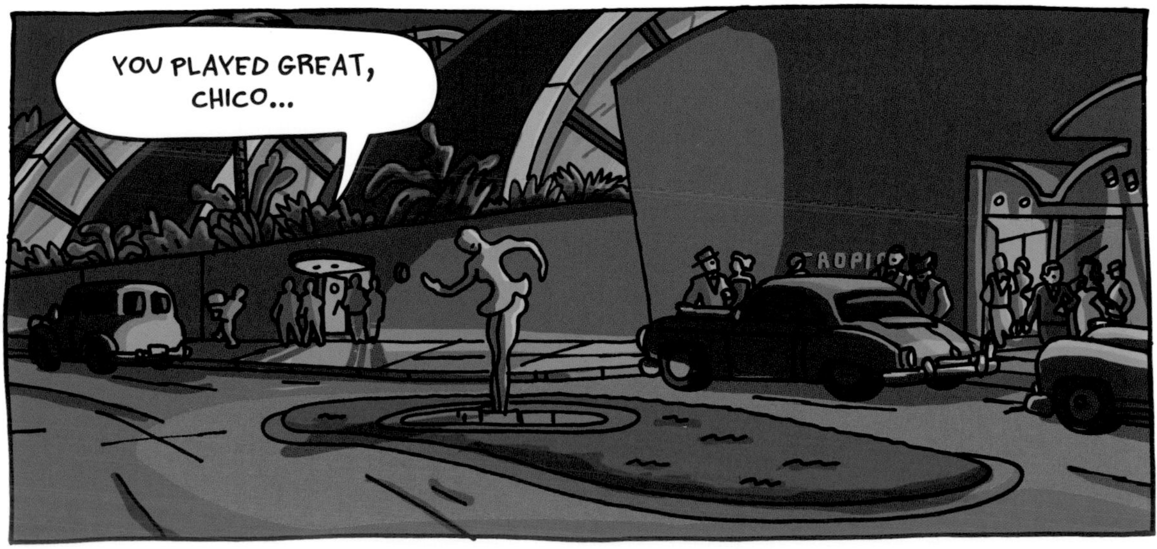
YOU PLAYED GREAT, CHICO...

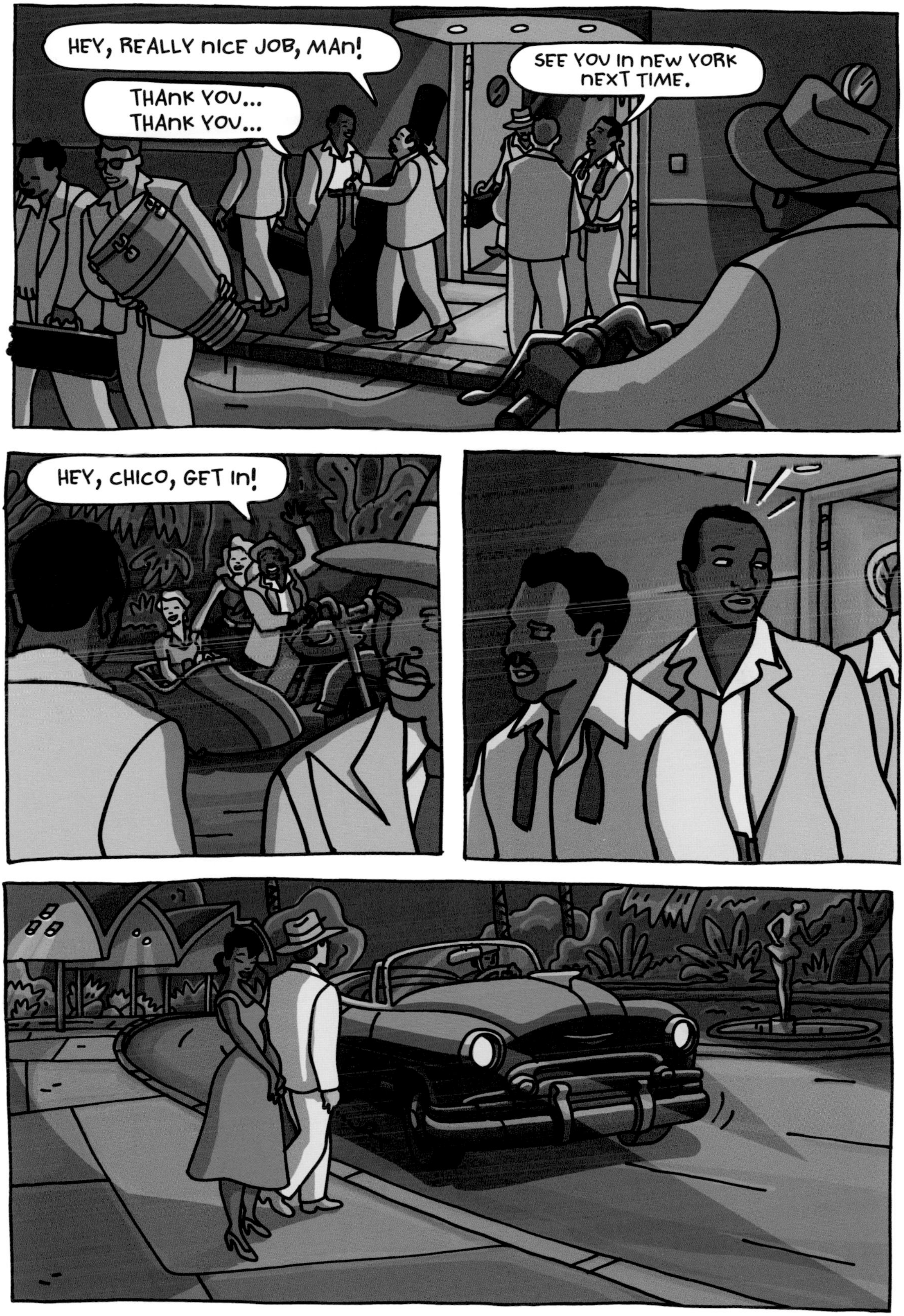

HEY, REALLY NICE JOB, MAN!
THANK YOU... THANK YOU...
SEE YOU IN NEW YORK NEXT TIME.
HEY, CHICO, GET IN!

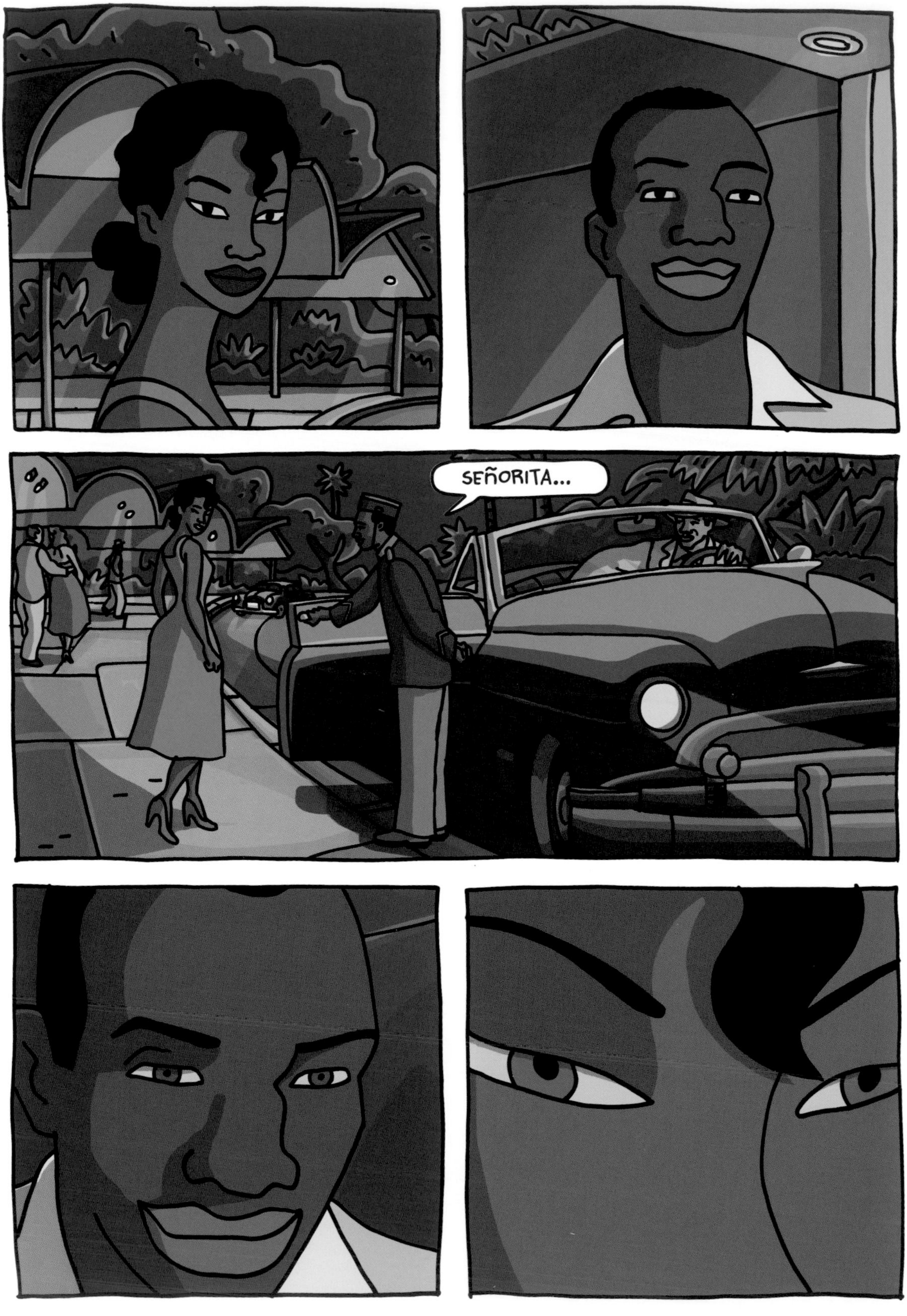
SEÑORITA...

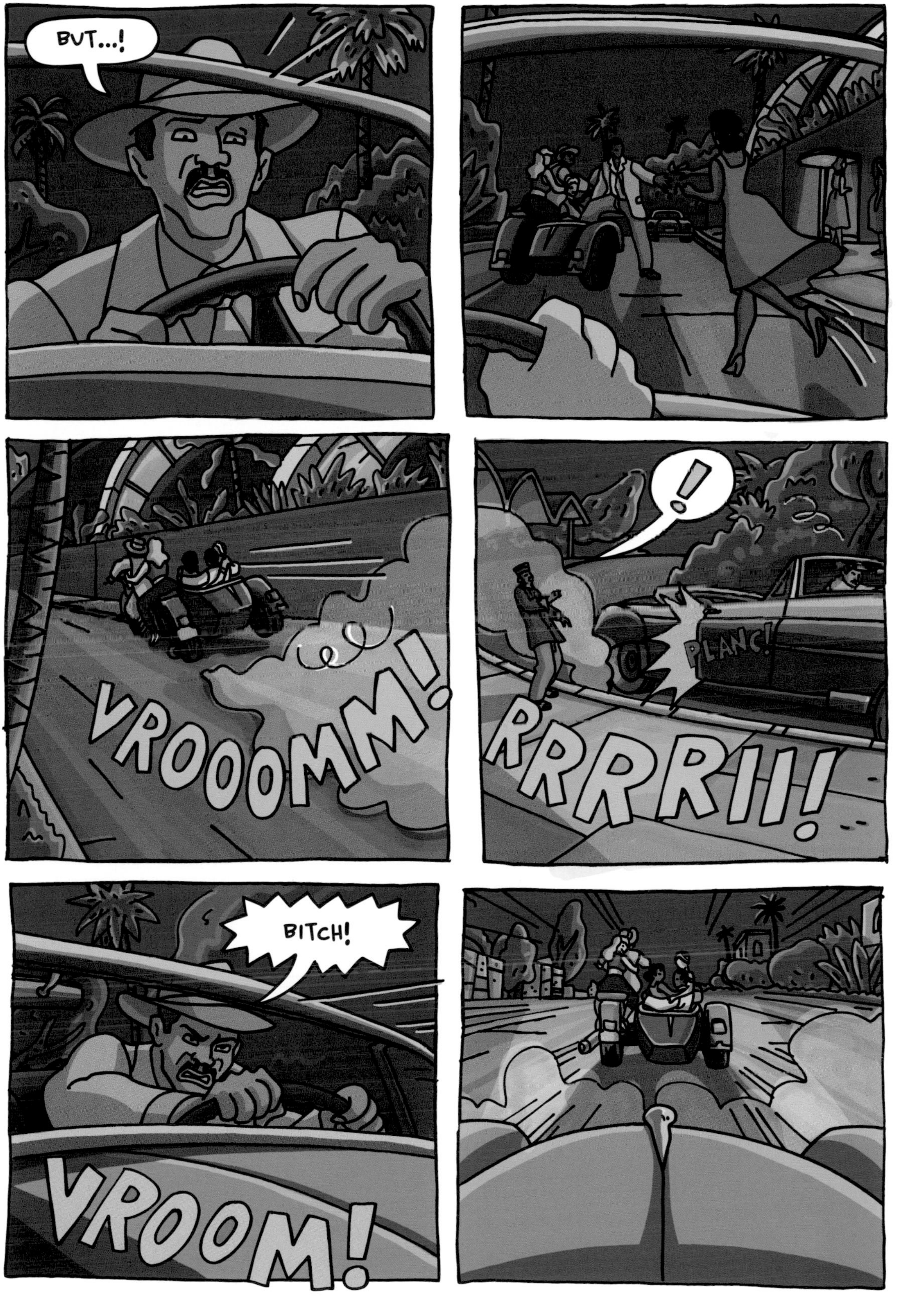
BUT...!
VROOOMM!
!
PLANC!
RRRRII!
BITCH!
VROOM!

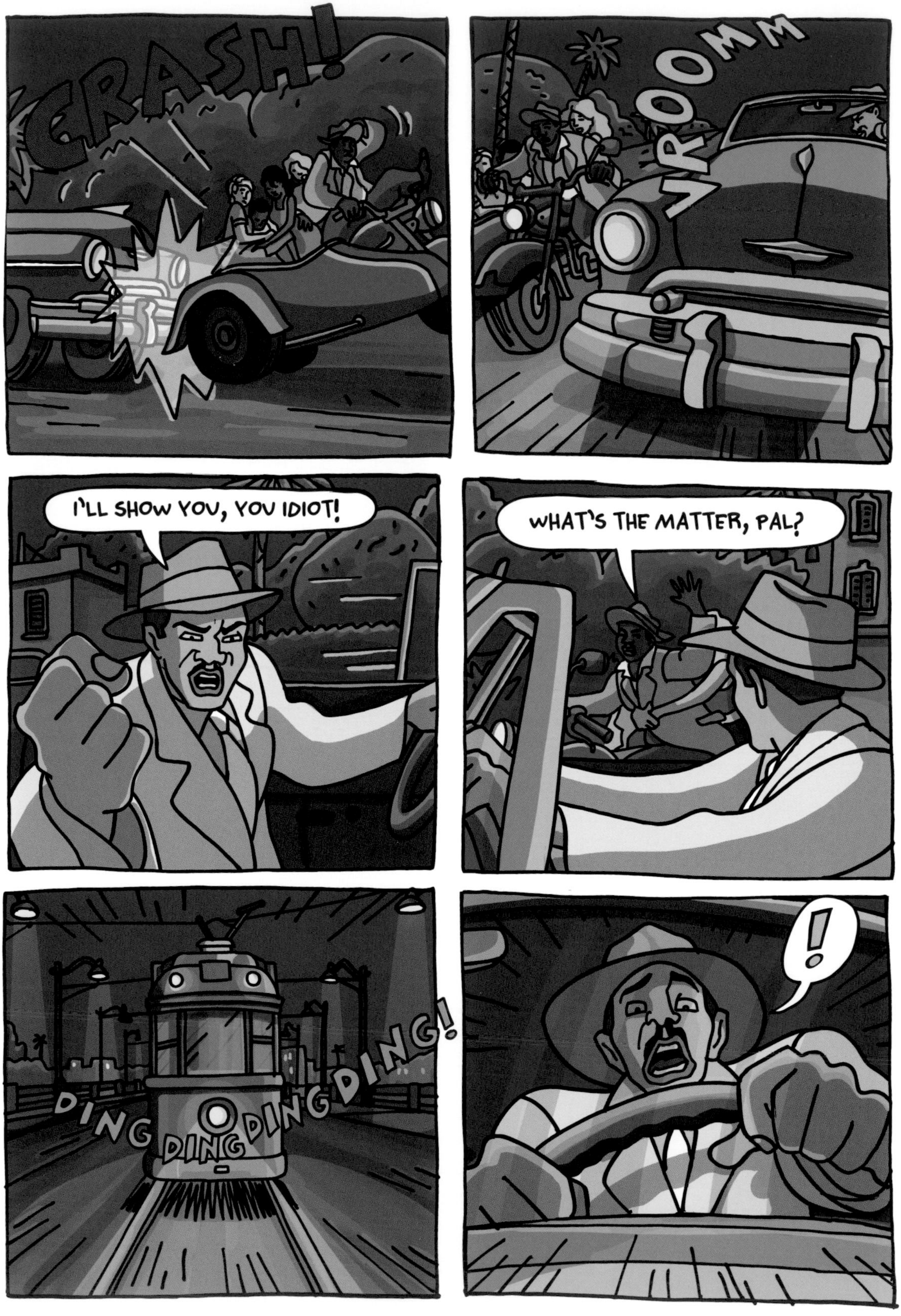
CRASH!
VROOMM
I'LL SHOW YOU, YOU IDIOT!
WHAT'S THE MATTER, PAL?
DING DING DING DING!
!?

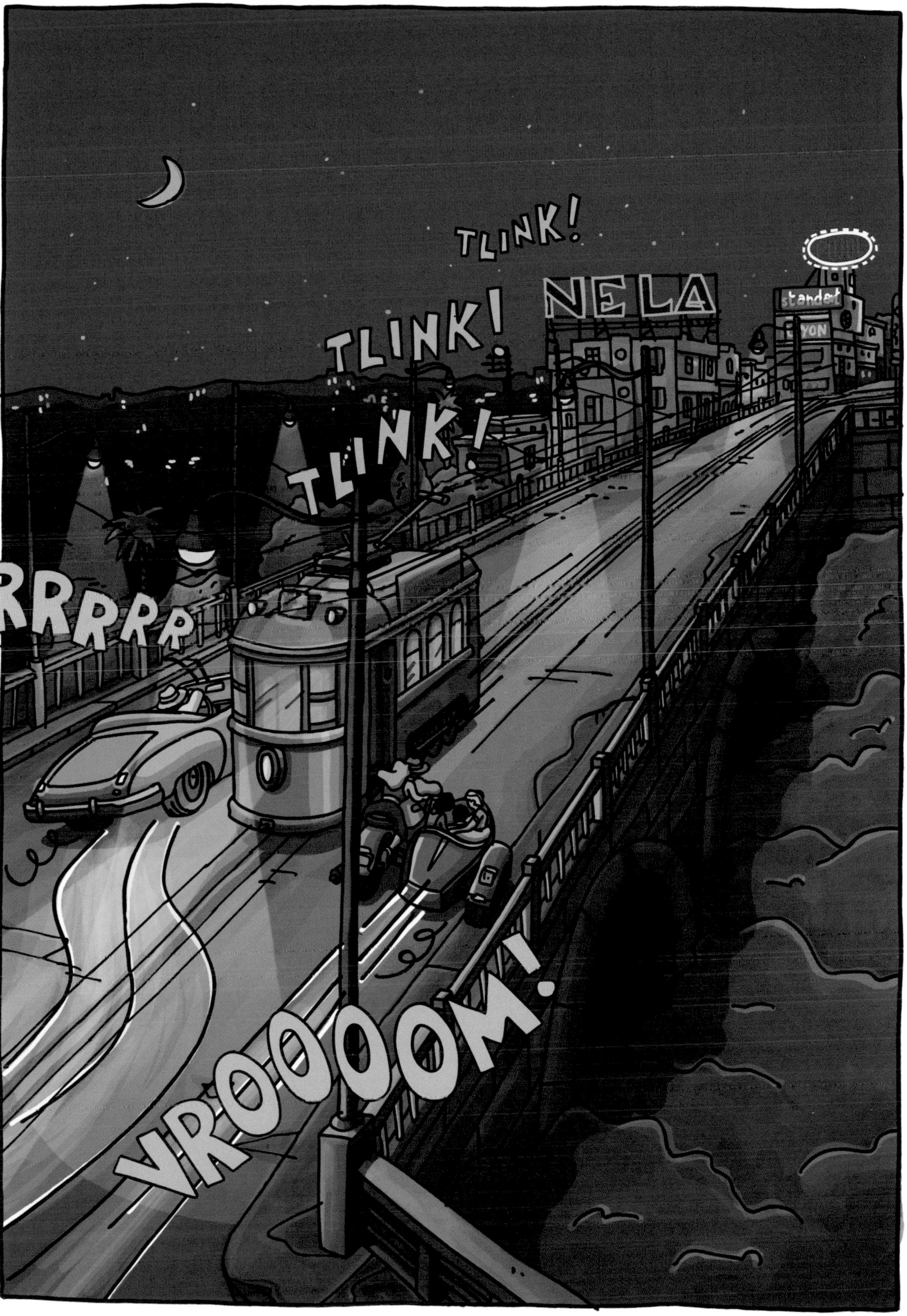
TLINK!
NELA
TLINK!
TLINK!
TLINK!
RRRRR
VROOOOM!

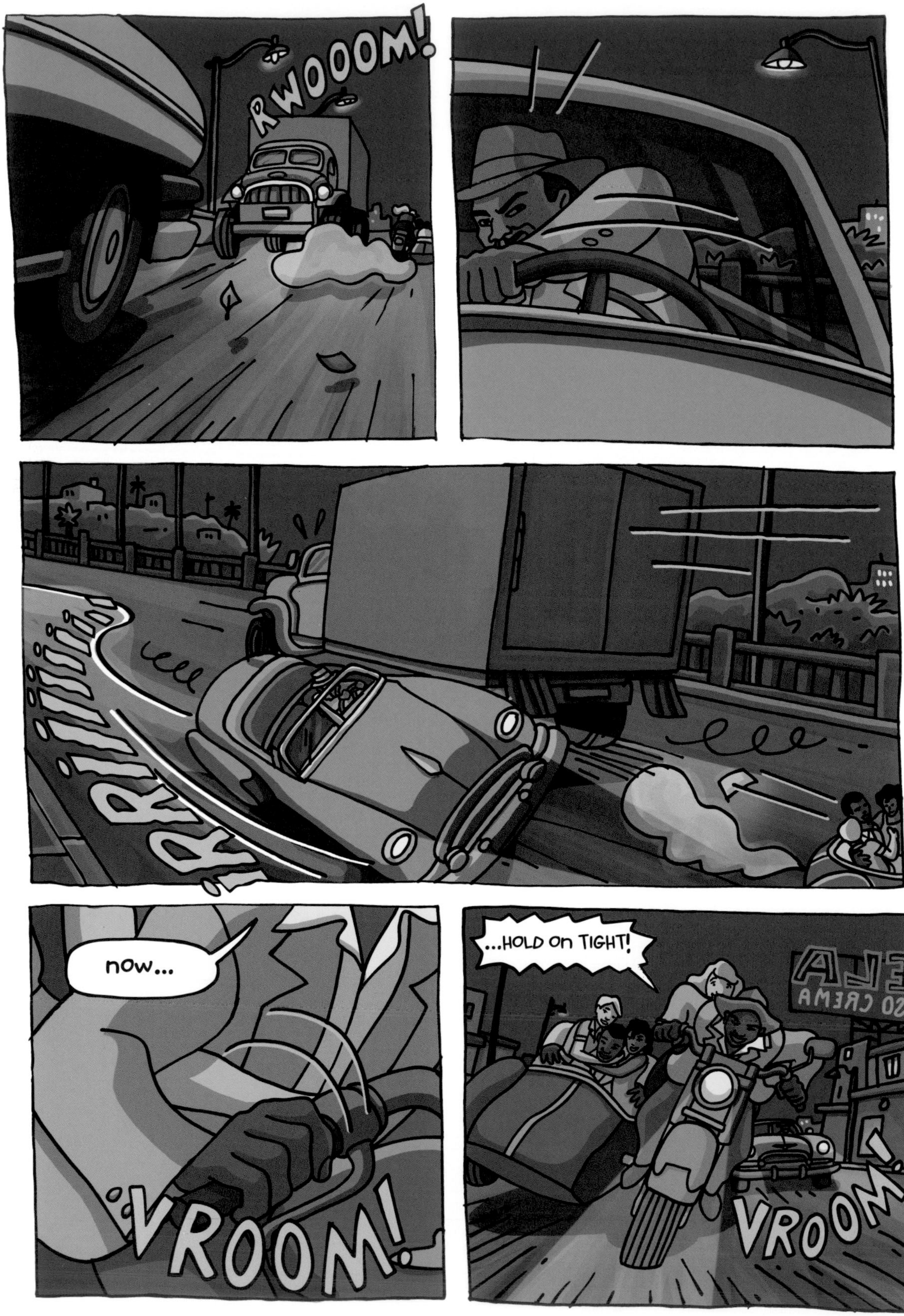
RWOOOM!
now...
VROOM!
...HOLD on TIGHT!
VROOM!

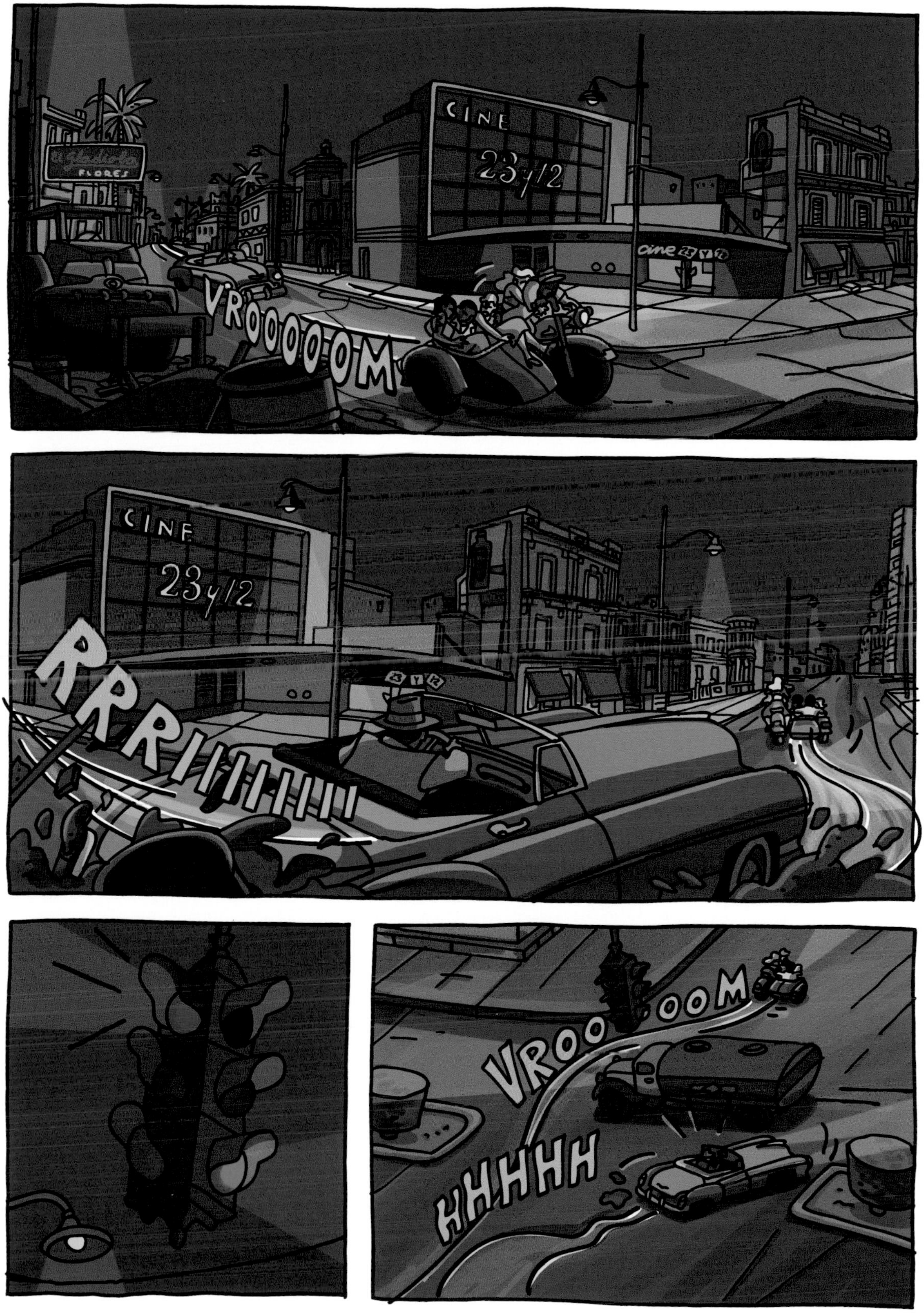
CINE
23y12
cine 23 y 12
VROOOOOM
CINE
23y12
RRRIIIIIIII
VROO OOM
HHHHH

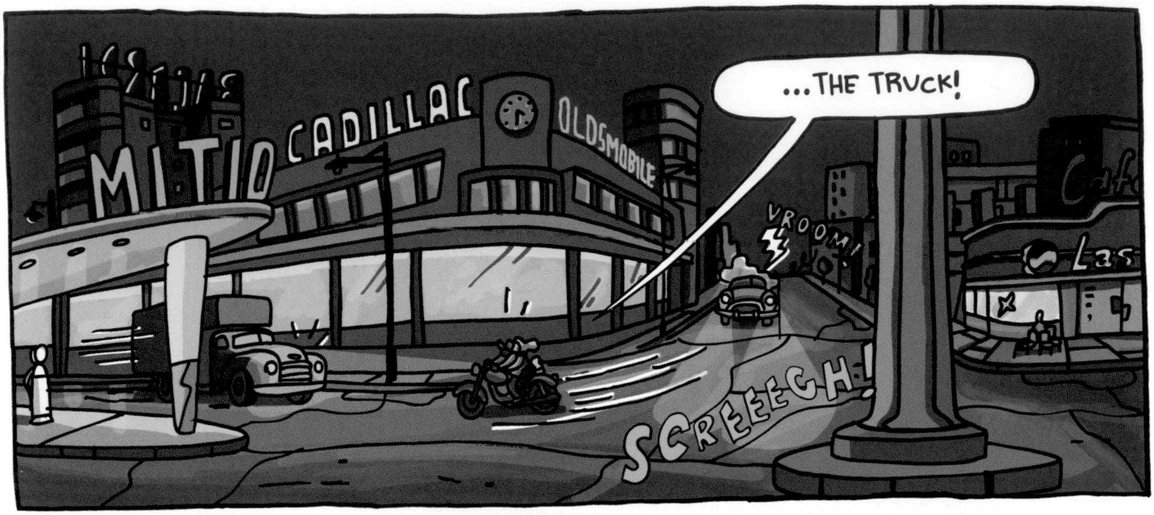
MITIO
CADILLAC
OLDSMOBILE
...THE TRUCK!
VROOM!
SCREEECH!

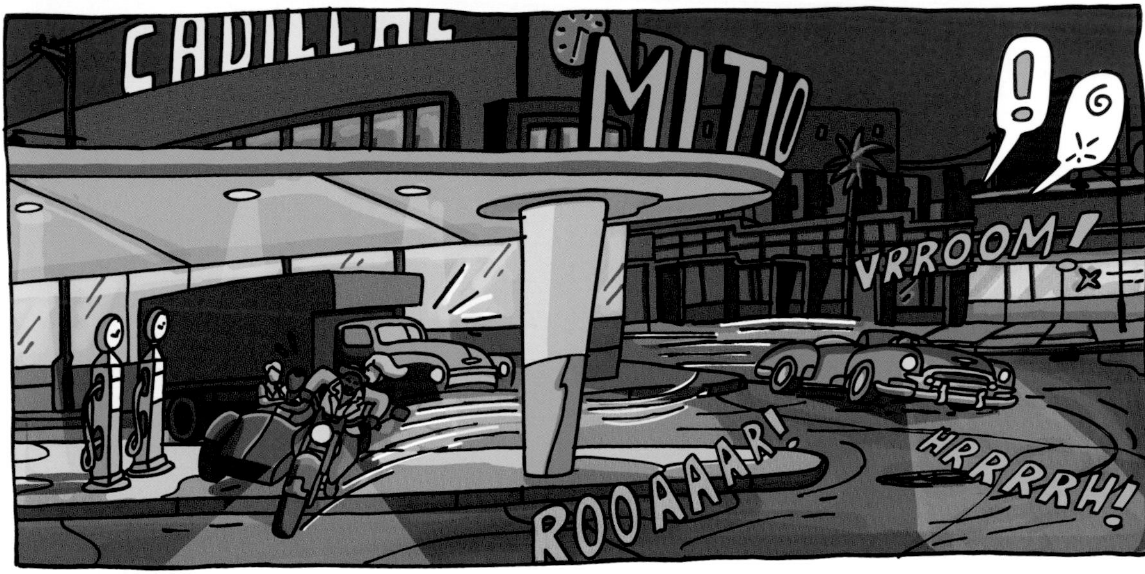
CADILLAC
MITIO
!
VRROOM!
ROOAAAR!
HRRRRRH!

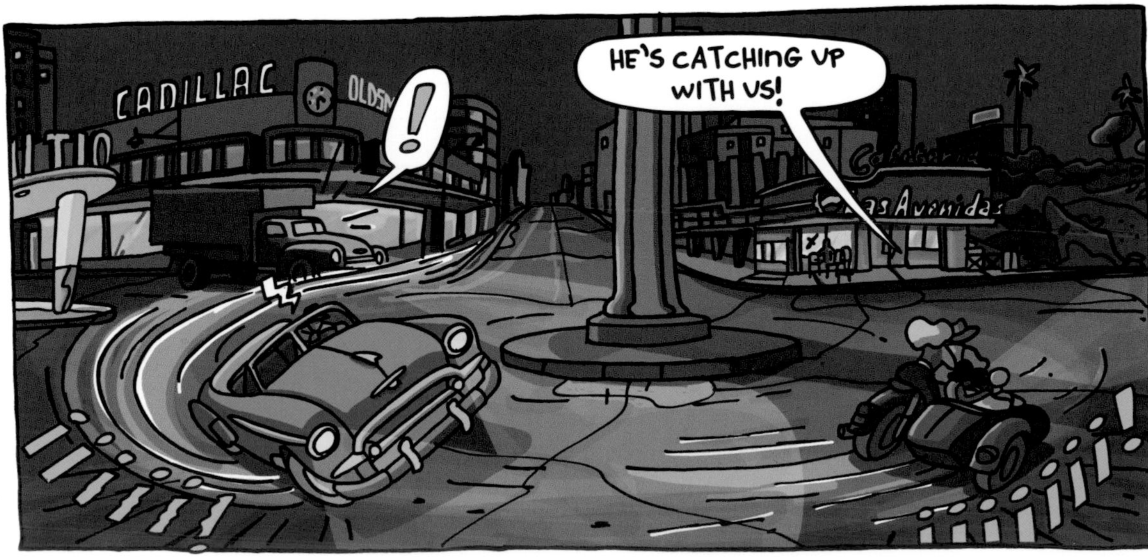
CADILLAC
!
HE'S CATCHING UP WITH US!
Las Avenidas

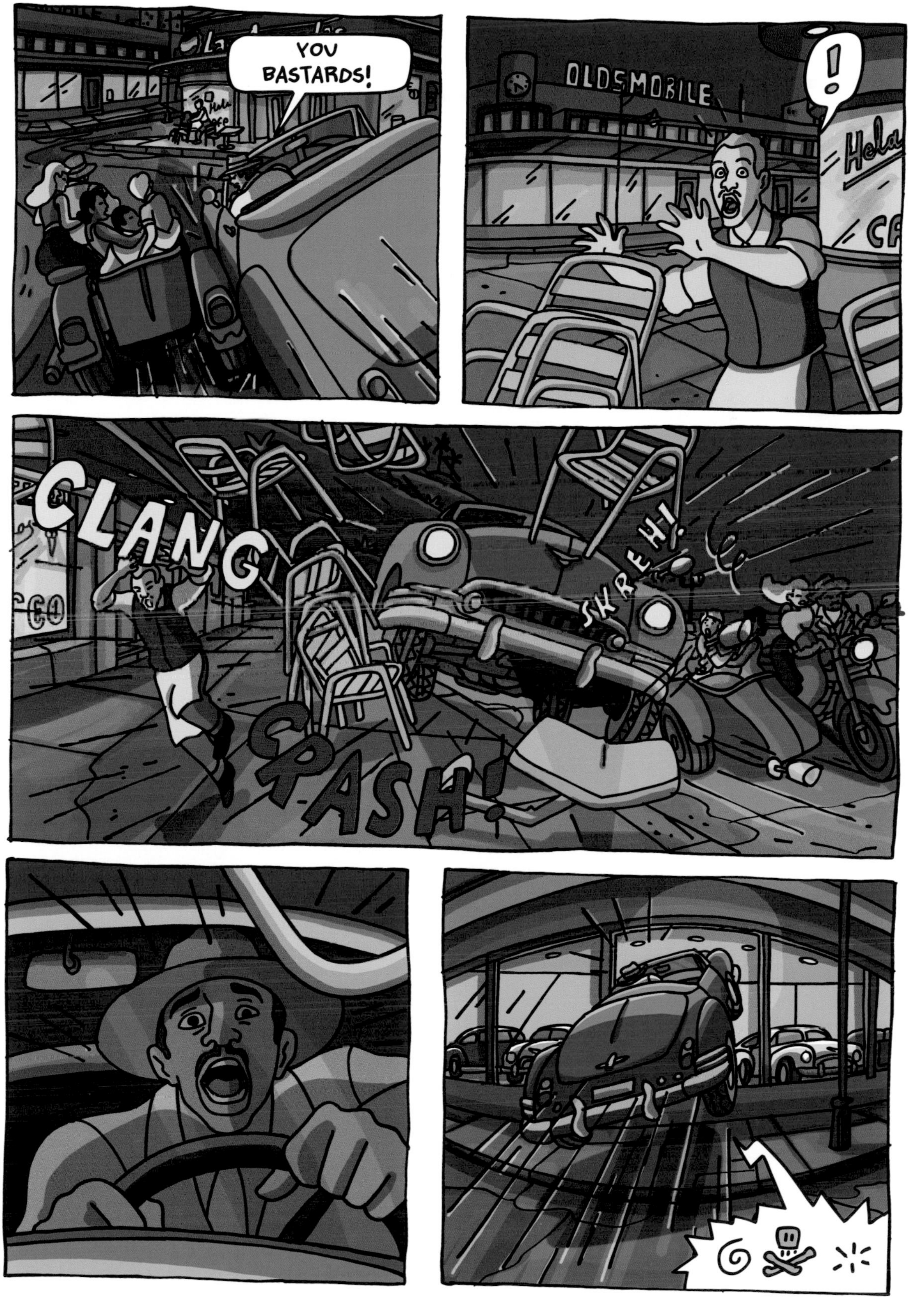
YOU BASTARDS!
OLDSMOBILE
!
CLANG
SKREH!
CRASH!

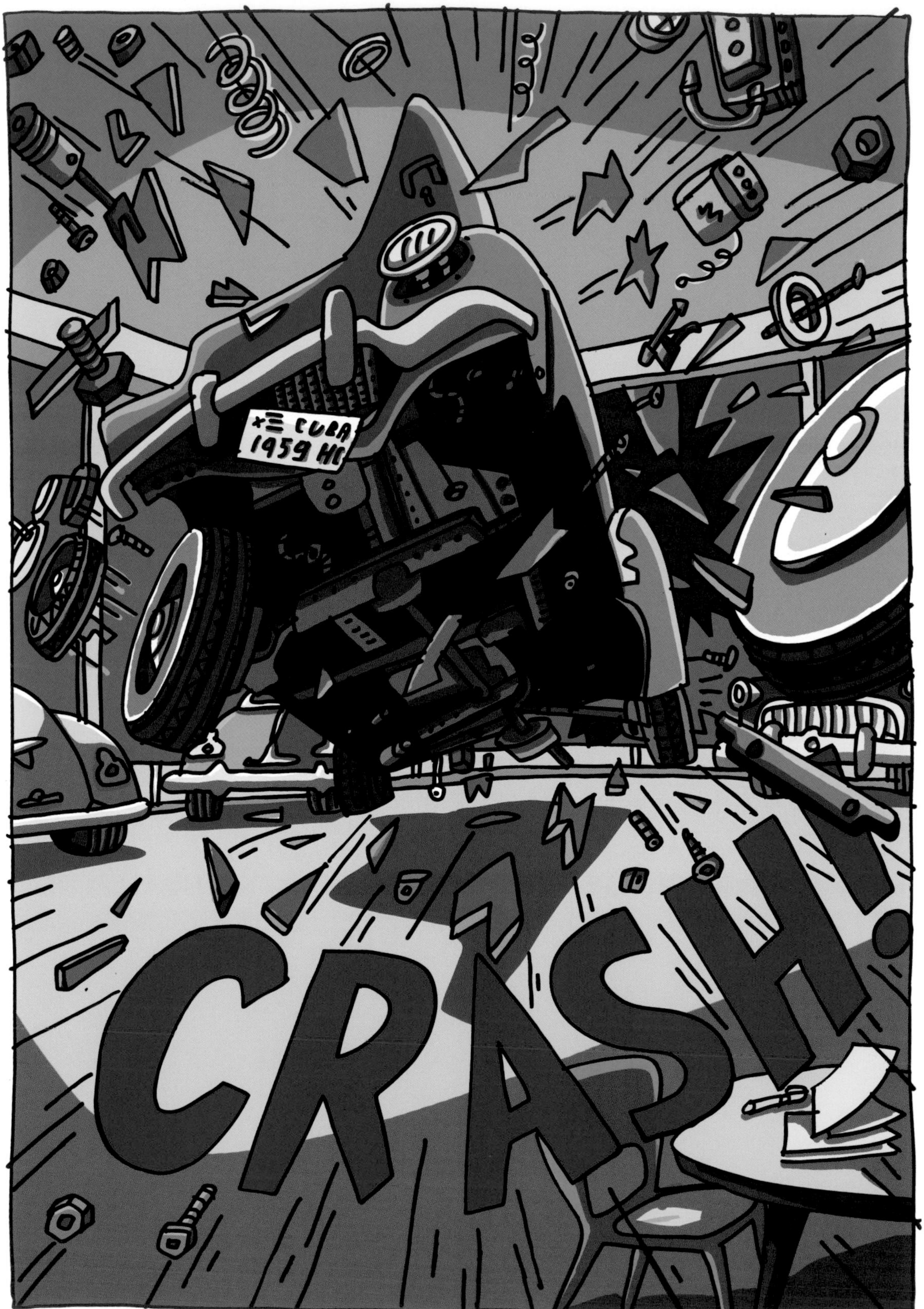
CUBA
1959 HC
CRASH!

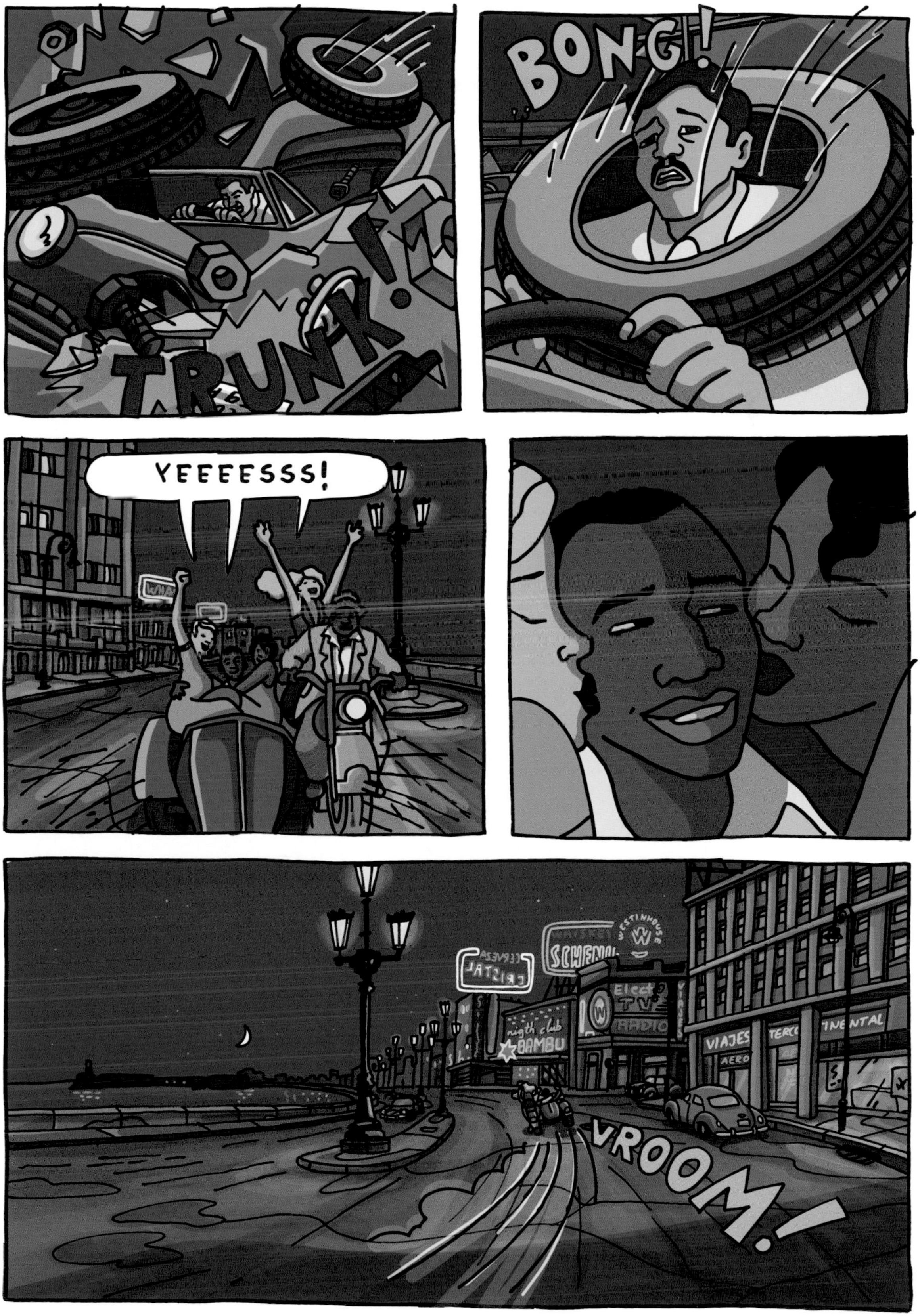
TRUNK!
BONG!
YEEEESSS!
WESTINGHOUSE
TV
RADIO
nigth club
BAMBU
VIAJES
VROOM!

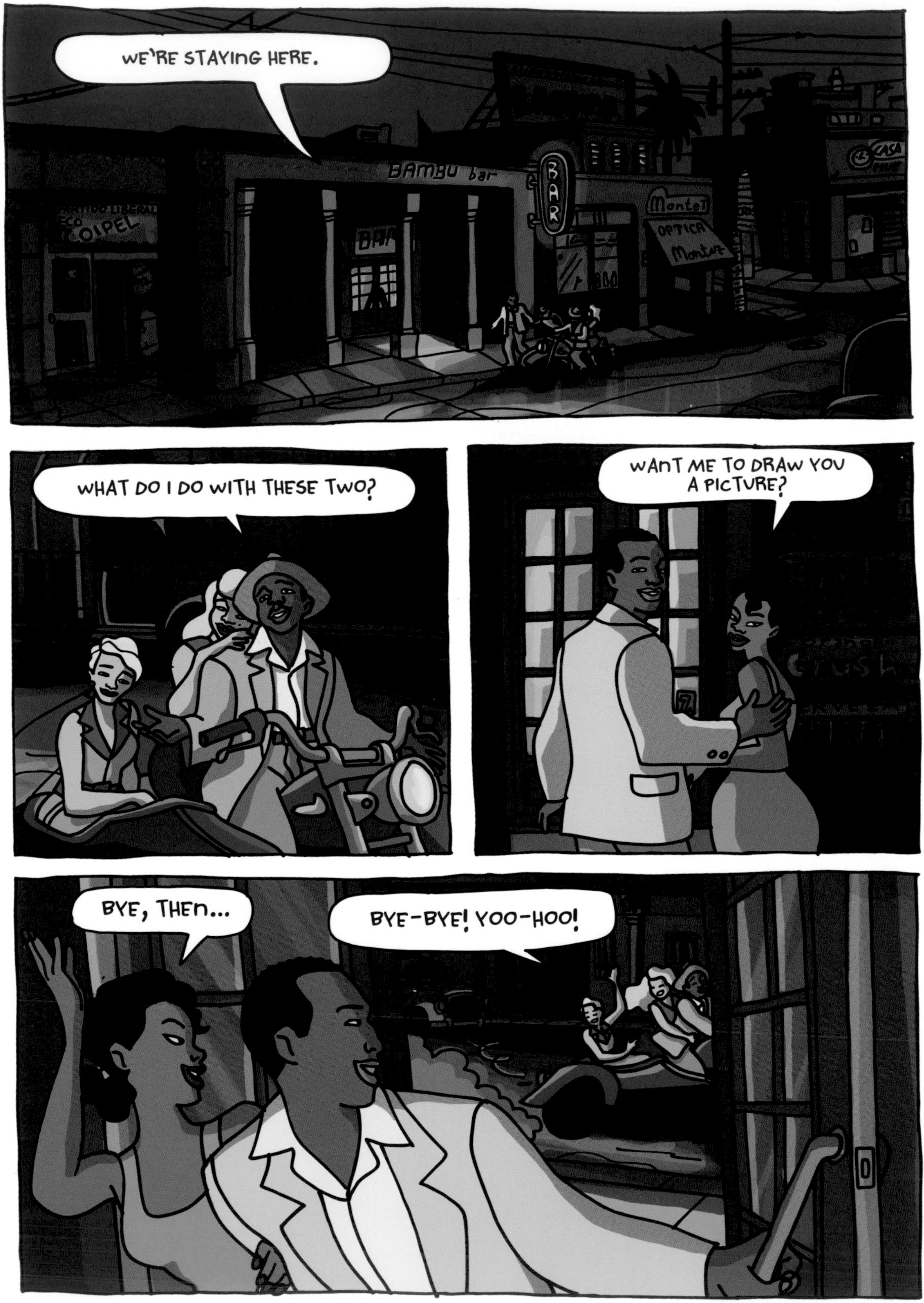
WE'RE STAYING HERE.
BAMBU bar
BAR
OPTICA
WHAT DO I DO WITH THESE TWO?
WANT ME TO DRAW YOU A PICTURE?
BYE, THEN...
BYE-BYE! YOO-HOO!

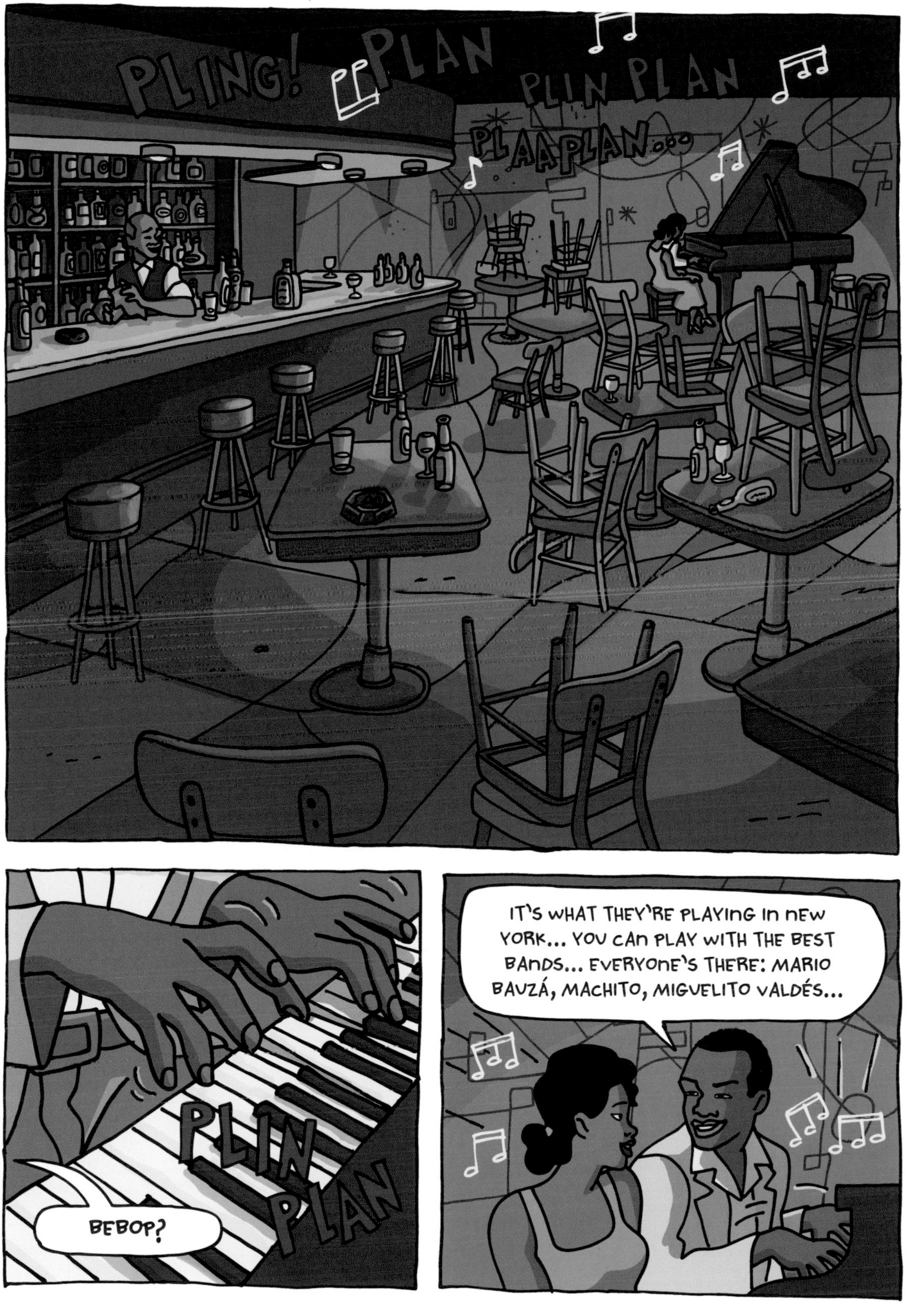
PLING! PLAN PLIN PLAN
PLAAPLAN...
PLIN PLAN
BEBOP?
IT'S WHAT THEY'RE PLAYING IN NEW YORK... YOU CAN PLAY WITH THE BEST BANDS... EVERYONE'S THERE: MARIO BAUZÁ, MACHITO, MIGUELITO VALDÉS...

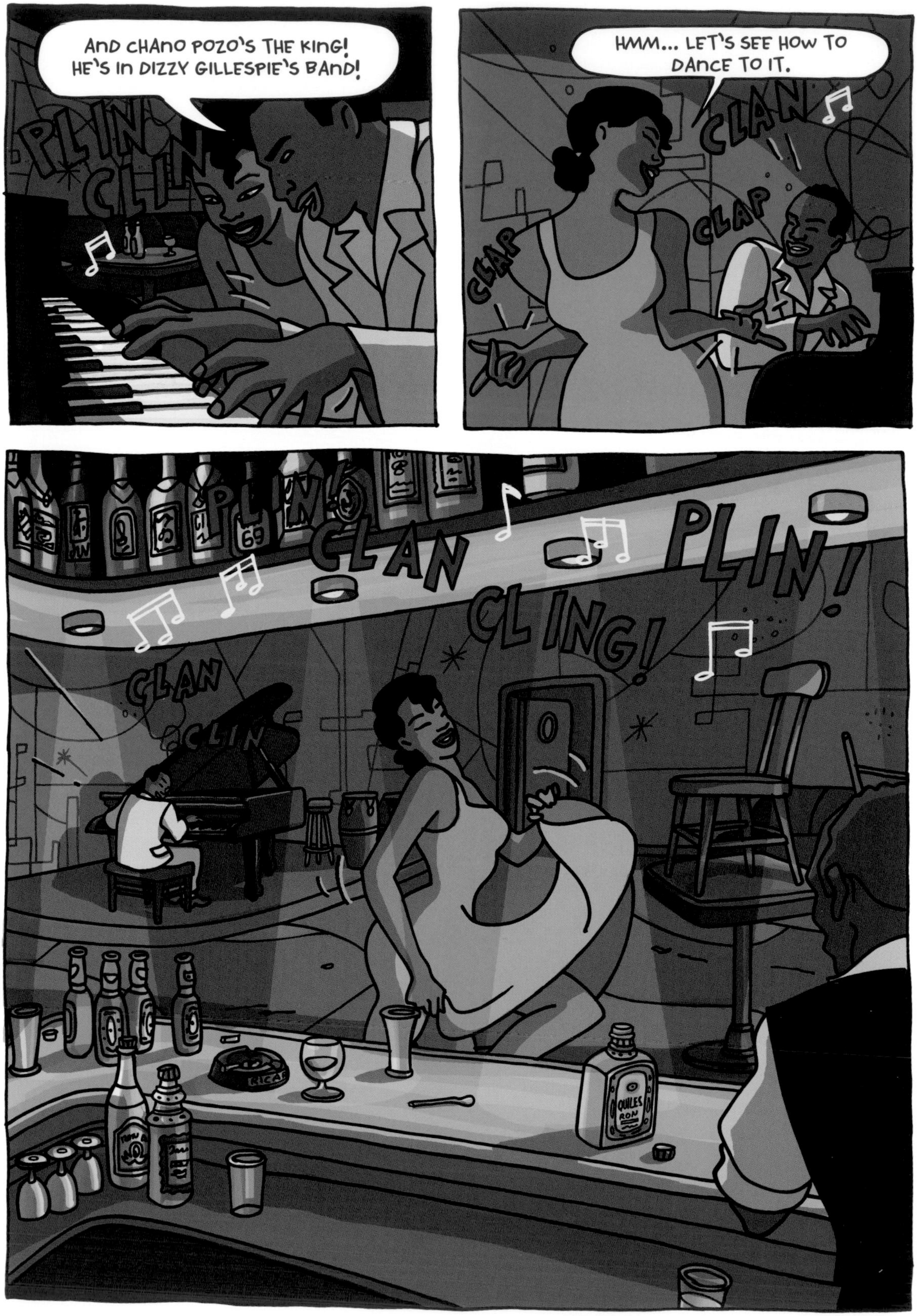

AND CHANO POZO'S THE KING! HE'S IN DIZZY GILLESPIE'S BAND!
PLIN
CLIN
HMM... LET'S SEE HOW TO DANCE TO IT.
CLAN
CLAP
CLAP
CLAP
PLIN!
CLAN
PLIN!
CLING!
CLAN
CLIN
QUILES
RON

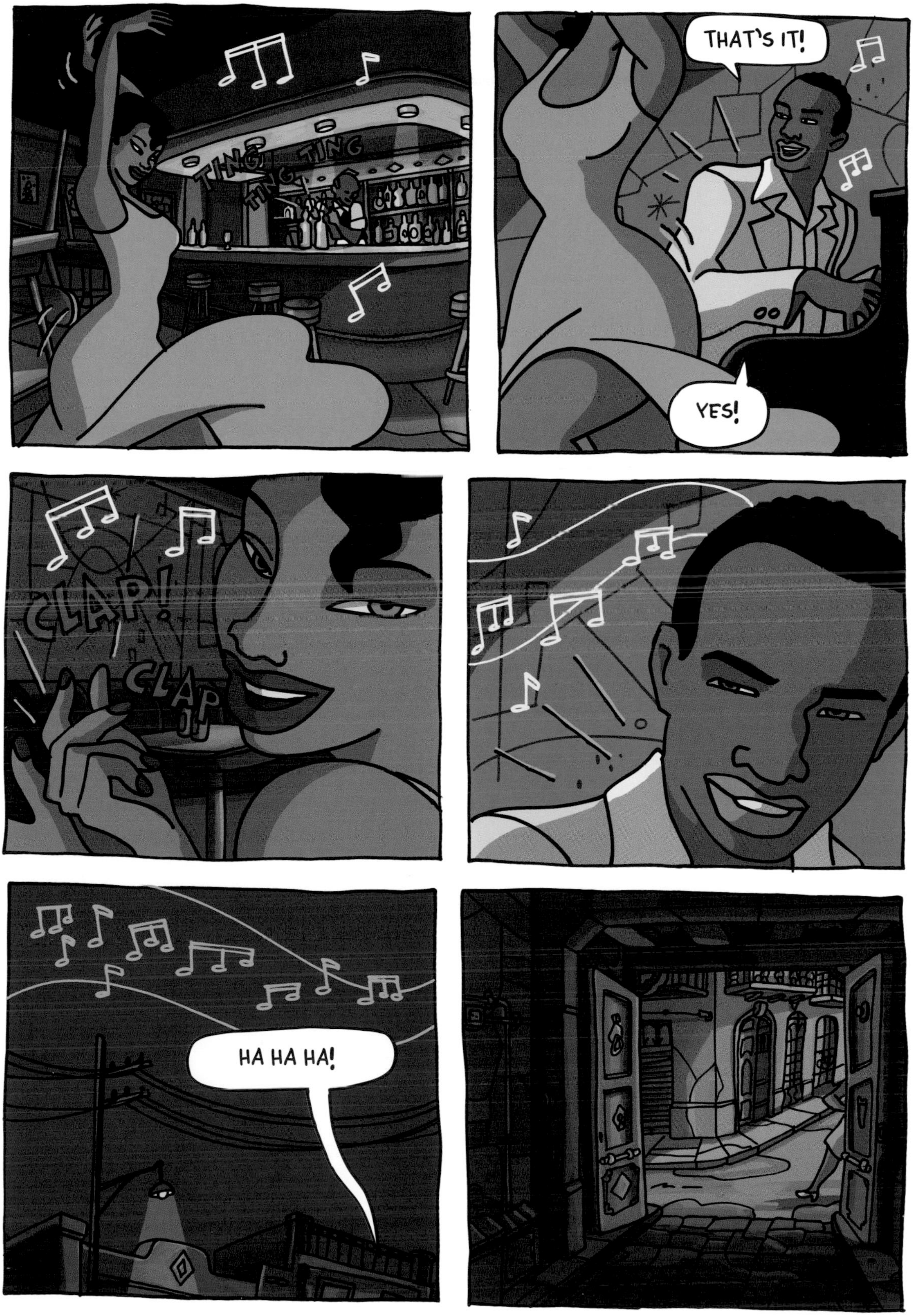
TING TING TING
THAT'S IT!
YES!
CLAP!
CLAP
HA HA HA!

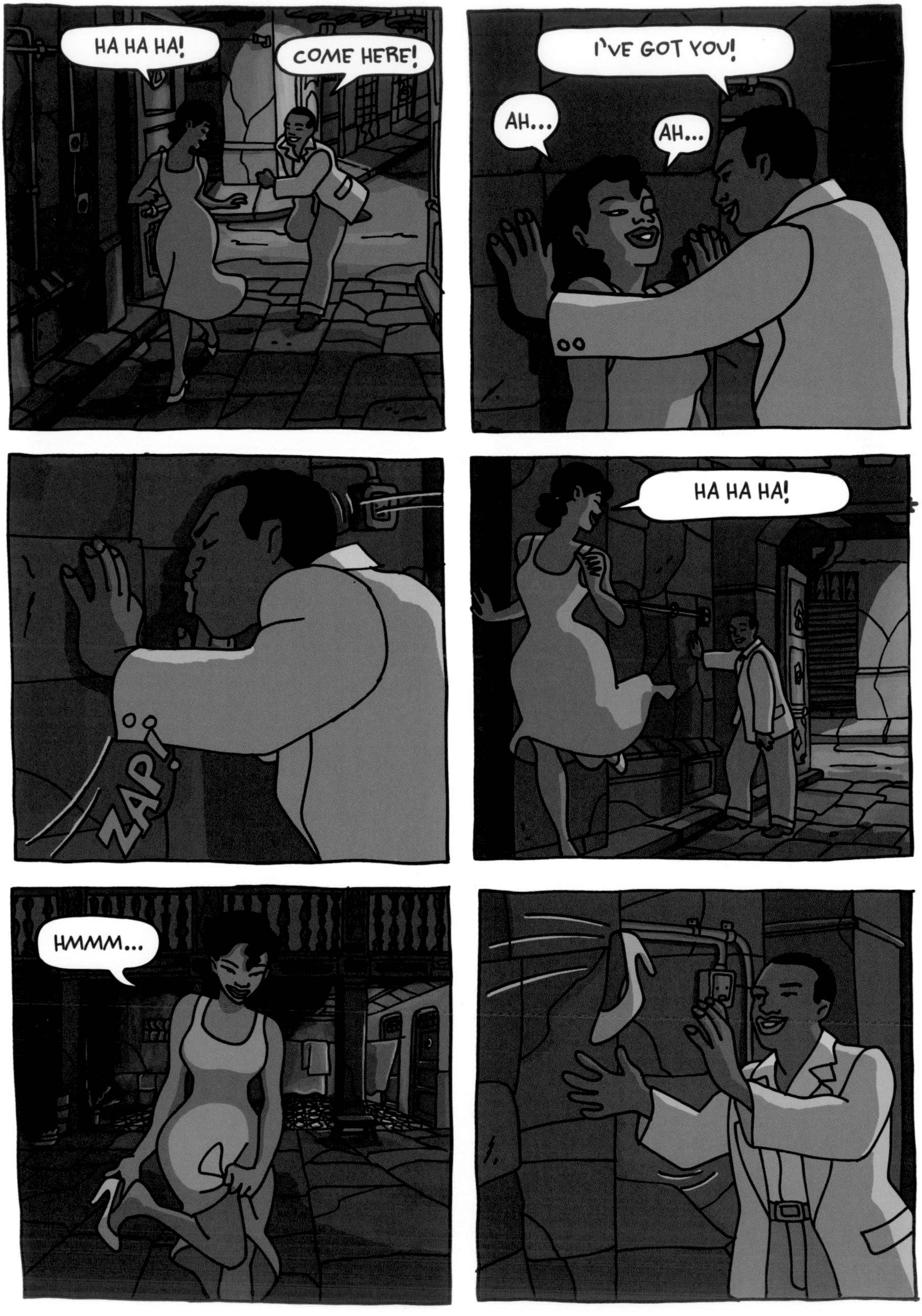
HA HA HA!
COME HERE!
I'VE GOT YOU!
AH...
AH...
ZAP!
HA HA HA!
HMMM...

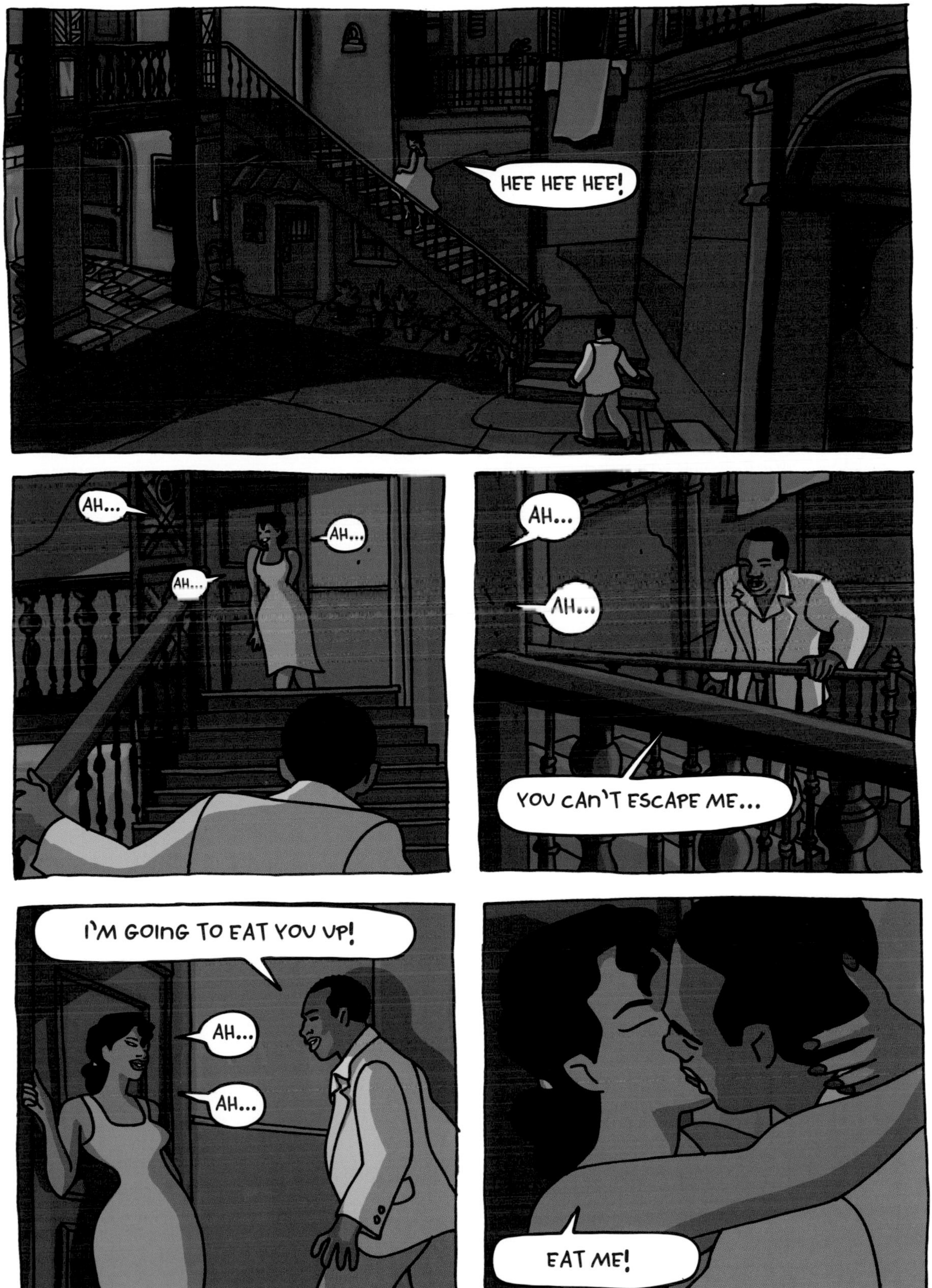
HEE HEE HEE!
AH...
AH...
AH...
AH...
AH...
YOU CAN'T ESCAPE ME...
I'M GOING TO EAT YOU UP!
AH...
AH...
EAT ME!

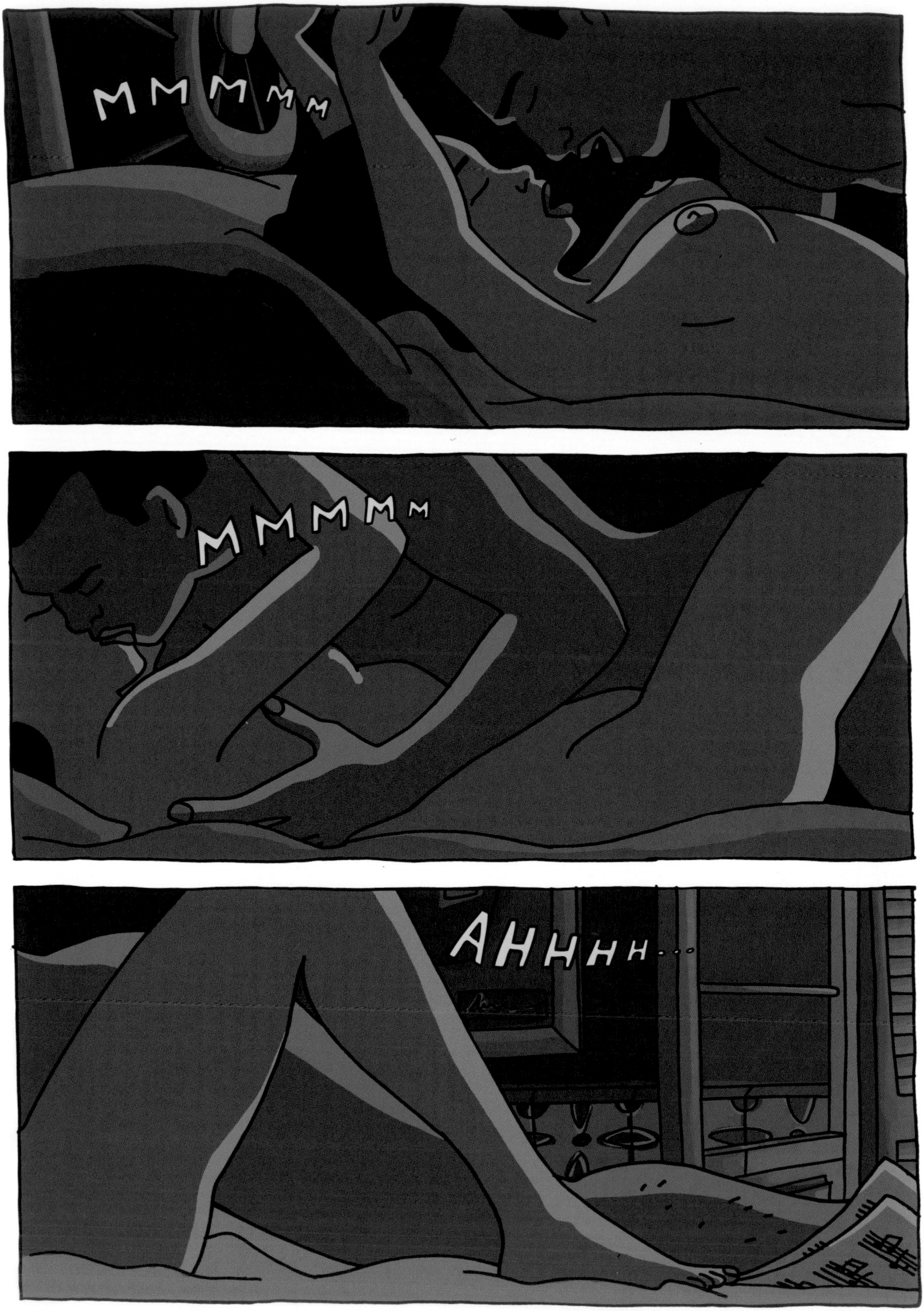
MMMMM
MMMMMM
AHHHH...

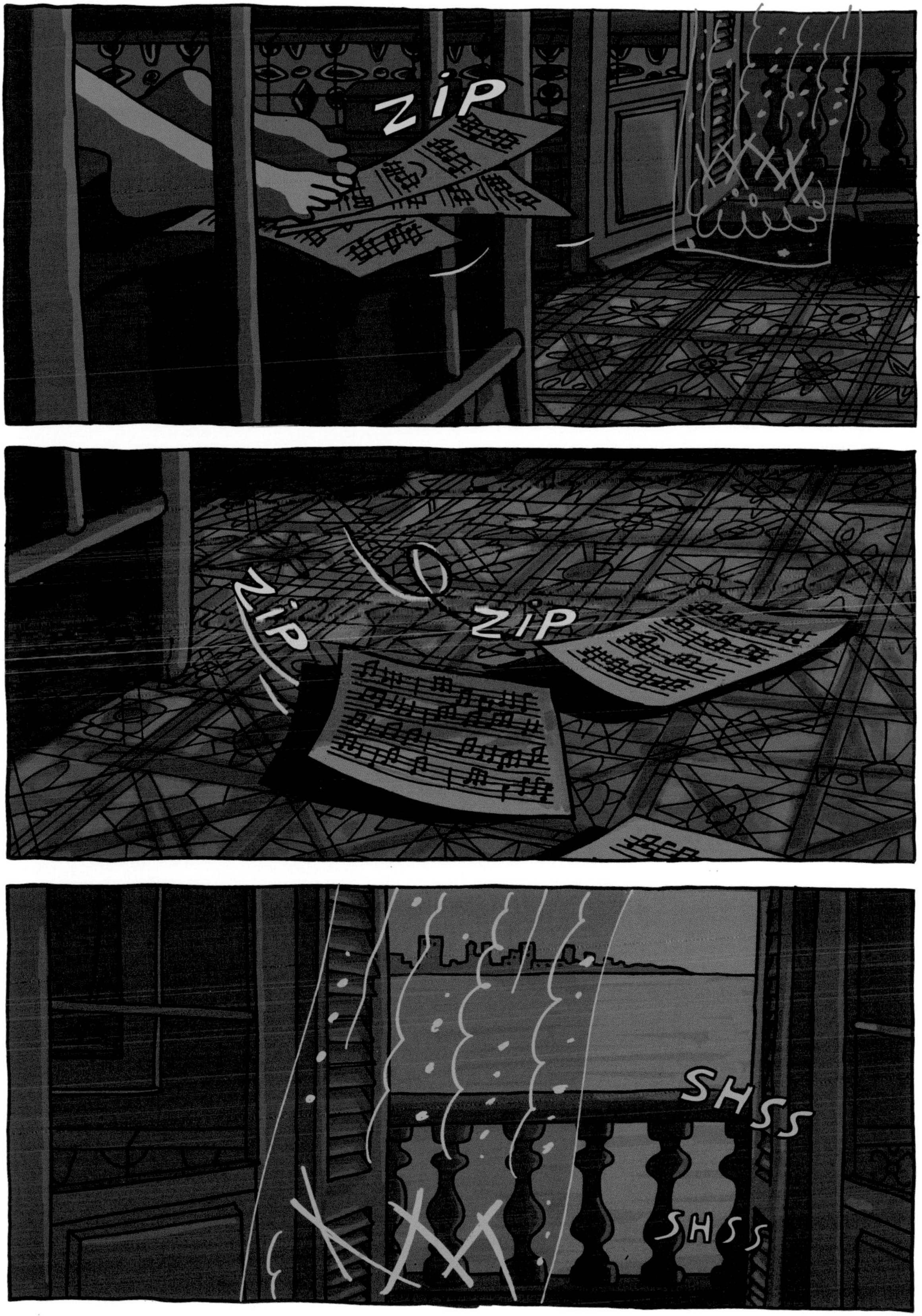
ZIP
ZIP
ZIP
SHSS
SHSS

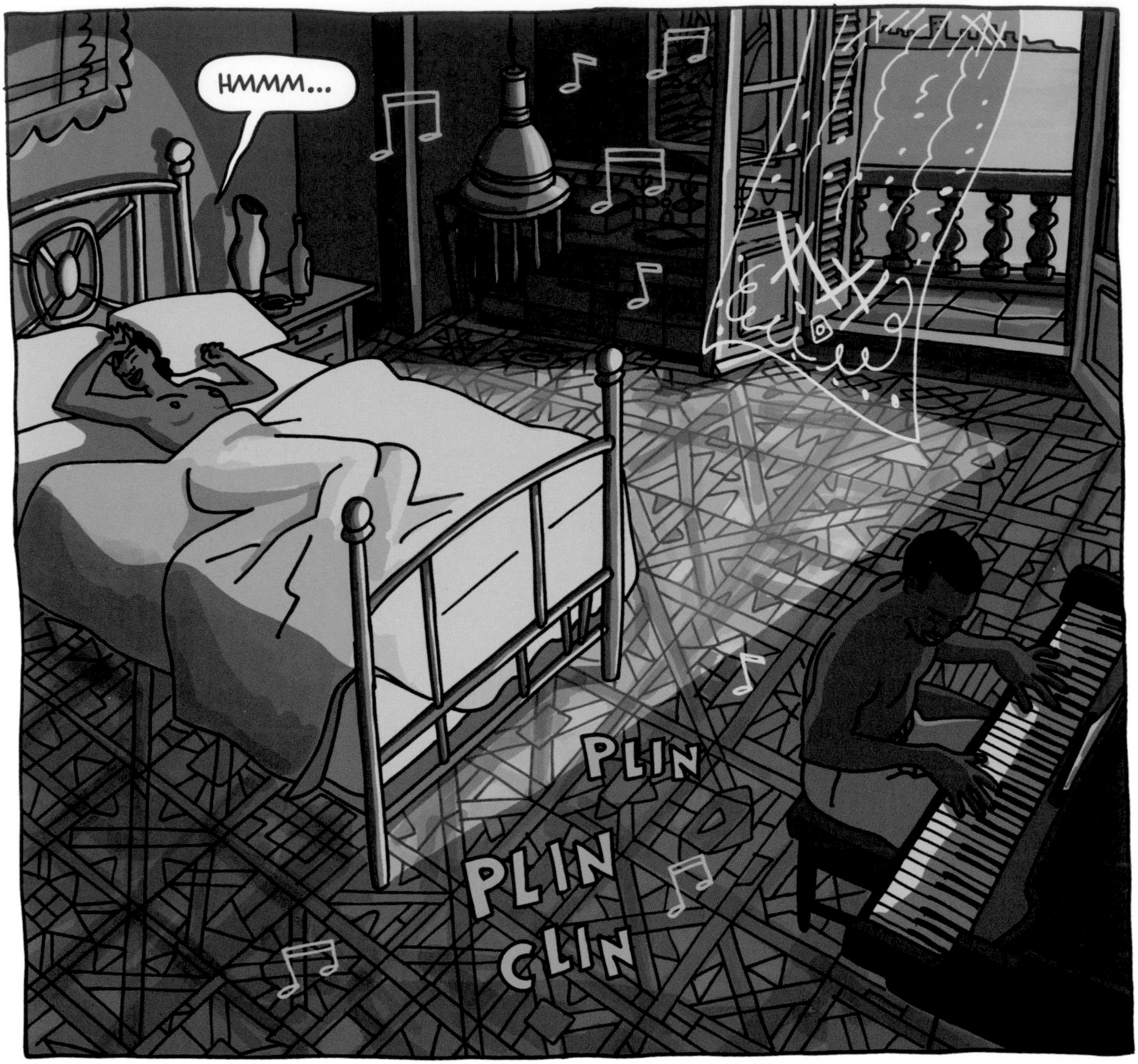
HMMM...
PLIN
PLIN
CLIN

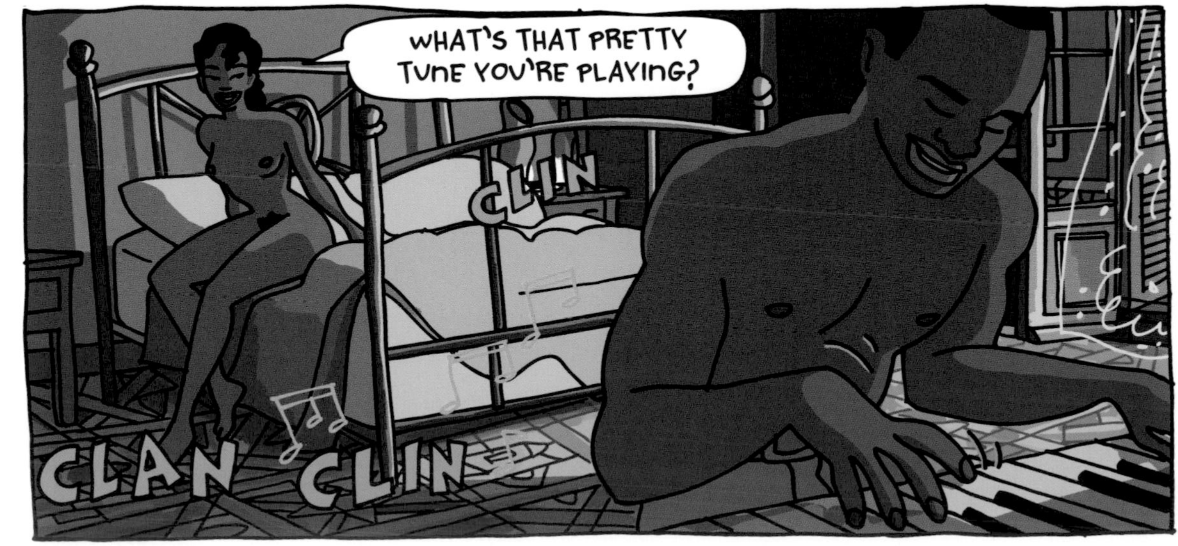
WHAT'S THAT PRETTY TUNE YOU'RE PLAYING?
CLIN
CLAN
CLIN

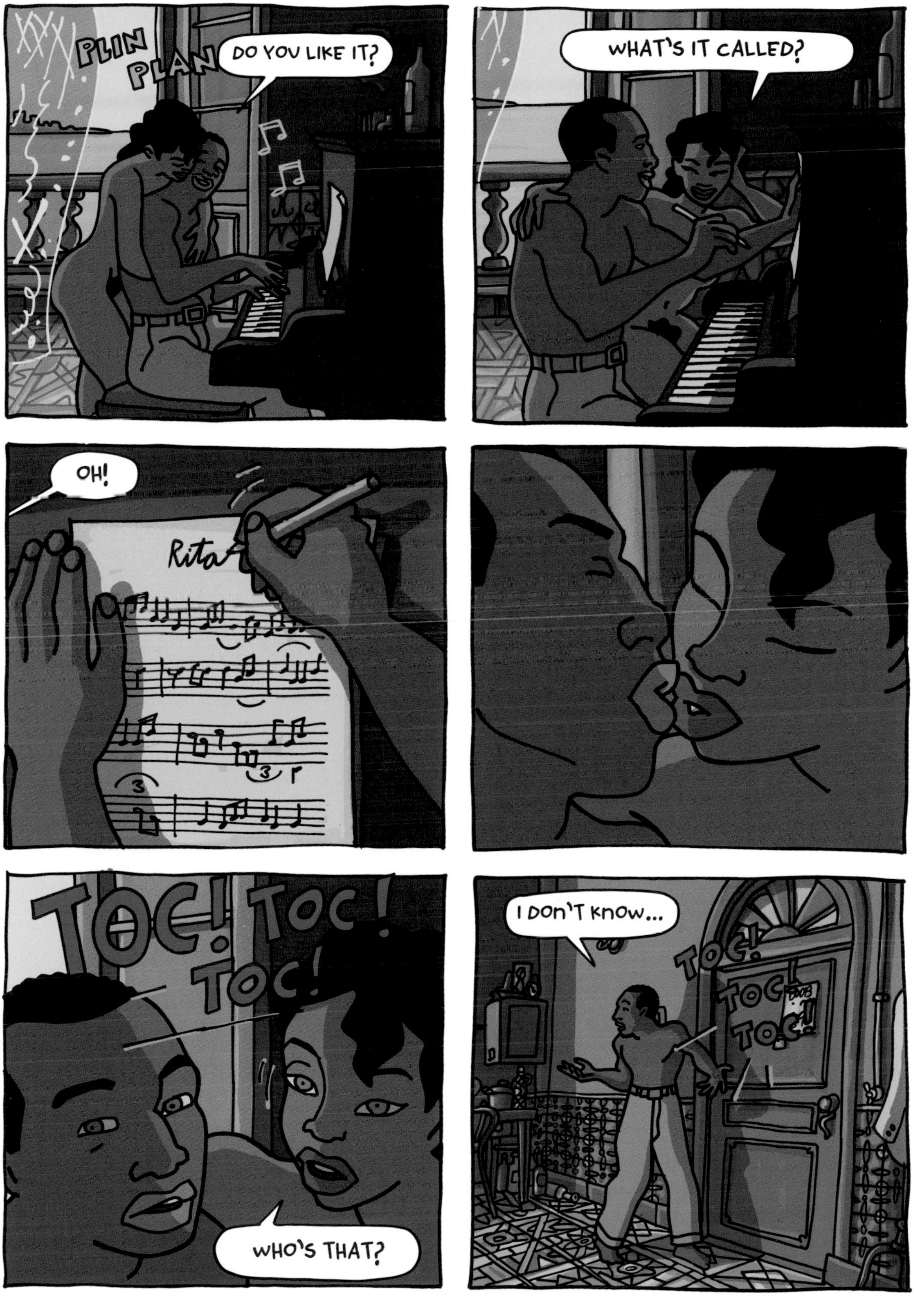
PLIN
PLAN
DO YOU LIKE IT?
WHAT'S IT CALLED?
OH!
Rita
TOC! TOC! TOC!
WHO'S THAT?
I DON'T KNOW...
TOC! TOC! TOC!

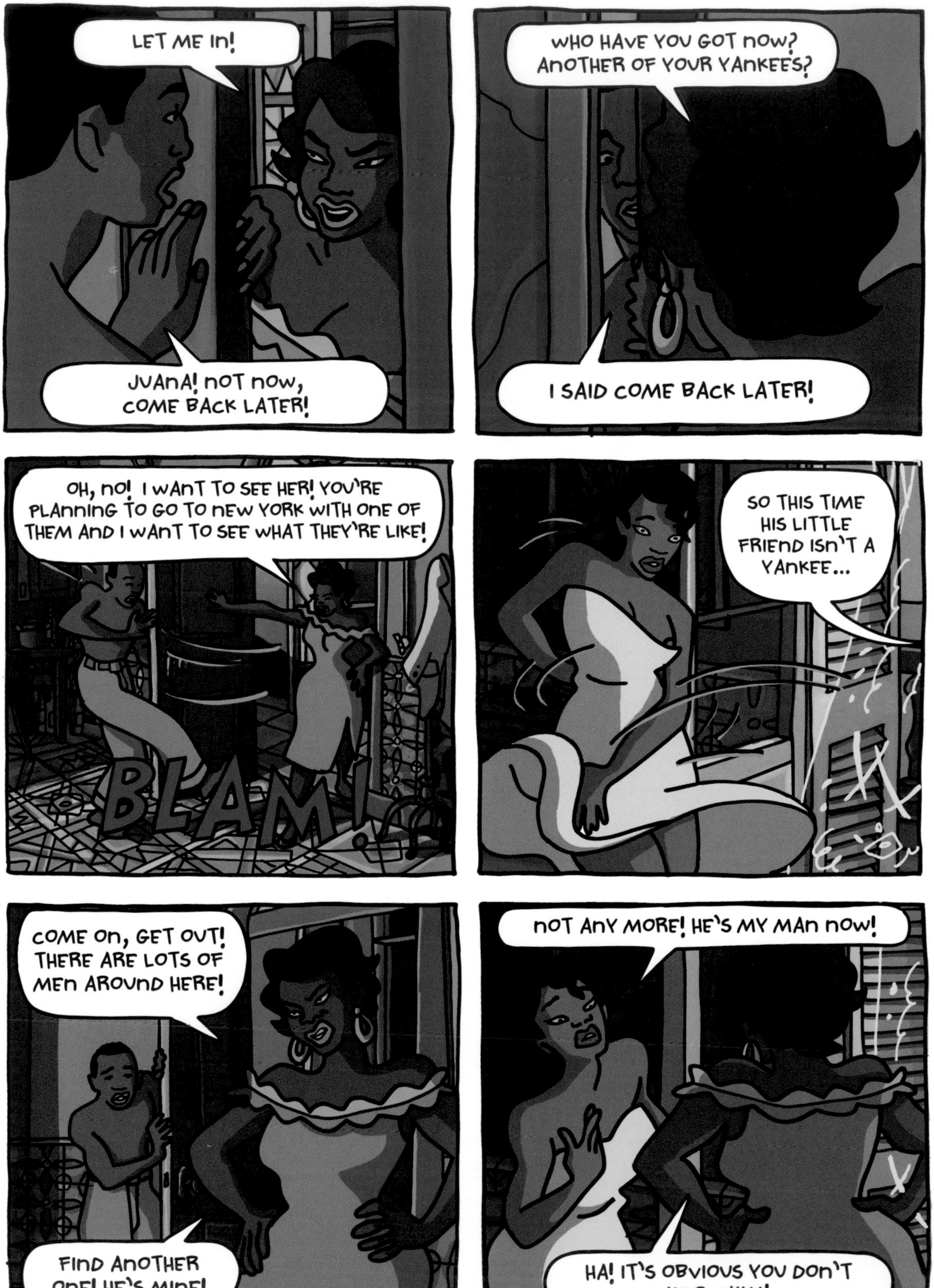
LET ME IN!
JUANA! NOT NOW, COME BACK LATER!
WHO HAVE YOU GOT NOW? ANOTHER OF YOUR YANKEES?
I SAID COME BACK LATER!
OH, NO! I WANT TO SEE HER! YOU'RE PLANNING TO GO TO NEW YORK WITH ONE OF THEM AND I WANT TO SEE WHAT THEY'RE LIKE!
BLAM!
SO THIS TIME HIS LITTLE FRIEND ISN'T A YANKEE...
COME ON, GET OUT! THERE ARE LOTS OF MEN AROUND HERE!
FIND ANOTHER ONE! HE'S MINE!
NOT ANY MORE! HE'S MY MAN NOW!
HA! IT'S OBVIOUS YOU DON'T KNOW HIM!

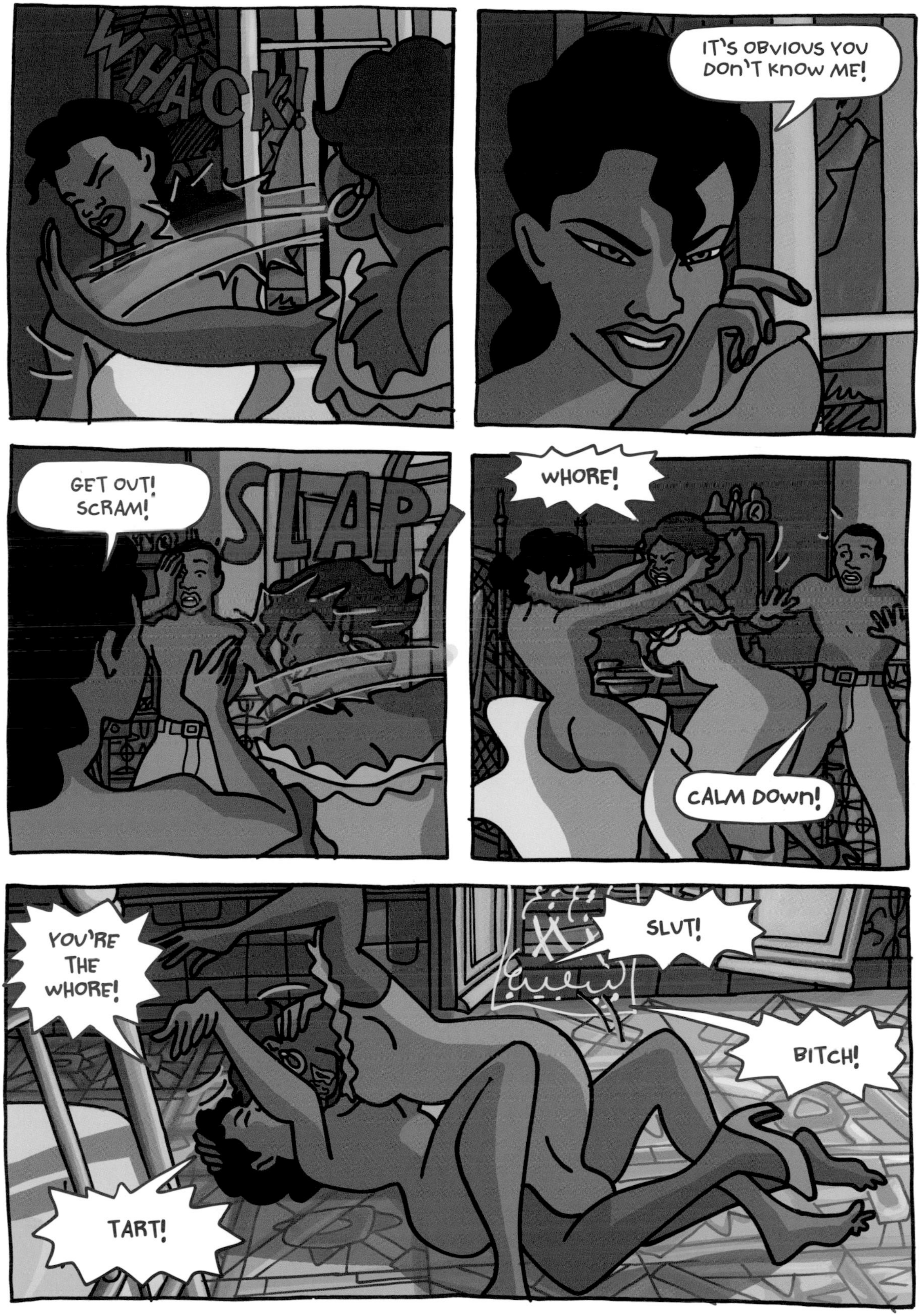
WHACK!
IT'S OBVIOUS YOU DON'T KNOW ME!
GET OUT! SCRAM!
SLAP!
WHORE!
CALM DOWN!
YOU'RE THE WHORE!
SLUT!
BITCH!
TART!

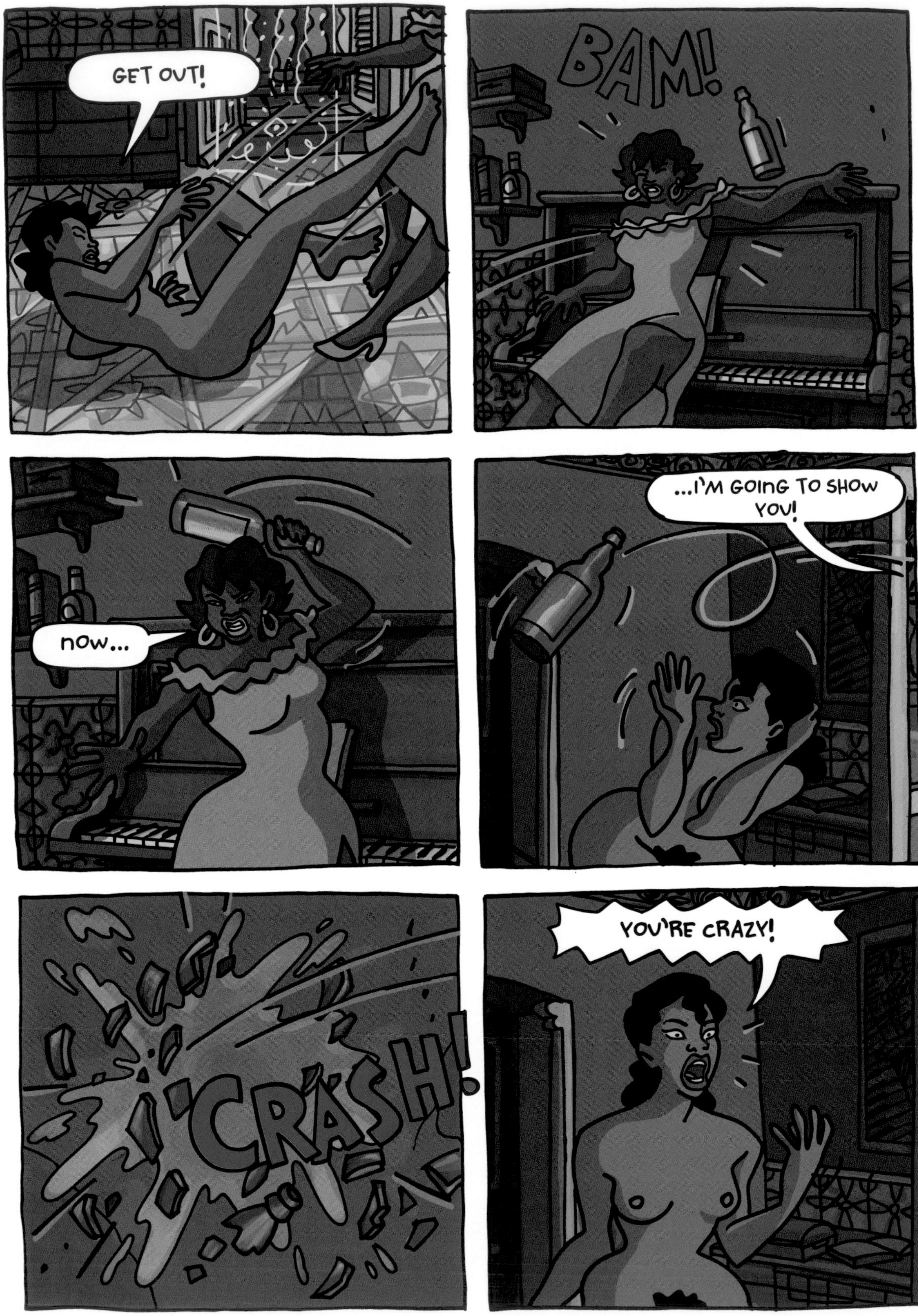
GET OUT!
BAM!
now...
...I'M GOING TO SHOW YOU!
CRASH!
YOU'RE CRAZY!

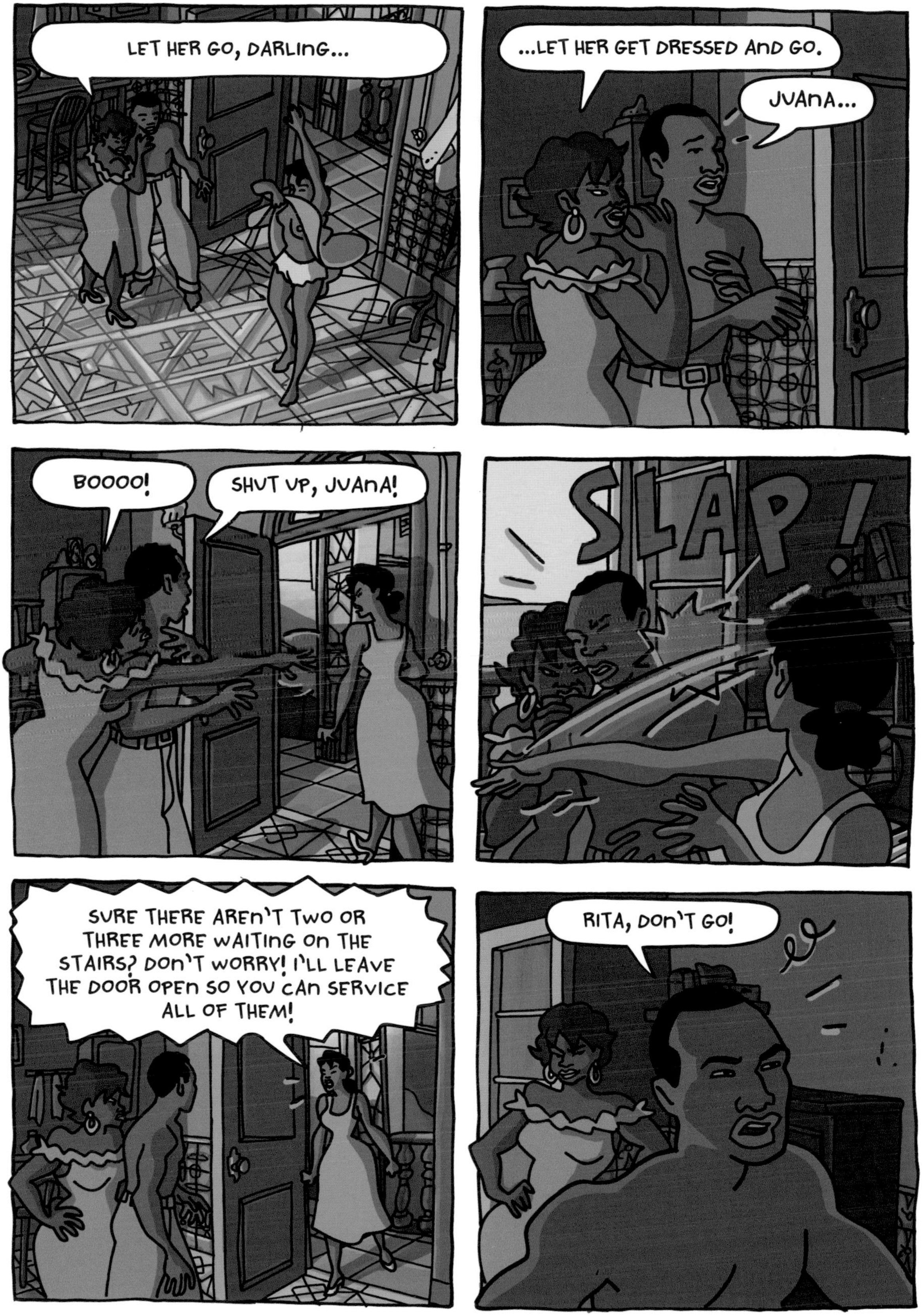
LET HER GO, DARLING...
...LET HER GET DRESSED AND GO.
JUANA...
BOOOO!
SHUT UP, JUANA!
SLAP!
SURE THERE AREN'T TWO OR THREE MORE WAITING ON THE STAIRS? DON'T WORRY! I'LL LEAVE THE DOOR OPEN SO YOU CAN SERVICE ALL OF THEM!
RITA, DON'T GO!

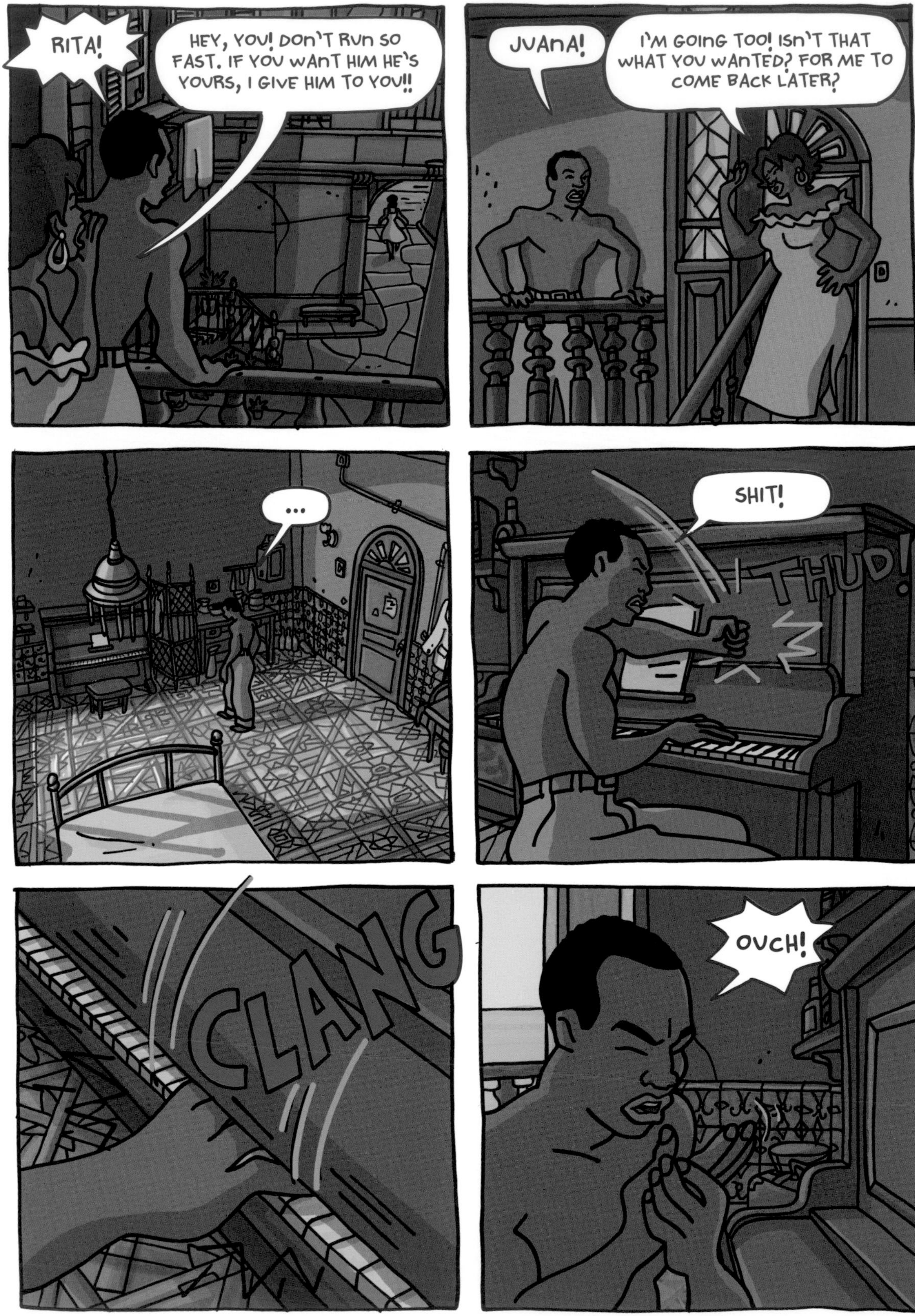
RITA!
HEY, YOU! DON'T RUN SO FAST. IF YOU WANT HIM HE'S YOURS, I GIVE HIM TO YOU!!
JUANA!
I'M GOING TOO! ISN'T THAT WHAT YOU WANTED? FOR ME TO COME BACK LATER?
...
SHIT!
THUD!
CLANG
OUCH!

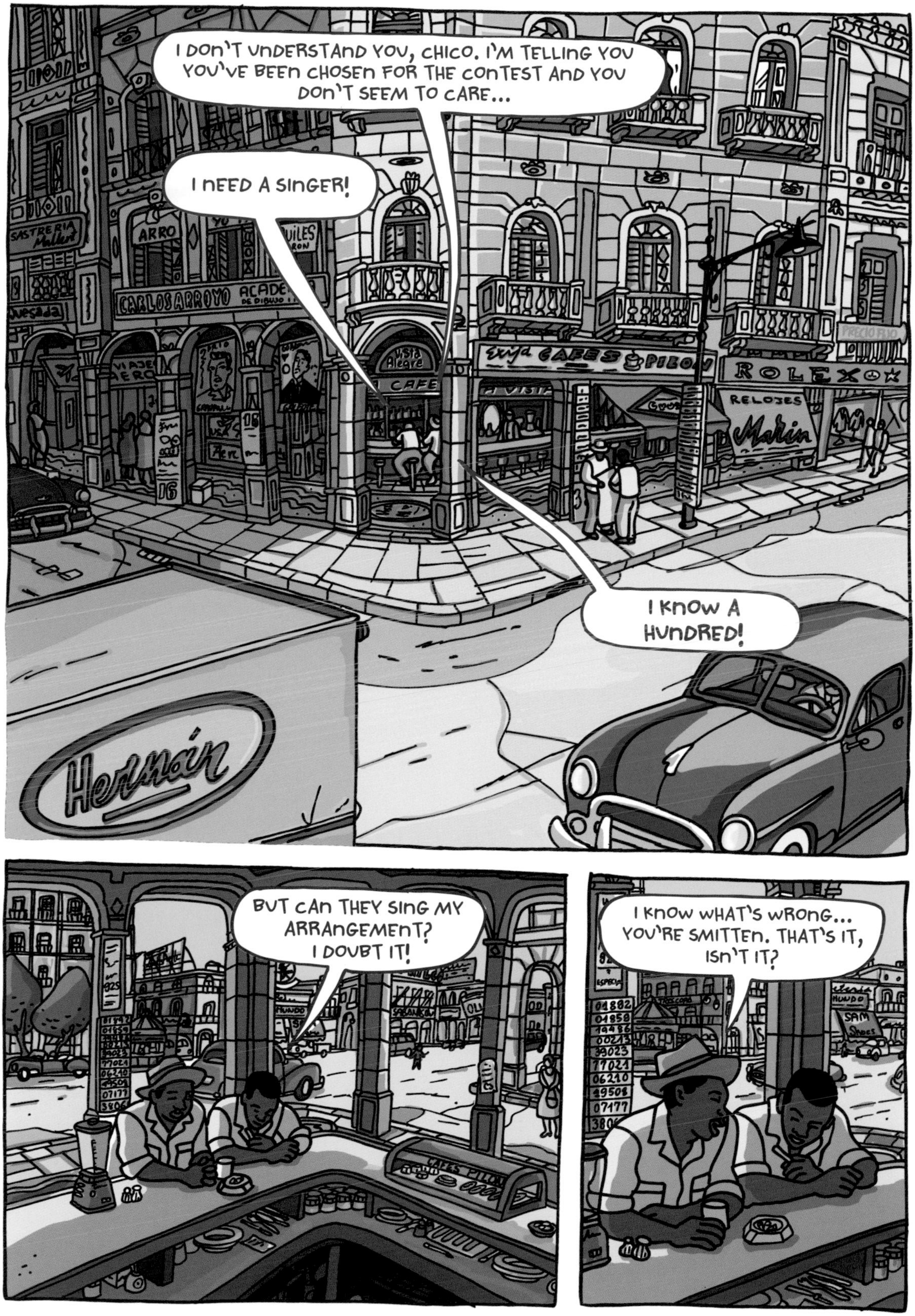

I DON'T UNDERSTAND YOU, CHICO. I'M TELLING YOU YOU'VE BEEN CHOSEN FOR THE CONTEST AND YOU DON'T SEEM TO CARE...
I NEED A SINGER!
I KNOW A HUNDRED!
CARLOS ARROYO
ROLEX
RELOJES
Marin
PRECIO FIJO
BUT CAN THEY SING MY ARRANGEMENT? I DOUBT IT!
I KNOW WHAT'S WRONG... YOU'RE SMITTEN. THAT'S IT, ISN'T IT?

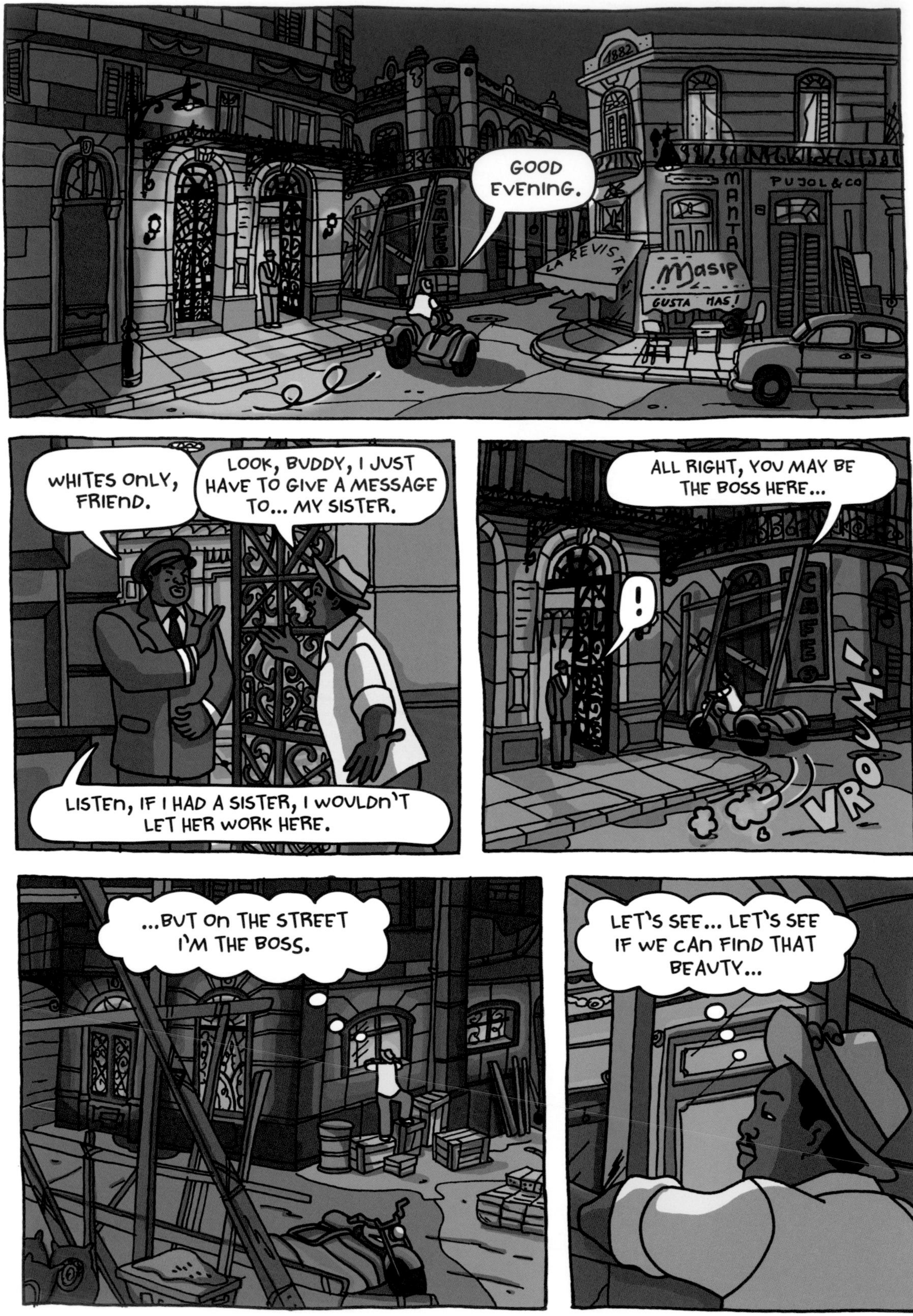
1882
GOOD EVENING.
CAFE
MANTA
PUJOL & CO
LA REVISTA
Masip
GUSTA MAS!
WHITES ONLY, FRIEND.
LOOK, BUDDY, I JUST HAVE TO GIVE A MESSAGE TO... MY SISTER.
LISTEN, IF I HAD A SISTER, I WOULDN'T LET HER WORK HERE.
ALL RIGHT, YOU MAY BE THE BOSS HERE...
!
VROOOM!
...BUT ON THE STREET I'M THE BOSS.
LET'S SEE... LET'S SEE IF WE CAN FIND THAT BEAUTY...

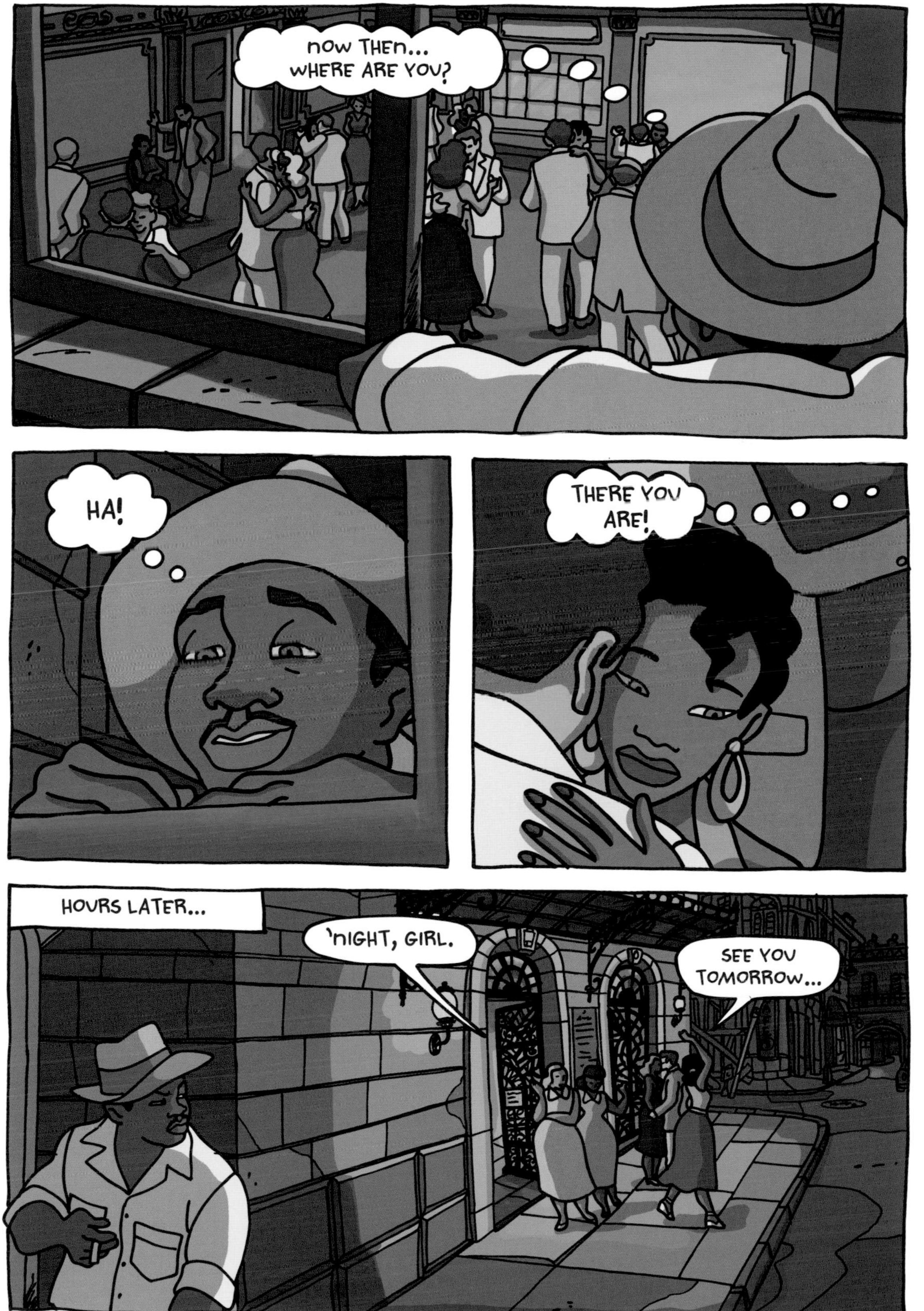
NOW THEN...
WHERE ARE YOU?
HA!
THERE YOU ARE!
HOURS LATER...
'NIGHT, GIRL.
SEE YOU TOMORROW...

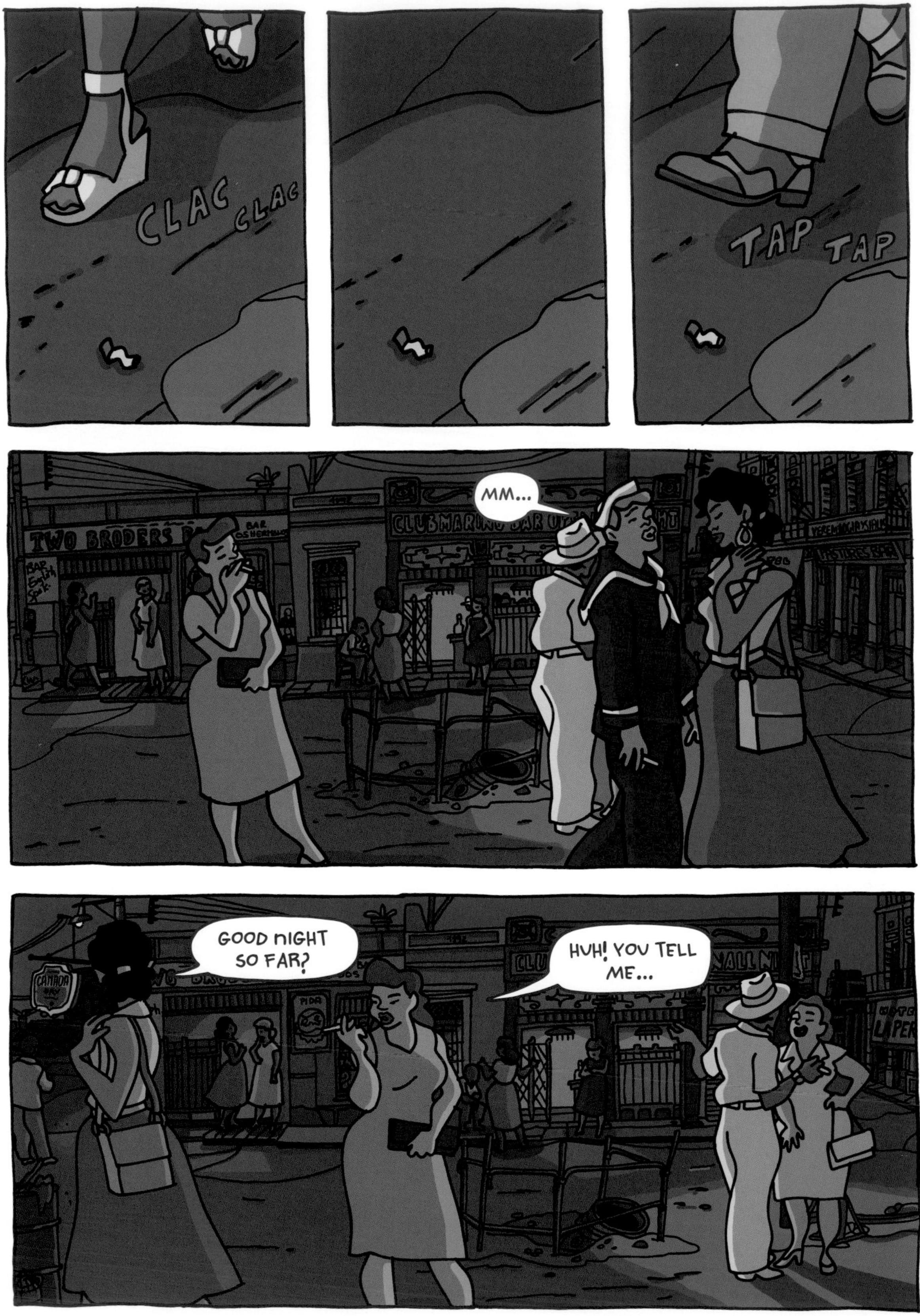
CLAC CLAC
TAP TAP
MM...
GOOD NIGHT SO FAR?
HUH! YOU TELL ME...

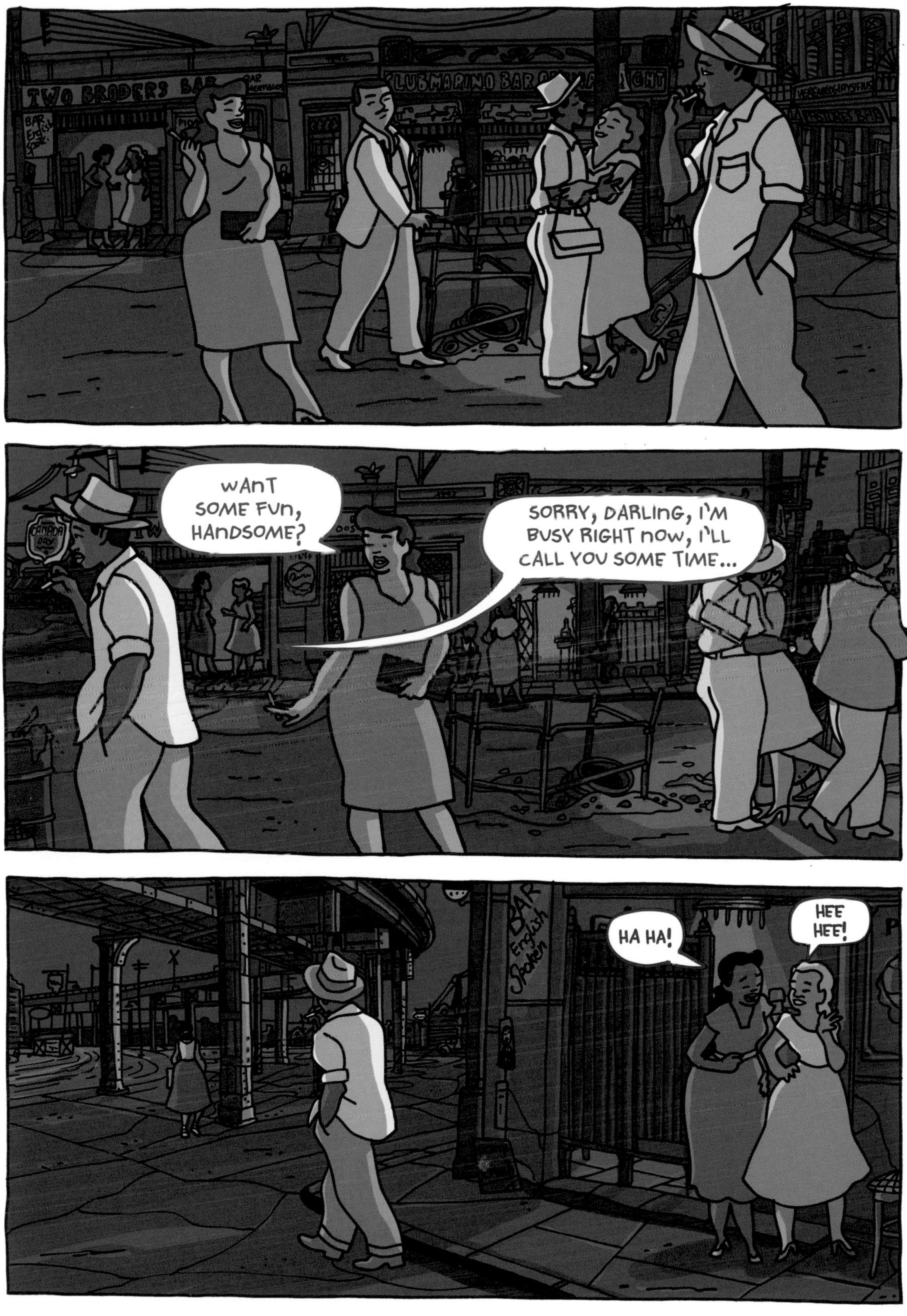
TWO BRODERS BAR
WANT SOME FUN, HANDSOME?
SORRY, DARLING, I'M BUSY RIGHT NOW, I'LL CALL YOU SOME TIME...
BAR English Spoken
HA HA!
HEE HEE!

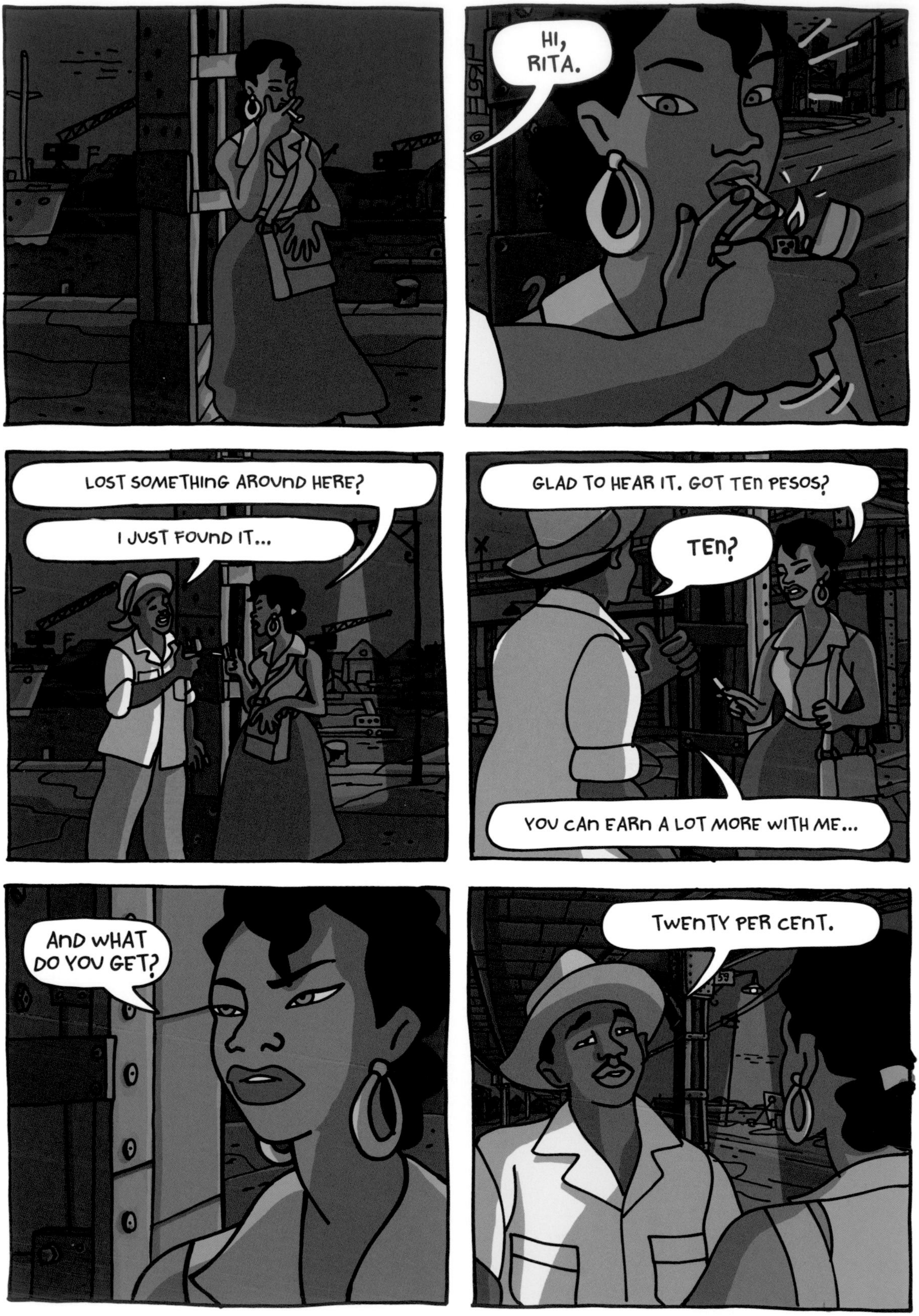
HI, RITA.
LOST SOMETHING AROUND HERE?
I JUST FOUND IT...
GLAD TO HEAR IT. GOT TEN PESOS?
TEN?
YOU CAN EARN A LOT MORE WITH ME...
AND WHAT DO YOU GET?
TWENTY PER CENT.

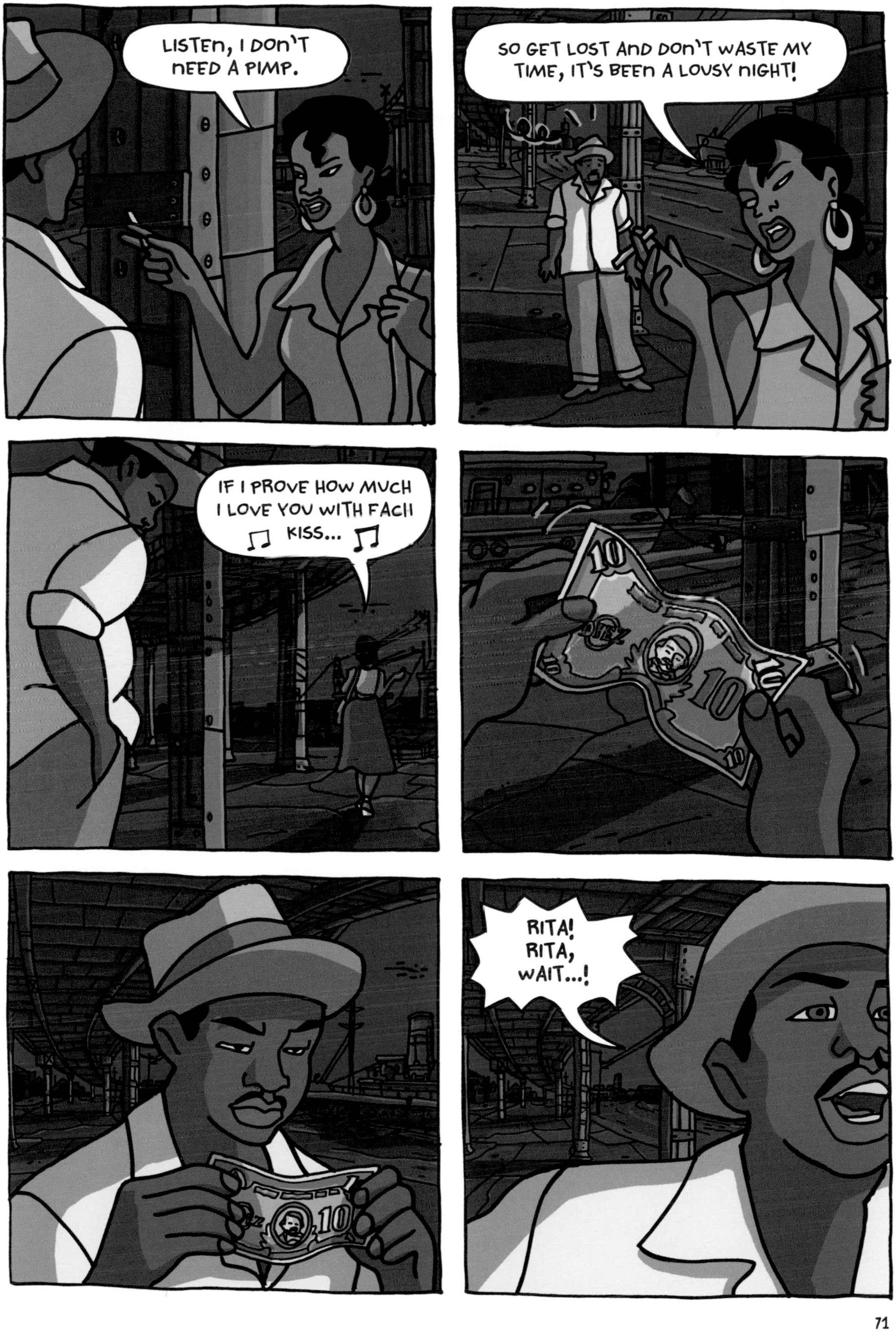
LISTEN, I DON'T NEED A PIMP.
SO GET LOST AND DON'T WASTE MY TIME, IT'S BEEN A LOUSY NIGHT!
IF I PROVE HOW MUCH I LOVE YOU WITH EACH ♫ KISS... ♫
RITA! RITA, WAIT...!

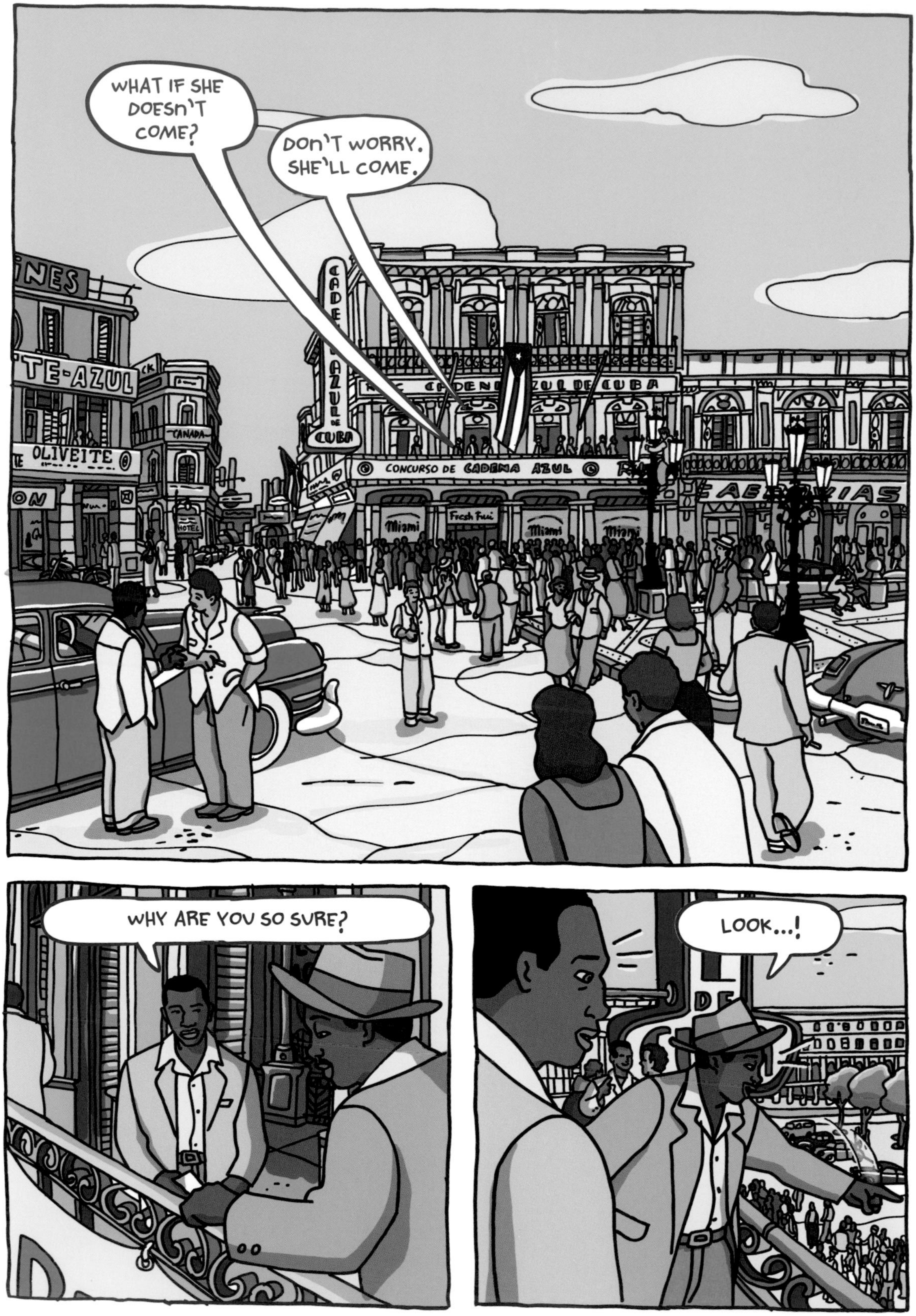
WHAT IF SHE DOESN'T COME?
DON'T WORRY. SHE'LL COME.
CONCURSO DE CADENA AZUL
CADENA AZUL DE CUBA
WHY ARE YOU SO SURE?
LOOK...!

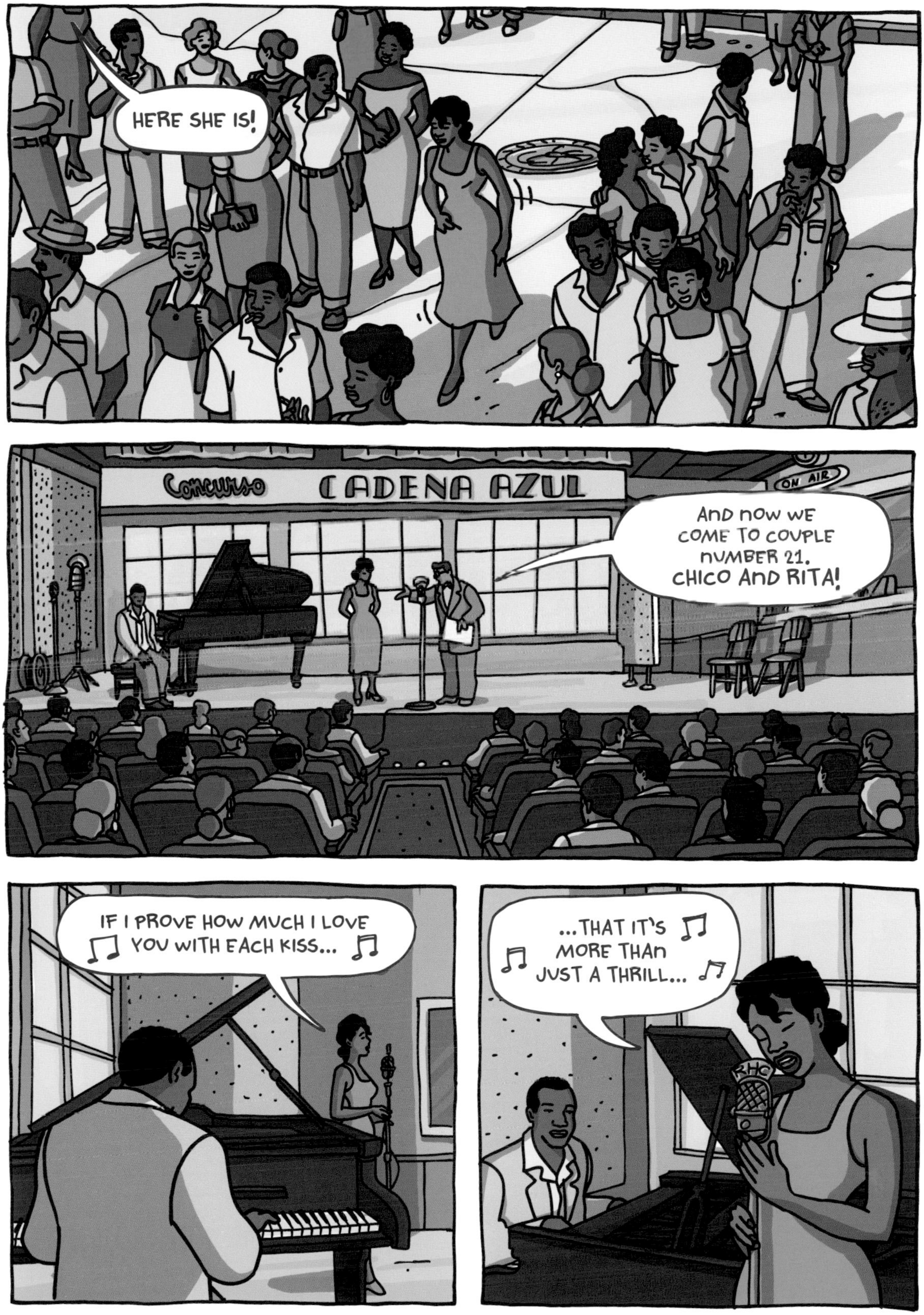
HERE SHE IS!
Concurso CADENA AZUL
ON AIR
AND NOW WE COME TO COUPLE NUMBER 21. CHICO AND RITA!
IF I PROVE HOW MUCH I LOVE YOU WITH EACH KISS...
...THAT IT'S MORE THAN JUST A THRILL...
RHC

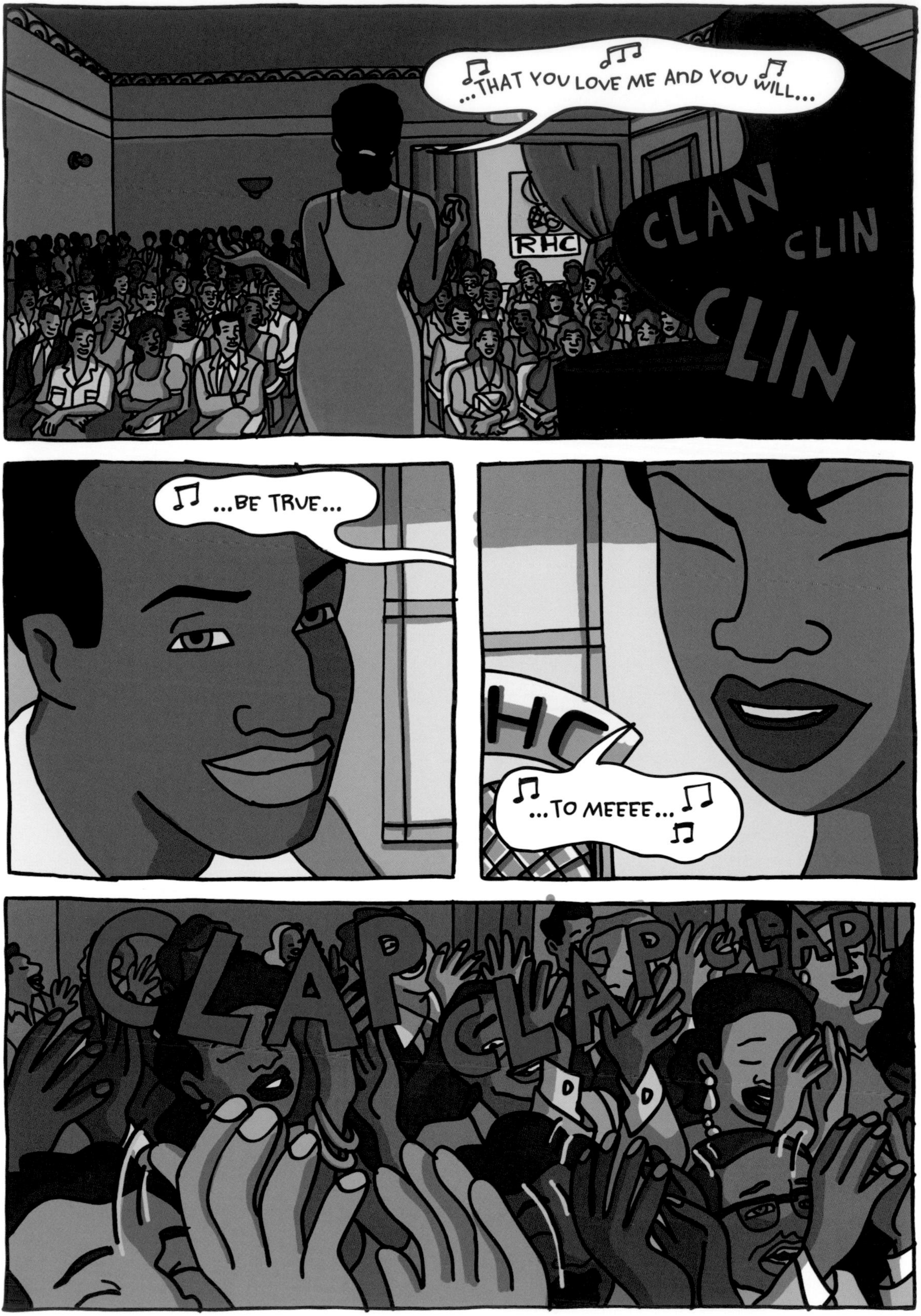
...THAT YOU LOVE ME AND YOU WILL...
RHC
CLAN CLIN CLIN
...BE TRUE...
...TO MEEEE...
CLAP CLAP CLAP!

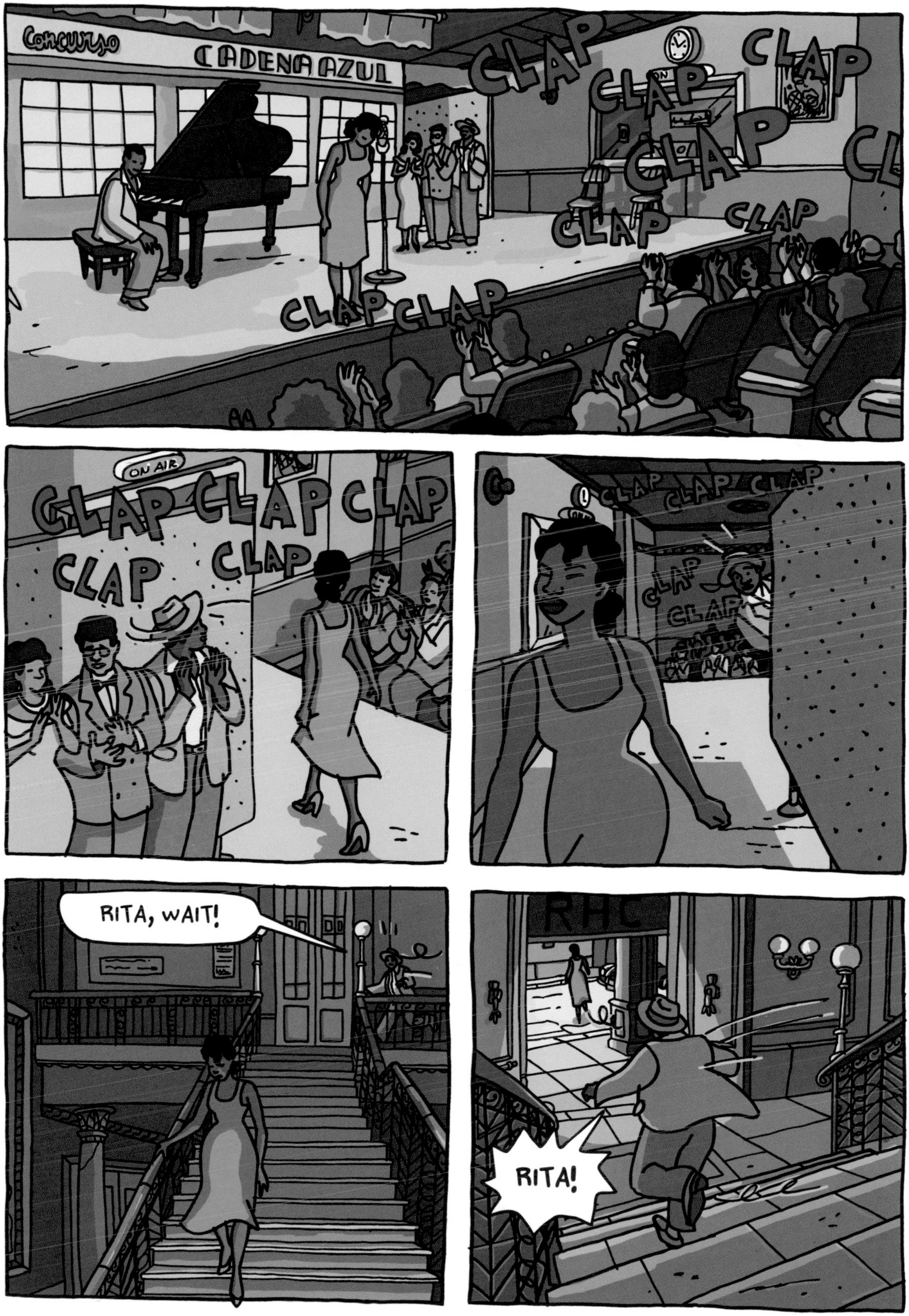
Concurso
CADENA AZUL
CLAP
CLAP
CLAP
CLAP
CLAP
CLAP
CLAP CLAP
ON AIR
CLAP CLAP CLAP
CLAP
CLAP
CLAP CLAP CLAP
CLAP
CLAP
RITA, WAIT!
RHC
RITA!

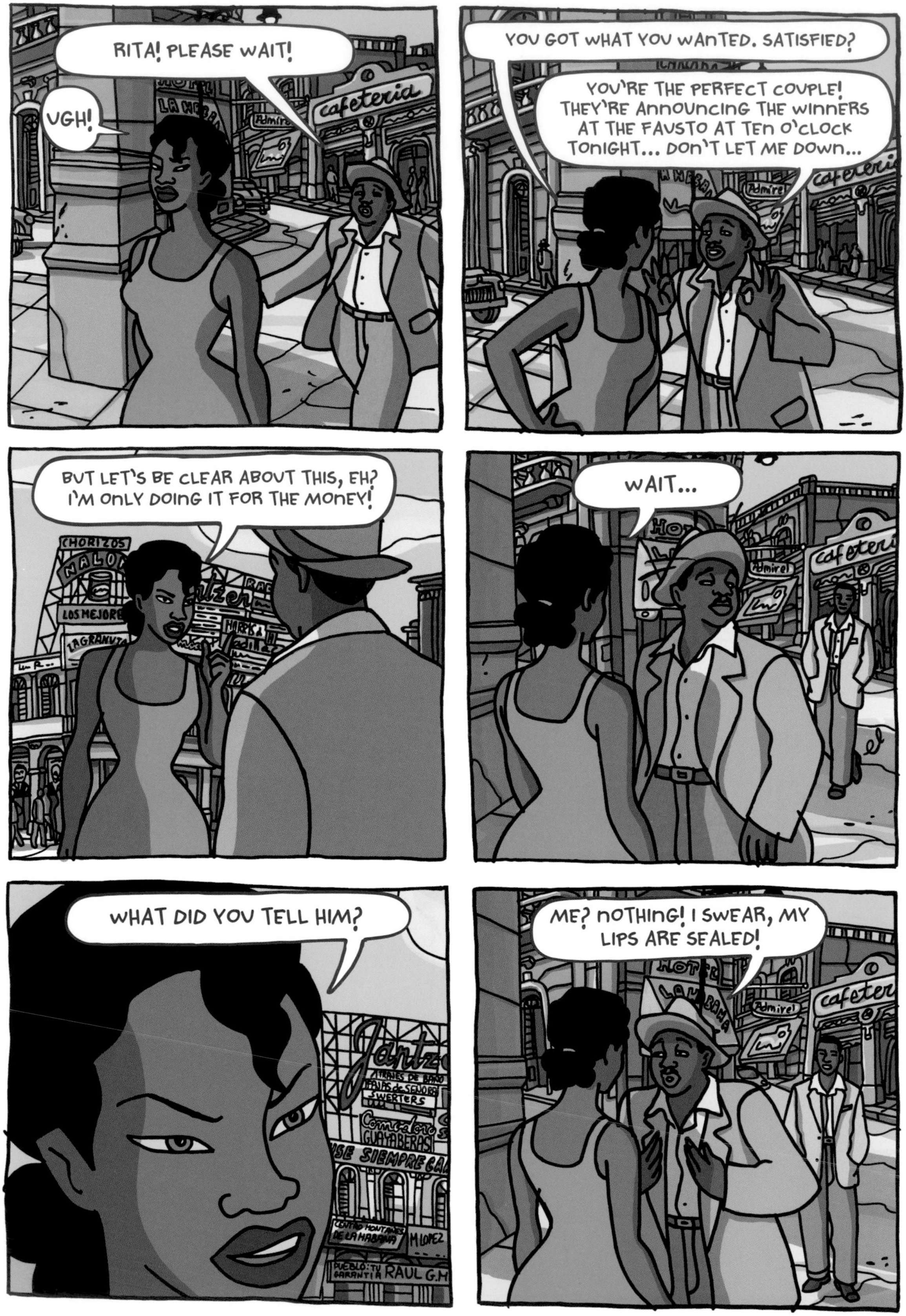
RITA! PLEASE WAIT!
UGH!
YOU GOT WHAT YOU WANTED. SATISFIED?
YOU'RE THE PERFECT COUPLE! THEY'RE ANNOUNCING THE WINNERS AT THE FAUSTO AT TEN O'CLOCK TONIGHT... DON'T LET ME DOWN...
BUT LET'S BE CLEAR ABOUT THIS, EH? I'M ONLY DOING IT FOR THE MONEY!
WAIT...
WHAT DID YOU TELL HIM?
ME? NOTHING! I SWEAR, MY LIPS ARE SEALED!

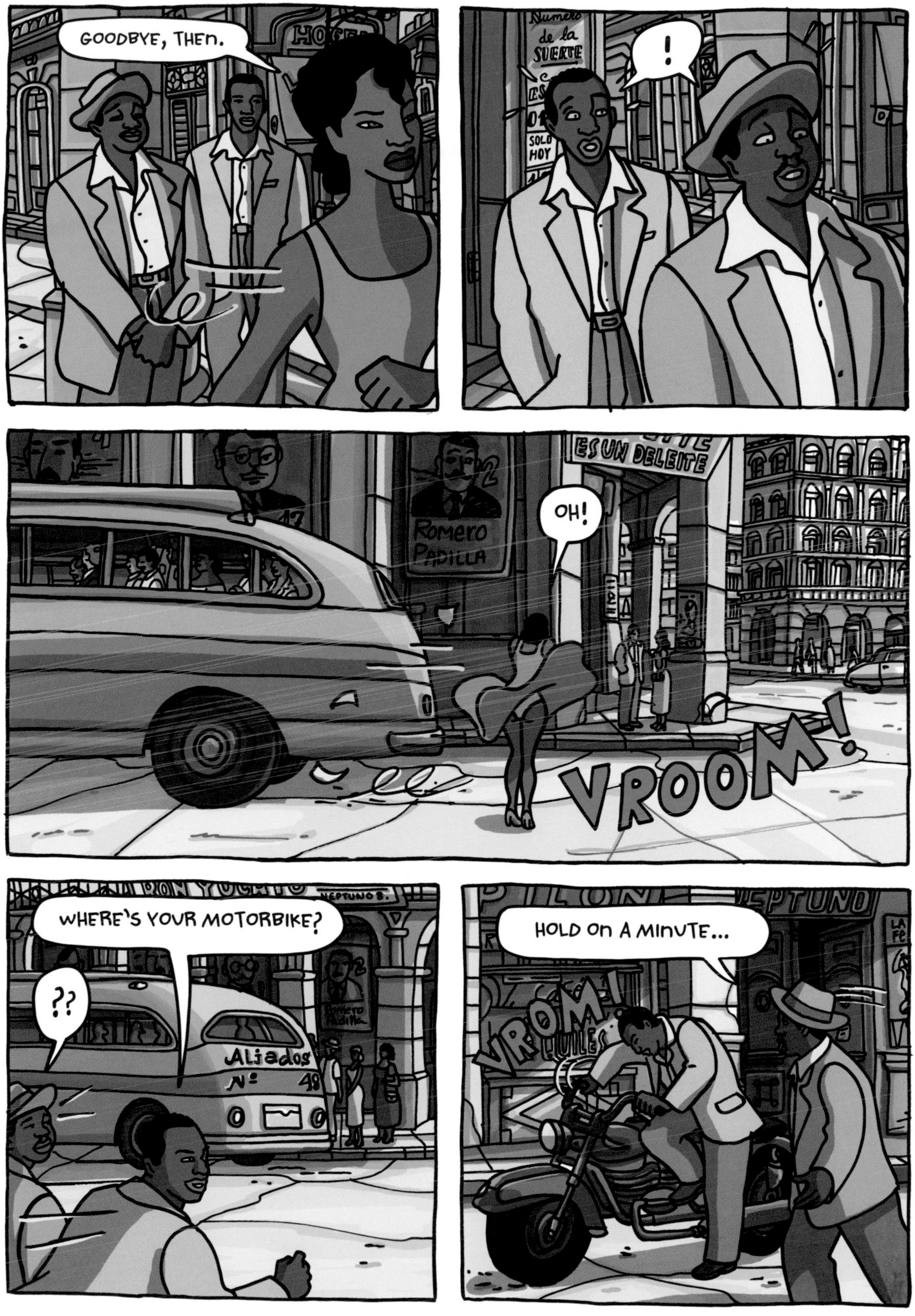
GOODBYE, THEN.
Numero de la SUERTE
SOLO HOY
!
ES UN DELEITE
Romero PADILLA
OH!
VROOM!
WHERE'S YOUR MOTORBIKE?
??
Aliados Nº 48
HOLD ON A MINUTE...
VROOM!
NEPTUNO

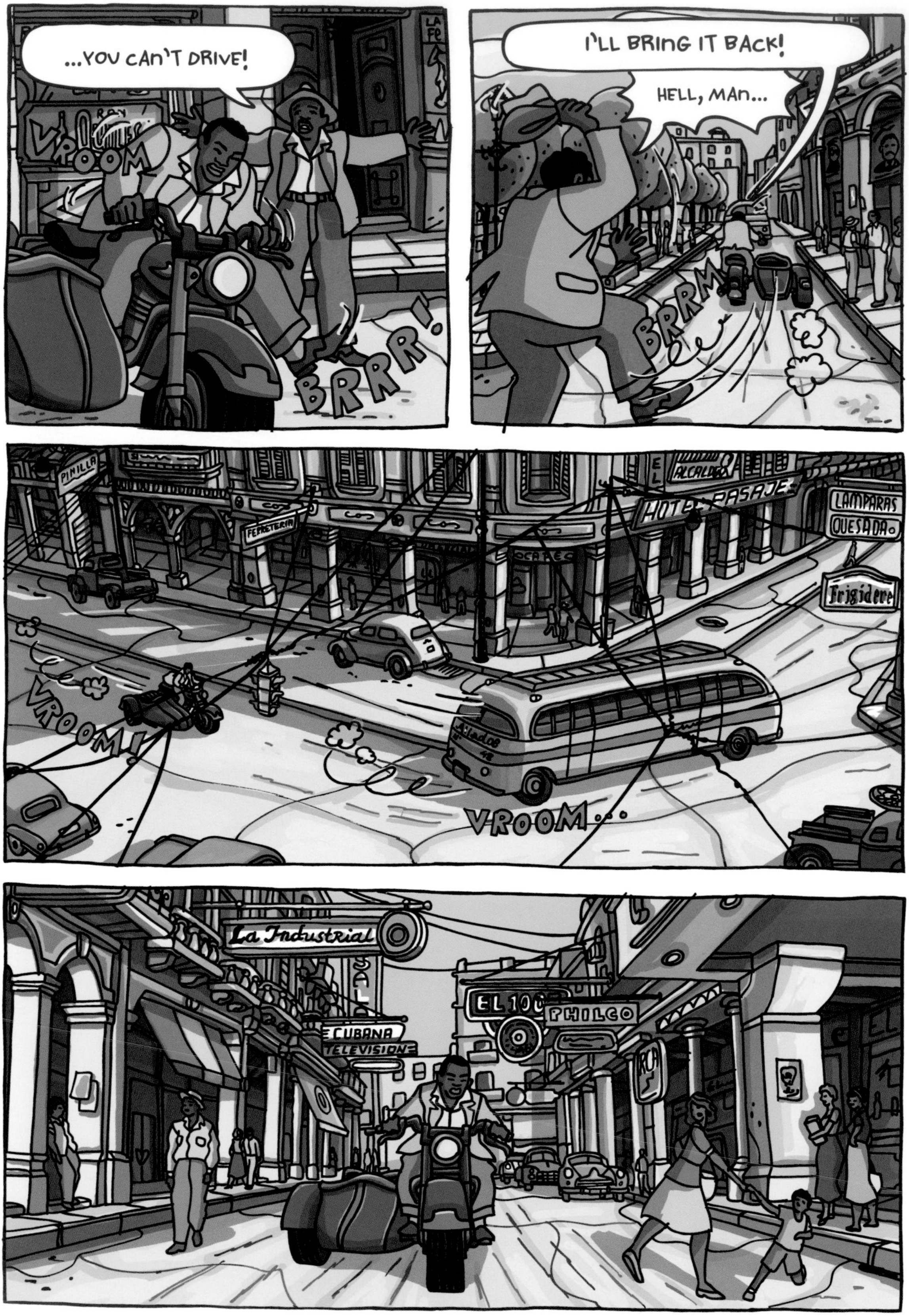
...YOU CAN'T DRIVE!
VROOM
BRRRR!
I'LL BRING IT BACK!
HELL, MAN...
BRRRM
PINILLA
FERRETERIA
HOTEL PASAJE
LAMPARAS QUESADA
Frigidere
VROOM!
VROOM...
La Industrial
CUBANA TELEVISION
PHILCO
RCA

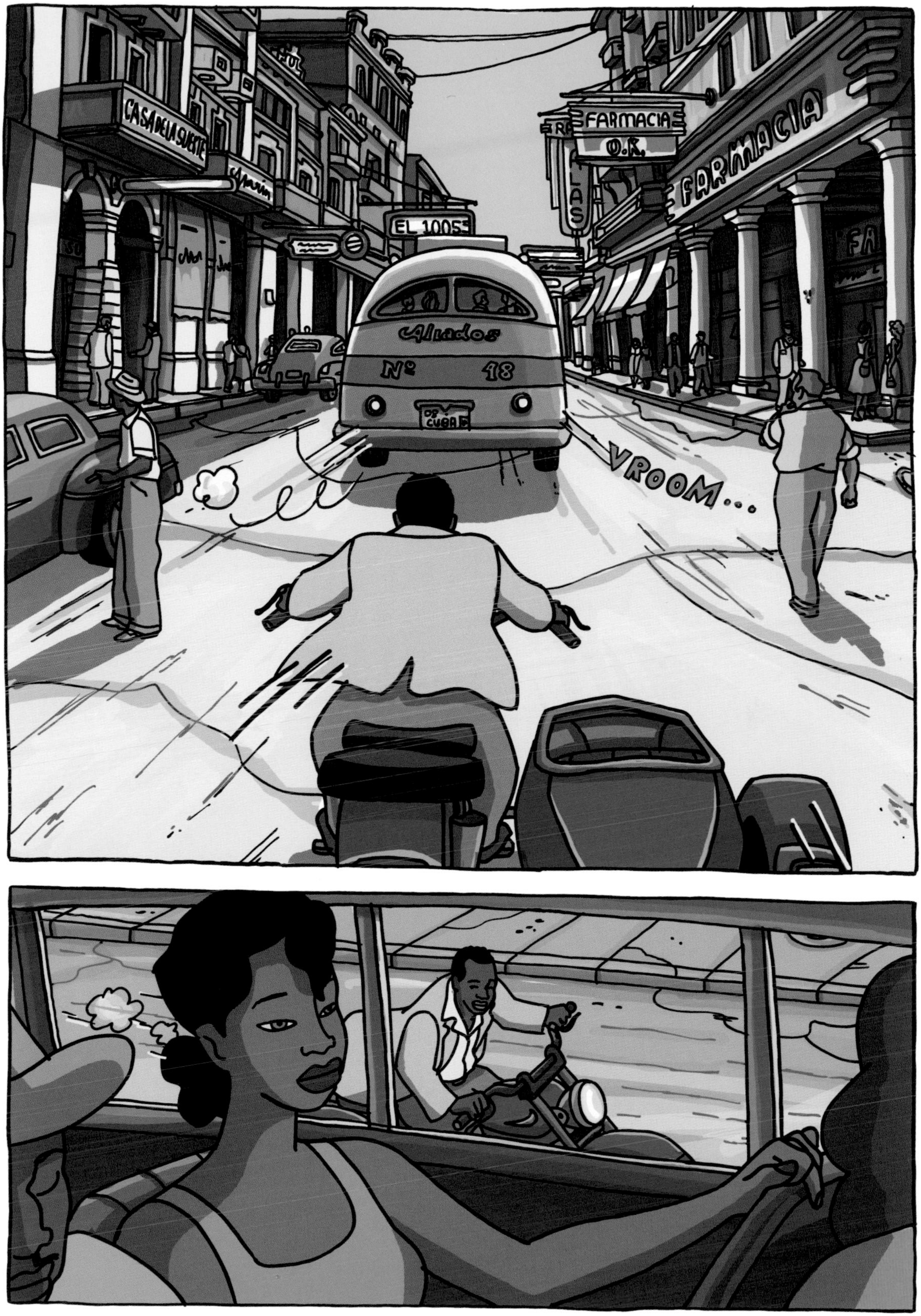
CASA DE LA SUERTE
FARMACIA
O.K.
FARMACIA
EL 1005
Aliados
Nº 48
VROOM...

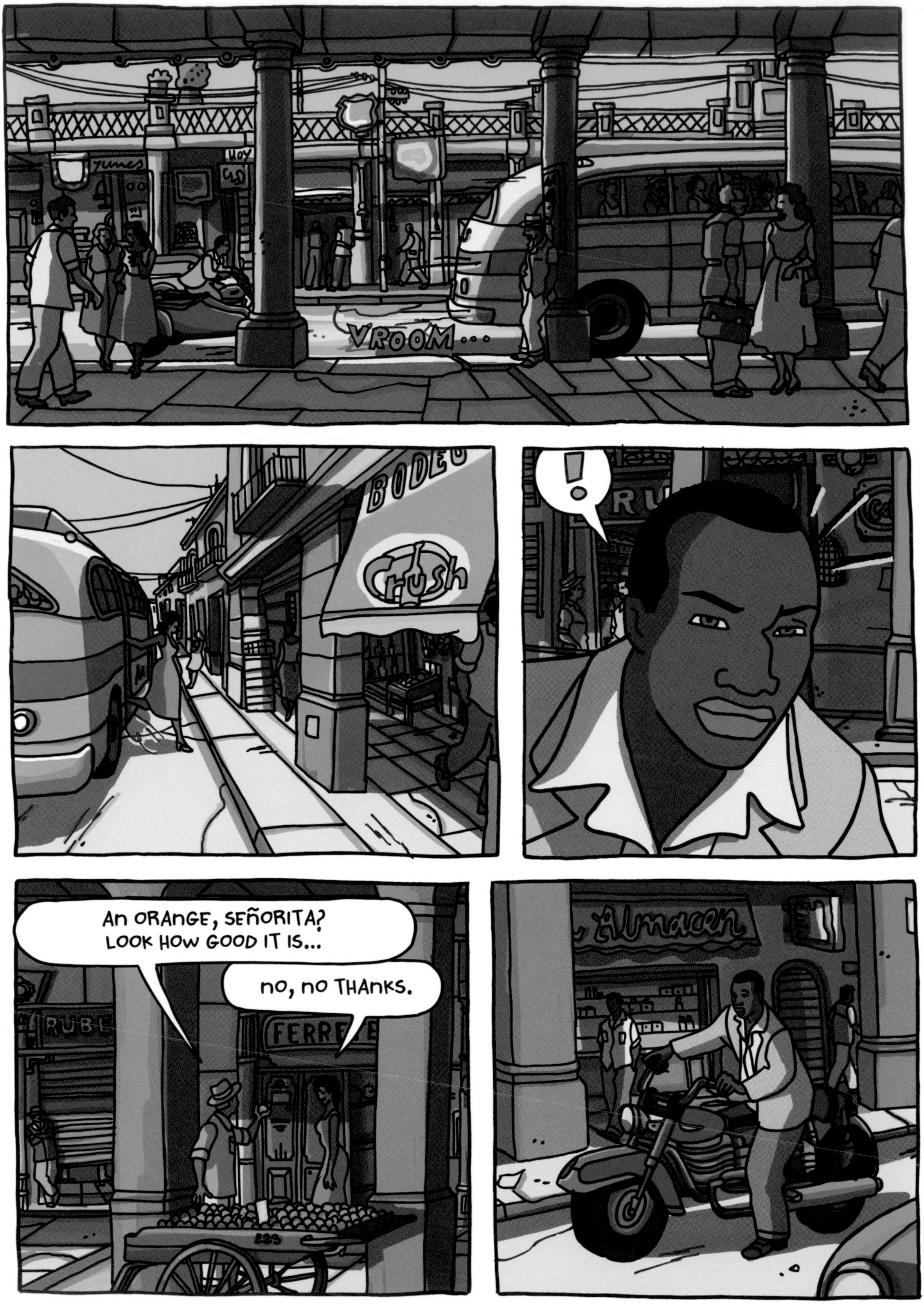
HOY
VROOM...
Crush
!
An ORANGE, SEÑORITA? LOOK HOW GOOD IT IS...
no, no THANKS.
Almacen

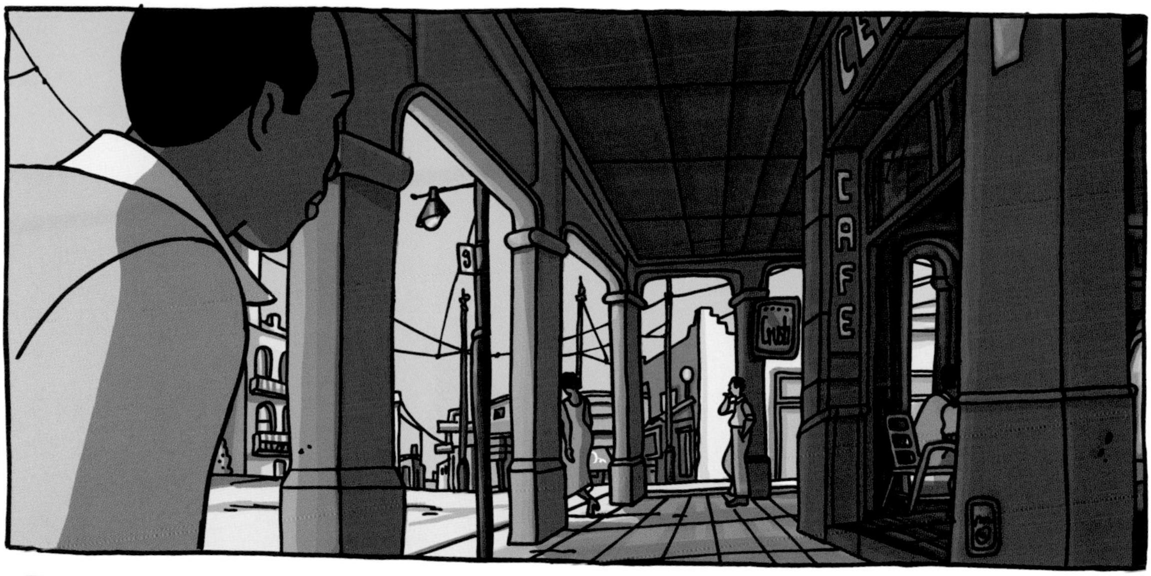
CAFE

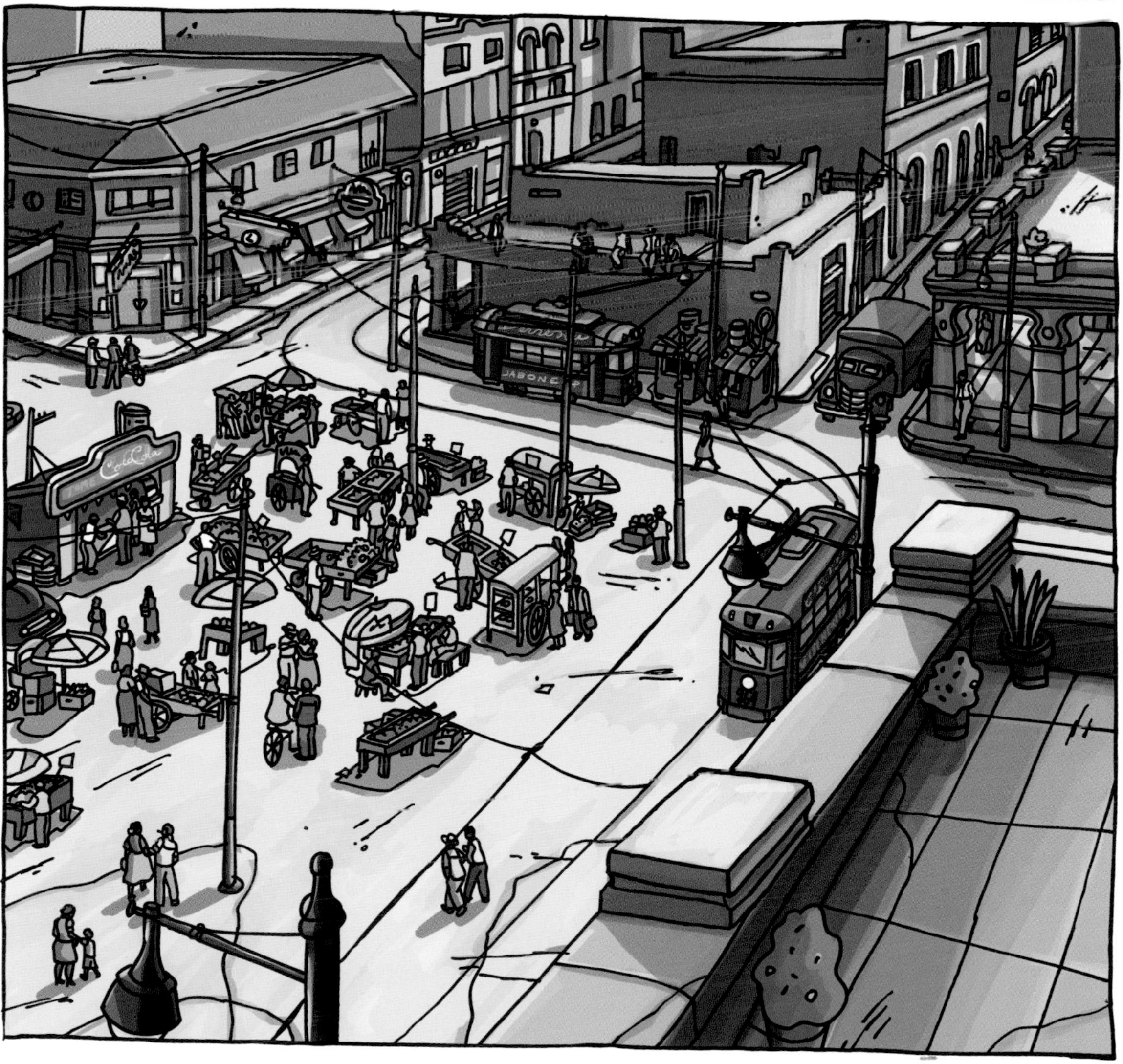

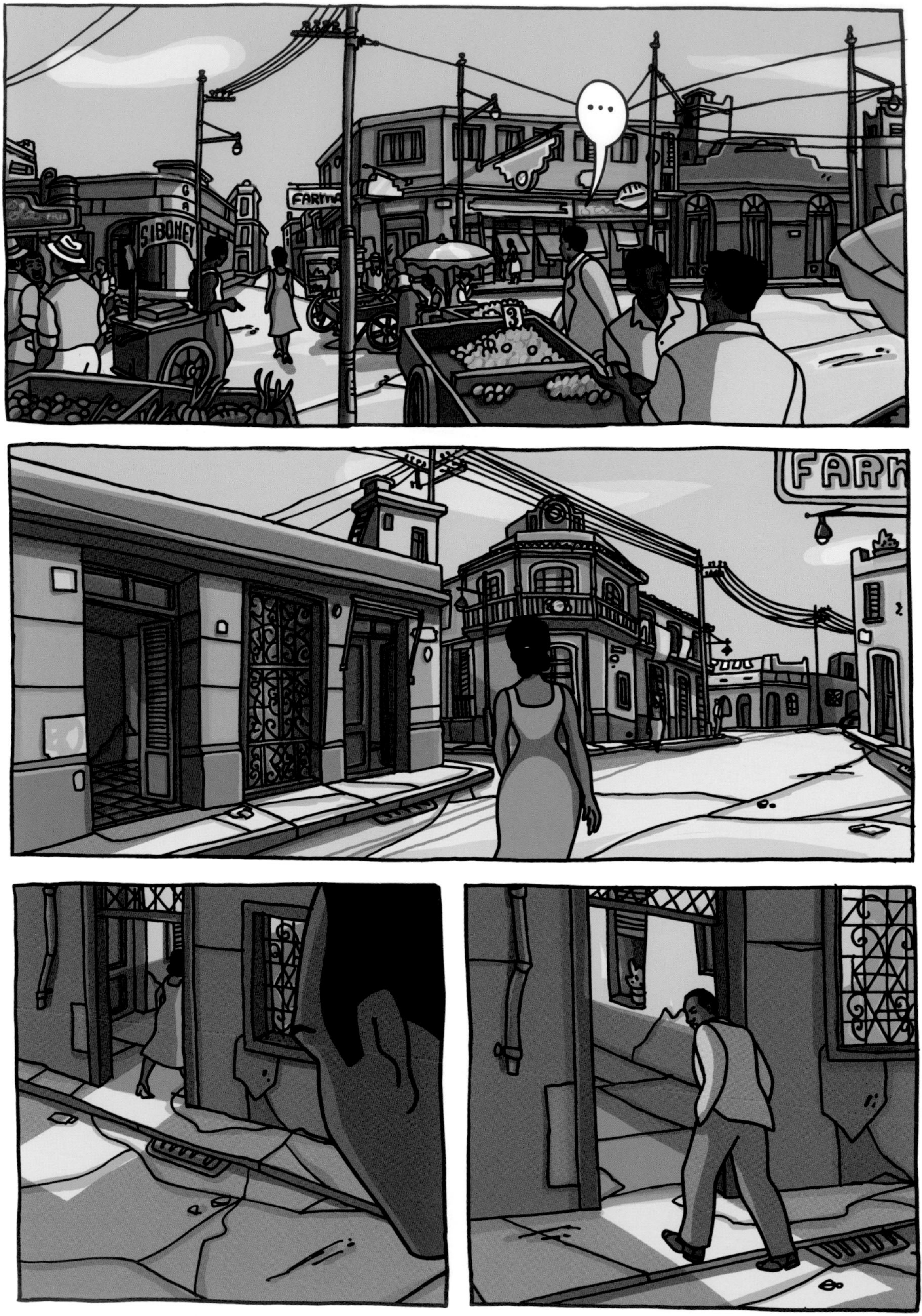
...
SIBONEY
FARMA
FARM

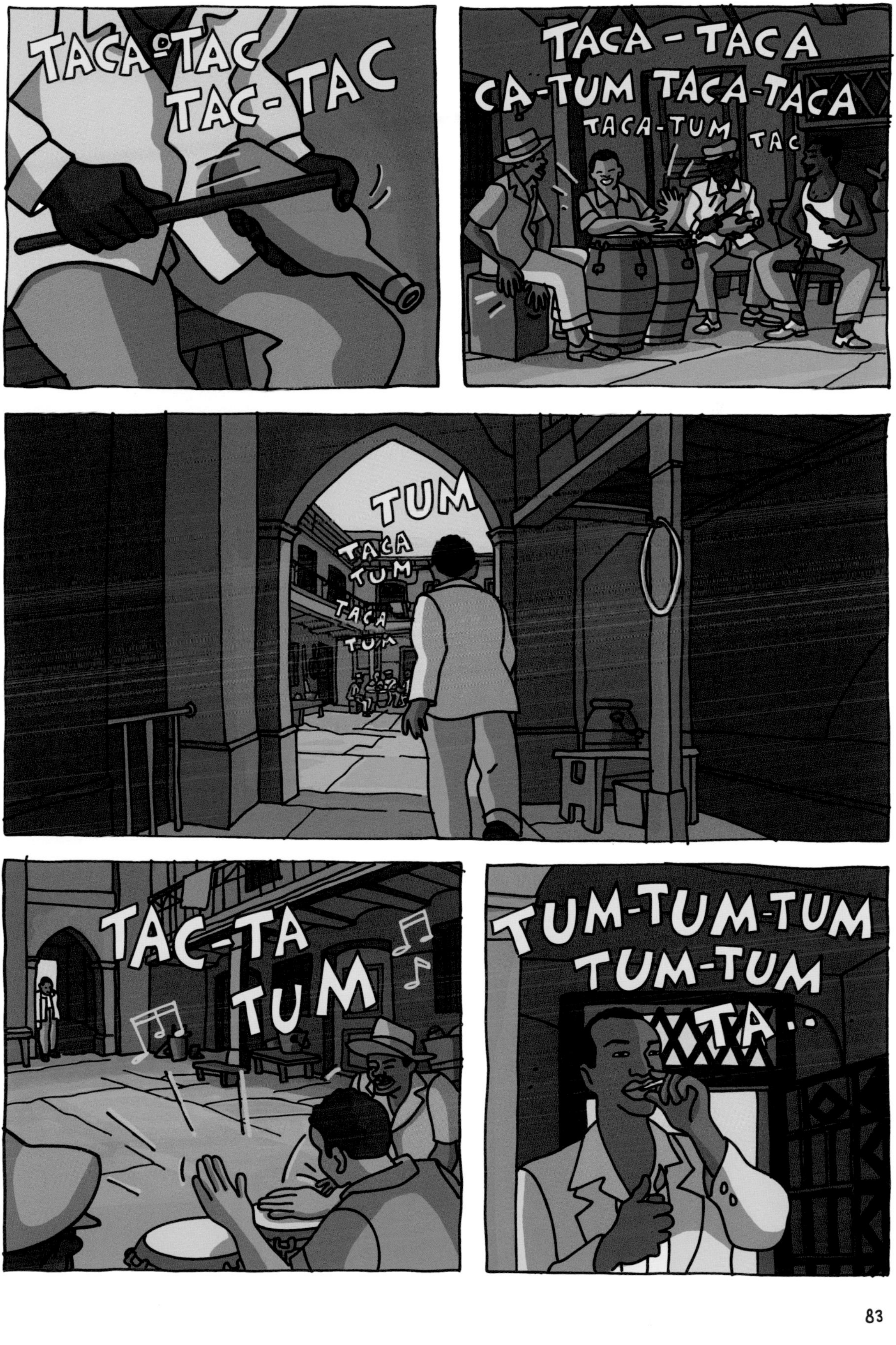
TACA-TAC
TAC-TAC
TACA - TACA
CA-TUM TACA-TACA
TACA-TUM TAC
TUM
TACA
TUM
TACA
TUM
TAC-TA
TUM
TUM-TUM-TUM
TUM-TUM
TA..

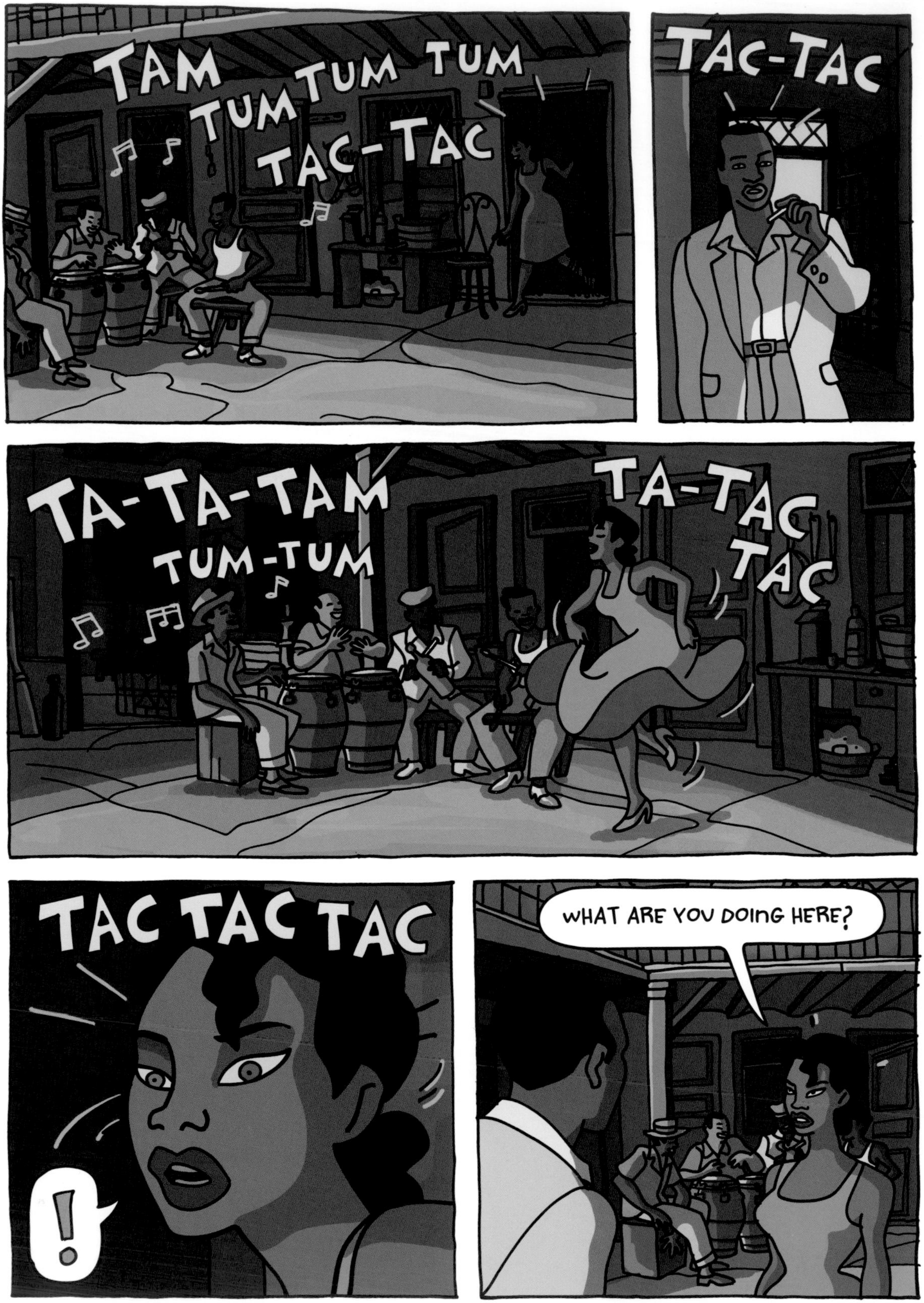
TAM TUM TUM TUM TUM
TAC-TAC
TAC-TAC
TA-TA-TAM
TUM-TUM
TA-TAC TAC
TAC TAC TAC
!
WHAT ARE YOU DOING HERE?

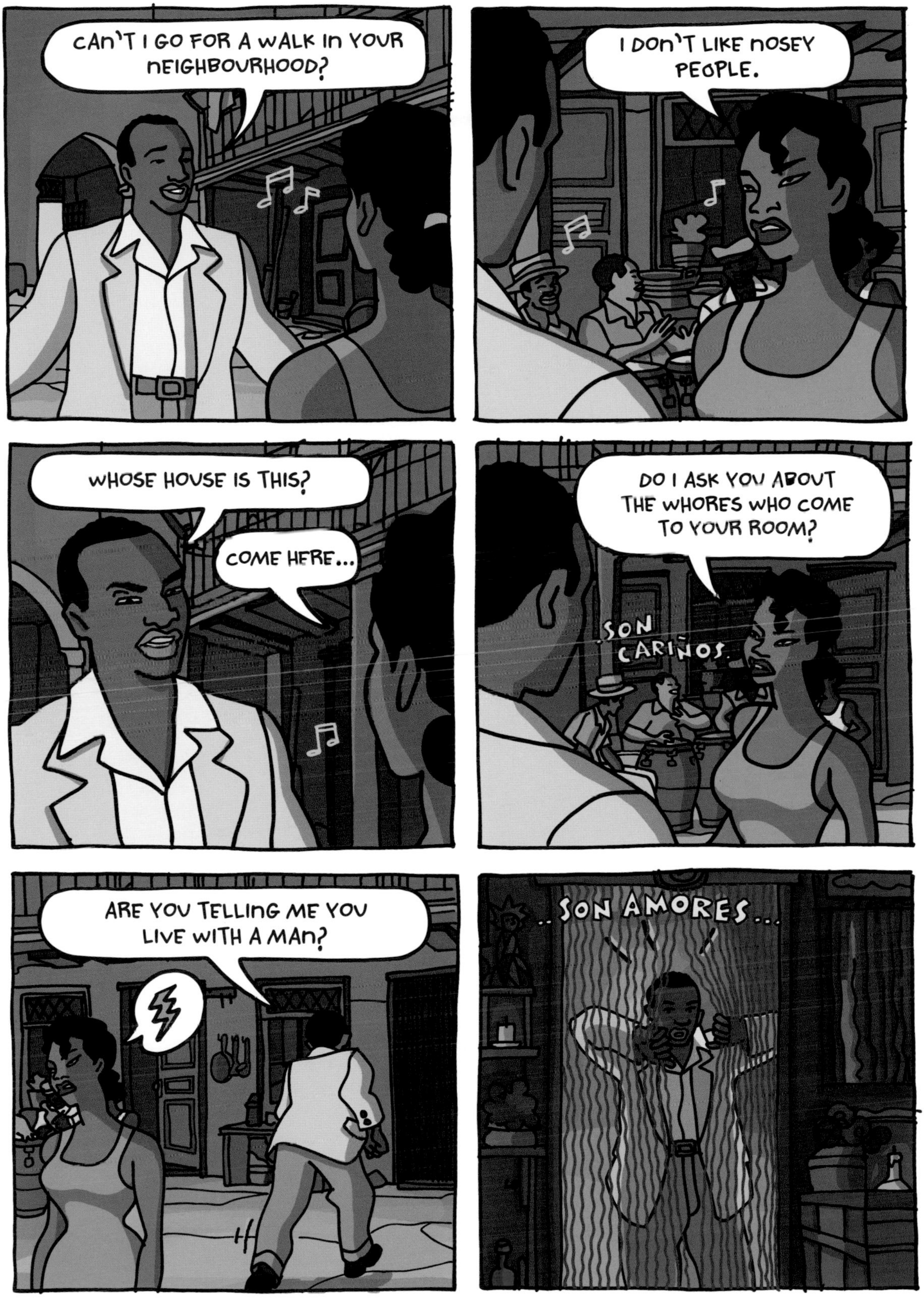
CAN'T I GO FOR A WALK IN YOUR NEIGHBOURHOOD?
I DON'T LIKE NOSEY PEOPLE.
WHOSE HOUSE IS THIS?
COME HERE...
DO I ASK YOU ABOUT THE WHORES WHO COME TO YOUR ROOM?
SON CARIÑOS
ARE YOU TELLING ME YOU LIVE WITH A MAN?
..SON AMORES...

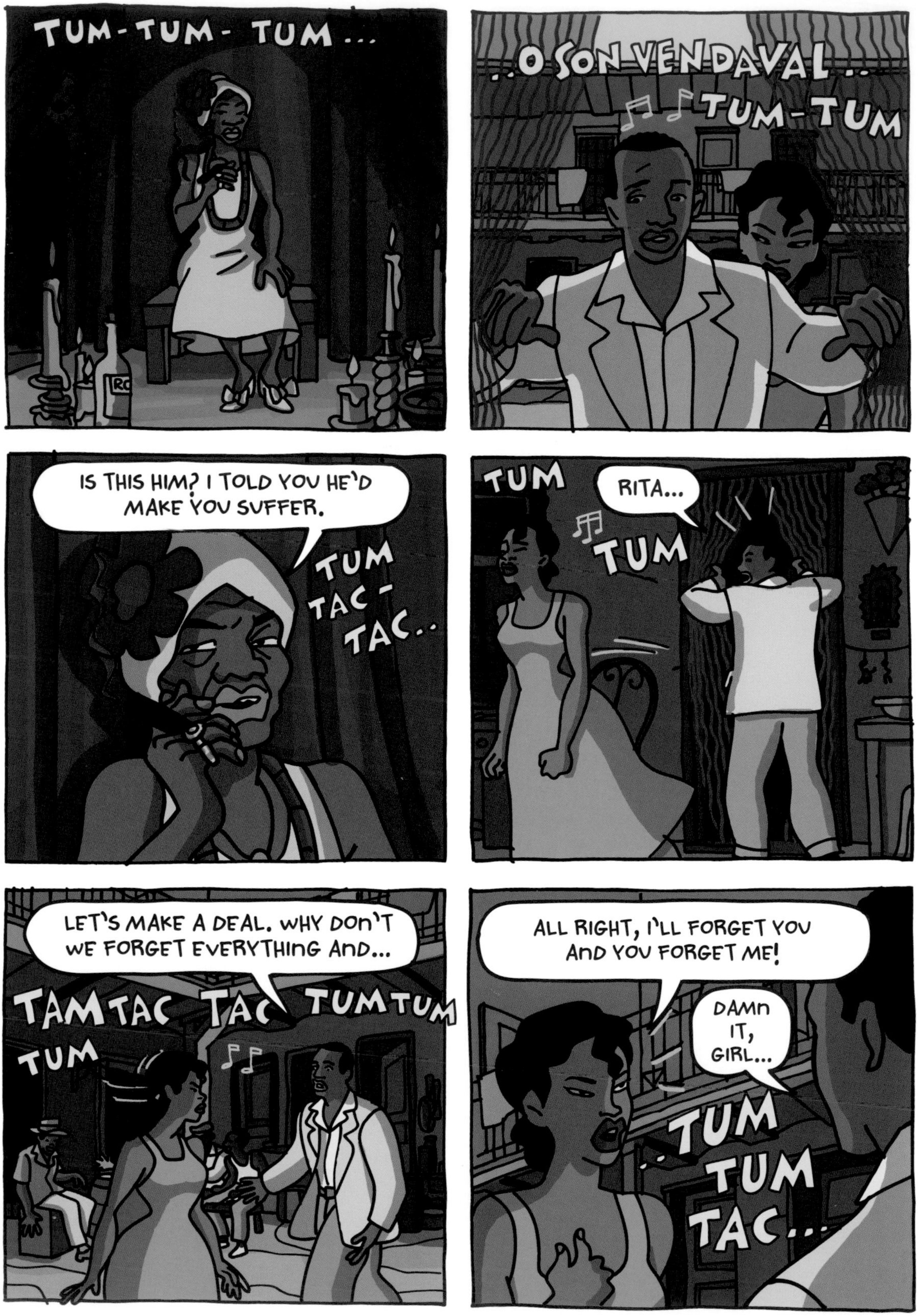
TUM-TUM-TUM...
..O SON VENDAVAL..
TUM-TUM
IS THIS HIM? I TOLD YOU HE'D MAKE YOU SUFFER.
TUM TAC-TAC..
TUM
RITA...
TUM
LET'S MAKE A DEAL. WHY DON'T WE FORGET EVERYTHING AND...
TAM TAC TAC TUM TUM
TUM
ALL RIGHT, I'LL FORGET YOU AND YOU FORGET ME!
DAMN IT, GIRL...
TUM TUM TAC...

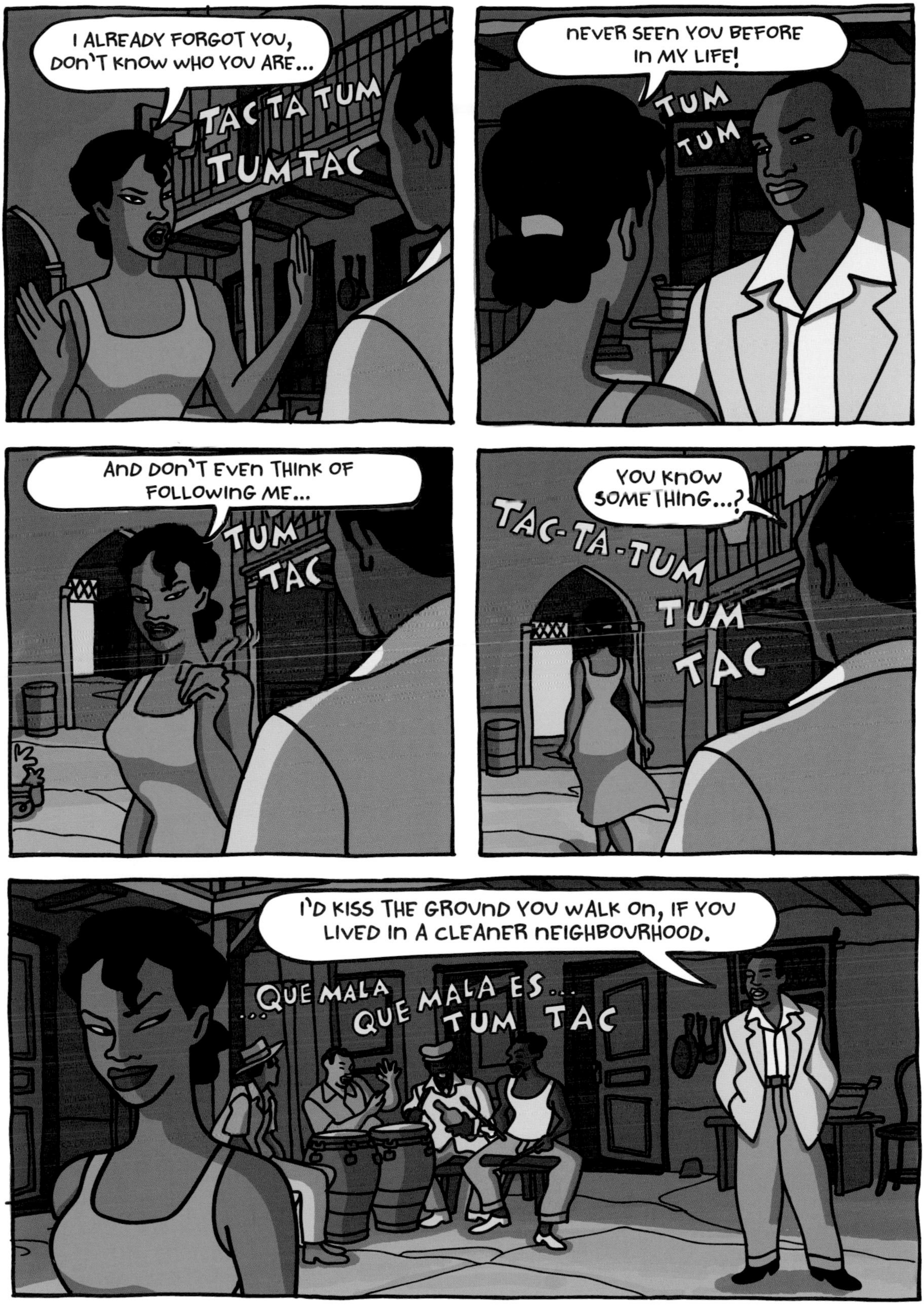
I ALREADY FORGOT YOU, DON'T KNOW WHO YOU ARE...
TAC TA TUM
TUM TAC
NEVER SEEN YOU BEFORE IN MY LIFE!
TUM
TUM
AND DON'T EVEN THINK OF FOLLOWING ME...
TUM
TAC
YOU KNOW SOMETHING...?
TAC-TA-TUM
TUM
TAC
I'D KISS THE GROUND YOU WALK ON, IF YOU LIVED IN A CLEANER NEIGHBOURHOOD.
...QUE MALA
QUE MALA ES...
TUM TAC

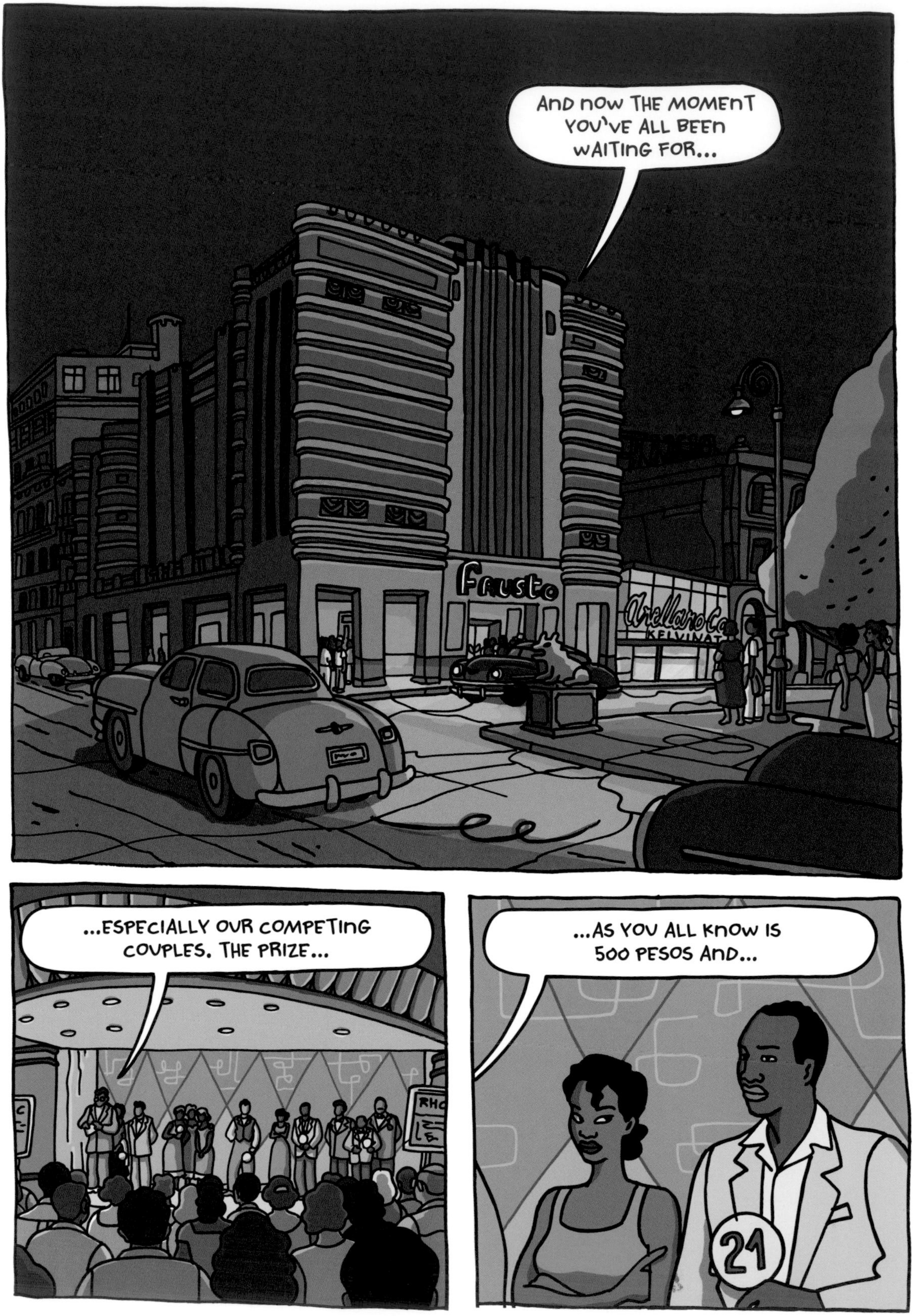
AND NOW THE MOMENT YOU'VE ALL BEEN WAITING FOR...
Fausto
...ESPECIALLY OUR COMPETING COUPLES. THE PRIZE...
...AS YOU ALL KNOW IS 500 PESOS AND...
21

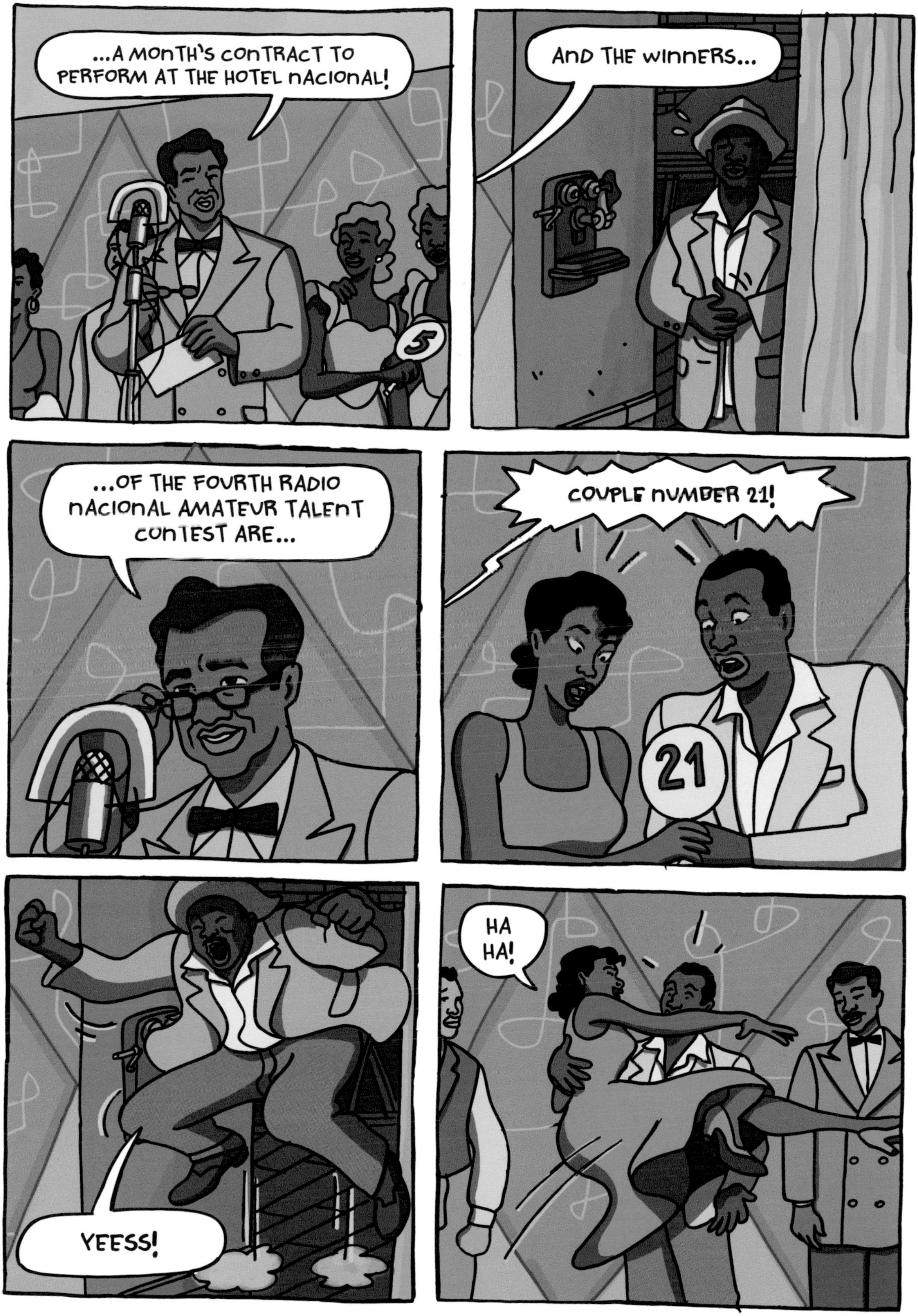
...A MONTH'S CONTRACT TO PERFORM AT THE HOTEL NACIONAL!
AND THE WINNERS...
...OF THE FOURTH RADIO NACIONAL AMATEUR TALENT CONTEST ARE...
COUPLE NUMBER 21!
21
YEESS!
HA HA!

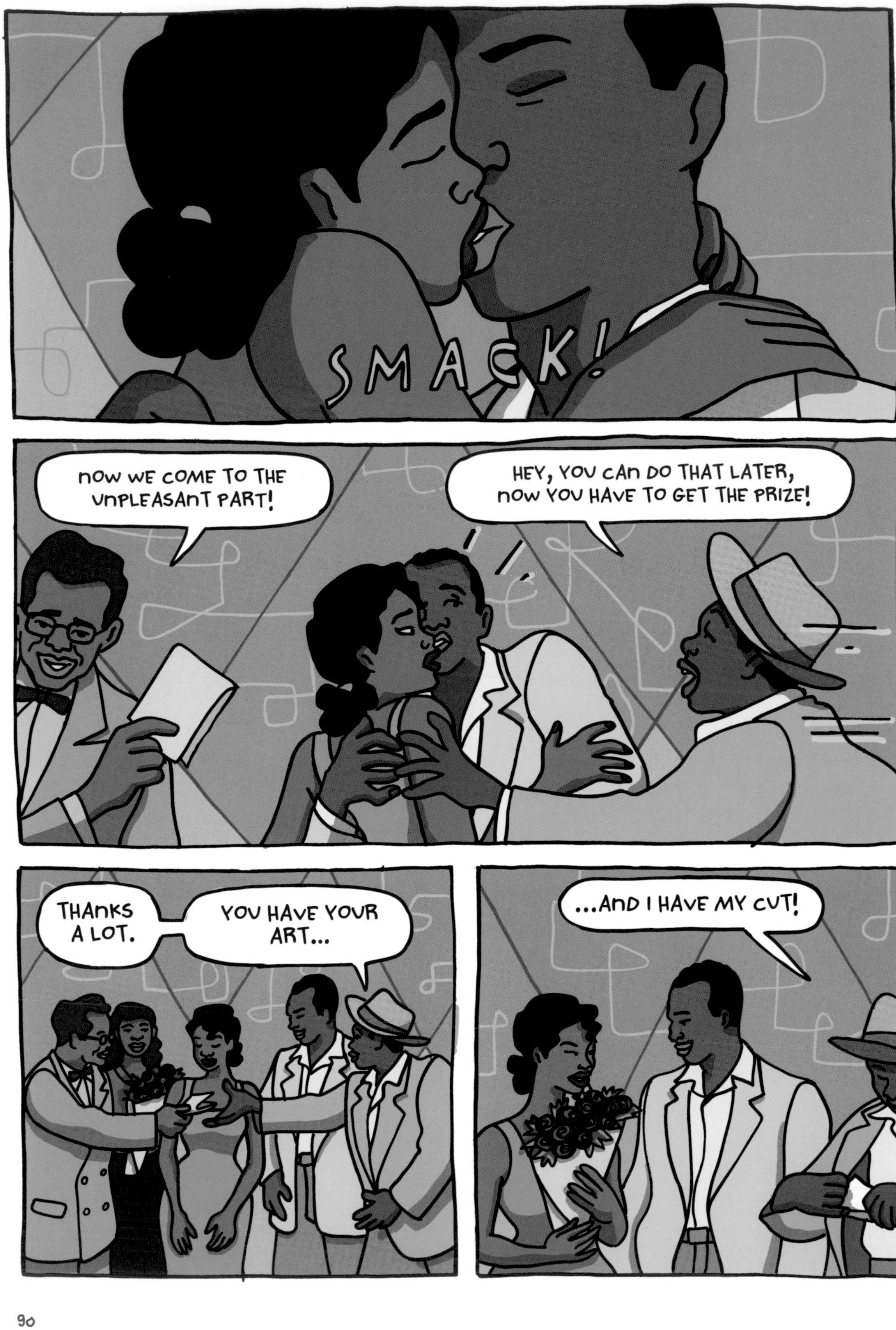
SMACK!
NOW WE COME TO THE UNPLEASANT PART!
HEY, YOU CAN DO THAT LATER, NOW YOU HAVE TO GET THE PRIZE!
THANKS A LOT.
YOU HAVE YOUR ART...
...AND I HAVE MY CUT!

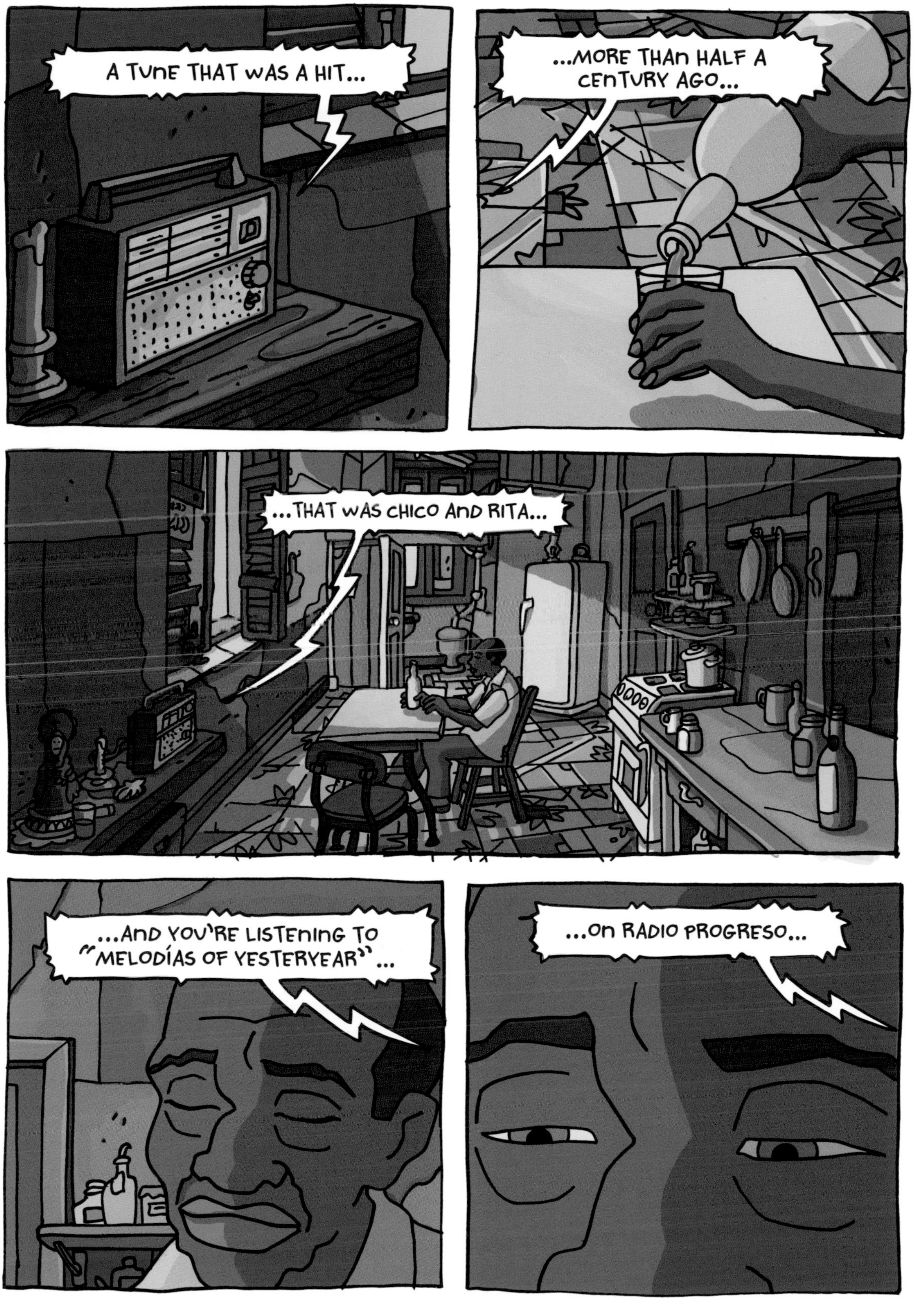
A TUNE THAT WAS A HIT...
...MORE THAN HALF A CENTURY AGO...
...THAT WAS CHICO AND RITA...
...AND YOU'RE LISTENING TO "MELODÍAS OF YESTERYEAR"...
...ON RADIO PROGRESO...

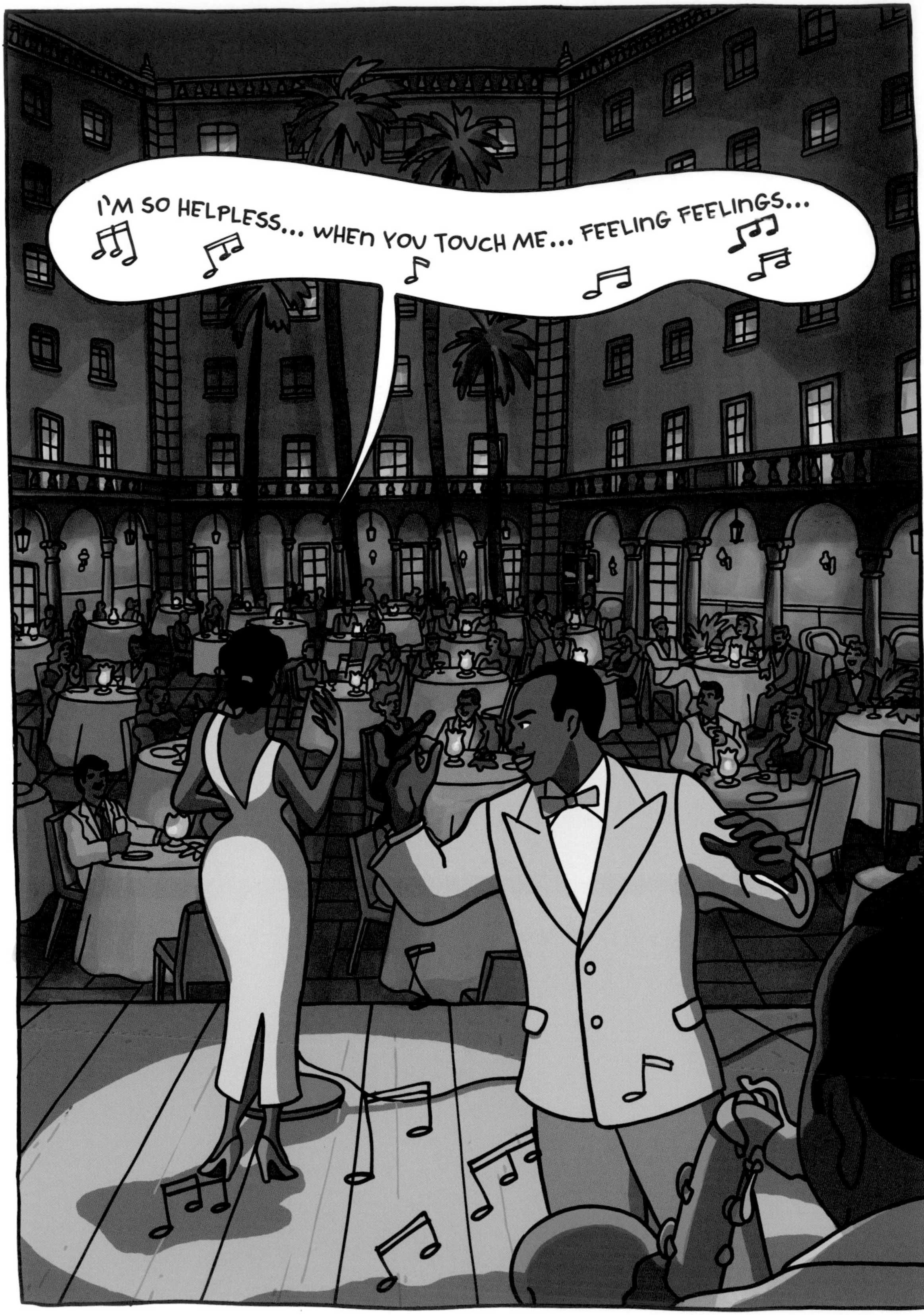
I'M SO HELPLESS... WHEN YOU TOUCH ME... FEELING FEELINGS...

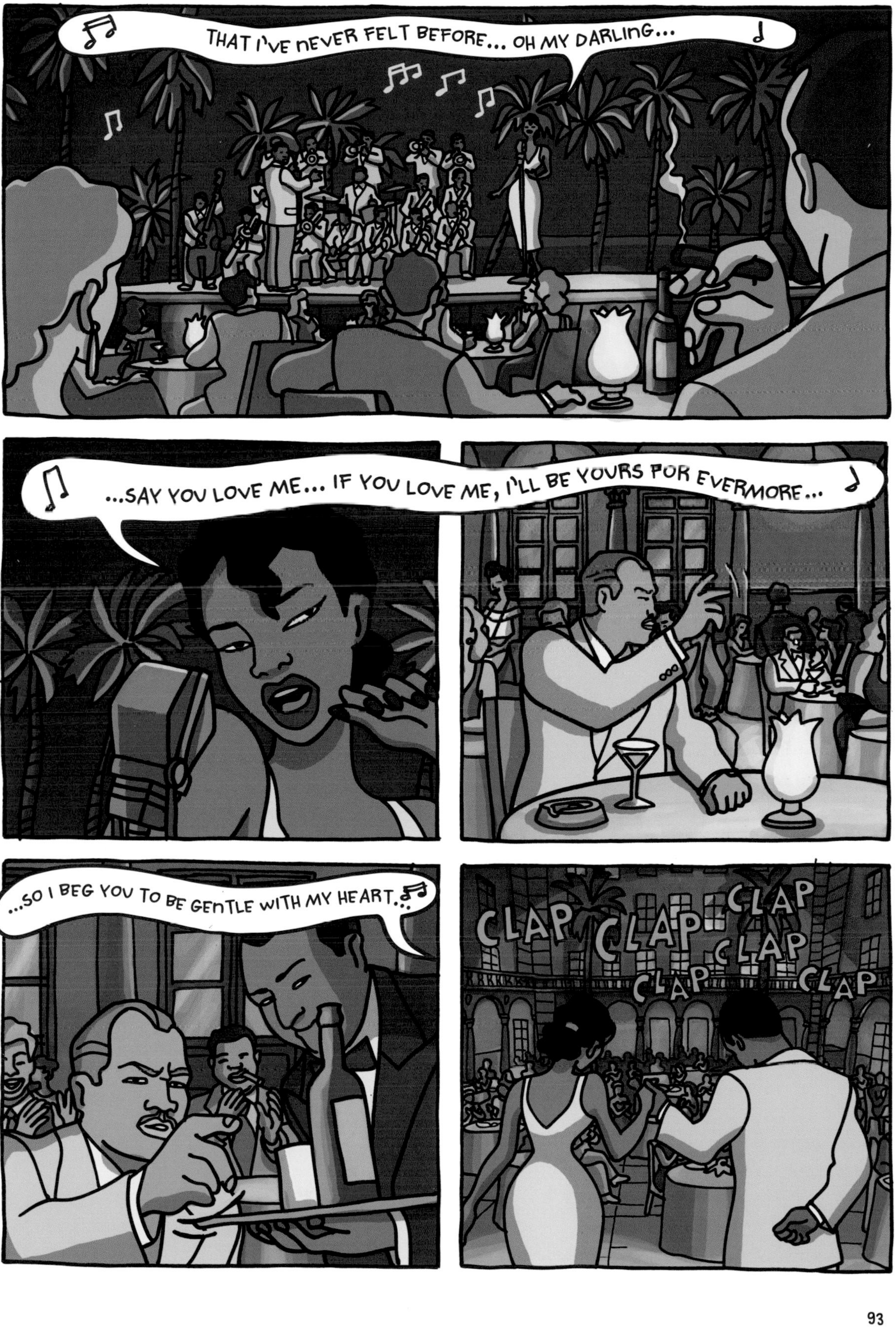
THAT I'VE NEVER FELT BEFORE... OH MY DARLING...
...SAY YOU LOVE ME... IF YOU LOVE ME, I'LL BE YOURS FOR EVERMORE...
...SO I BEG YOU TO BE GENTLE WITH MY HEART...
CLAP CLAP CLAP CLAP CLAP CLAP

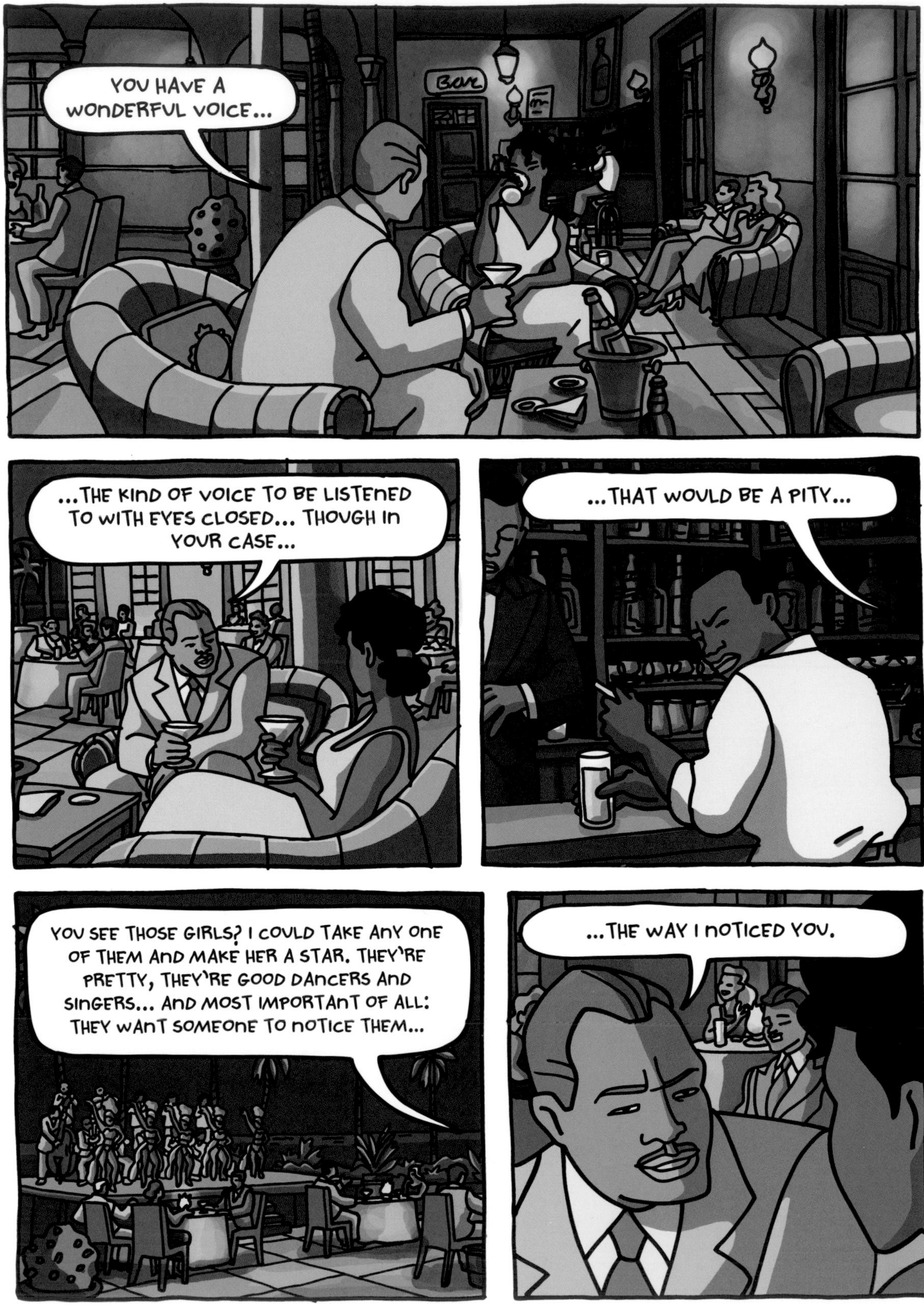
YOU HAVE A WONDERFUL VOICE...
...THE KIND OF VOICE TO BE LISTENED TO WITH EYES CLOSED... THOUGH IN YOUR CASE...
...THAT WOULD BE A PITY...
YOU SEE THOSE GIRLS? I COULD TAKE ANY ONE OF THEM AND MAKE HER A STAR. THEY'RE PRETTY, THEY'RE GOOD DANCERS AND SINGERS... AND MOST IMPORTANT OF ALL: THEY WANT SOMEONE TO NOTICE THEM...
...THE WAY I NOTICED YOU.

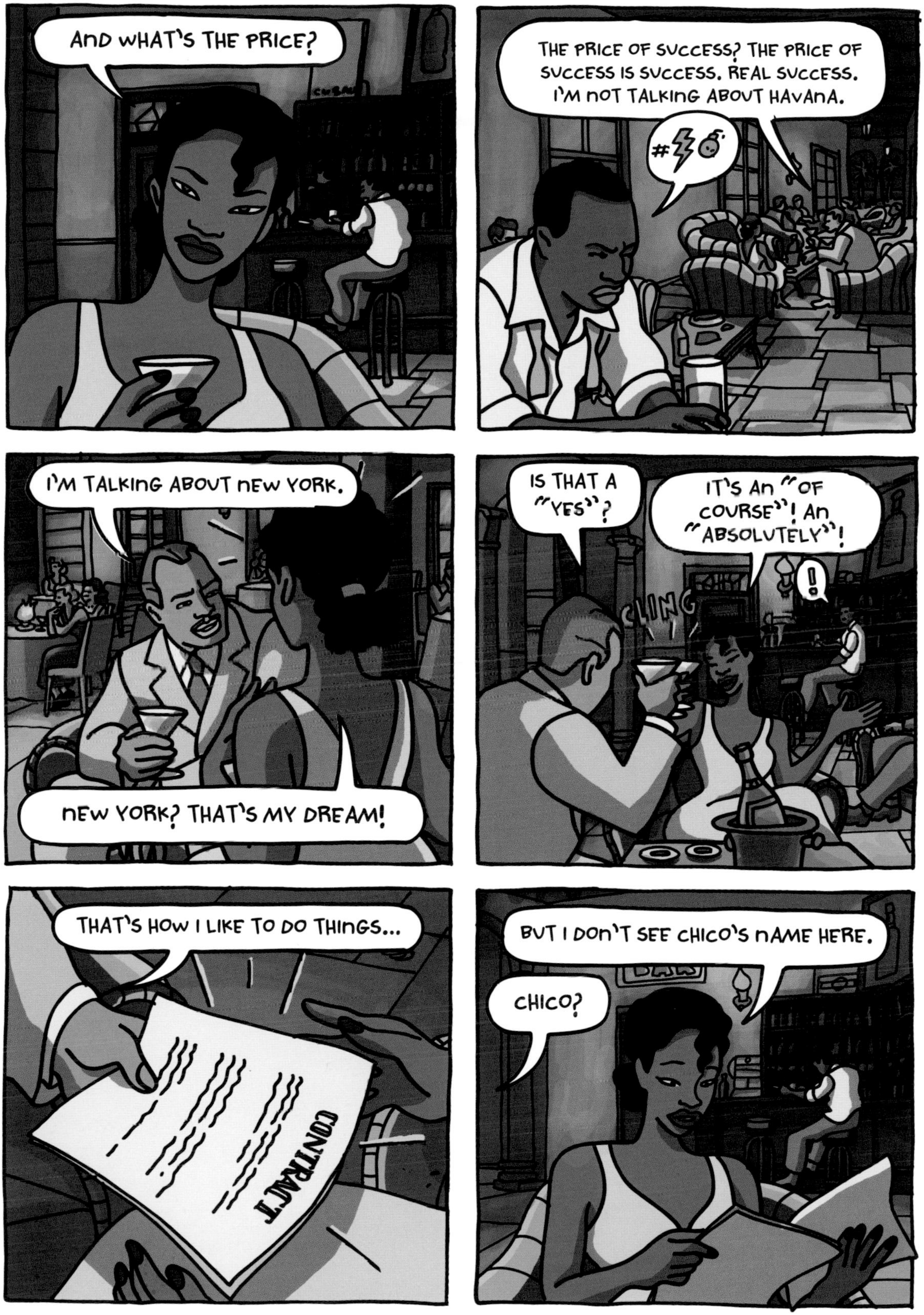
AND WHAT'S THE PRICE?
THE PRICE OF SUCCESS? THE PRICE OF SUCCESS IS SUCCESS. REAL SUCCESS. I'M NOT TALKING ABOUT HAVANA.
#
I'M TALKING ABOUT NEW YORK.
NEW YORK? THAT'S MY DREAM!
IS THAT A "YES"?
IT'S AN "OF COURSE"! AN "ABSOLUTELY"!
CLING
!
THAT'S HOW I LIKE TO DO THINGS...
CONTRACT
BUT I DON'T SEE CHICO'S NAME HERE.
CHICO?

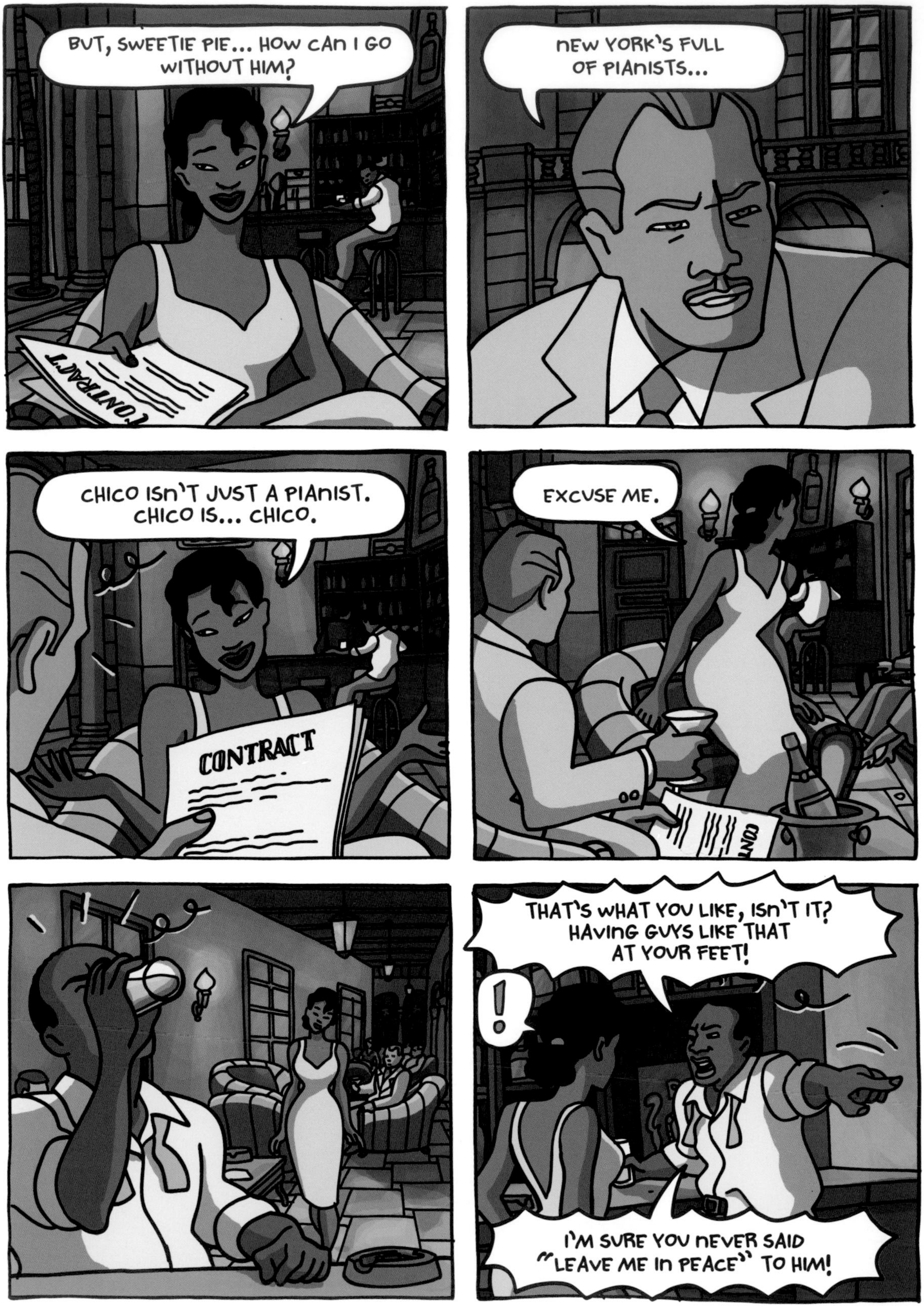
BUT, SWEETIE PIE... HOW CAN I GO WITHOUT HIM?
CONTRACT
NEW YORK'S FULL OF PIANISTS...
CHICO ISN'T JUST A PIANIST. CHICO IS... CHICO.
CONTRACT
EXCUSE ME.
CONT
THAT'S WHAT YOU LIKE, ISN'T IT? HAVING GUYS LIKE THAT AT YOUR FEET!
!
I'M SURE YOU NEVER SAID "LEAVE ME IN PEACE" TO HIM!

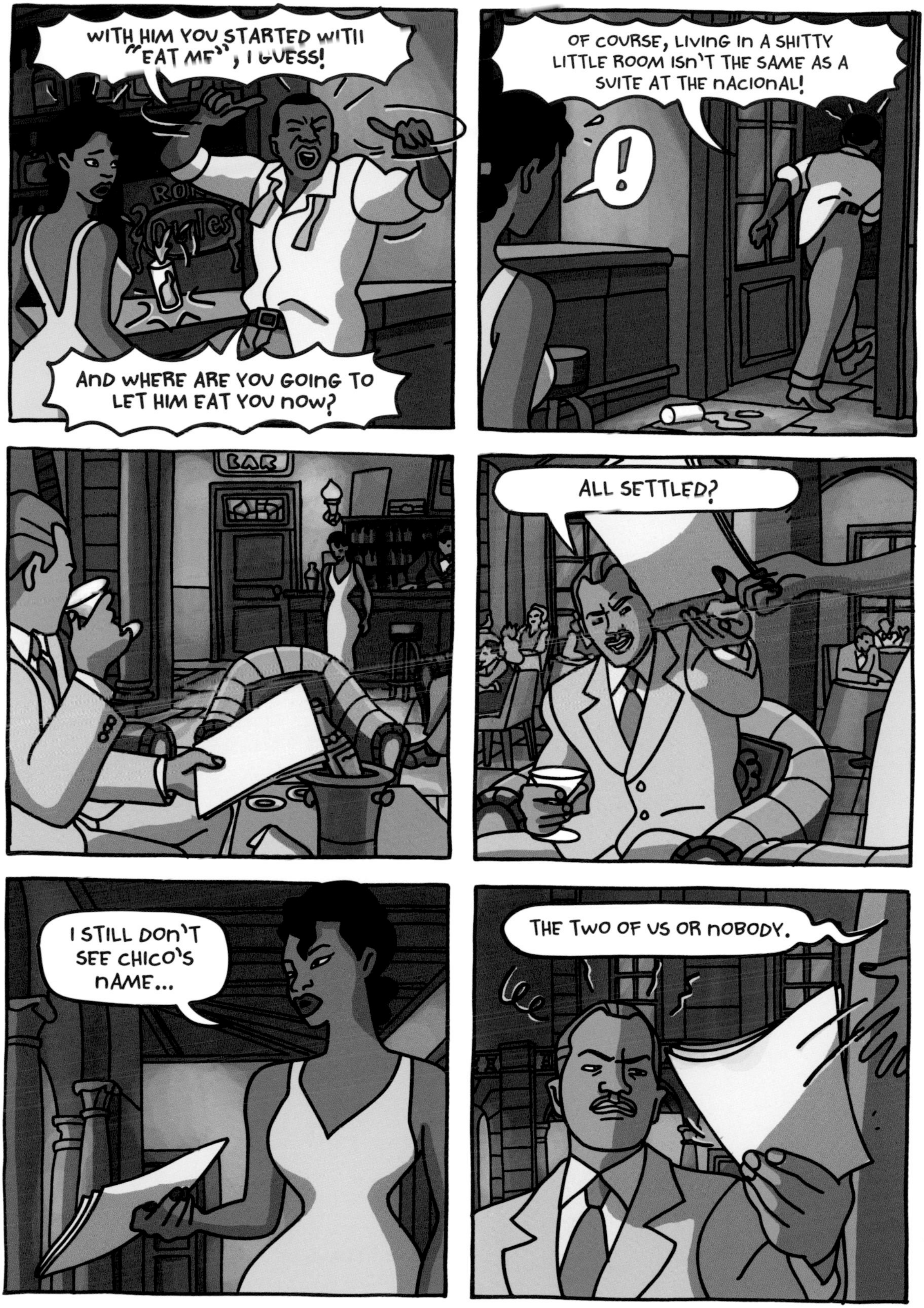
WITH HIM YOU STARTED WITH "EAT ME", I GUESS!
AND WHERE ARE YOU GOING TO LET HIM EAT YOU NOW?
OF COURSE, LIVING IN A SHITTY LITTLE ROOM ISN'T THE SAME AS A SUITE AT THE NACIONAL!
!
ROMULES
BAR
ALL SETTLED?
I STILL DON'T SEE CHICO'S NAME...
THE TWO OF US OR NOBODY.

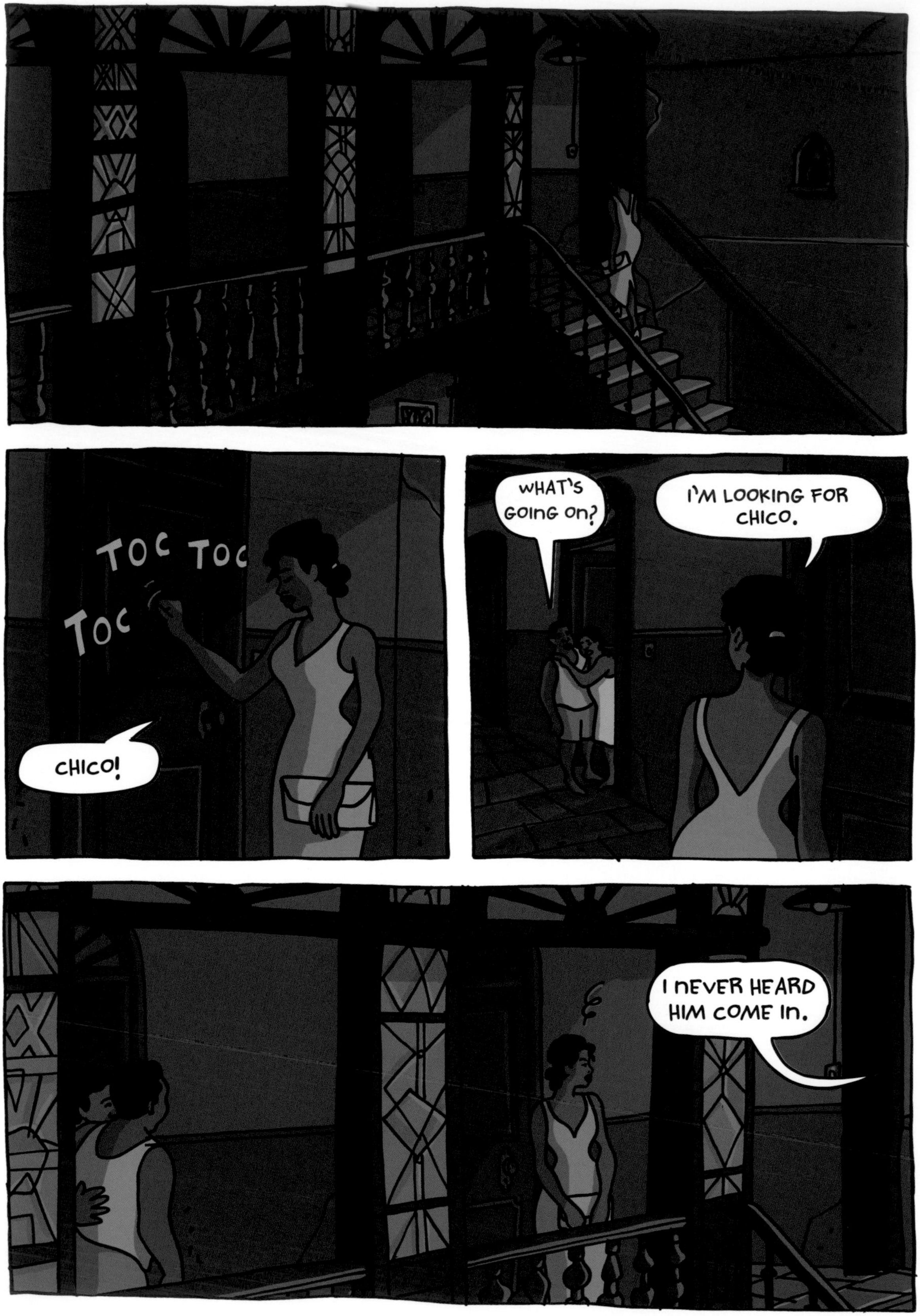
TOC TOC
TOC
CHICO!
WHAT'S GOING ON?
I'M LOOKING FOR CHICO.
I NEVER HEARD HIM COME IN.

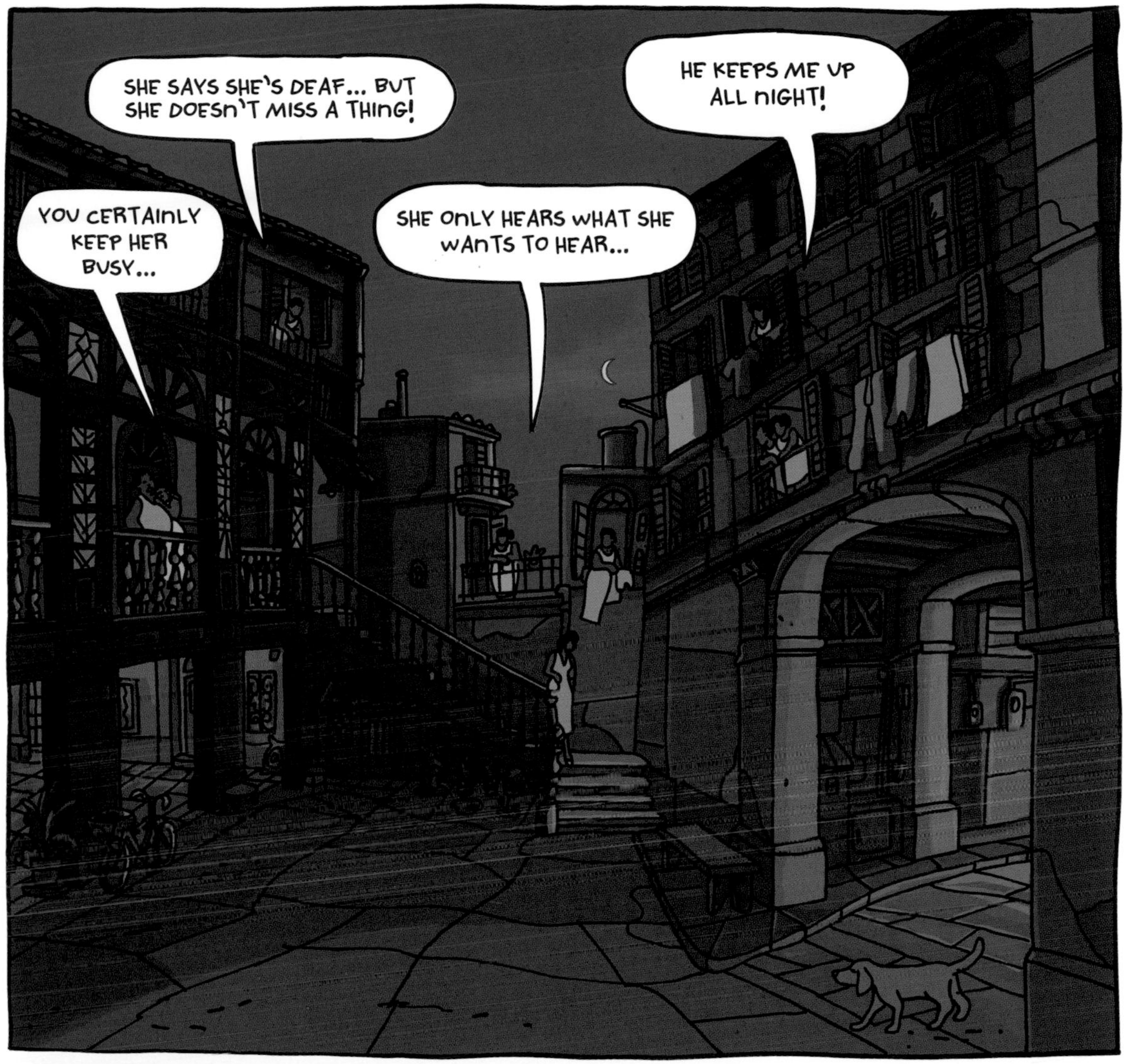

SHE SAYS SHE'S DEAF... BUT SHE DOESN'T MISS A THING!
YOU CERTAINLY KEEP HER BUSY...
SHE ONLY HEARS WHAT SHE WANTS TO HEAR...
HE KEEPS ME UP ALL NIGHT!

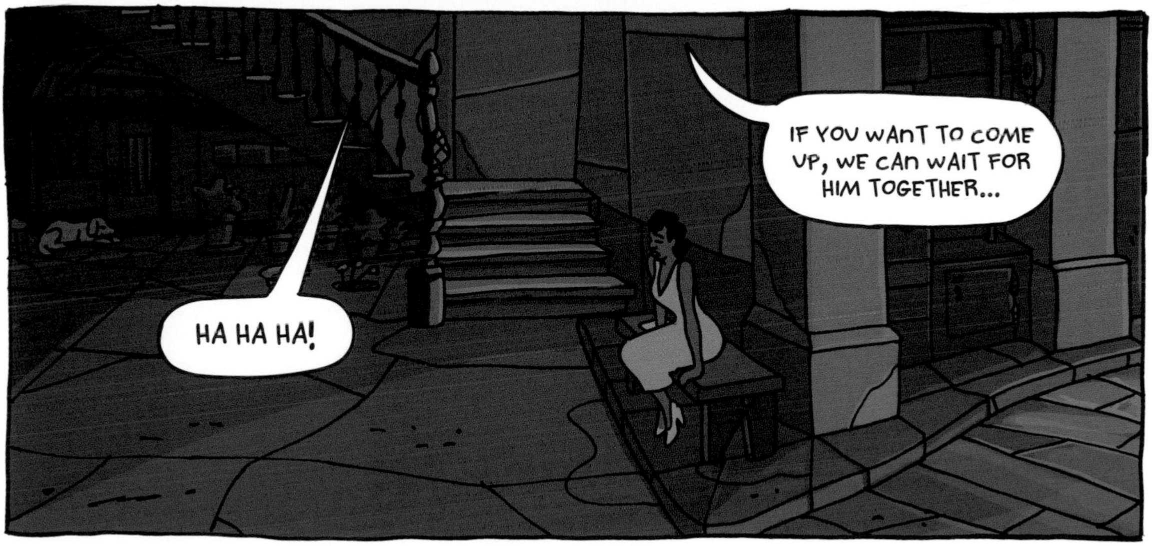

HA HA HA!
IF YOU WANT TO COME UP, WE CAN WAIT FOR HIM TOGETHER...

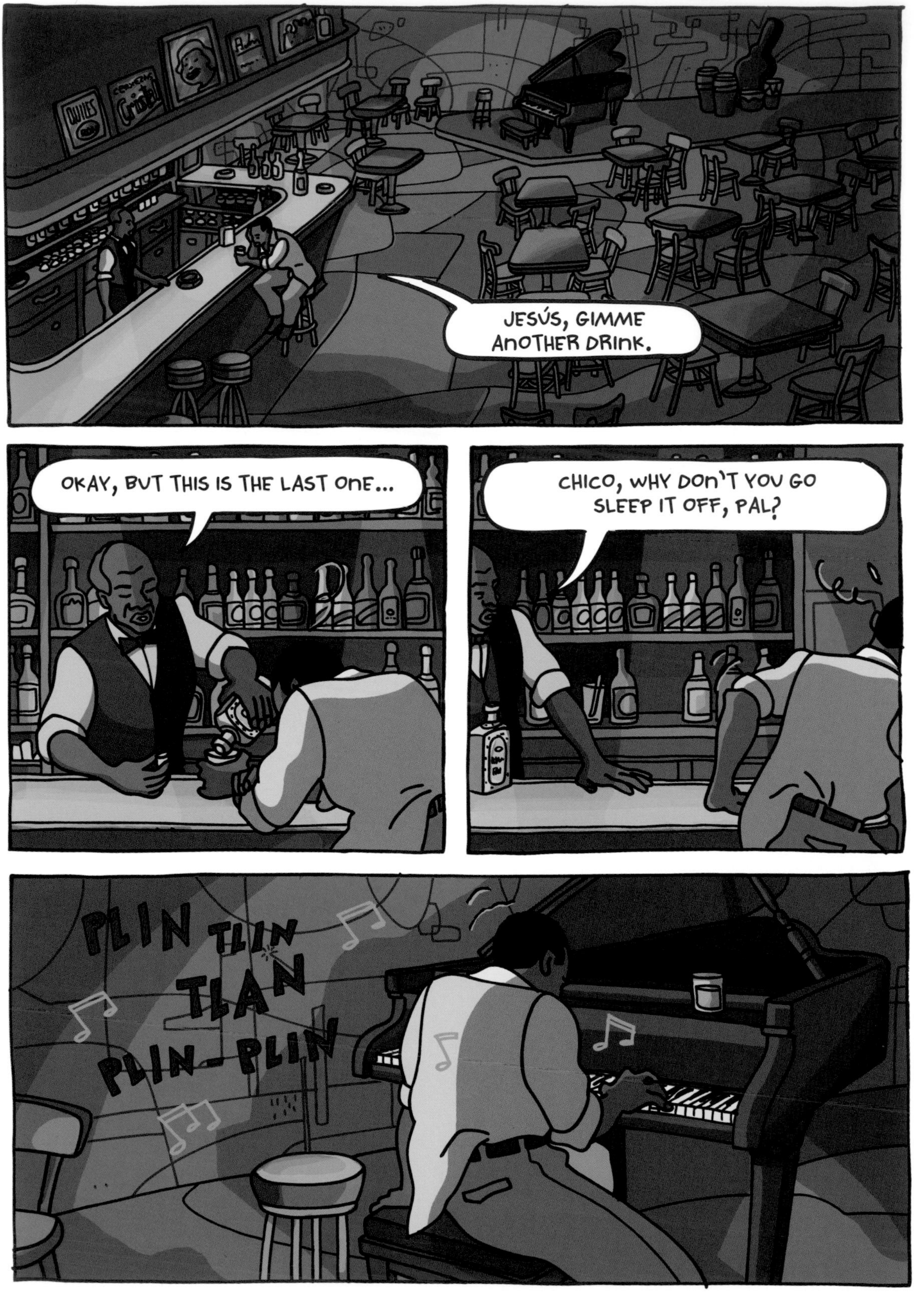
JESÚS, GIMME ANOTHER DRINK.
OKAY, BUT THIS IS THE LAST ONE...
CHICO, WHY DON'T YOU GO SLEEP IT OFF, PAL?
PLIN TLIN
TLAN
PLIN-PLIN

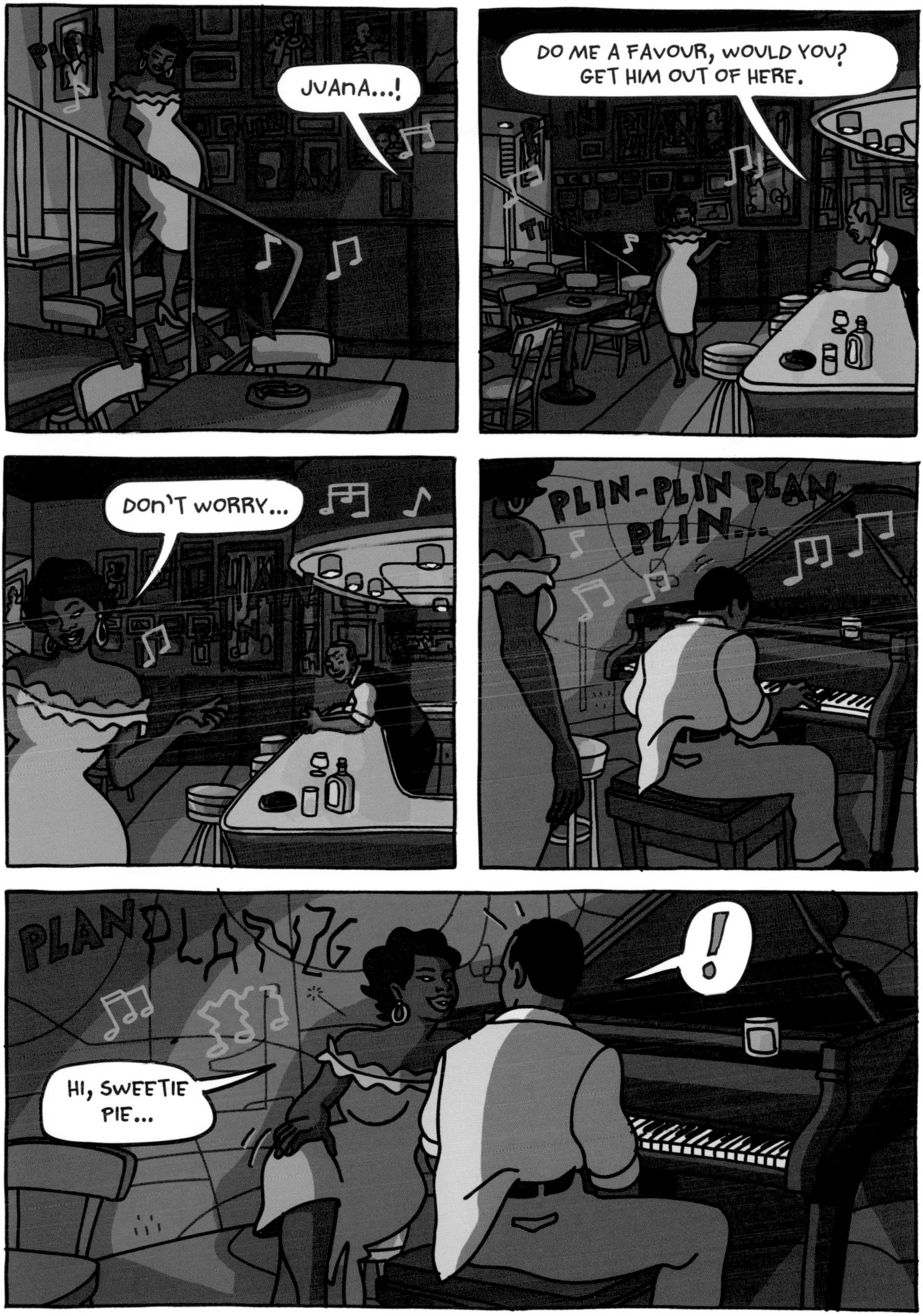
JUANA...!
DO ME A FAVOUR, WOULD YOU? GET HIM OUT OF HERE.
DON'T WORRY...
PLIN-PLIN PLAN PLIN...
!
HI, SWEETIE PIE...

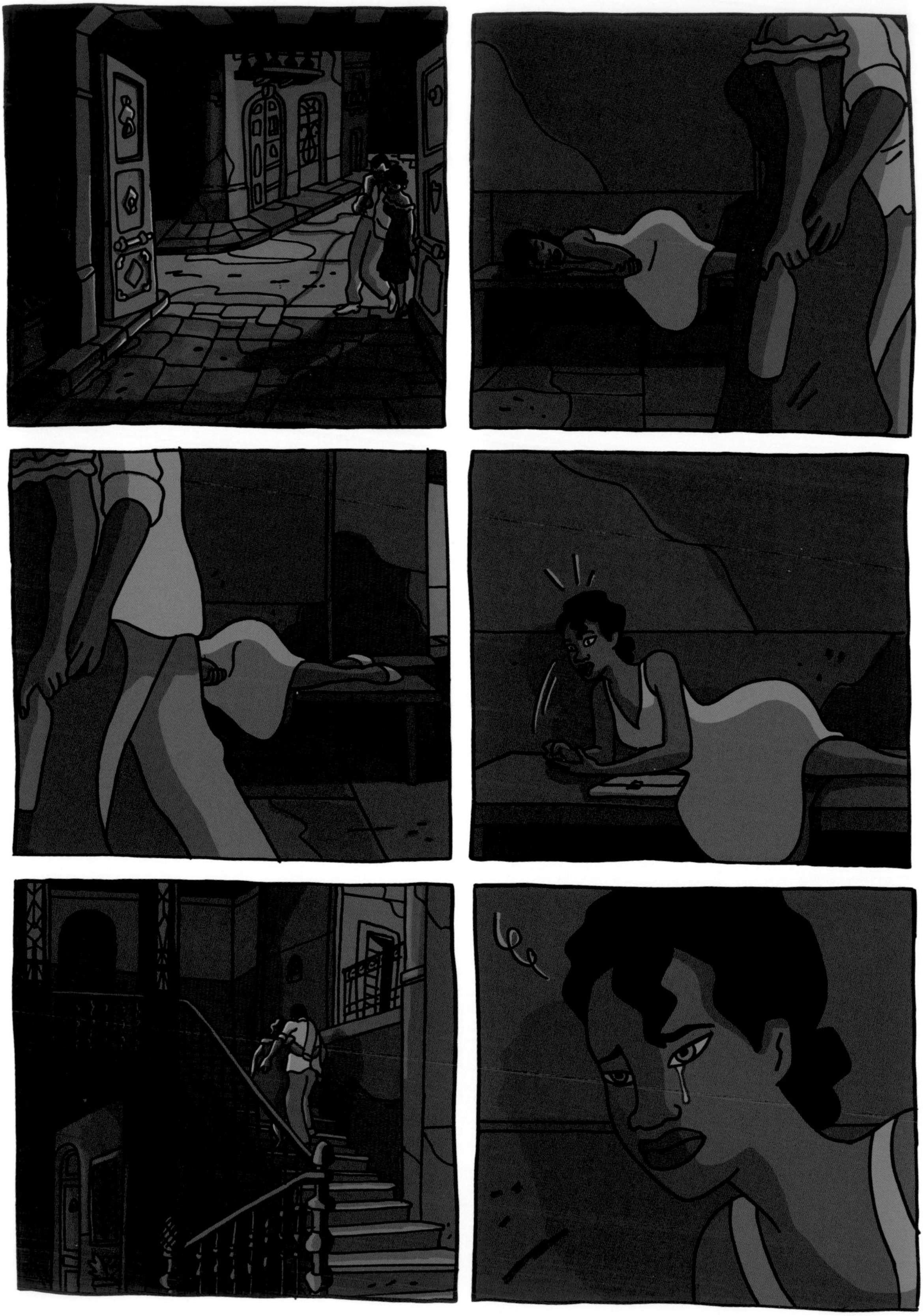

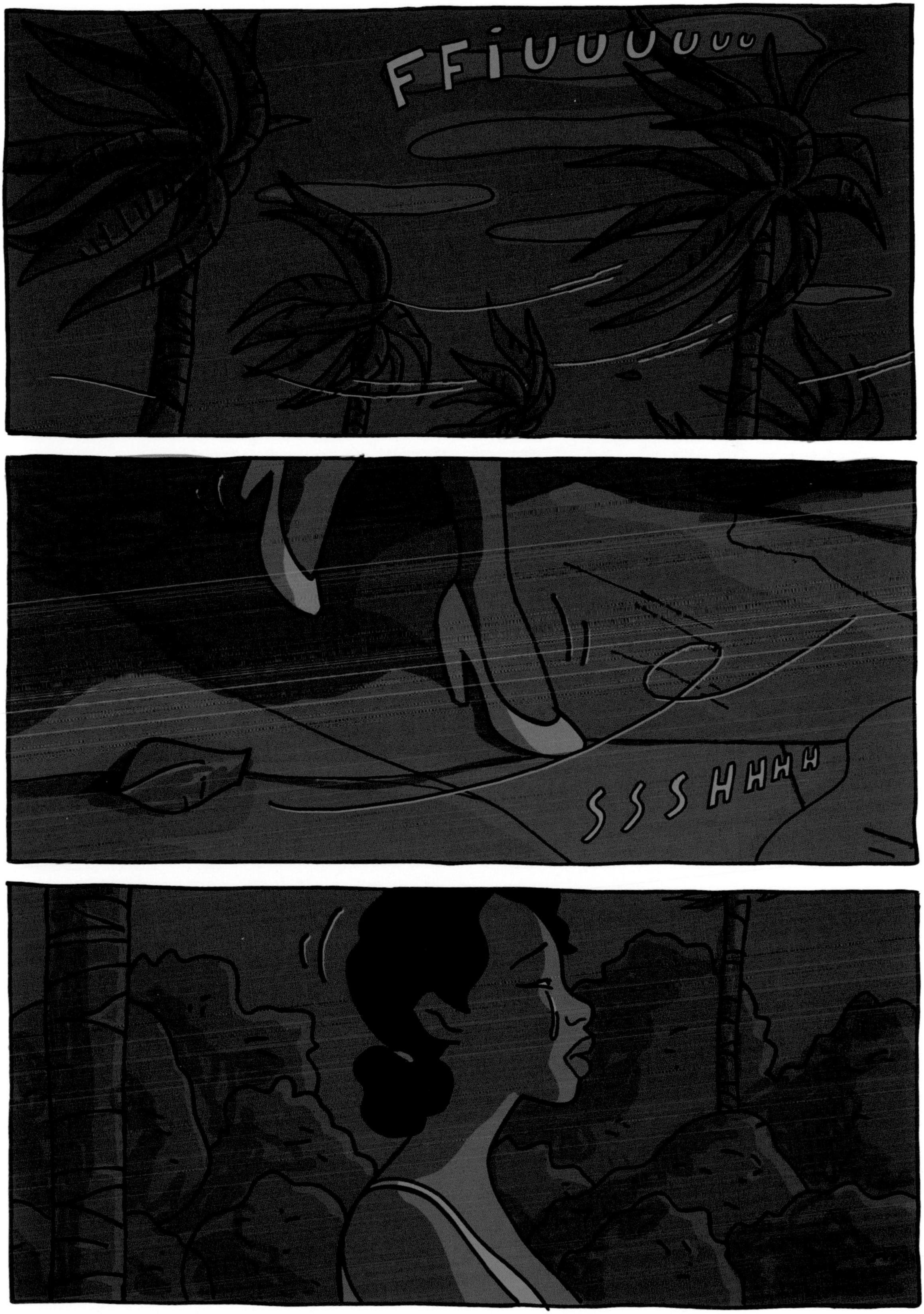
FFiUUUUUU
SSSHHHH

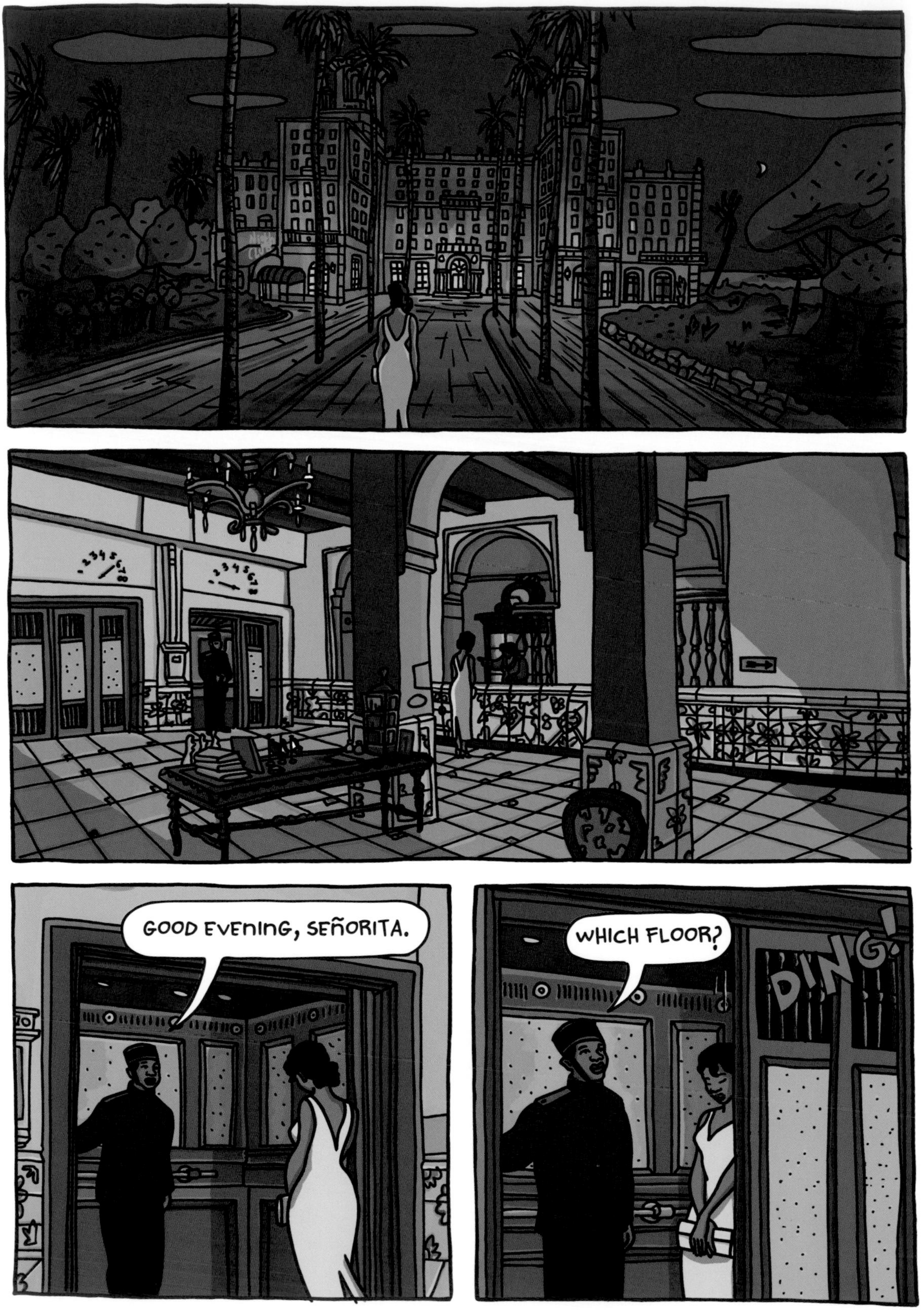

GOOD EVENING, SEÑORITA.
WHICH FLOOR?
DING!

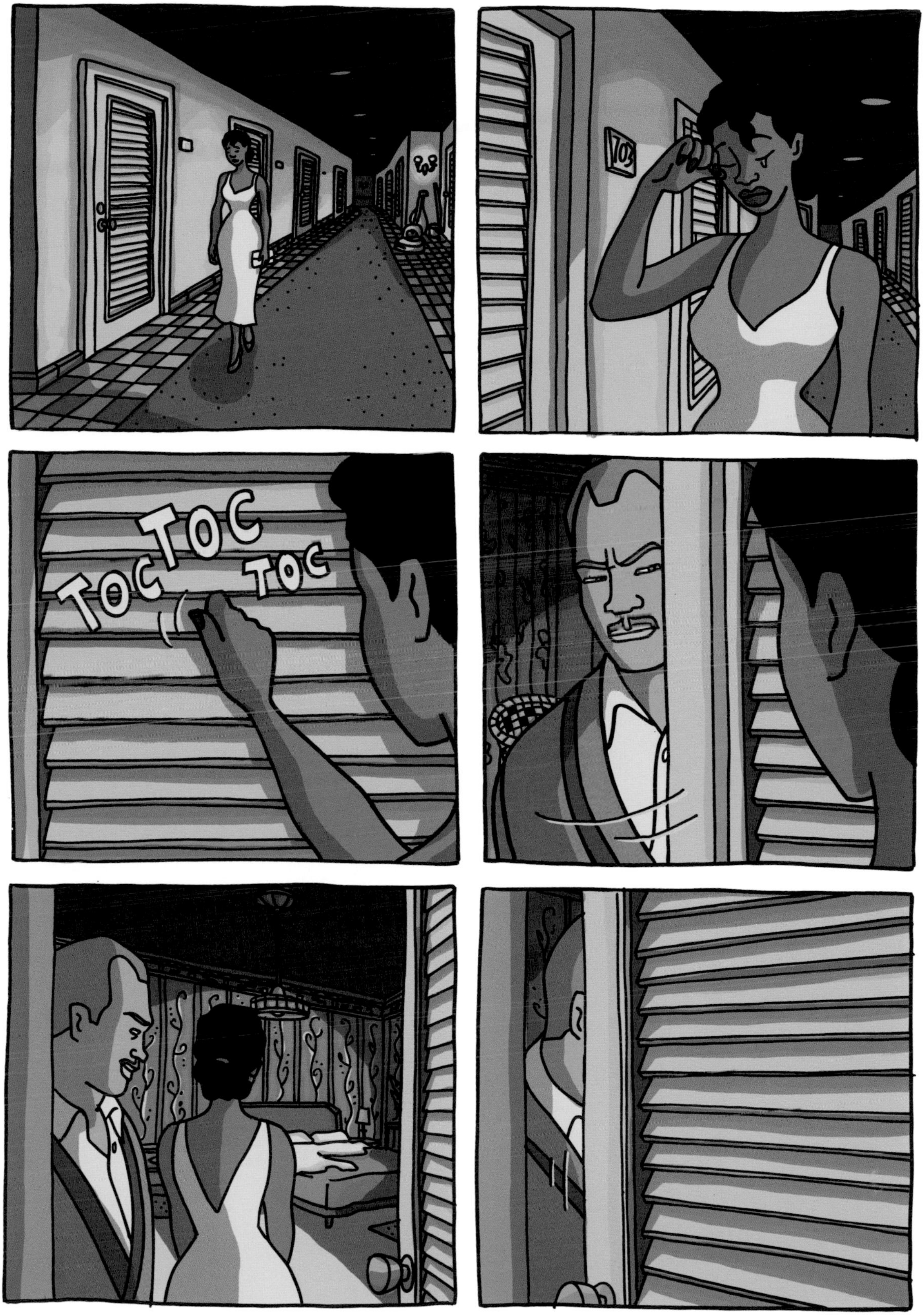
TOC TOC TOC

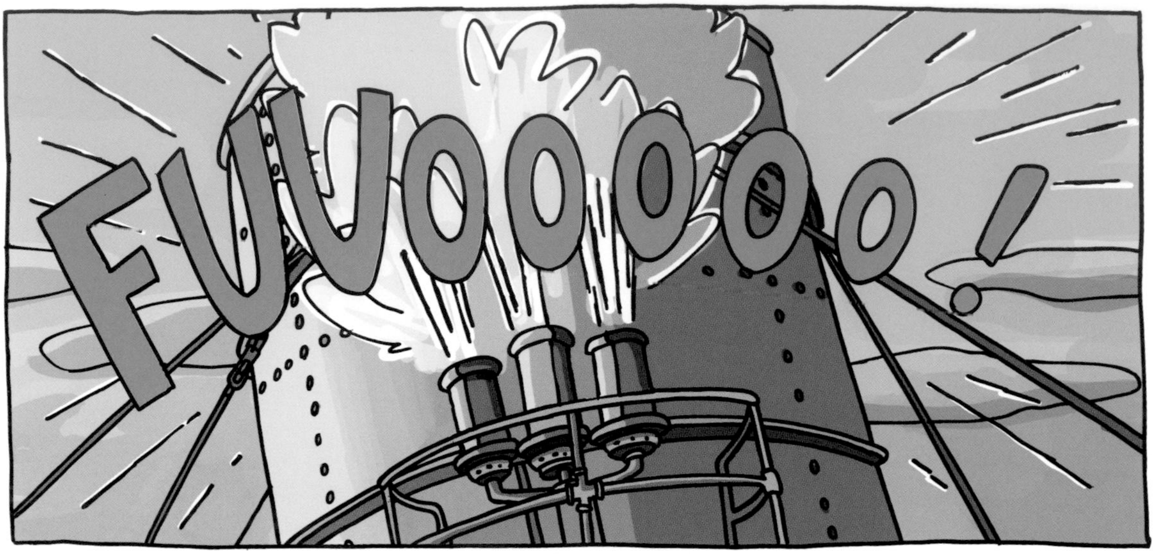
FUUOOOOO!

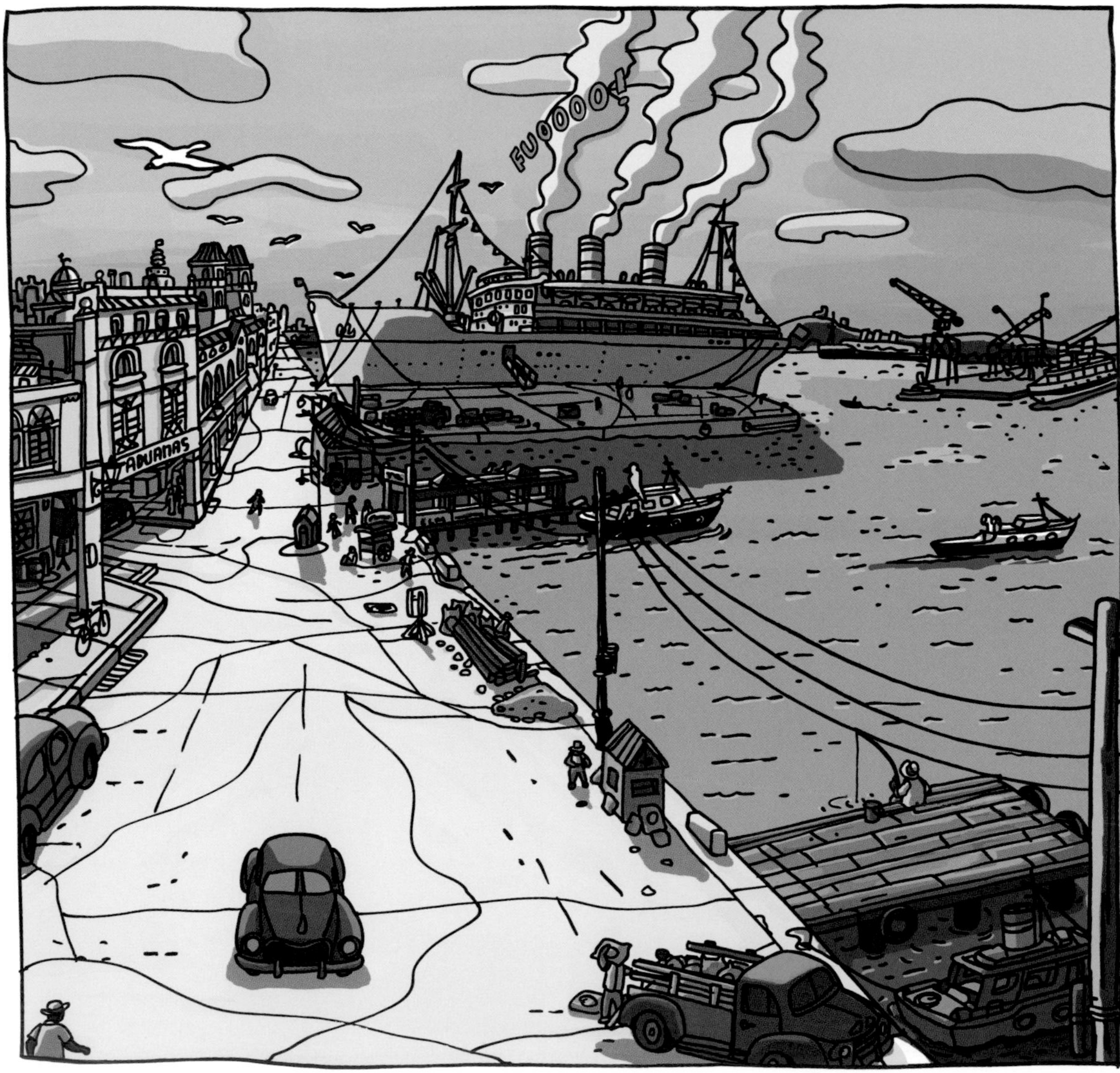
FUOOOO!
ADUANAS

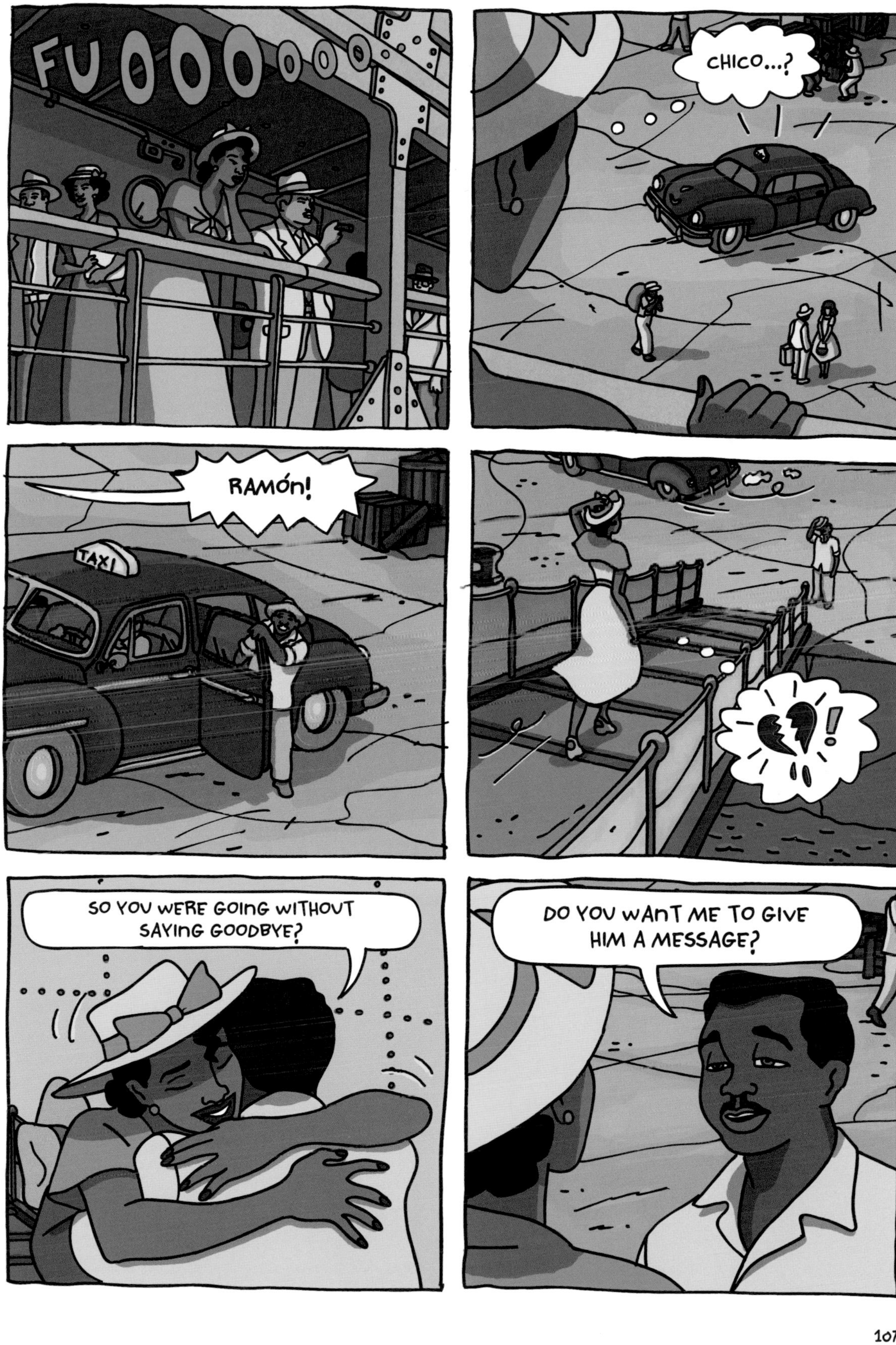

FUOOOooo
CHICO...?
RAMÓN!
SO YOU WERE GOING WITHOUT SAYING GOODBYE?
DO YOU WANT ME TO GIVE HIM A MESSAGE?

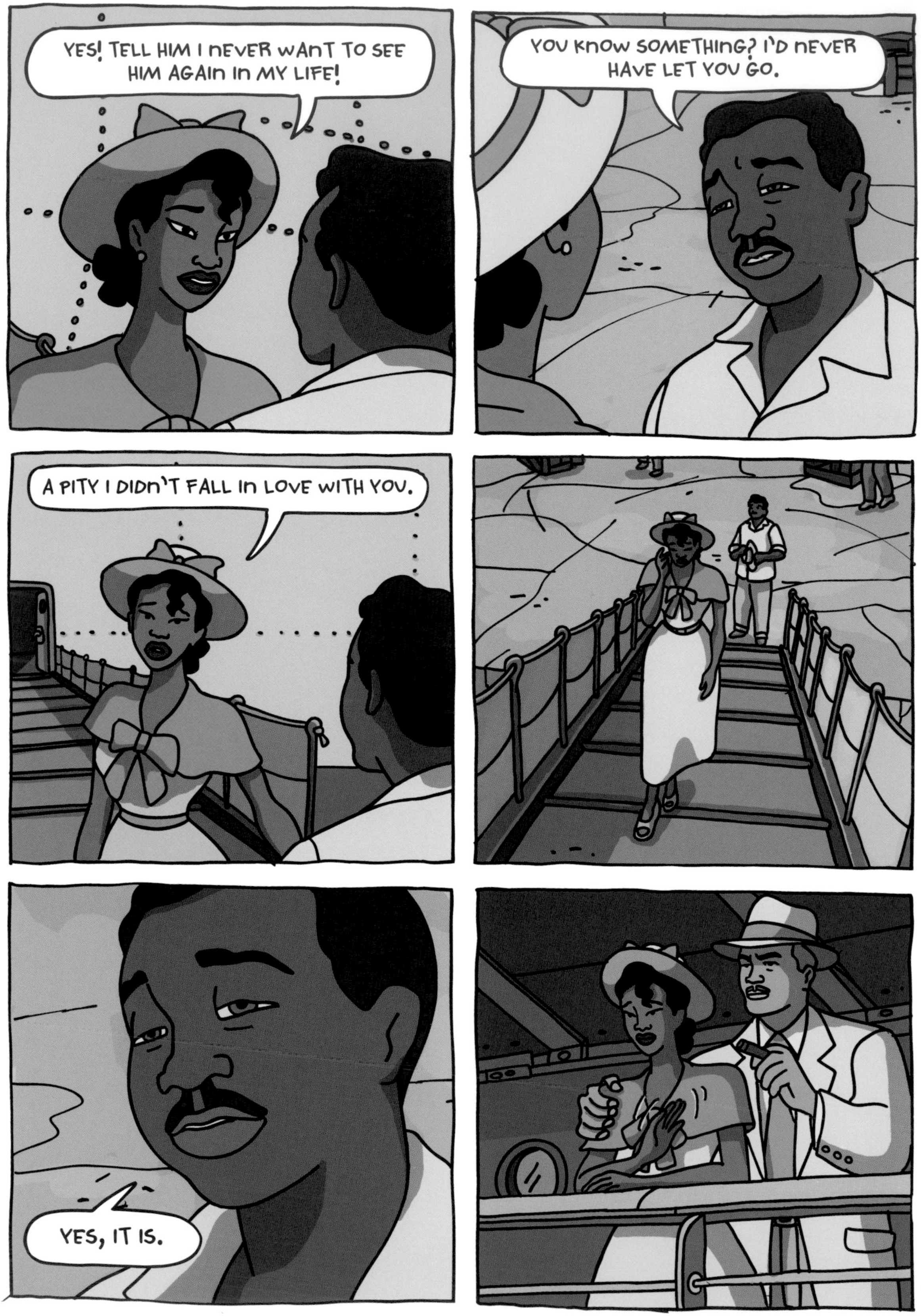
YES! TELL HIM I NEVER WANT TO SEE HIM AGAIN IN MY LIFE!
YOU KNOW SOMETHING? I'D NEVER HAVE LET YOU GO.
A PITY I DIDN'T FALL IN LOVE WITH YOU.
YES, IT IS.

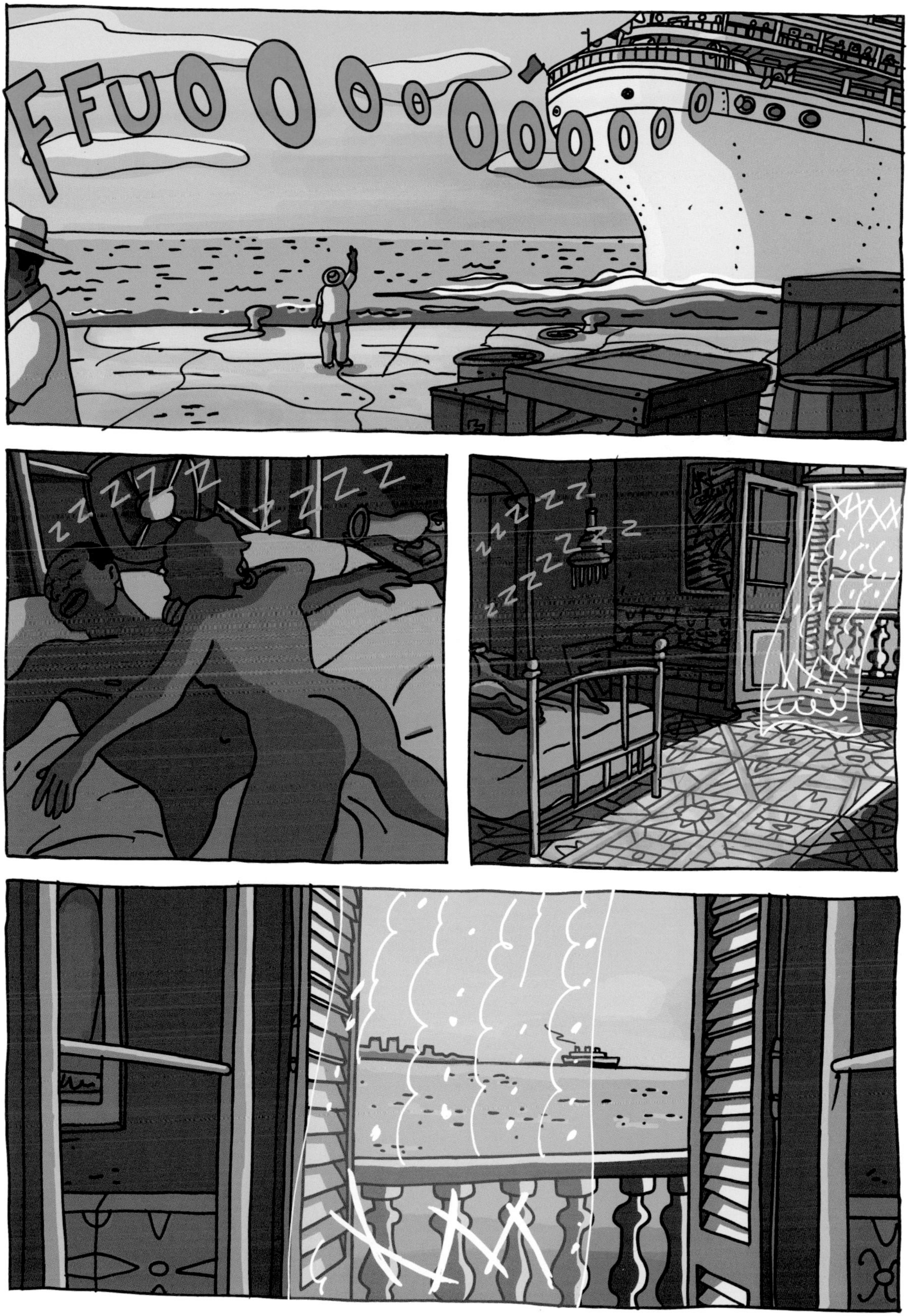
FFUOOOOooOOOOOOO
ZZZZZ
ZZZZ
ZZZZZ
ZZZZZZ

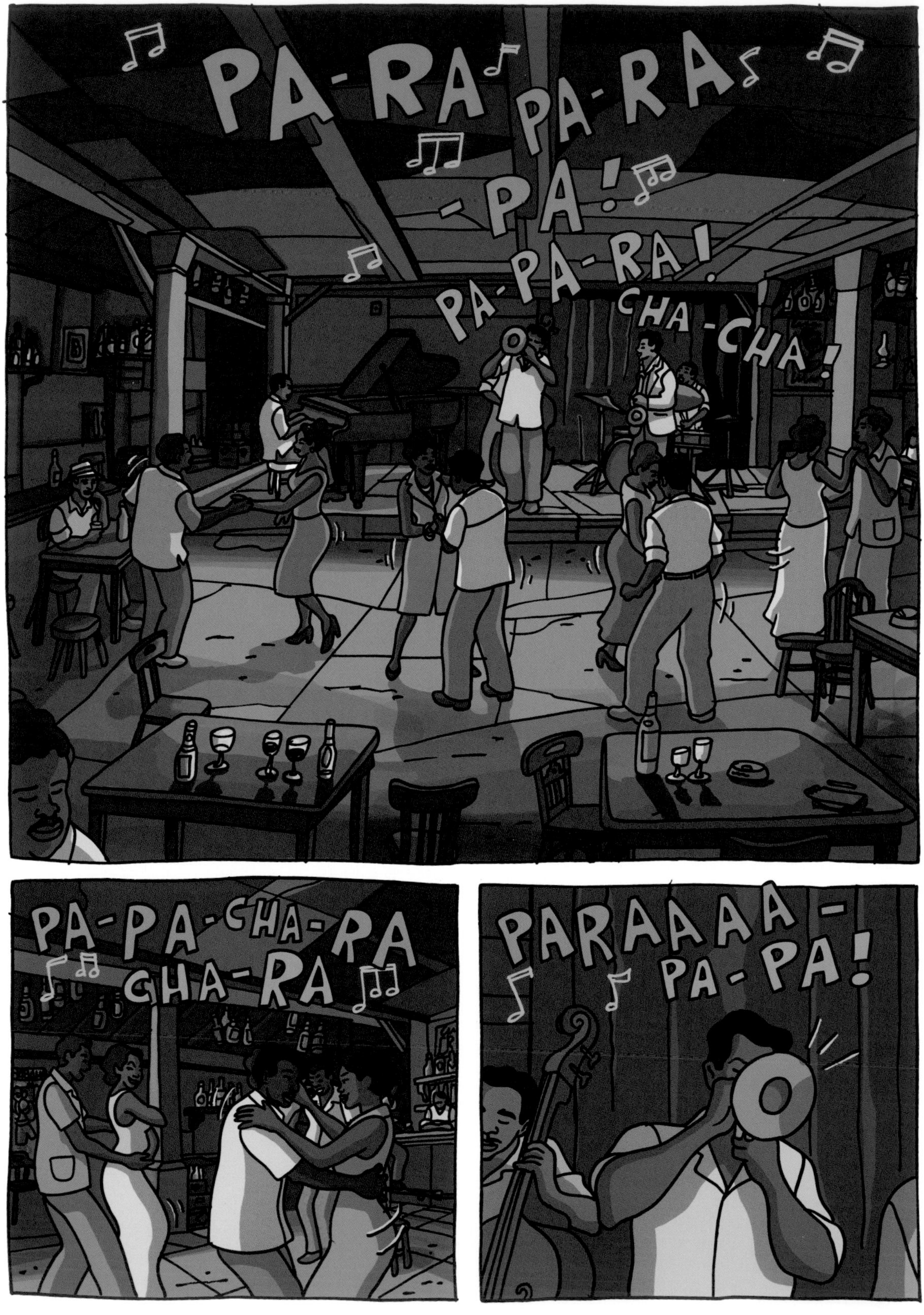
PA-RA PA-RA
-PA!
PA-PA-RA!
CHA-CHA!
PA-PA-CHA-RA
CHA-RA
PARAAAA-
PA-PA!

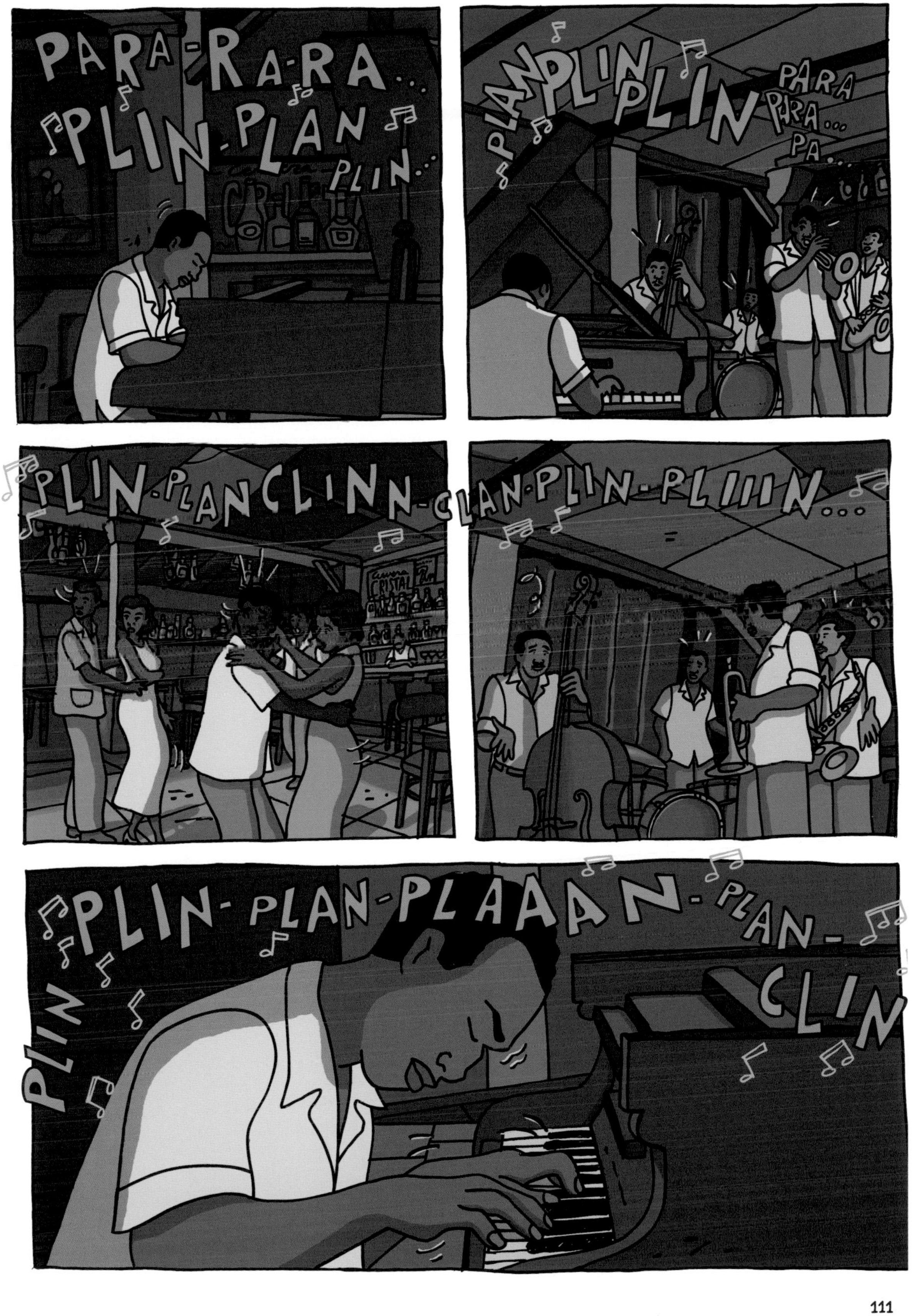
PARA-RA-RA-RA...
PLIN-PLAN
PLIN...
PLAN PLIN PLIN
PARA PARA... PA...
PLIN-PLAN CLINN-CLAN-PLIN-PLIIIN...
CRISTAL
PLIN
PLIN-PLAN-PLAAAN-PLAN-
CLIN

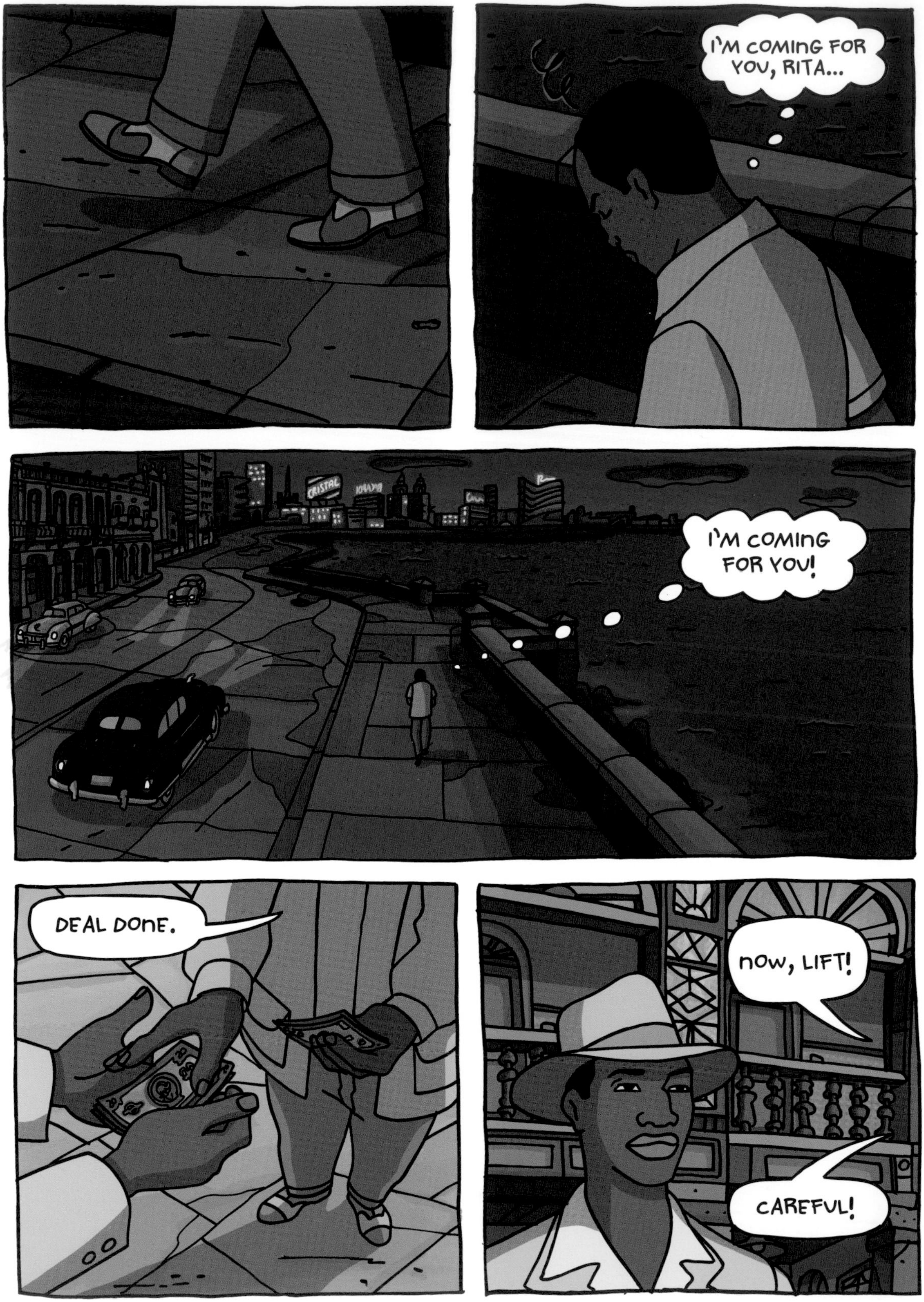
I'M COMING FOR YOU, RITA...
CRISTAL
I'M COMING FOR YOU!
DEAL DONE.
NOW, LIFT!
CAREFUL!

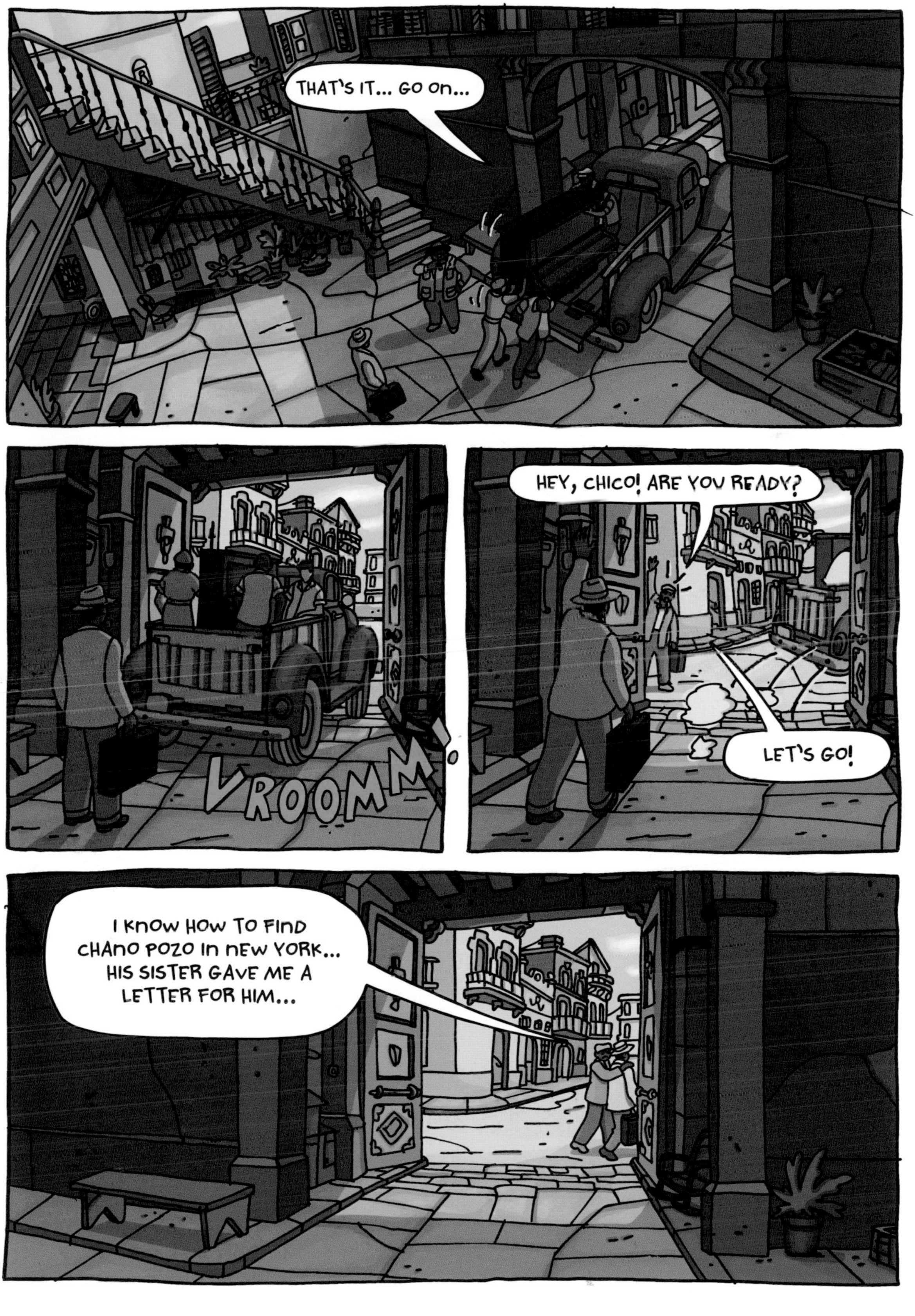
THAT'S IT... GO ON...
VROOMM
HEY, CHICO! ARE YOU READY?
LET'S GO!
I KNOW HOW TO FIND CHANO POZO IN NEW YORK... HIS SISTER GAVE ME A LETTER FOR HIM...

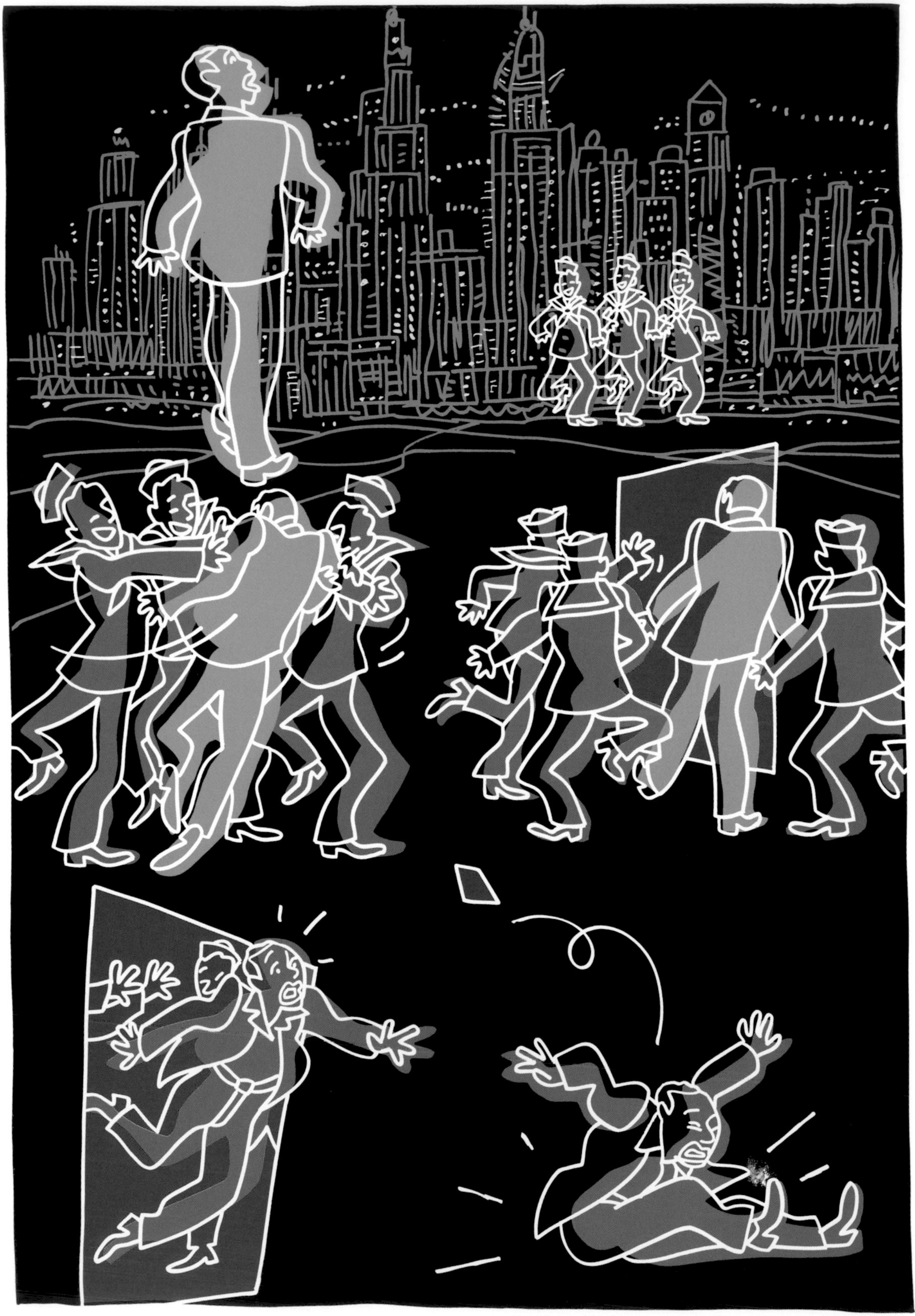

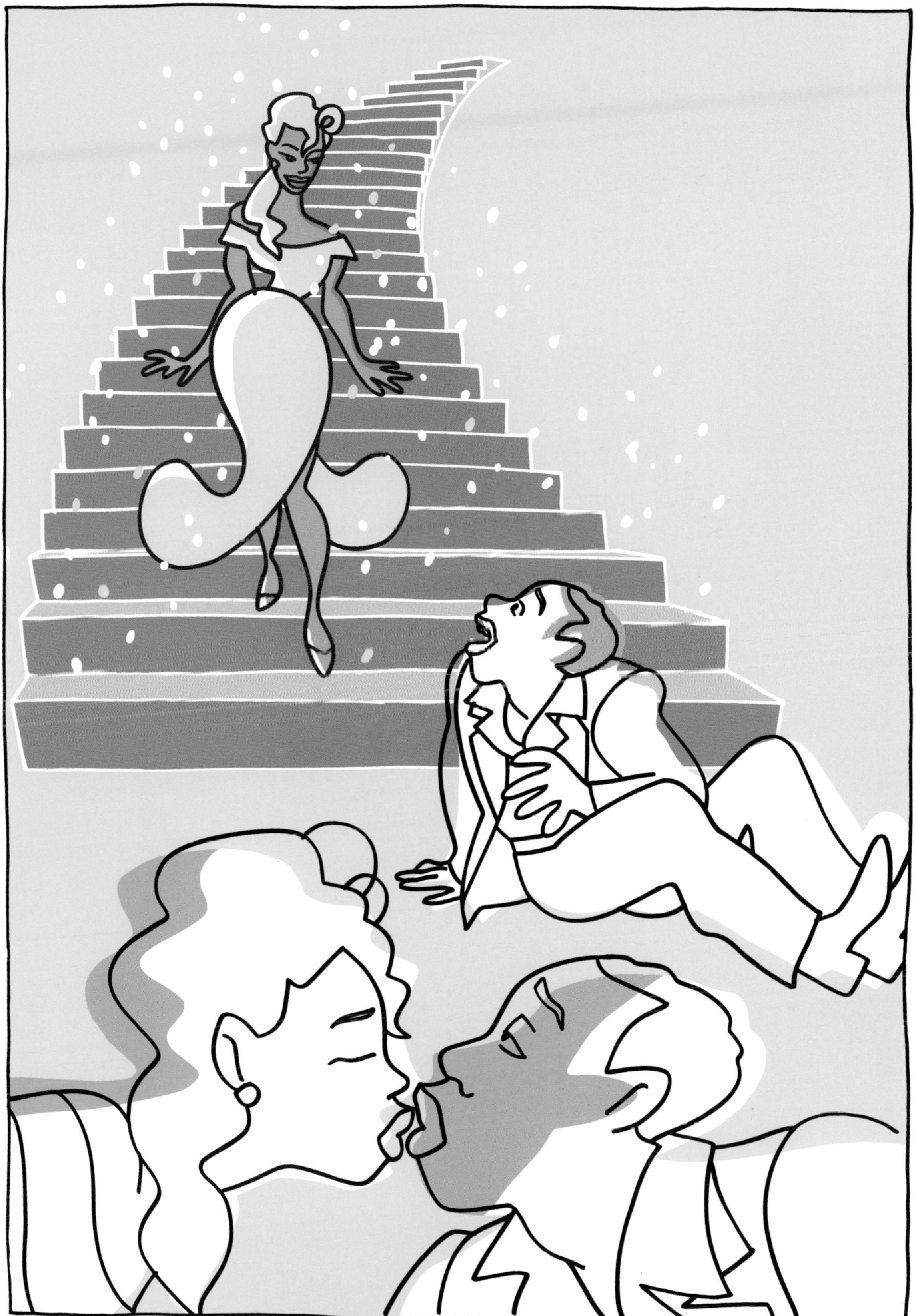

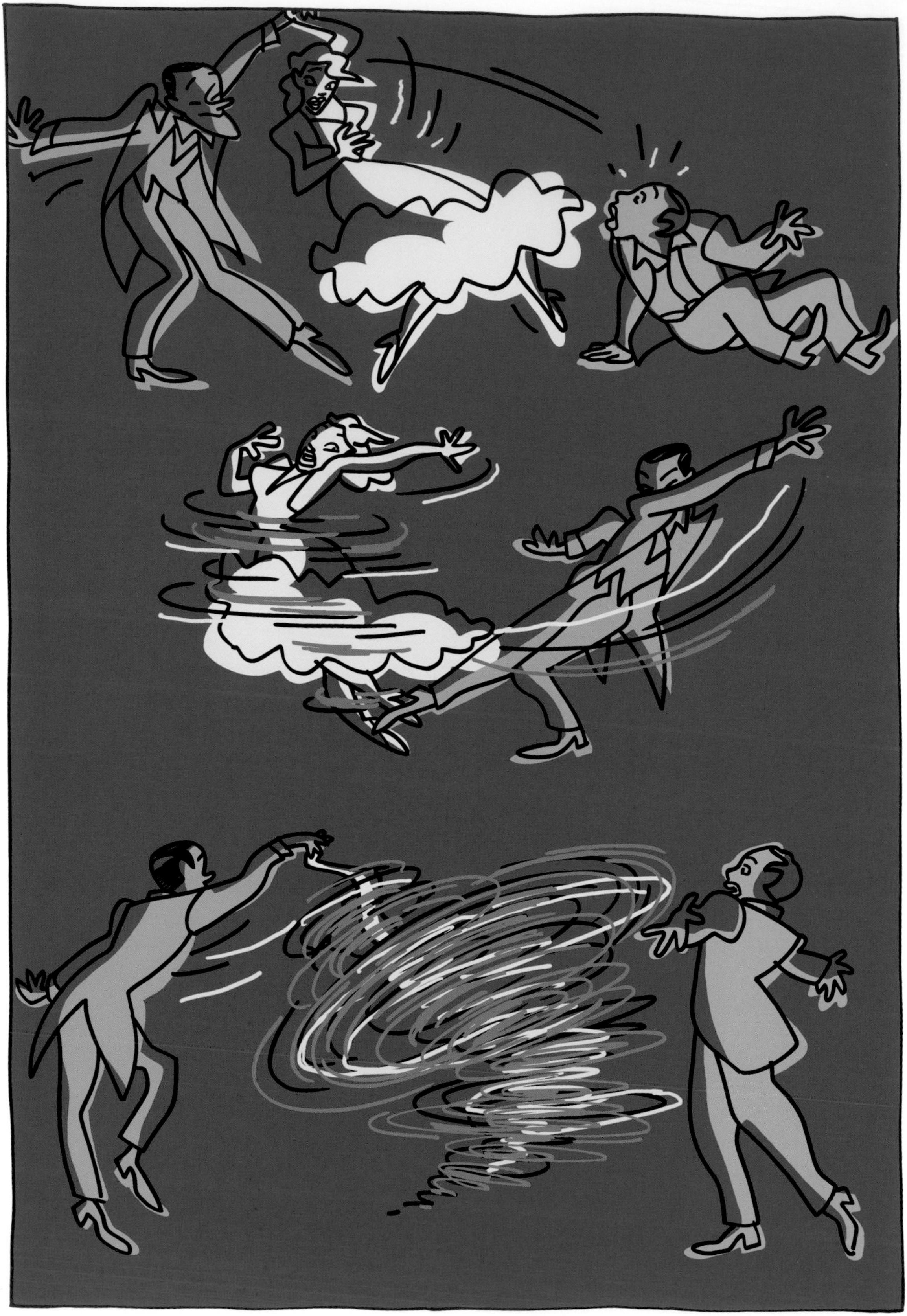

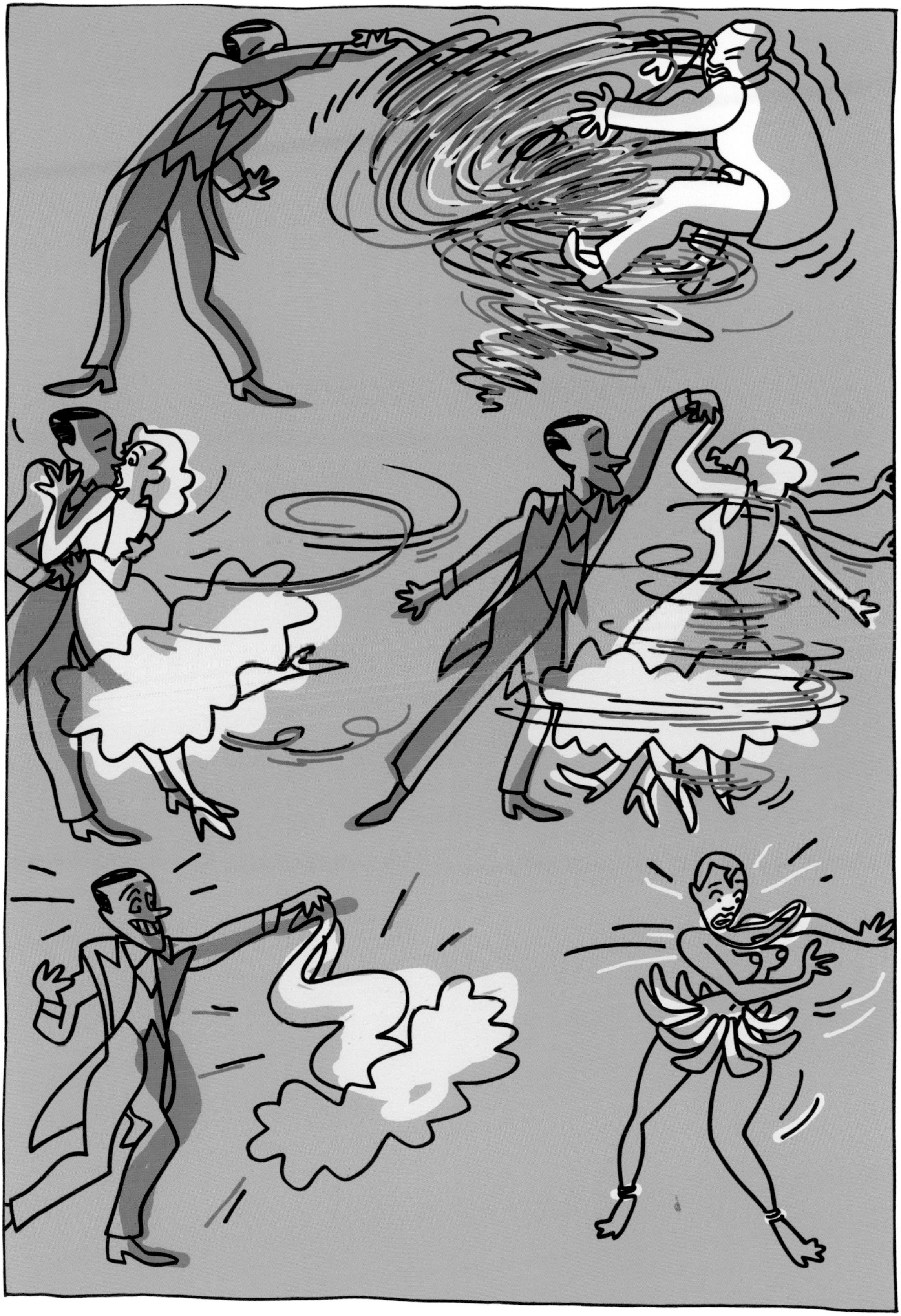

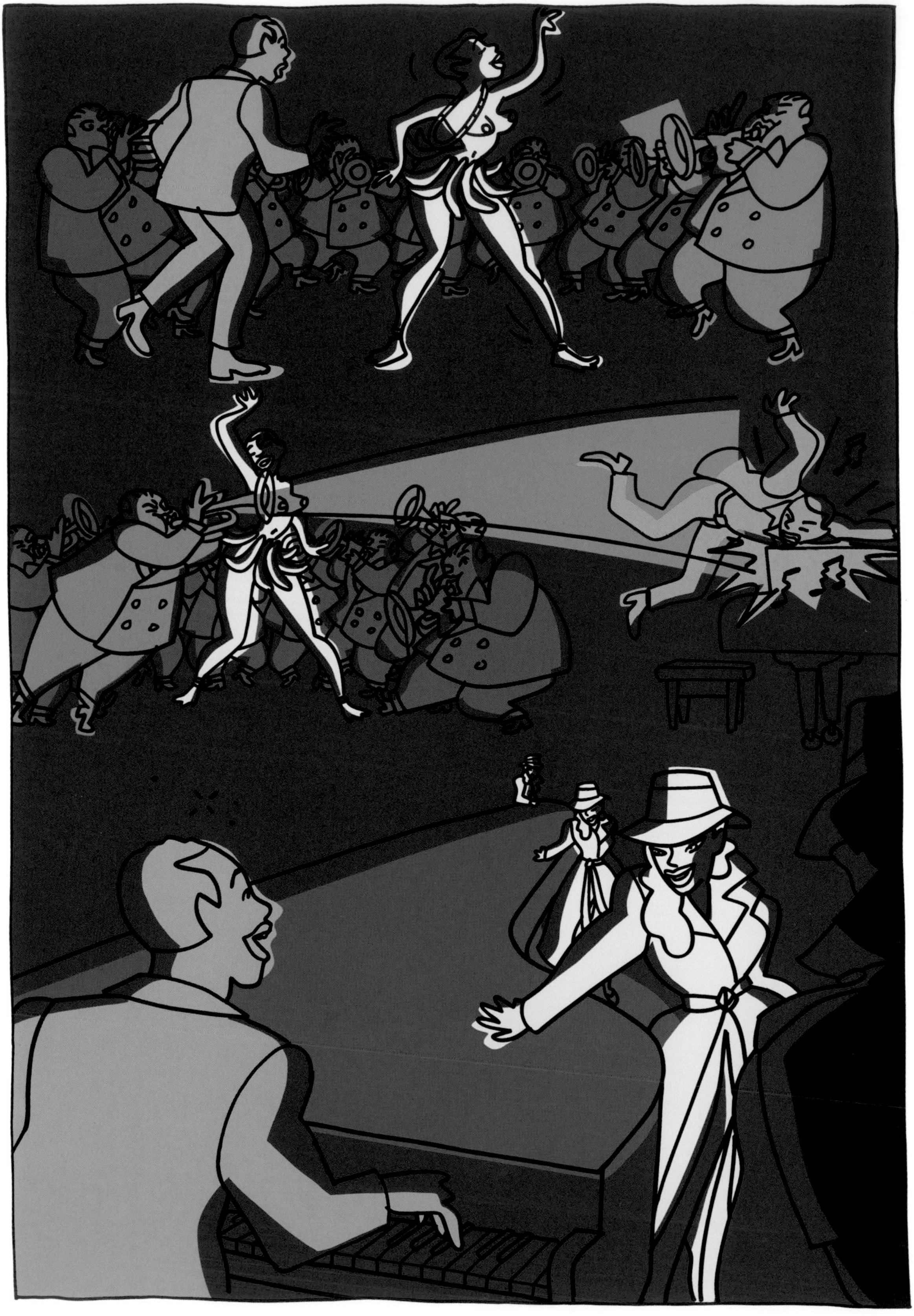

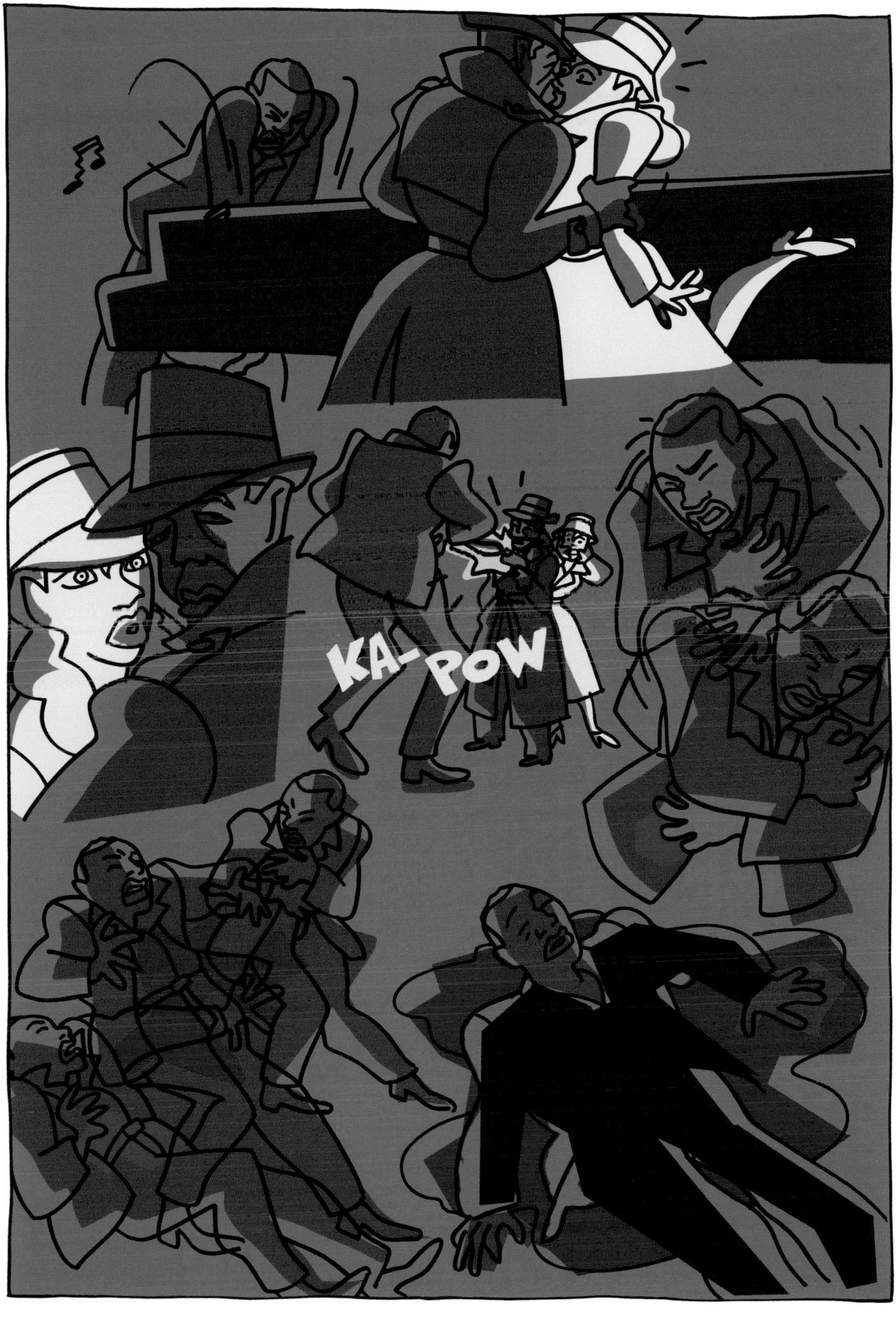
KA-POW

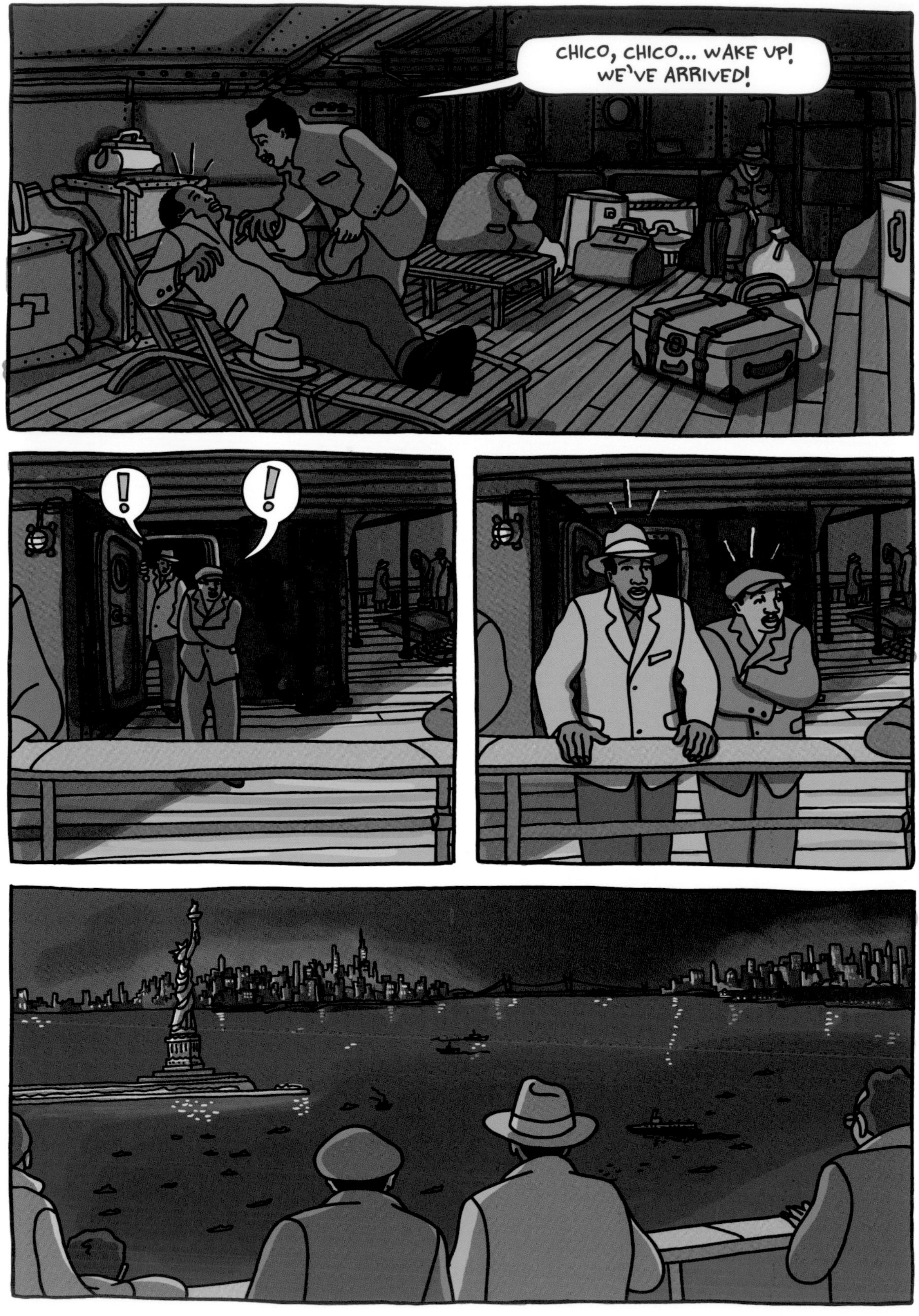
CHICO, CHICO... WAKE UP! WE'VE ARRIVED!
!
!

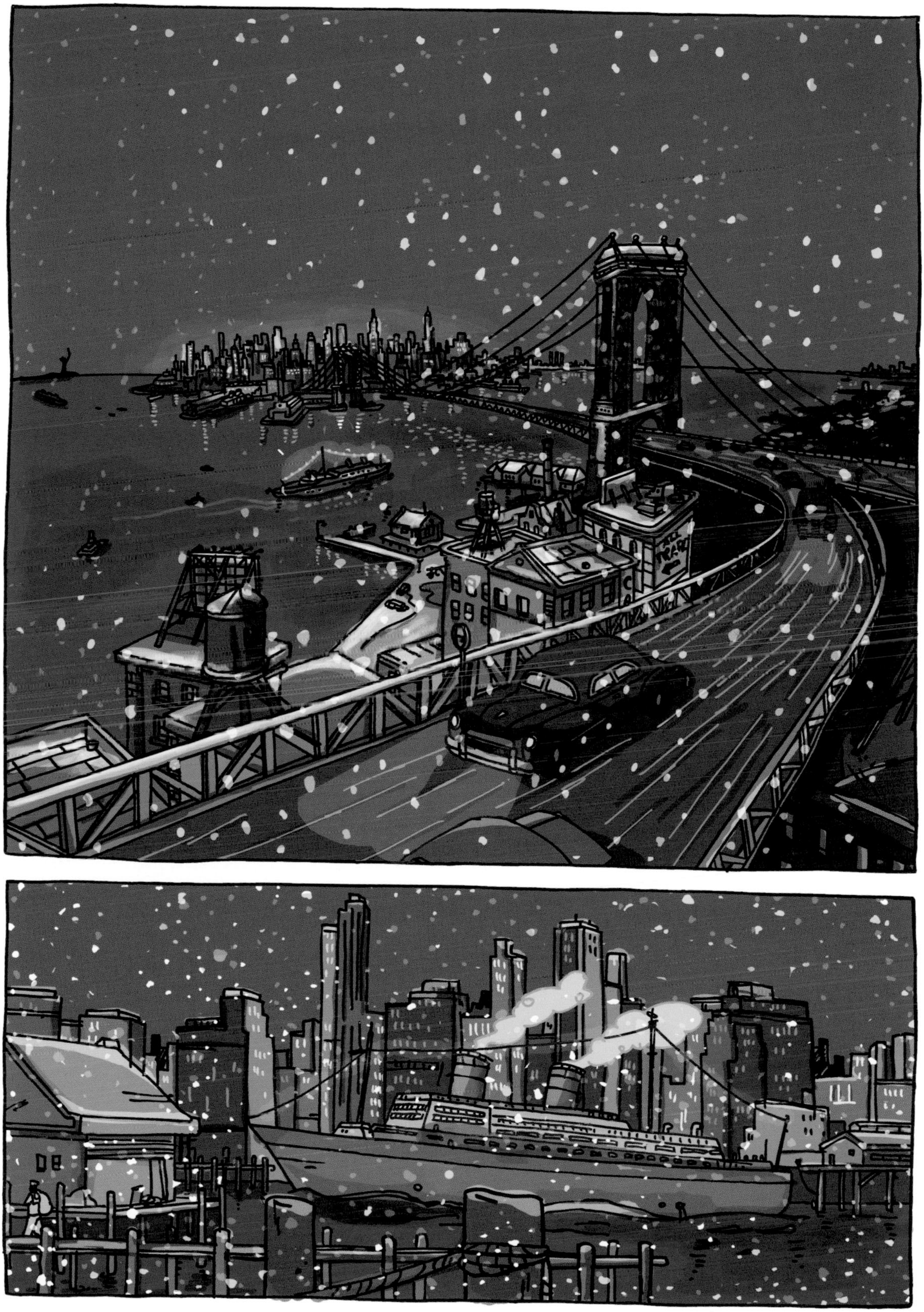

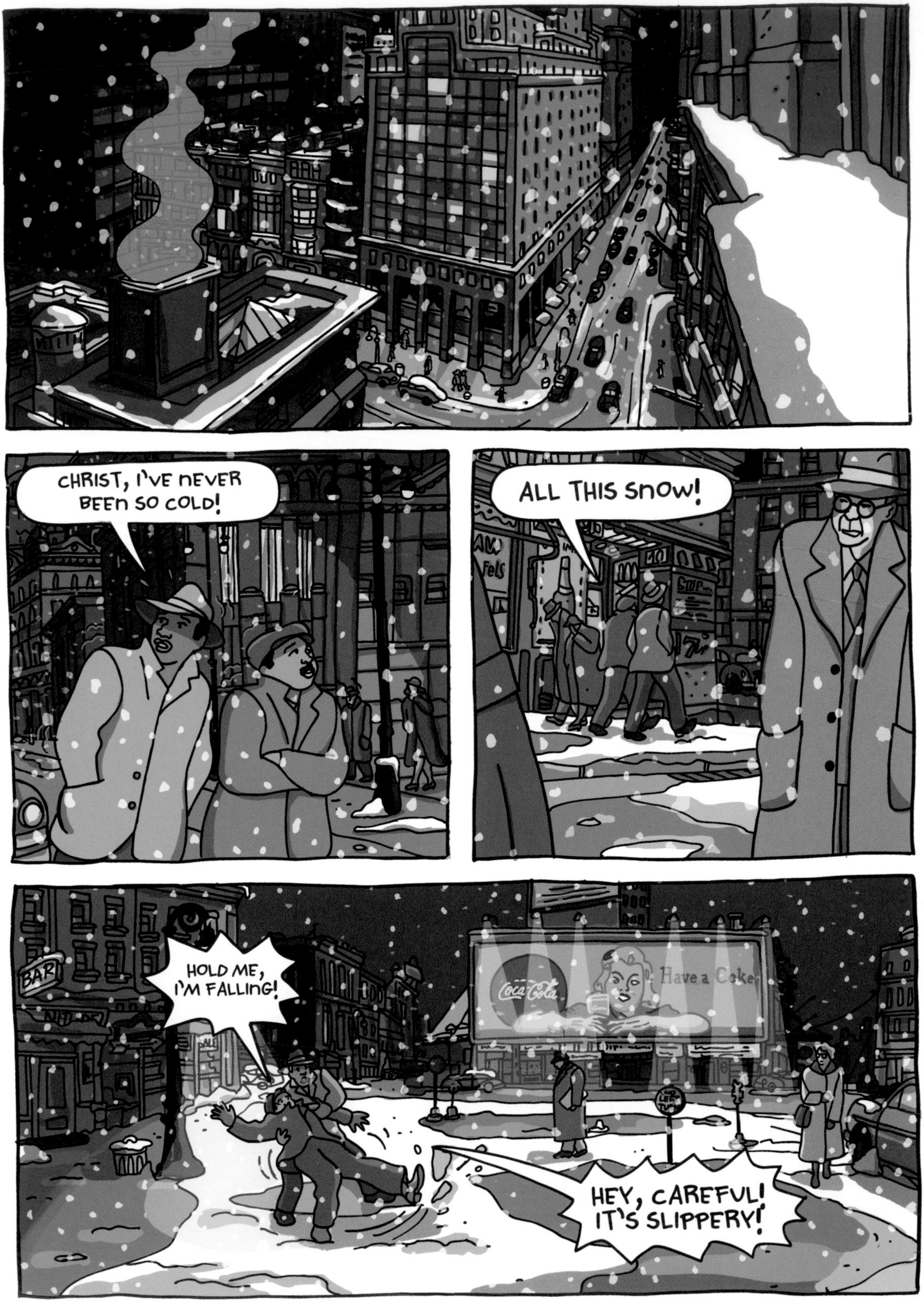
CHRIST, I'VE NEVER BEEN SO COLD!
ALL THIS SNOW!
BAR
HOLD ME, I'M FALLING!
Coca-Cola
Have a Coke
HEY, CAREFUL! IT'S SLIPPERY!

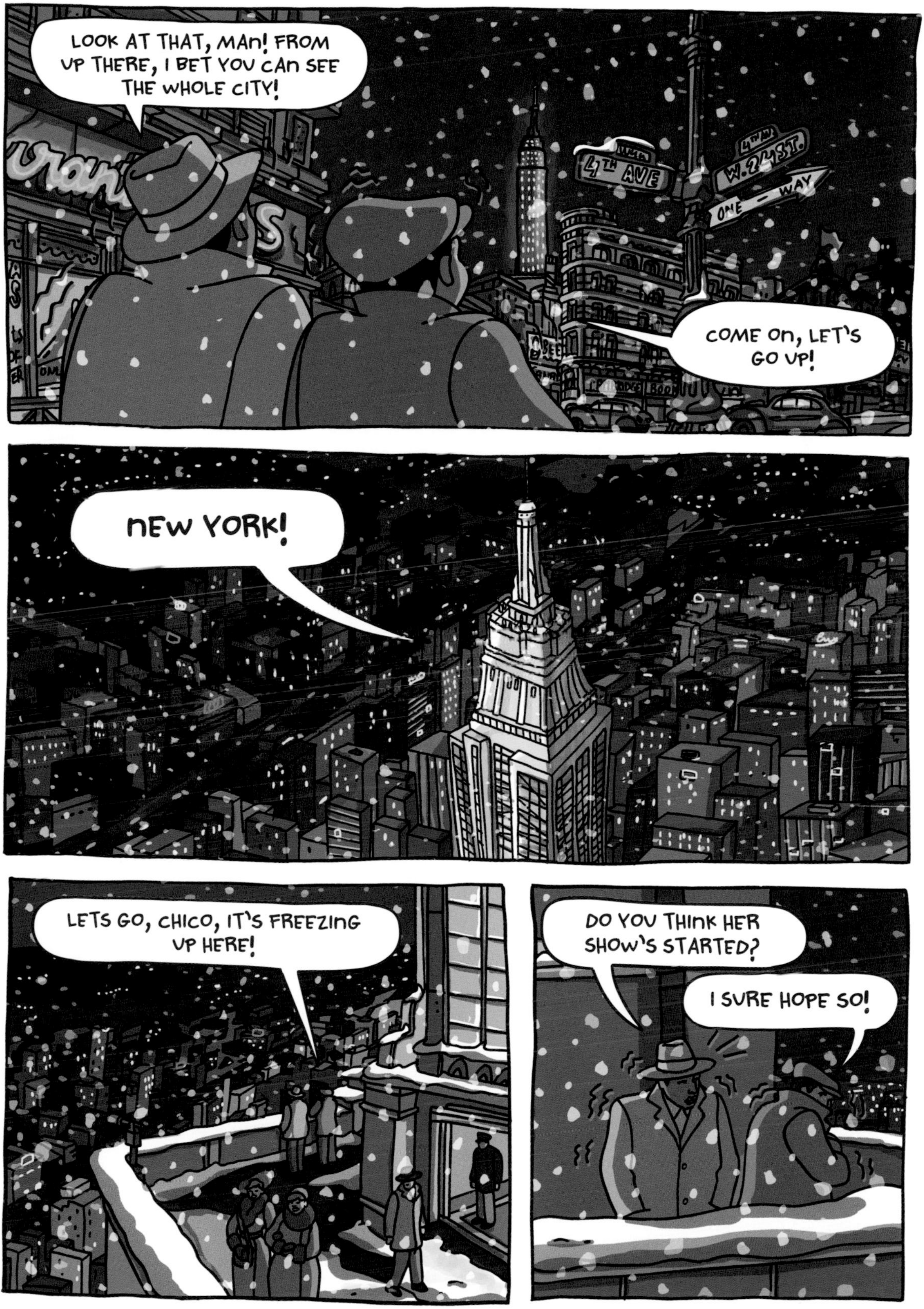
LOOK AT THAT, MAN! FROM UP THERE, I BET YOU CAN SEE THE WHOLE CITY!
4TH AVE
W. 24 ST.
ONE WAY
COME ON, LET'S GO UP!
NEW YORK!
LETS GO, CHICO, IT'S FREEZING UP HERE!
DO YOU THINK HER SHOW'S STARTED?
I SURE HOPE SO!

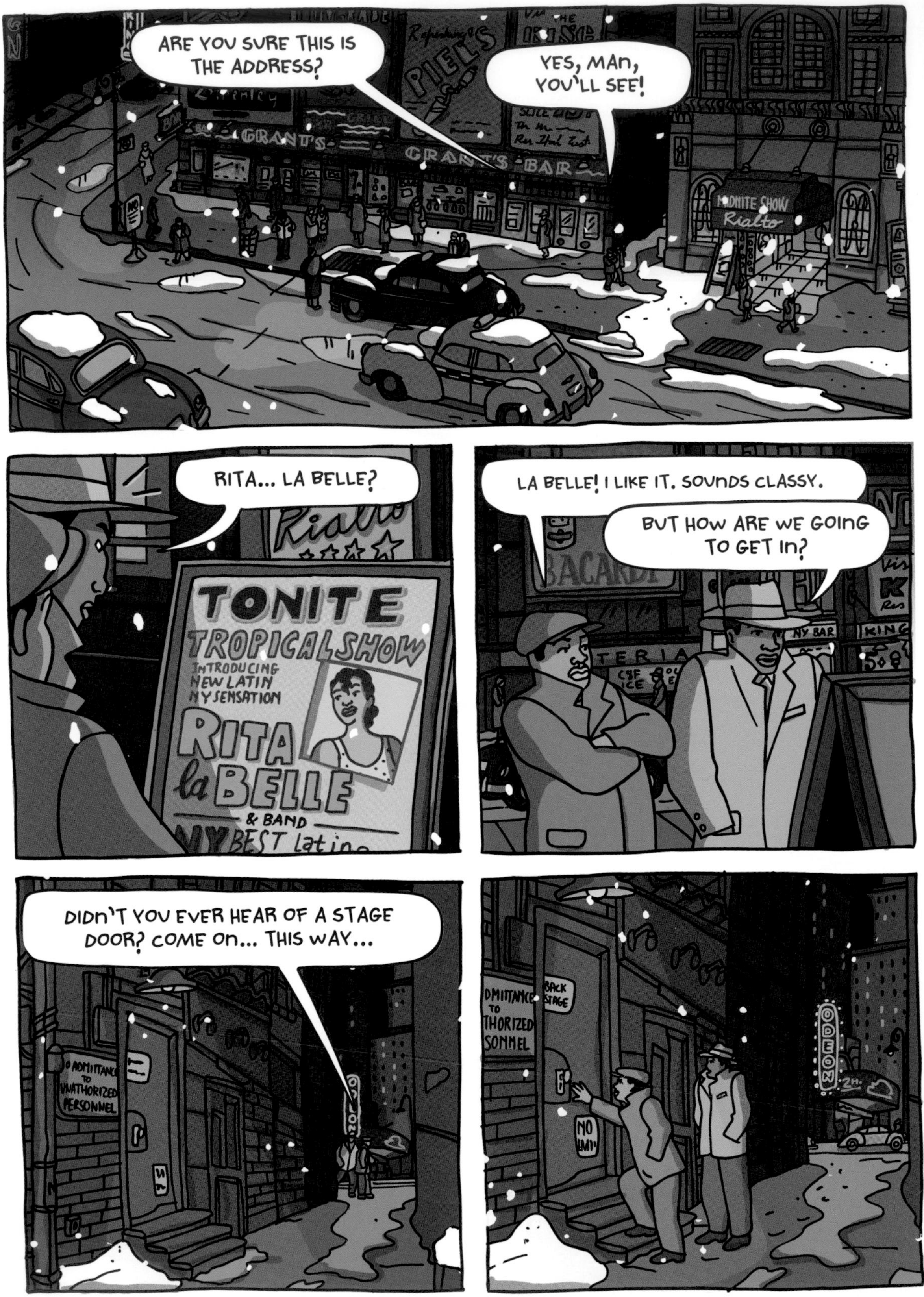

ARE YOU SURE THIS IS THE ADDRESS?
YES, MAN, YOU'LL SEE!
GRANT'S BAR
MIDNITE SHOW
Rialto
RITA... LA BELLE?
TONITE
TROPICAL SHOW
INTRODUCING NEW LATIN NY SENSATION
RITA la BELLE
& BAND
LA BELLE! I LIKE IT. SOUNDS CLASSY.
BUT HOW ARE WE GOING TO GET IN?
DIDN'T YOU EVER HEAR OF A STAGE DOOR? COME ON... THIS WAY...
NO ADMITTANCE TO UNAUTHORIZED PERSONNEL
BACK STAGE
ODEON

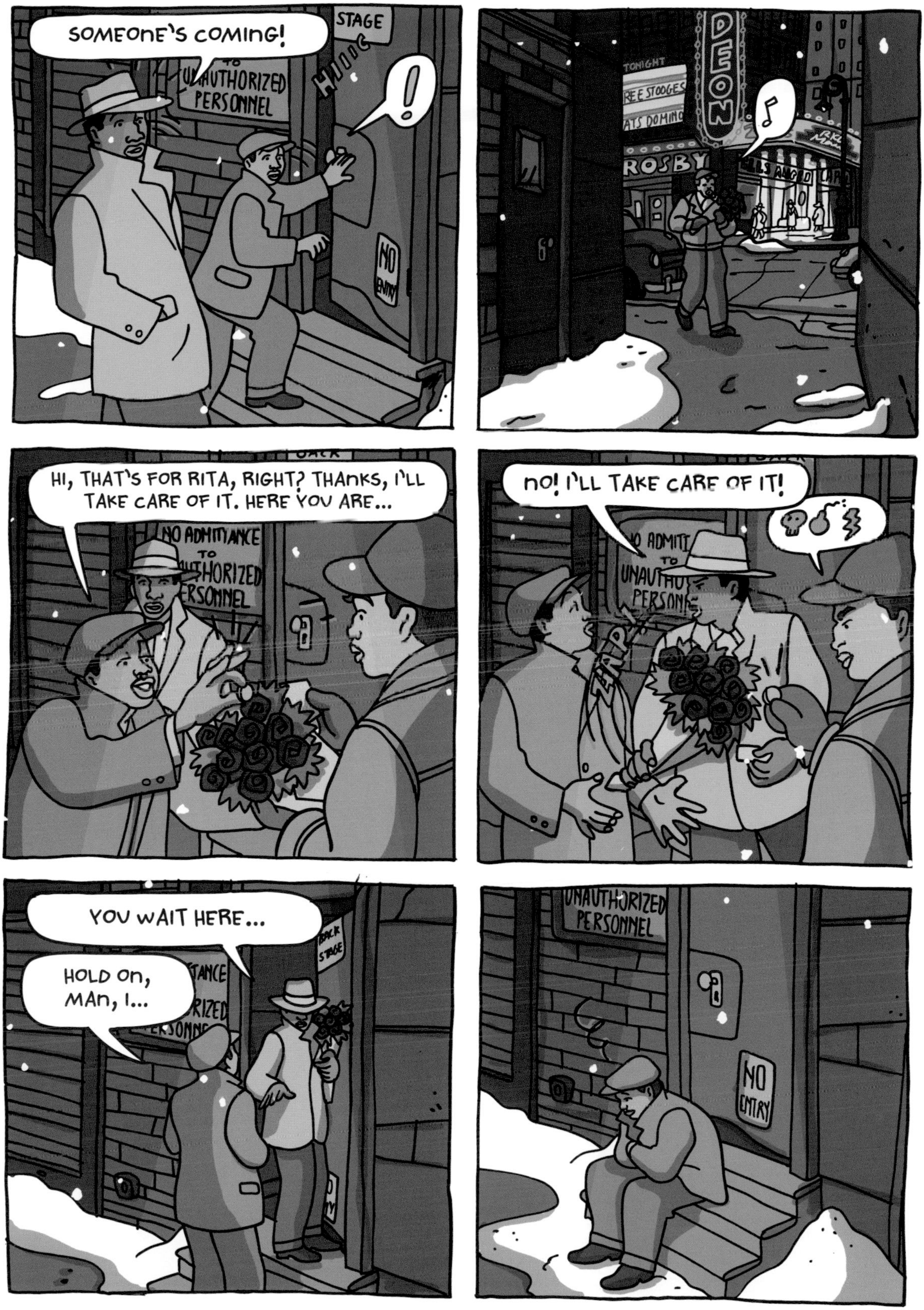
SOMEONE'S COMING!
STAGE
UNAUTHORIZED PERSONNEL
!
NO ENTRY
TONIGHT
DEON
ROSBY
HI, THAT'S FOR RITA, RIGHT? THANKS, I'LL TAKE CARE OF IT. HERE YOU ARE...
NO ADMITTANCE TO UNAUTHORIZED PERSONNEL
NO! I'LL TAKE CARE OF IT!
ZAP!
YOU WAIT HERE...
HOLD ON, MAN, I...
BACK STAGE
UNAUTHORIZED PERSONNEL
NO ENTRY

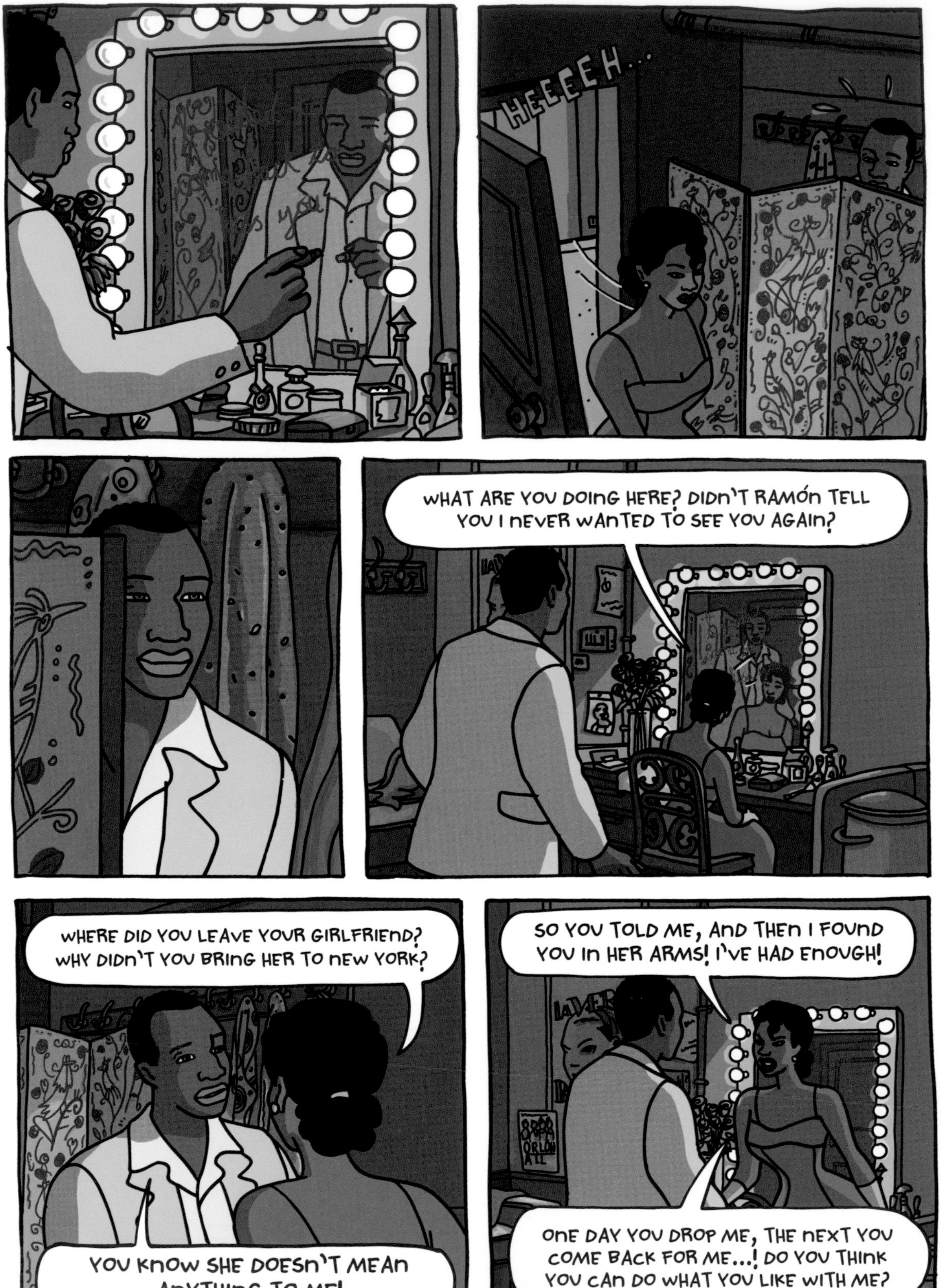
HEEEEH...
WHAT ARE YOU DOING HERE? DIDN'T RAMÓN TELL YOU I NEVER WANTED TO SEE YOU AGAIN?
WHERE DID YOU LEAVE YOUR GIRLFRIEND? WHY DIDN'T YOU BRING HER TO NEW YORK?
YOU KNOW SHE DOESN'T MEAN ANYTHING TO ME!
SO YOU TOLD ME, AND THEN I FOUND YOU IN HER ARMS! I'VE HAD ENOUGH!
ONE DAY YOU DROP ME, THE NEXT YOU COME BACK FOR ME...! DO YOU THINK YOU CAN DO WHAT YOU LIKE WITH ME?

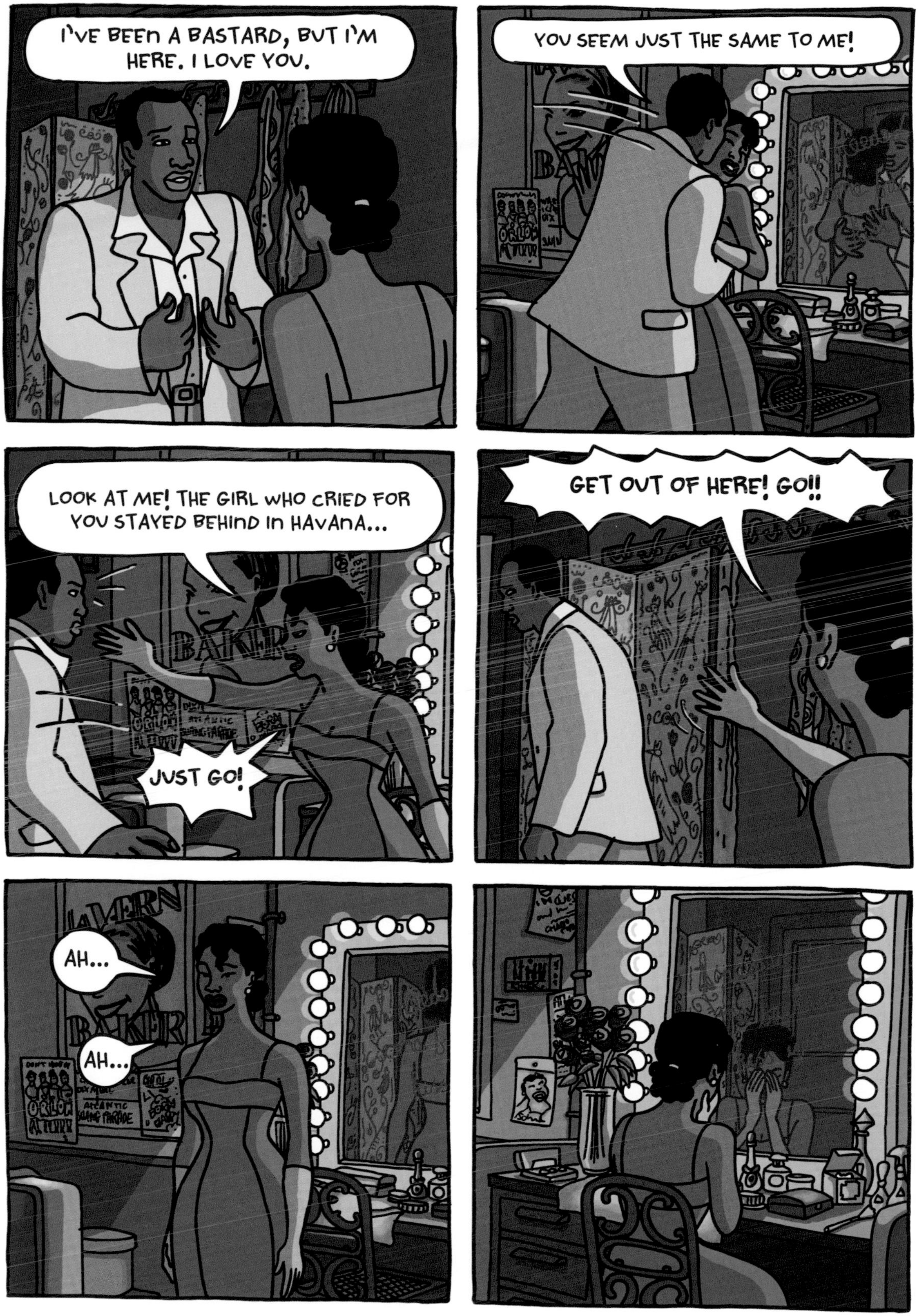
I'VE BEEN A BASTARD, BUT I'M HERE. I LOVE YOU.
YOU SEEM JUST THE SAME TO ME!
LOOK AT ME! THE GIRL WHO CRIED FOR YOU STAYED BEHIND IN HAVANA...
JUST GO!
GET OUT OF HERE! GO!!
AH...
AH...

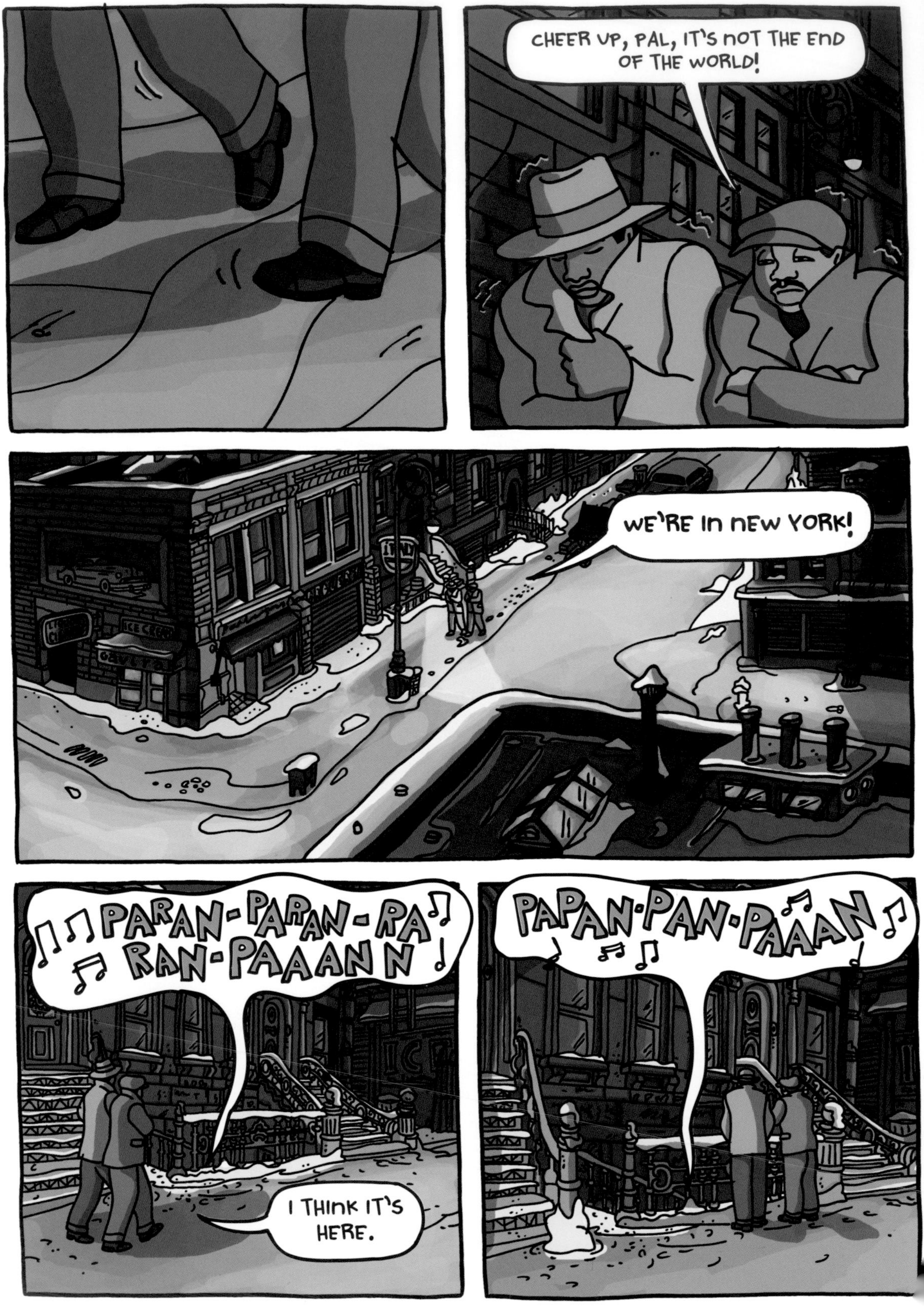
CHEER UP, PAL, IT'S NOT THE END OF THE WORLD!
WE'RE IN NEW YORK!
PARAN-PARAN-RA RAN-PAAANN
I THINK IT'S HERE.
PAPAN-PAN-PAAAN

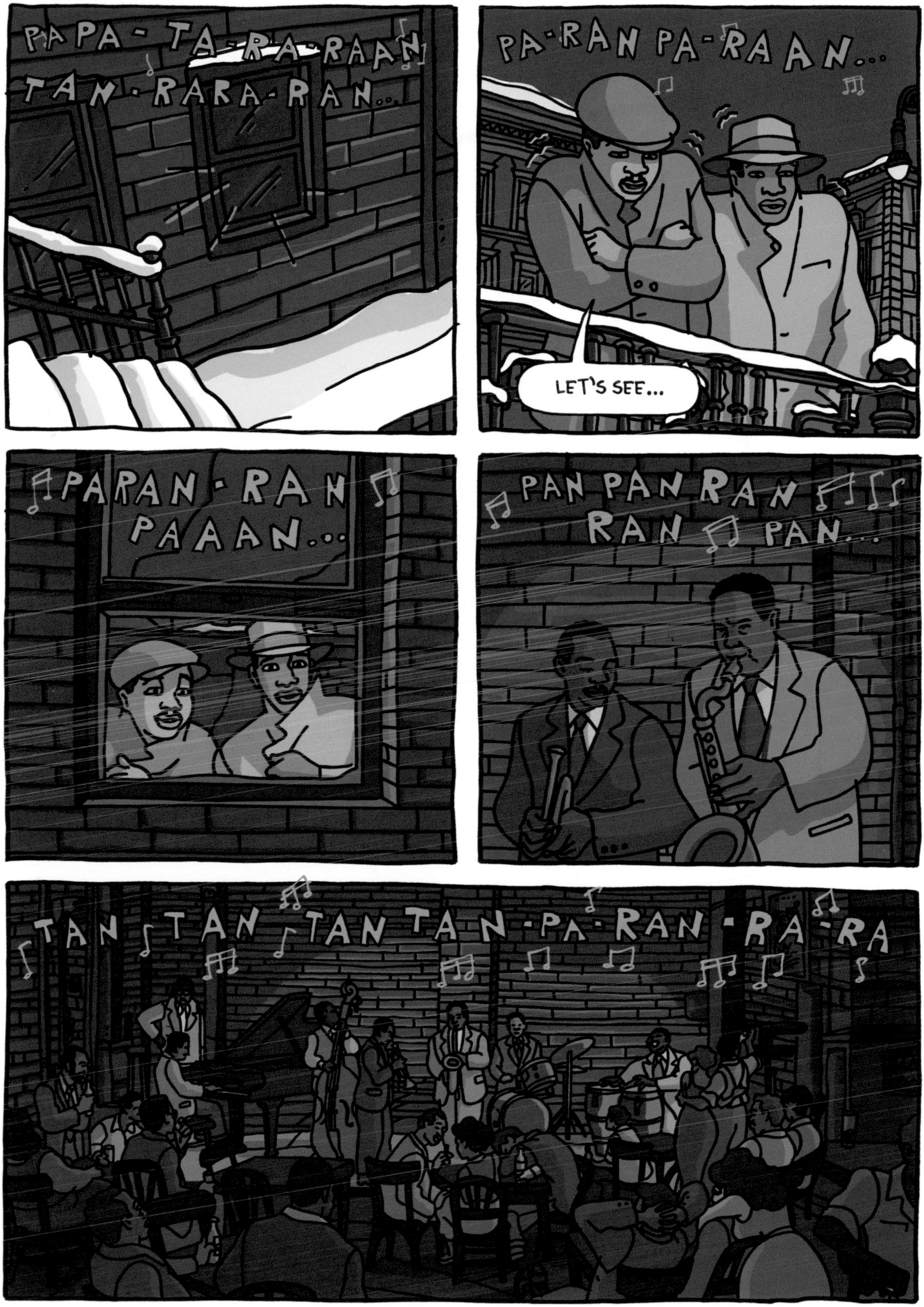
PAPA-TA-RA-RAAN
TAN-RARA-RAN...
PA-RAN PA-RAAN...
LET'S SEE...
PARAN-RAN
PAAAN...
PAN PAN RAN
RAN PAN...
TAN TAN TAN TAN-PA-RAN-RA-RA

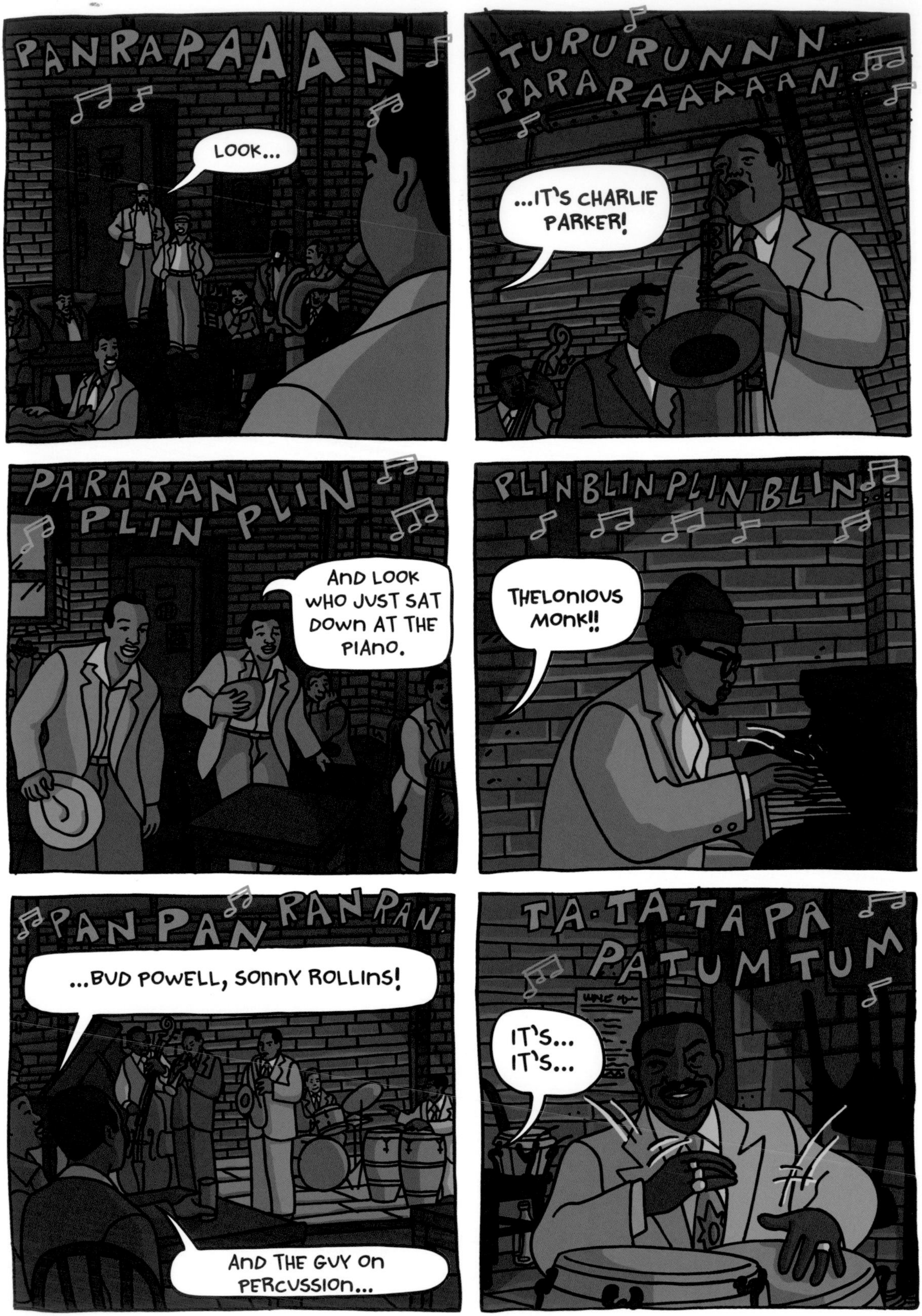
PANRARAAAN
LOOK...
TURURUNNN PARARAAAAAN
...IT'S CHARLIE PARKER!
PARARAN PLIN PLIN
AND LOOK WHO JUST SAT DOWN AT THE PIANO.
PLIN BLIN PLIN BLIN
THELONIOUS MONK!!
PAN PAN RAN PAN
...BUD POWELL, SONNY ROLLINS!
AND THE GUY ON PERCUSSION...
TA-TA-TAPA PATUM TUM
IT'S... IT'S...

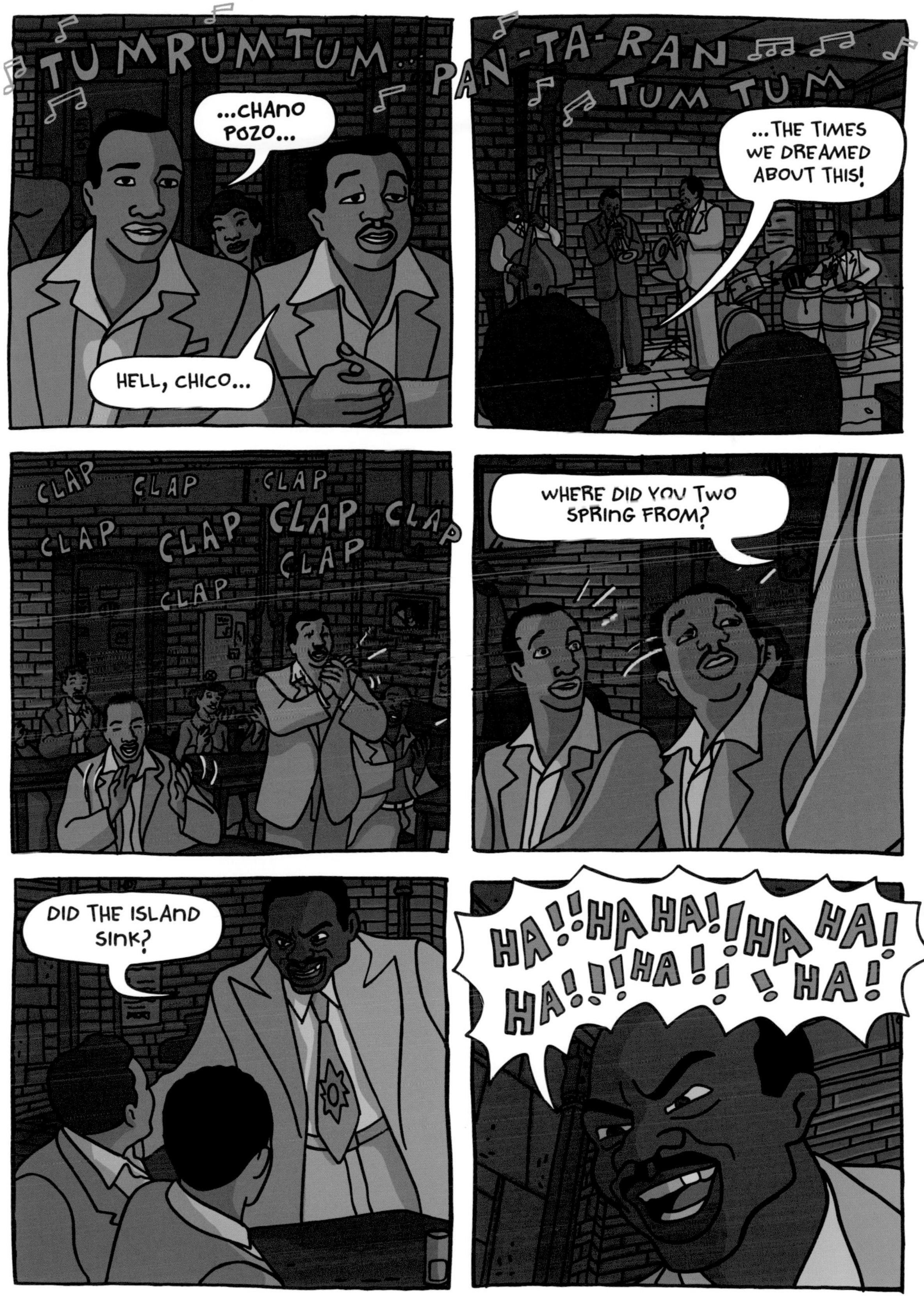

TUMRUMTUM... PAN-TA-RAN TUM TUM
...CHANO POZO...
HELL, CHICO...
...THE TIMES WE DREAMED ABOUT THIS!
CLAP CLAP CLAP CLAP CLAP CLAP CLAP CLAP CLAP
WHERE DID YOU TWO SPRING FROM?
DID THE ISLAND SINK?
HA! HA HA! HA HA! HA! HA! HA! HA!

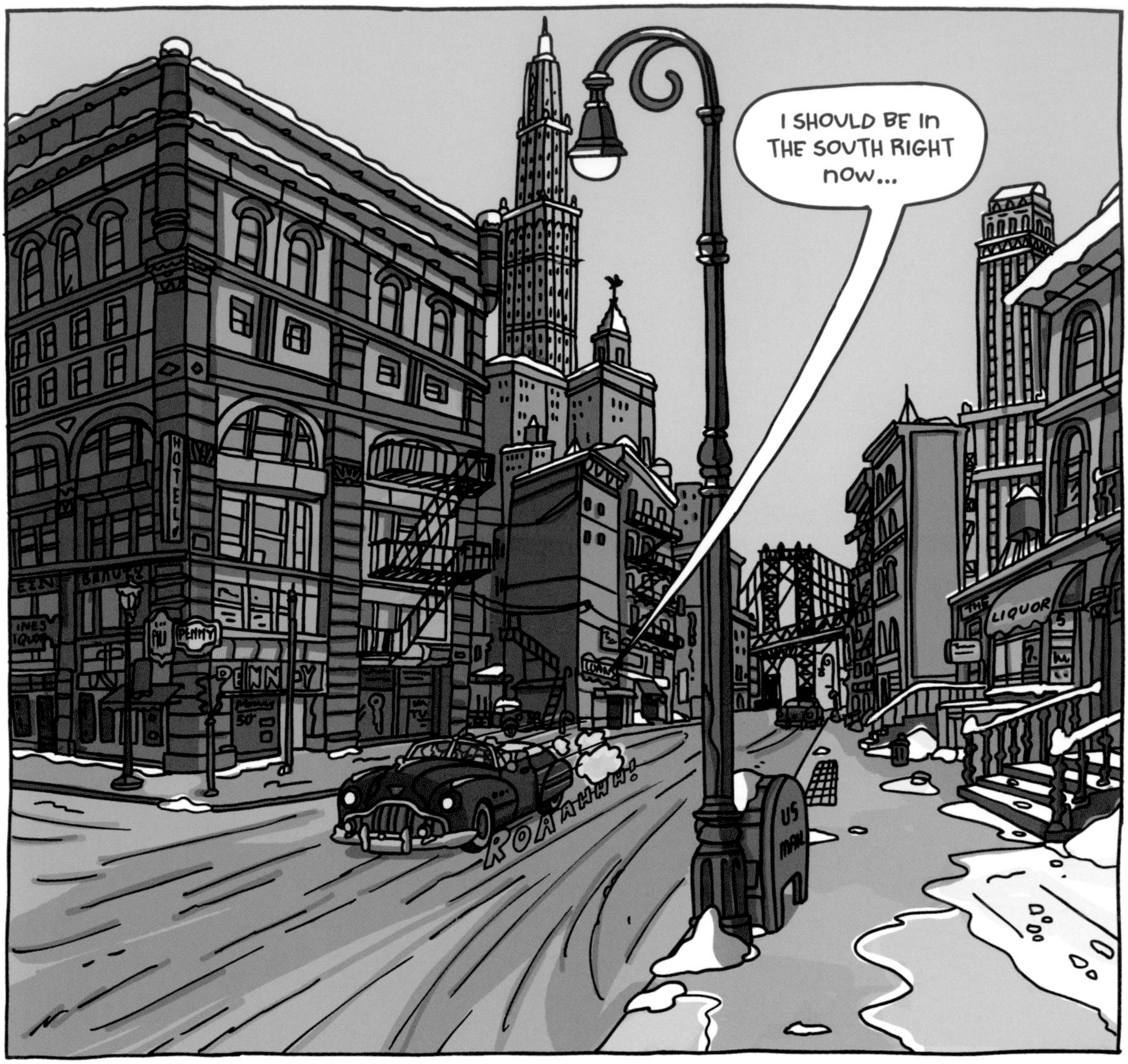
I SHOULD BE IN THE SOUTH RIGHT NOW...
HOTEL
PENNY
LIQUOR
US MAIL
ROAAHHHH!

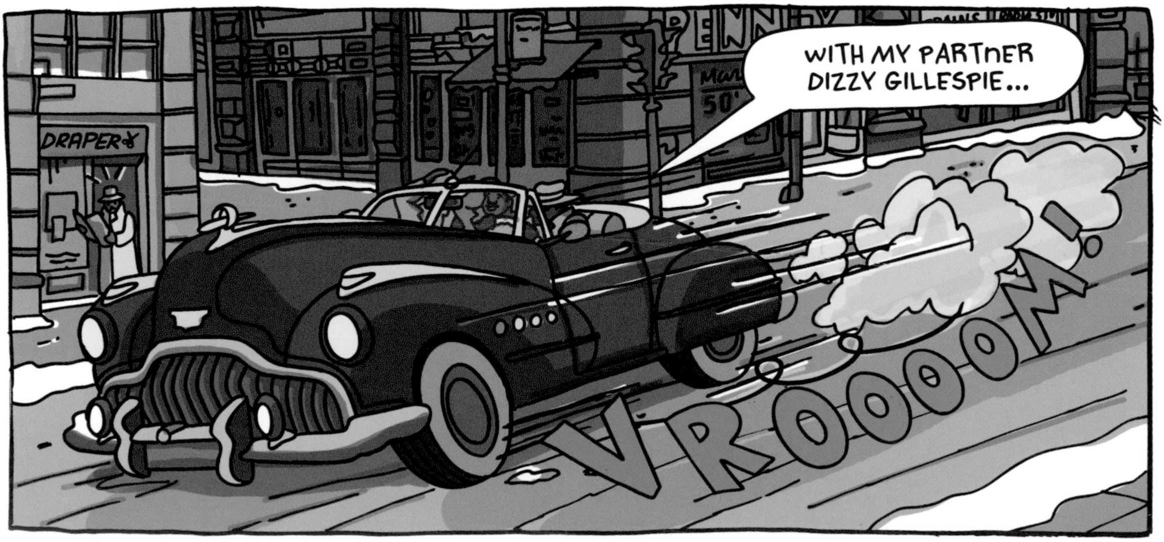
WITH MY PARTNER DIZZY GILLESPIE...
DRAPER
VROOOOM!

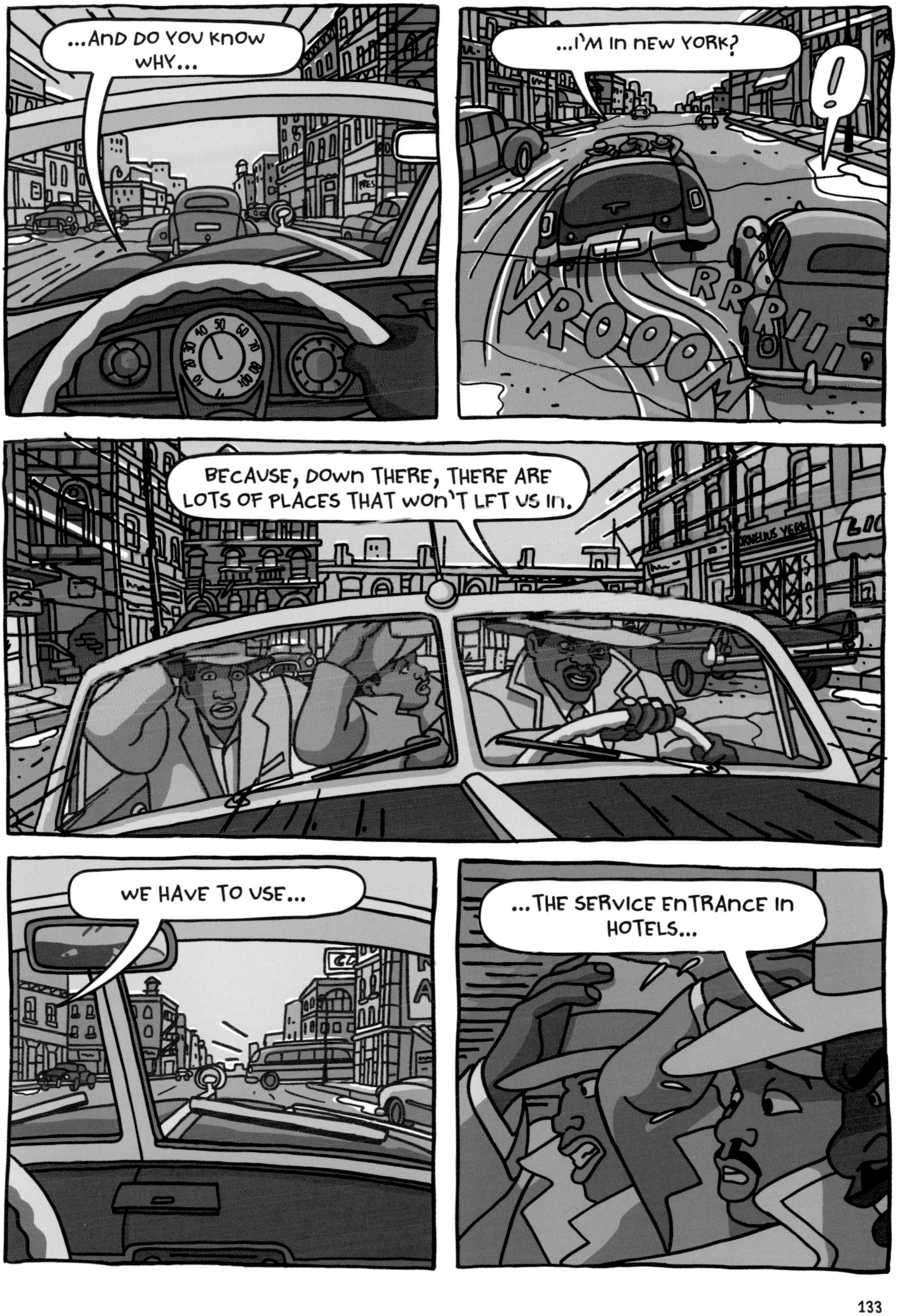

...AND DO YOU KNOW WHY...
...I'M IN NEW YORK?
!
VROOOOM
RRRIII
BECAUSE, DOWN THERE, THERE ARE LOTS OF PLACES THAT WON'T LET US IN.
WE HAVE TO USE...
...THE SERVICE ENTRANCE IN HOTELS...

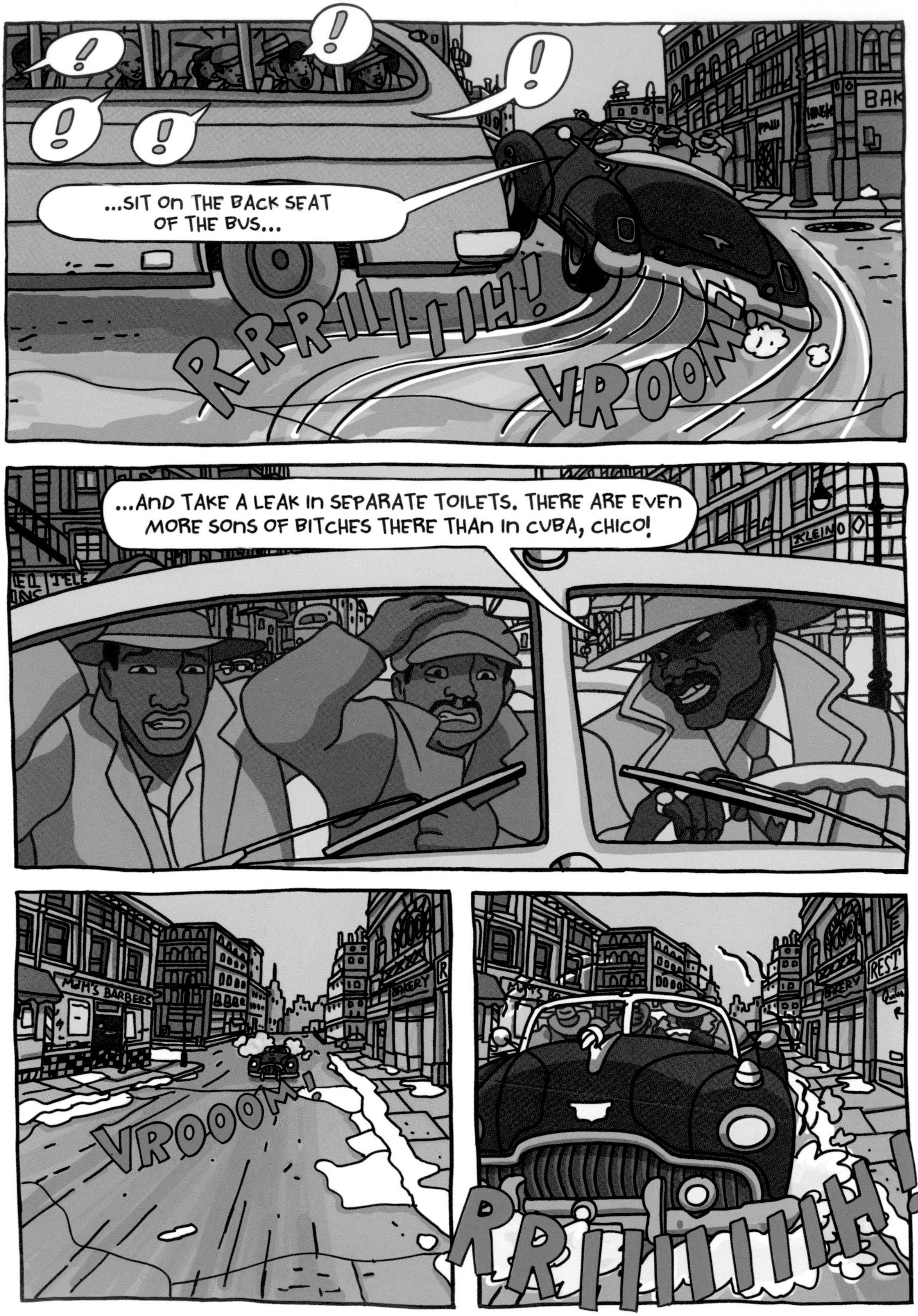
!
!
!
!
!
...SIT ON THE BACK SEAT OF THE BUS...
RRRIIIIIIH!
VROOM!
BAK
...AND TAKE A LEAK IN SEPARATE TOILETS. THERE ARE EVEN MORE SONS OF BITCHES THERE THAN IN CUBA, CHICO!
KLEINO
M&M'S BARBERS
BAKERY
VROOOM!
REST
RRIIIIIIIH!

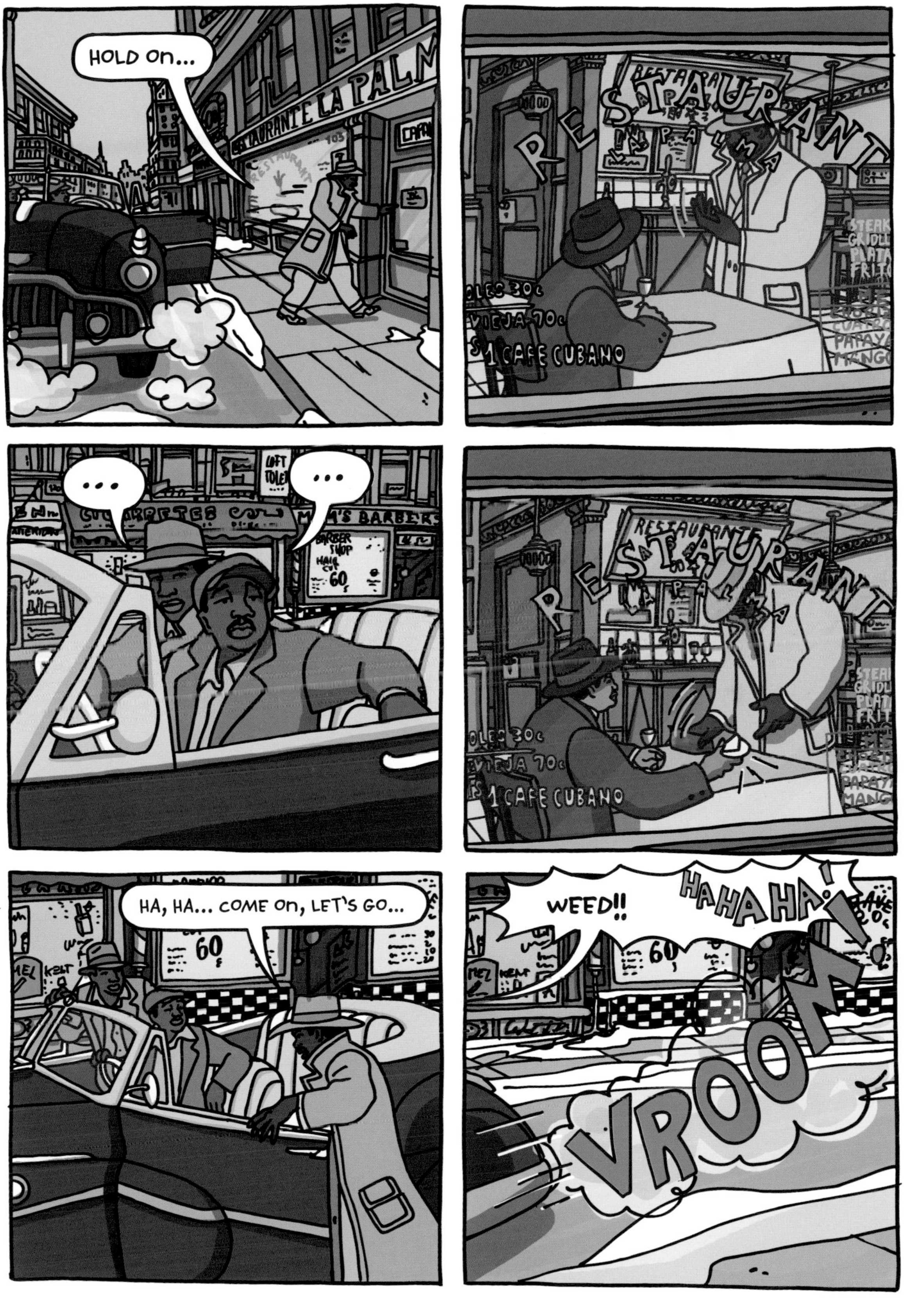
HOLD ON...
RESTAURANT
1 CAFE CUBANO
...
...
RESTAURANT
1 CAFE CUBANO
HA, HA... COME ON, LET'S GO...
WEED!!
HAHAHA!
VROOM!

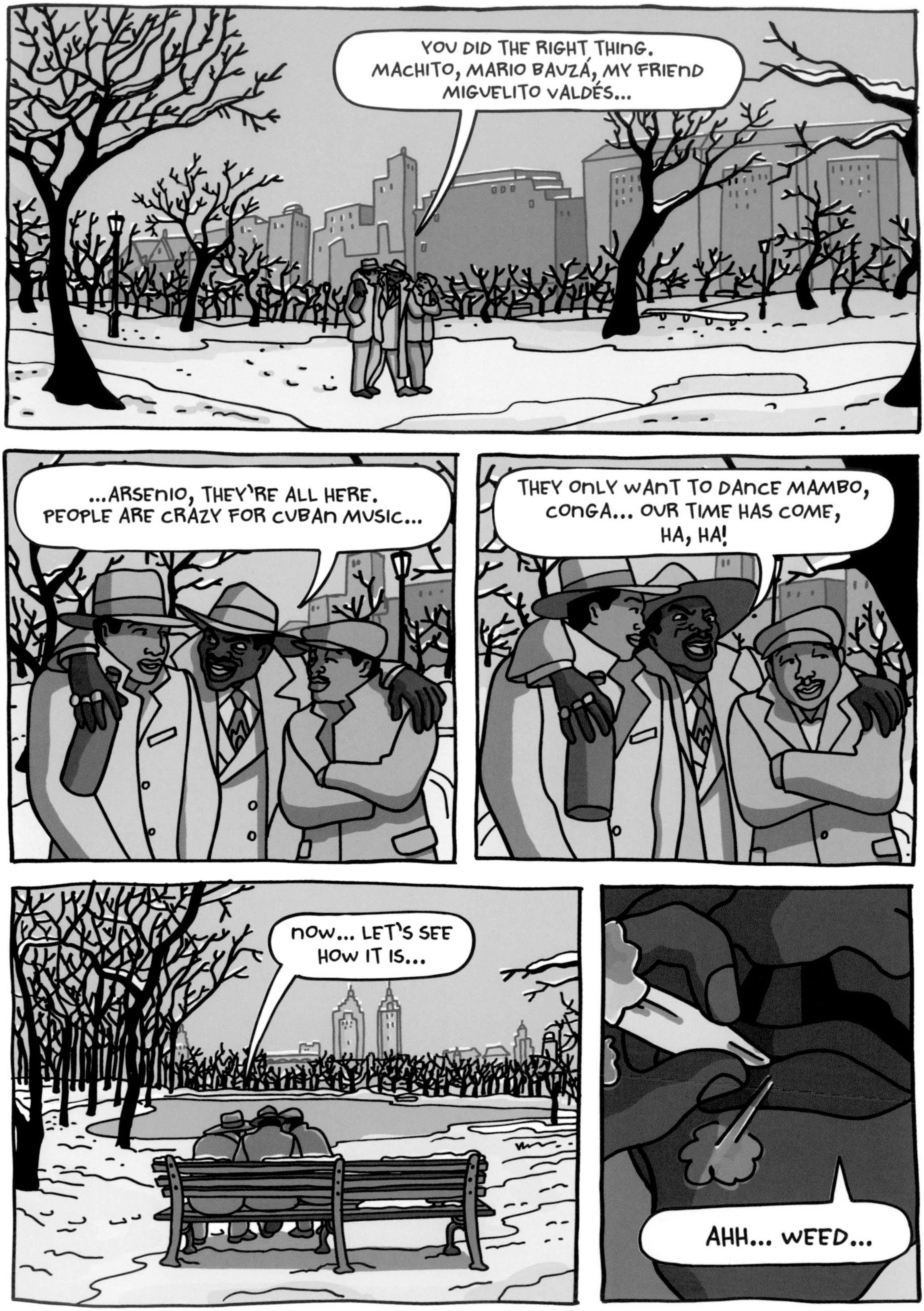
YOU DID THE RIGHT THING. MACHITO, MARIO BAUZÁ, MY FRIEND MIGUELITO VALDÉS...
...ARSENIO, THEY'RE ALL HERE. PEOPLE ARE CRAZY FOR CUBAN MUSIC...
THEY ONLY WANT TO DANCE MAMBO, CONGA... OUR TIME HAS COME, HA, HA!
NOW... LET'S SEE HOW IT IS...
AHH... WEED...

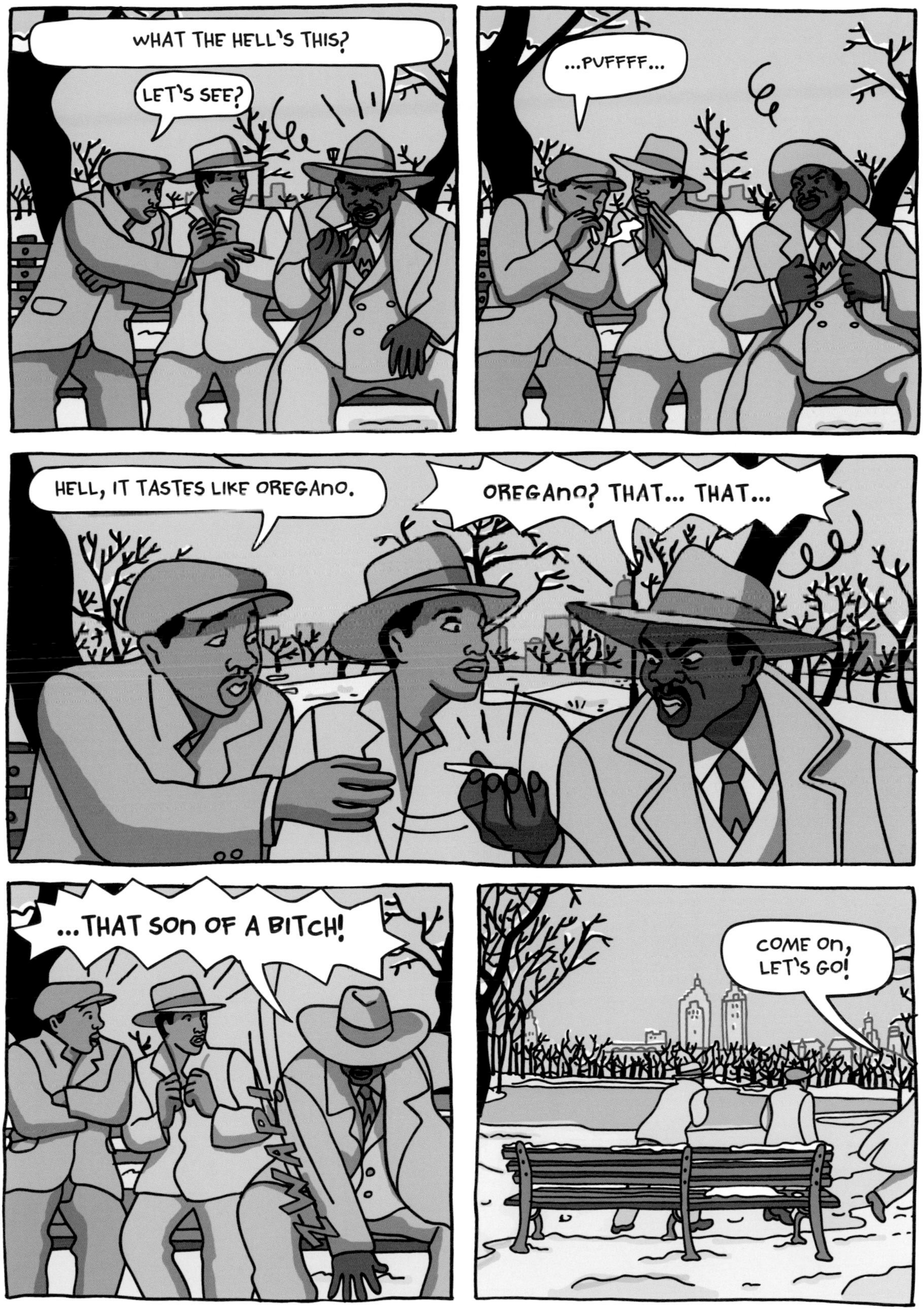
WHAT THE HELL'S THIS?
LET'S SEE?
...PUFFFF...
HELL, IT TASTES LIKE OREGANO.
OREGANO? THAT... THAT...
...THAT SON OF A BITCH!
COME ON, LET'S GO!

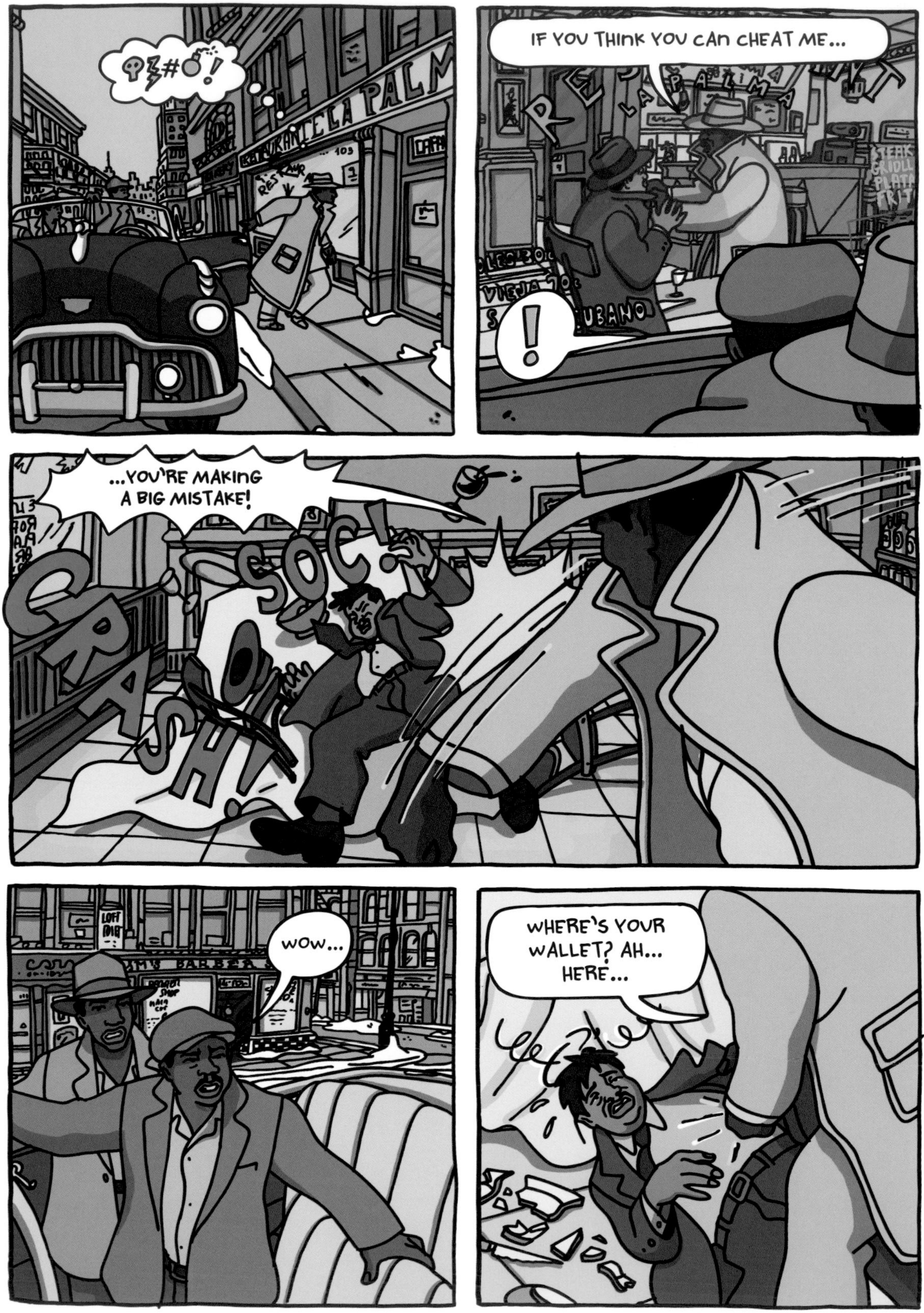
IF YOU THINK YOU CAN CHEAT ME...
!
...YOU'RE MAKING A BIG MISTAKE!
SOC!
CRASH!
WOW...
WHERE'S YOUR WALLET? AH... HERE...

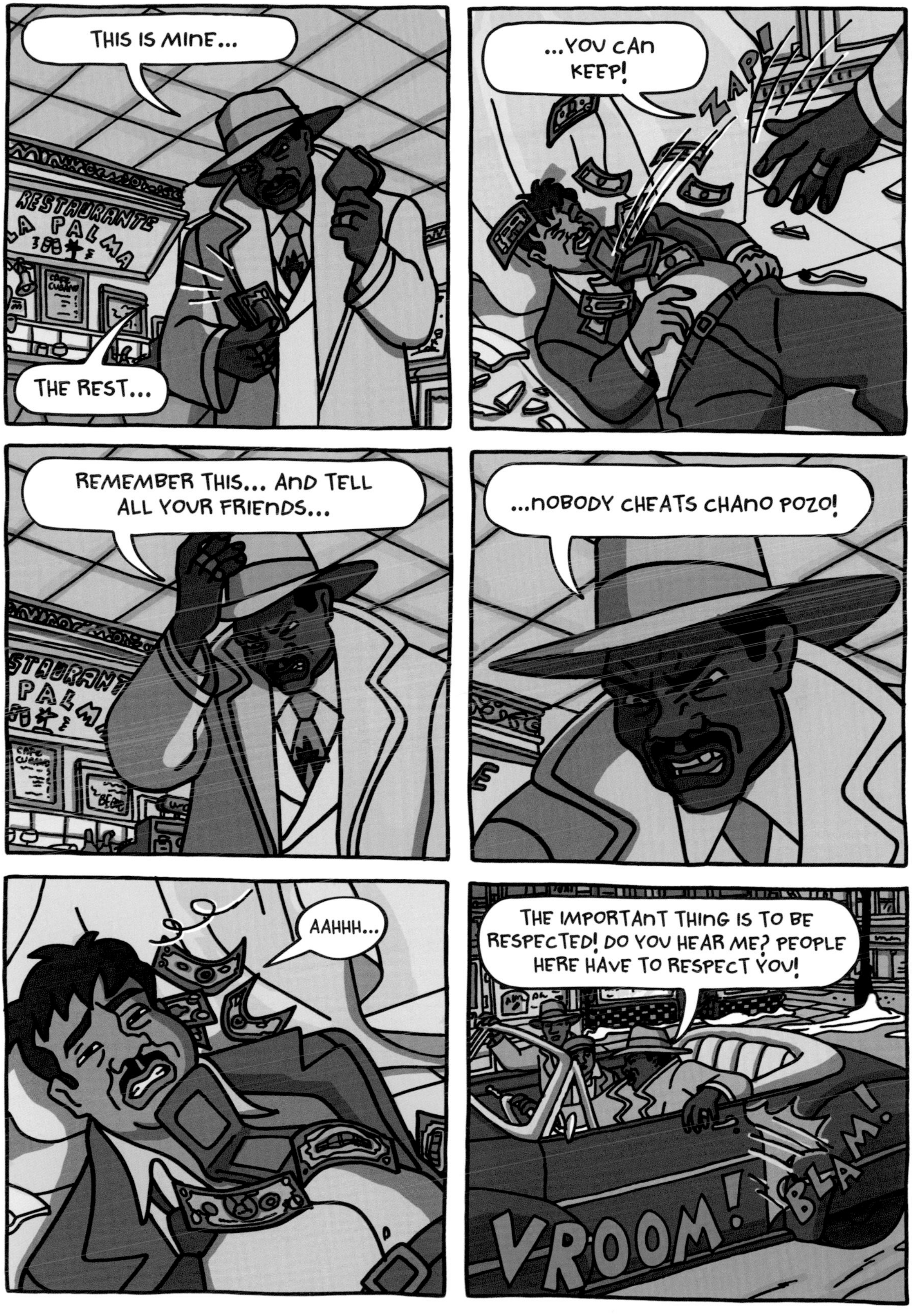
THIS IS MINE...
THE REST...
...YOU CAN KEEP!
ZAP!
RESTAURANTE LA PALMA
REMEMBER THIS... AND TELL ALL YOUR FRIENDS...
...NOBODY CHEATS CHANO POZO!
AAHHH...
THE IMPORTANT THING IS TO BE RESPECTED! DO YOU HEAR ME? PEOPLE HERE HAVE TO RESPECT YOU!
VROOM!
BLAM!

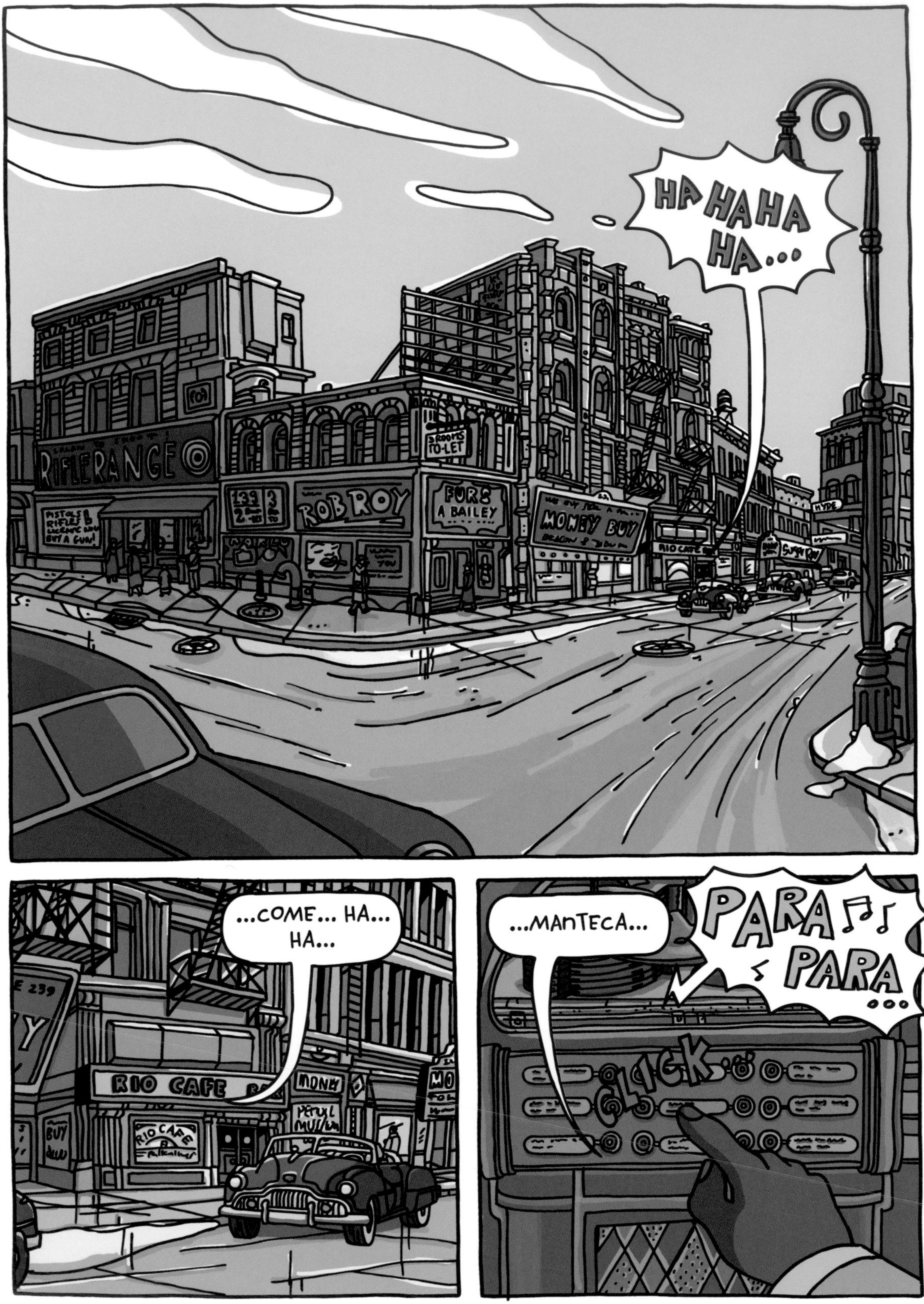
HAHAHA HA...
RIFLE RANGE
3 ROOMS TO-LET
ROB ROY
FURS A BAILEY
MONEY BUY
HYDE
RIO CAFE
...COME... HA... HA...
RIO CAFE
...MANTECA...
PARA PARA...
CLICK

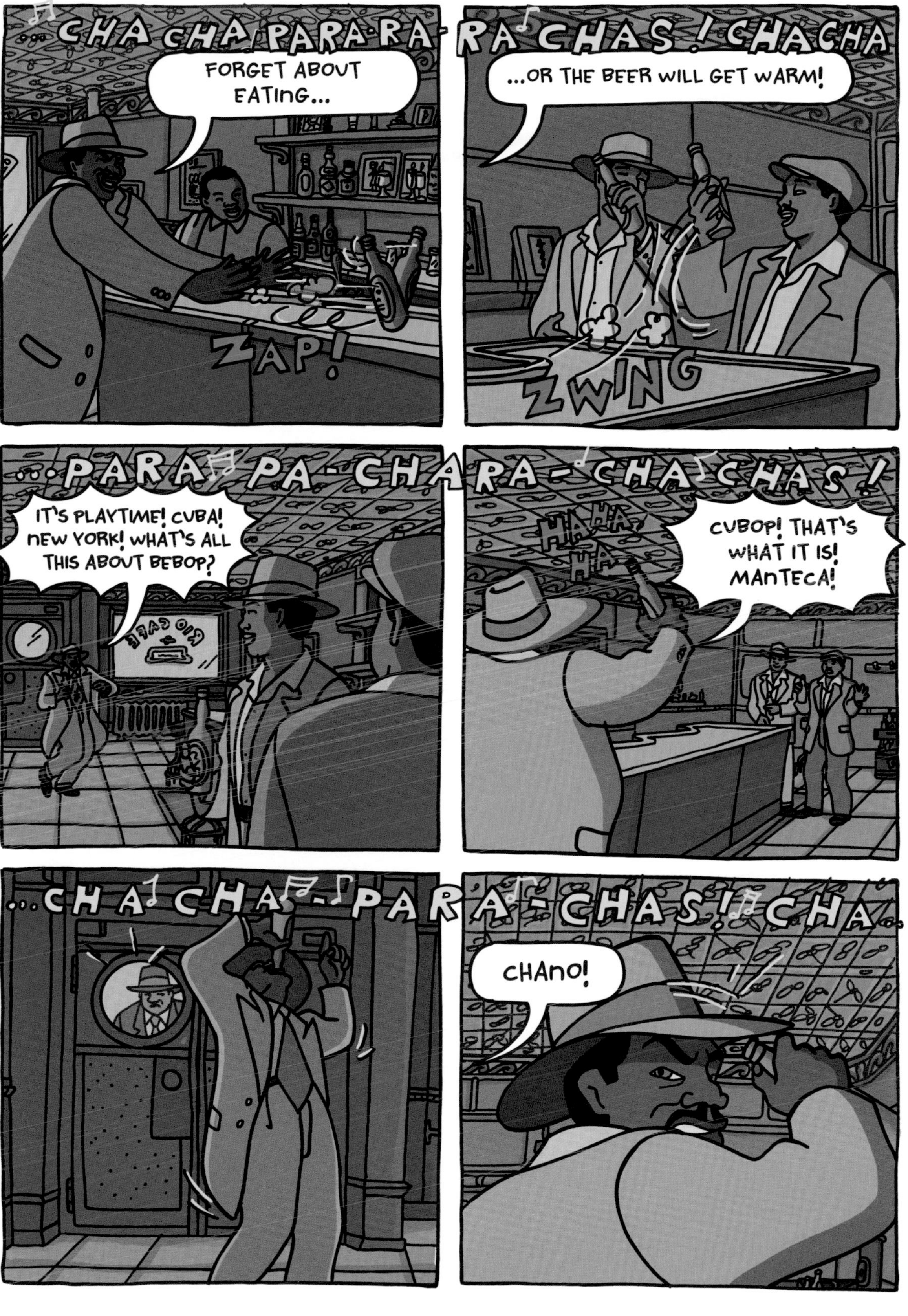
...CHA CHA PARA-RA-RA-RA CHAS! CHACHA
FORGET ABOUT EATING...
ZAP!
...OR THE BEER WILL GET WARM!
ZWING
...PARA PA-CHARA-CHA CHAS!
IT'S PLAYTIME! CUBA! NEW YORK! WHAT'S ALL THIS ABOUT BEBOP?
RIO CAFE
HA HA HA
CUBOP! THAT'S WHAT IT IS! MANTECA!
...CHA CHA-PARA-CHAS! CHA...
CHANO!

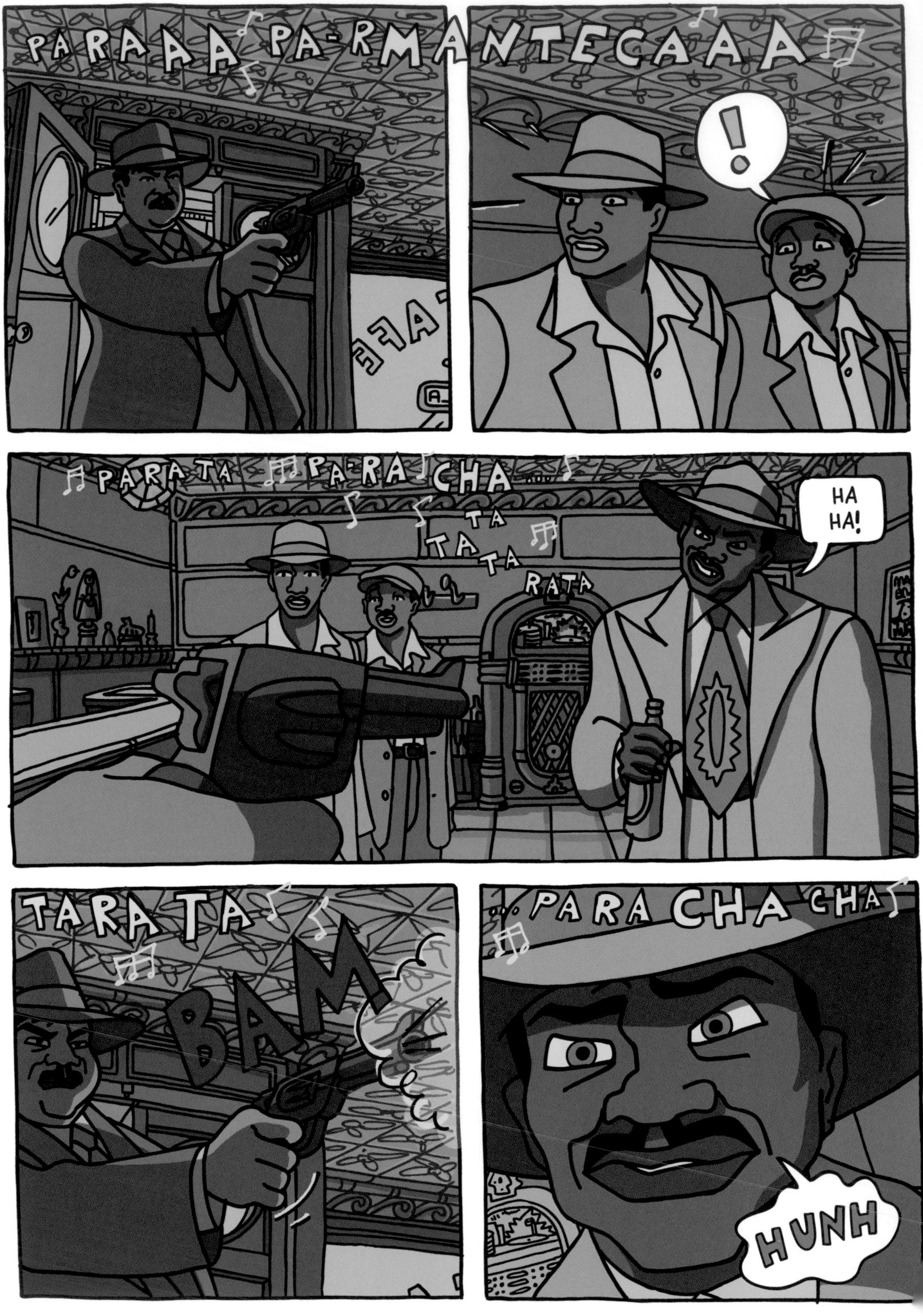

PARAAA PA-RMANTECAAA
!
PARATA PA-RA CHA...
TA TA TA RATA
HA HA!
TARATA
BAM
...PARA CHA CHA
HUNH

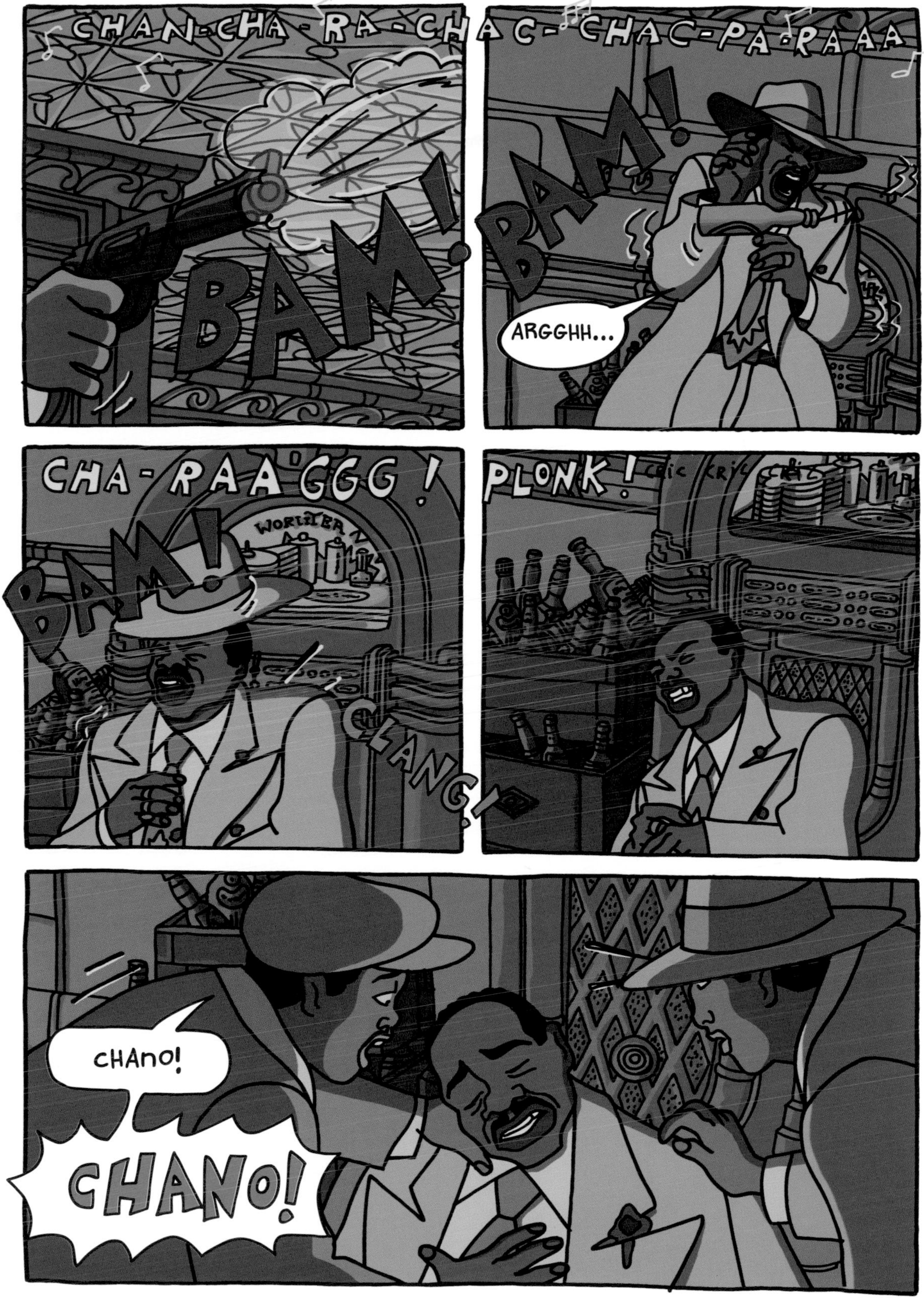
CHAN-CHA-RA-CHAC-CHAC-PA-RAAA
BAM!
BAM!
ARGGHH...
CHA-RAAGGG!
BAM!
CLANG!
PLONK!
CHANO!
CHANO!

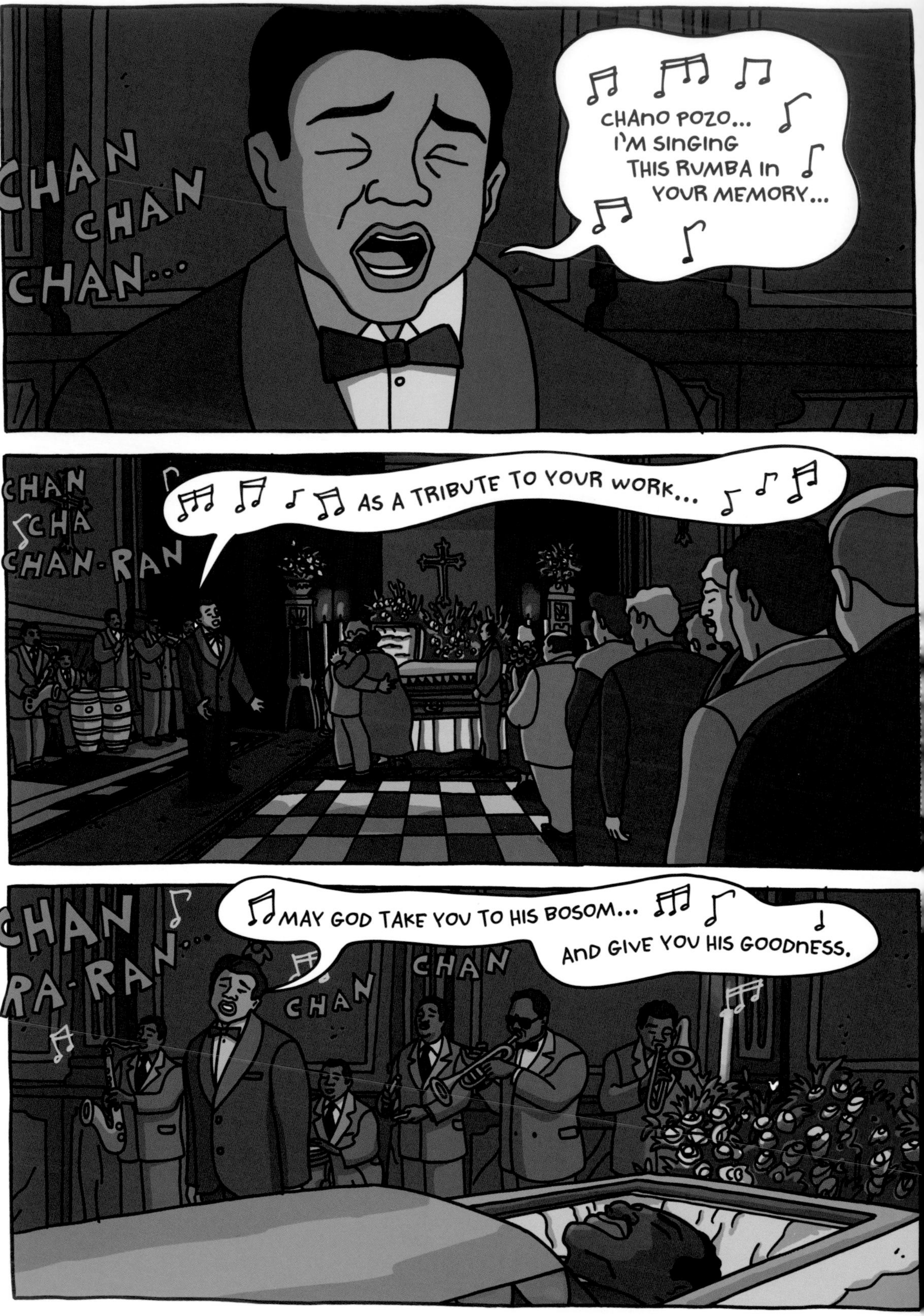
CHAN CHAN CHAN...
CHANO POZO... I'M SINGING THIS RUMBA IN YOUR MEMORY...
CHAN CHA CHAN-RAN
AS A TRIBUTE TO YOUR WORK...
CHAN RA-RAN...
MAY GOD TAKE YOU TO HIS BOSOM... AND GIVE YOU HIS GOODNESS.
CHAN
CHAN

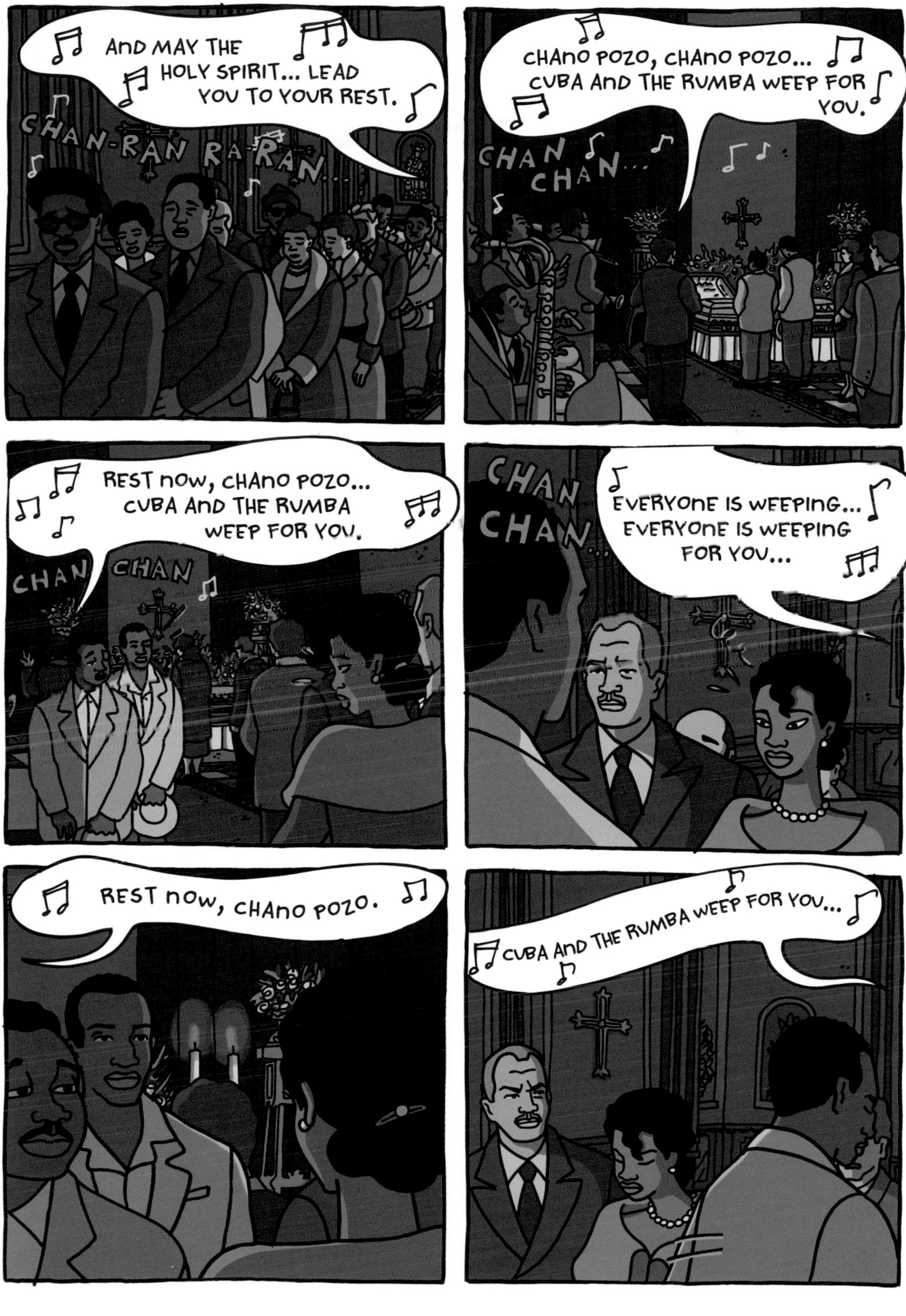
AND MAY THE HOLY SPIRIT... LEAD YOU TO YOUR REST.
CHAN-RAN RA-RAN...
CHANO POZO, CHANO POZO... CUBA AND THE RUMBA WEEP FOR YOU.
CHAN CHAN...
REST NOW, CHANO POZO... CUBA AND THE RUMBA WEEP FOR YOU.
CHAN CHAN
CHAN CHAN...
EVERYONE IS WEEPING... EVERYONE IS WEEPING FOR YOU...
REST NOW, CHANO POZO.
CUBA AND THE RUMBA WEEP FOR YOU...

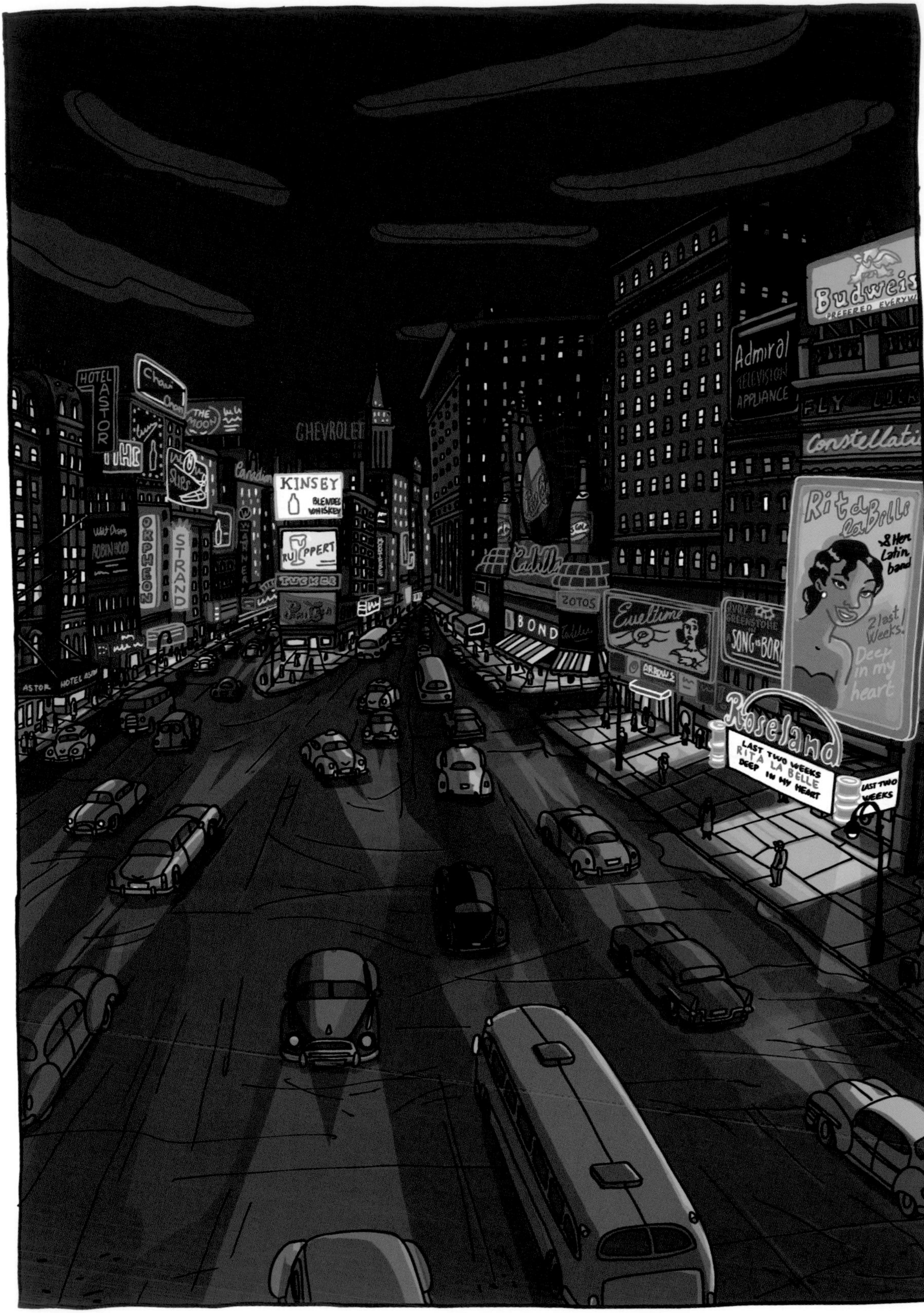

HOTEL ASTOR
THE MOON
CHEVROLET
KINSEY
BLENDED WHISKEY
RUPPERT
TUCKER
Walt Disney ROBIN HOOD
ORPHEON
STRAND
ASTOR HOTEL ASTOR
Admiral
TELEVISION APPLIANCE
ZOTOS
BOND
ARROWS
Rita la Belle
& Her Latin band
2 last weeks!
Deep in my heart
Roseland
LAST TWO WEEKS
RITA LA BELLE
DEEP IN MY HEART
LAST TWO WEEKS

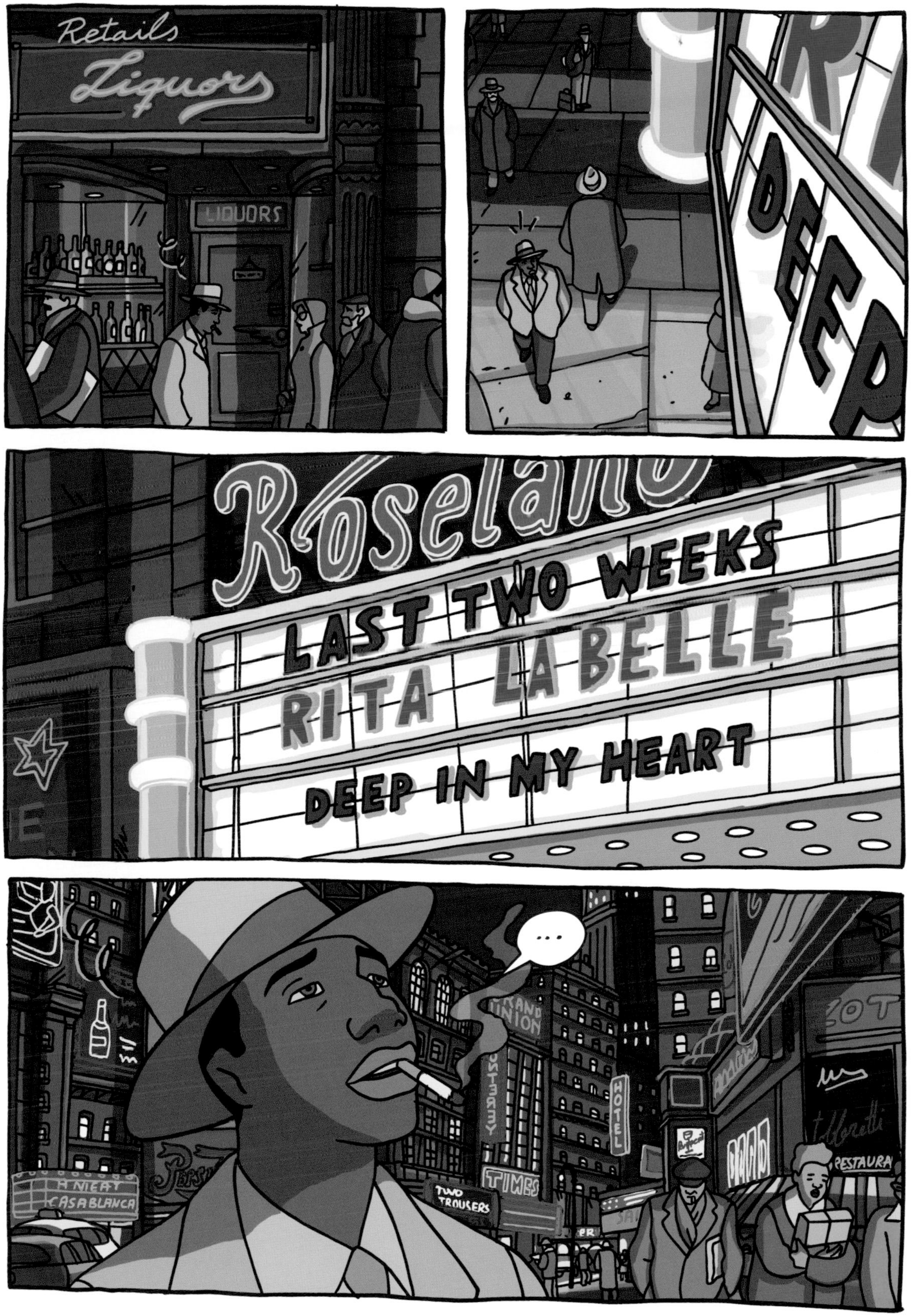
Retails
Liquors
LIQUORS
DEEP
LAST TWO WEEKS
RITA LA BELLE
DEEP IN MY HEART
...
HOTEL
TIMES
TWO TROUSERS
RESTAURA

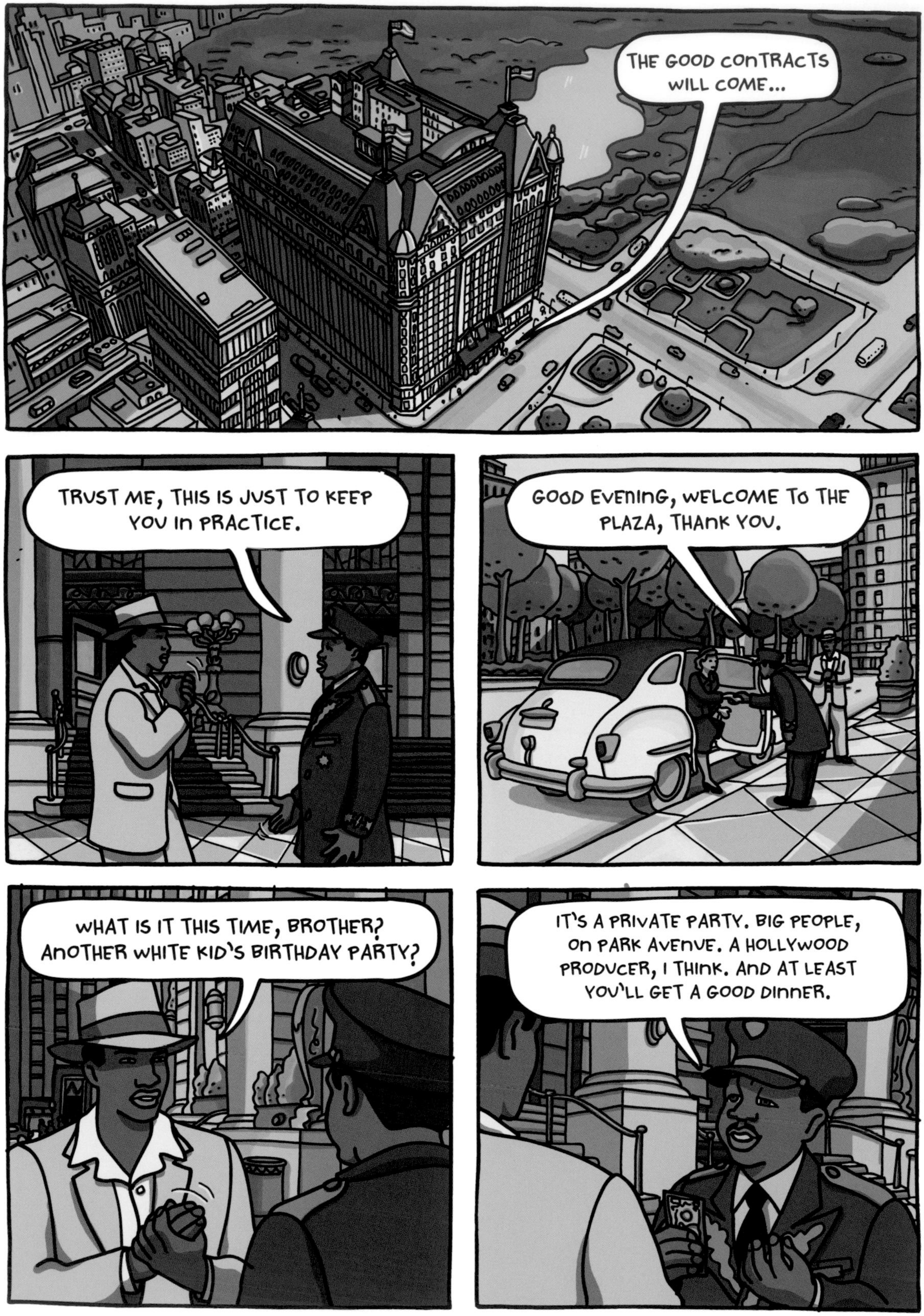
THE GOOD CONTRACTS WILL COME...
TRUST ME, THIS IS JUST TO KEEP YOU IN PRACTICE.
GOOD EVENING, WELCOME TO THE PLAZA, THANK YOU.
WHAT IS IT THIS TIME, BROTHER? ANOTHER WHITE KID'S BIRTHDAY PARTY?
IT'S A PRIVATE PARTY. BIG PEOPLE, ON PARK AVENUE. A HOLLYWOOD PRODUCER, I THINK. AND AT LEAST YOU'LL GET A GOOD DINNER.

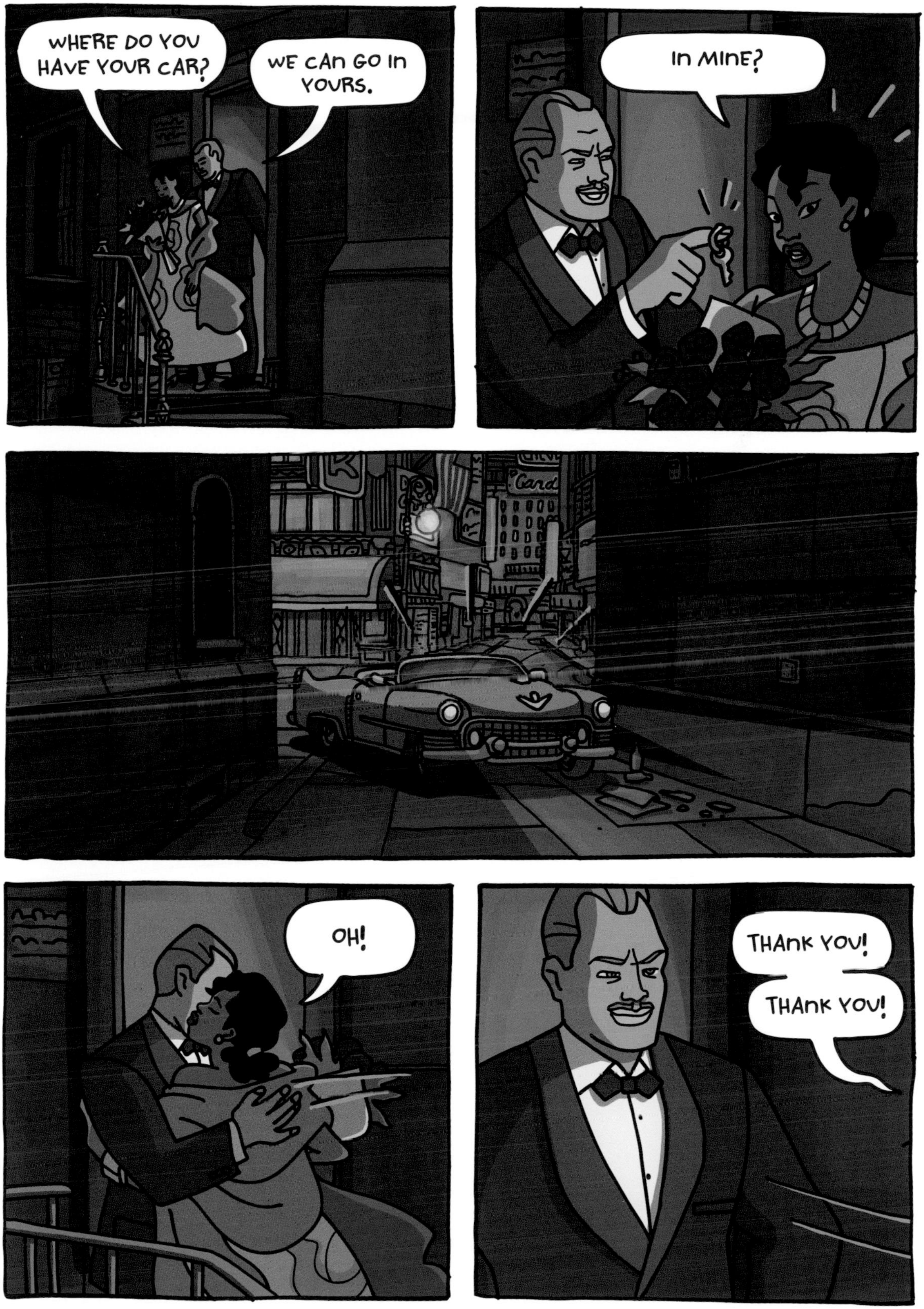
WHERE DO YOU HAVE YOUR CAR?
WE CAN GO IN YOURS.
IN MINE?
OH!
THANK YOU!
THANK YOU!

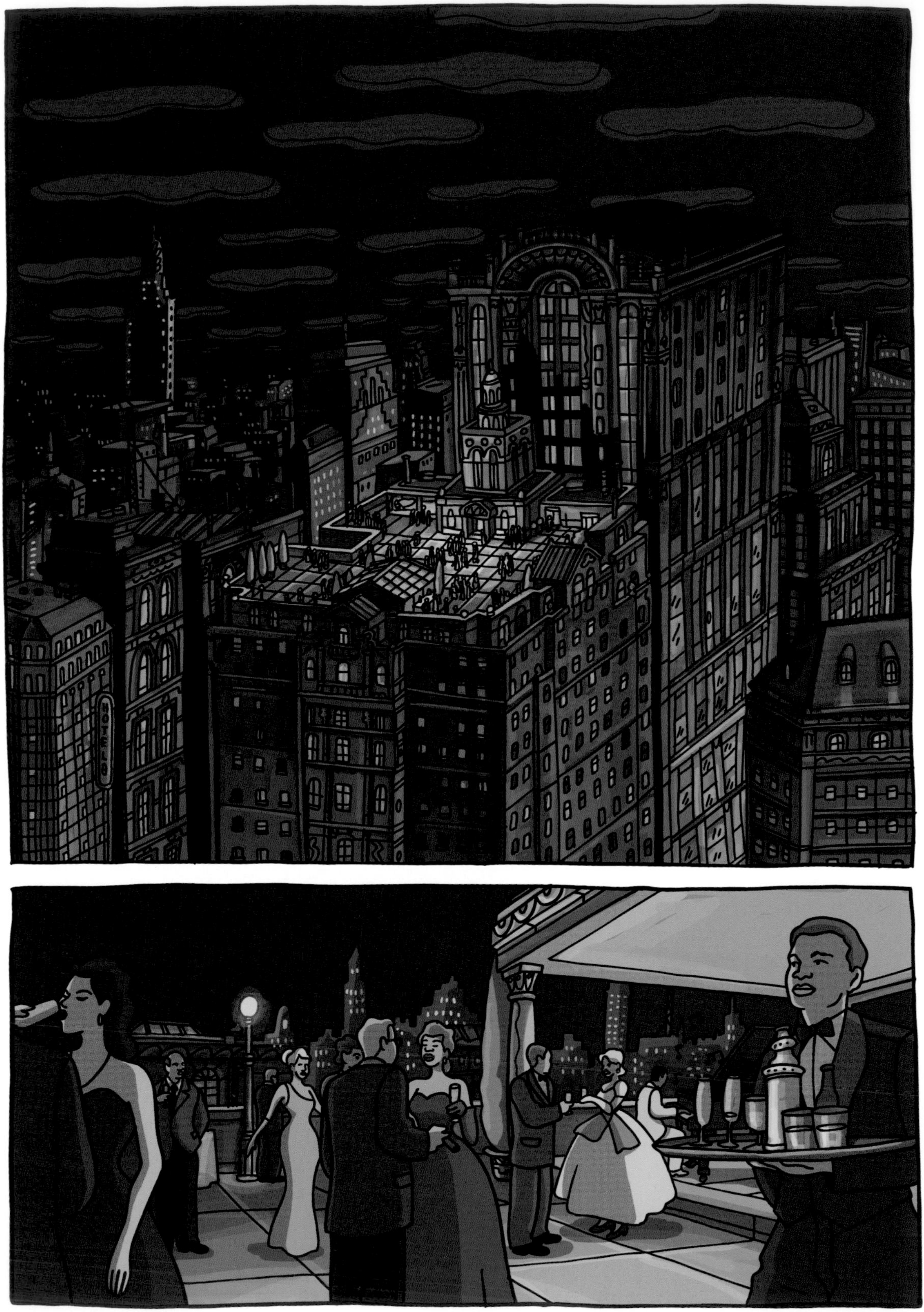
HOTEL

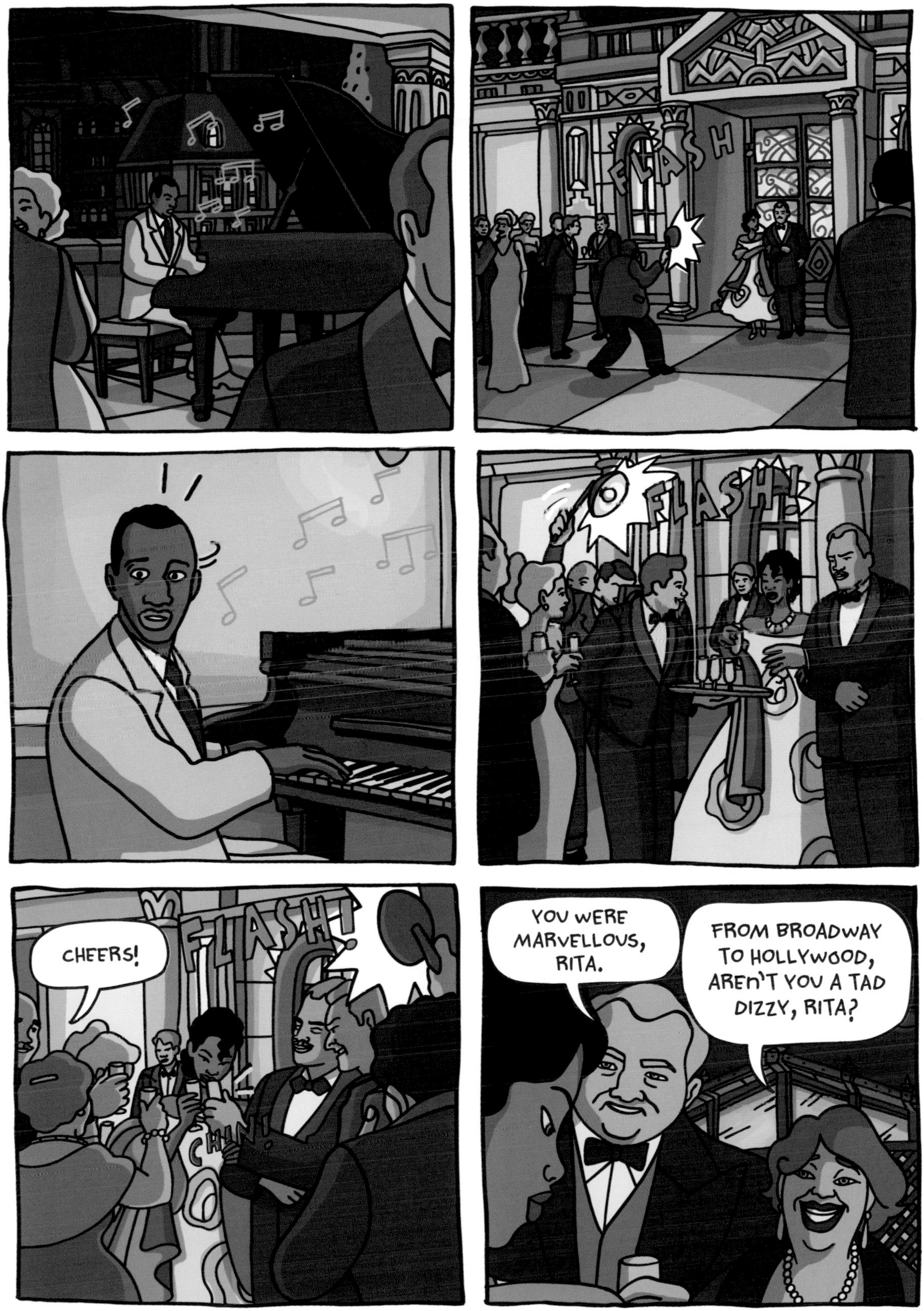
FLASH!
FLASH!
CHEERS!
FLASH!
CHIN!
YOU WERE MARVELLOUS, RITA.
FROM BROADWAY TO HOLLYWOOD, AREN'T YOU A TAD DIZZY, RITA?

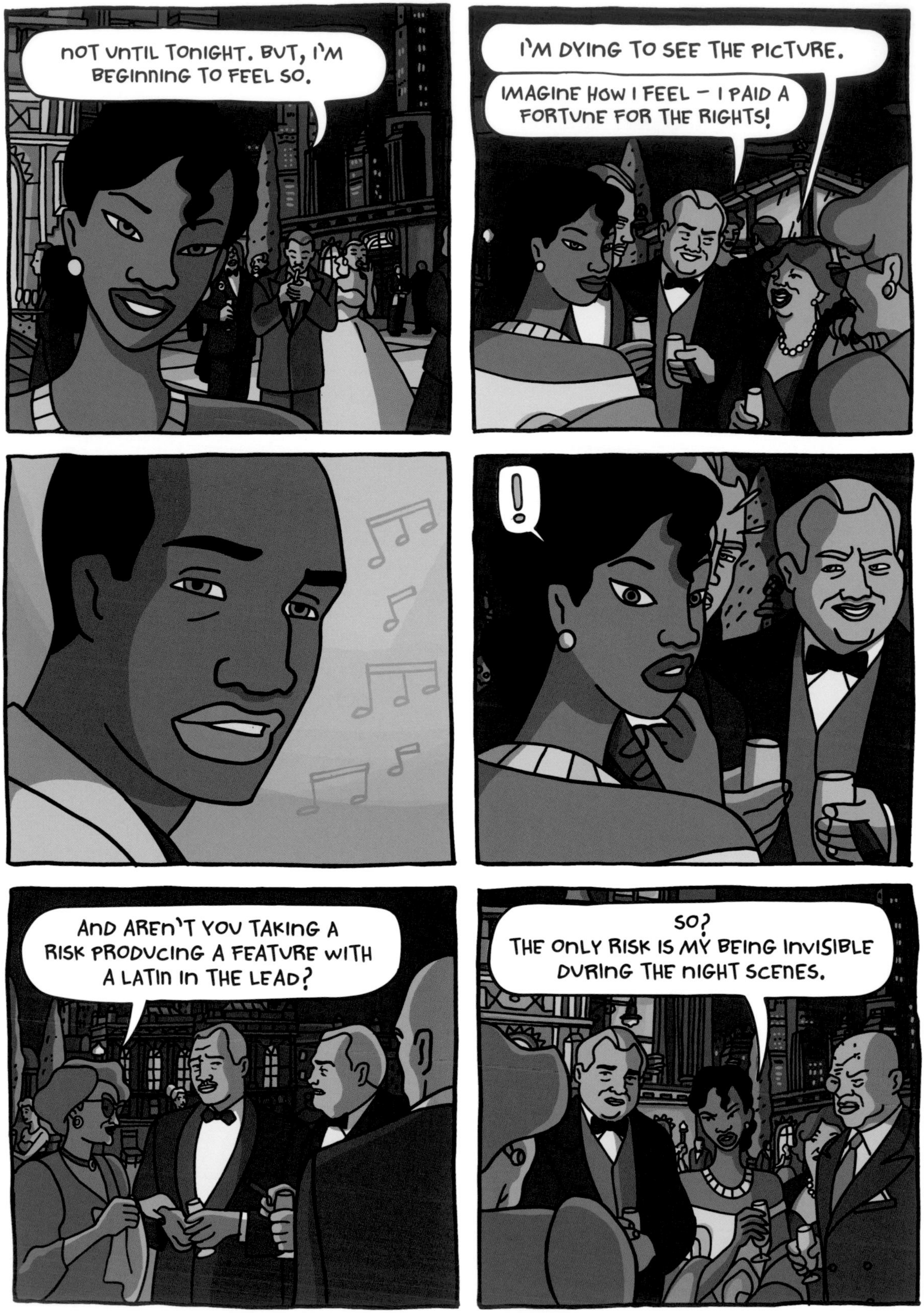
NOT UNTIL TONIGHT. BUT, I'M BEGINNING TO FEEL SO.
I'M DYING TO SEE THE PICTURE.
IMAGINE HOW I FEEL – I PAID A FORTUNE FOR THE RIGHTS!
!
AND AREN'T YOU TAKING A RISK PRODUCING A FEATURE WITH A LATIN IN THE LEAD?
SO?
THE ONLY RISK IS MY BEING INVISIBLE DURING THE NIGHT SCENES.

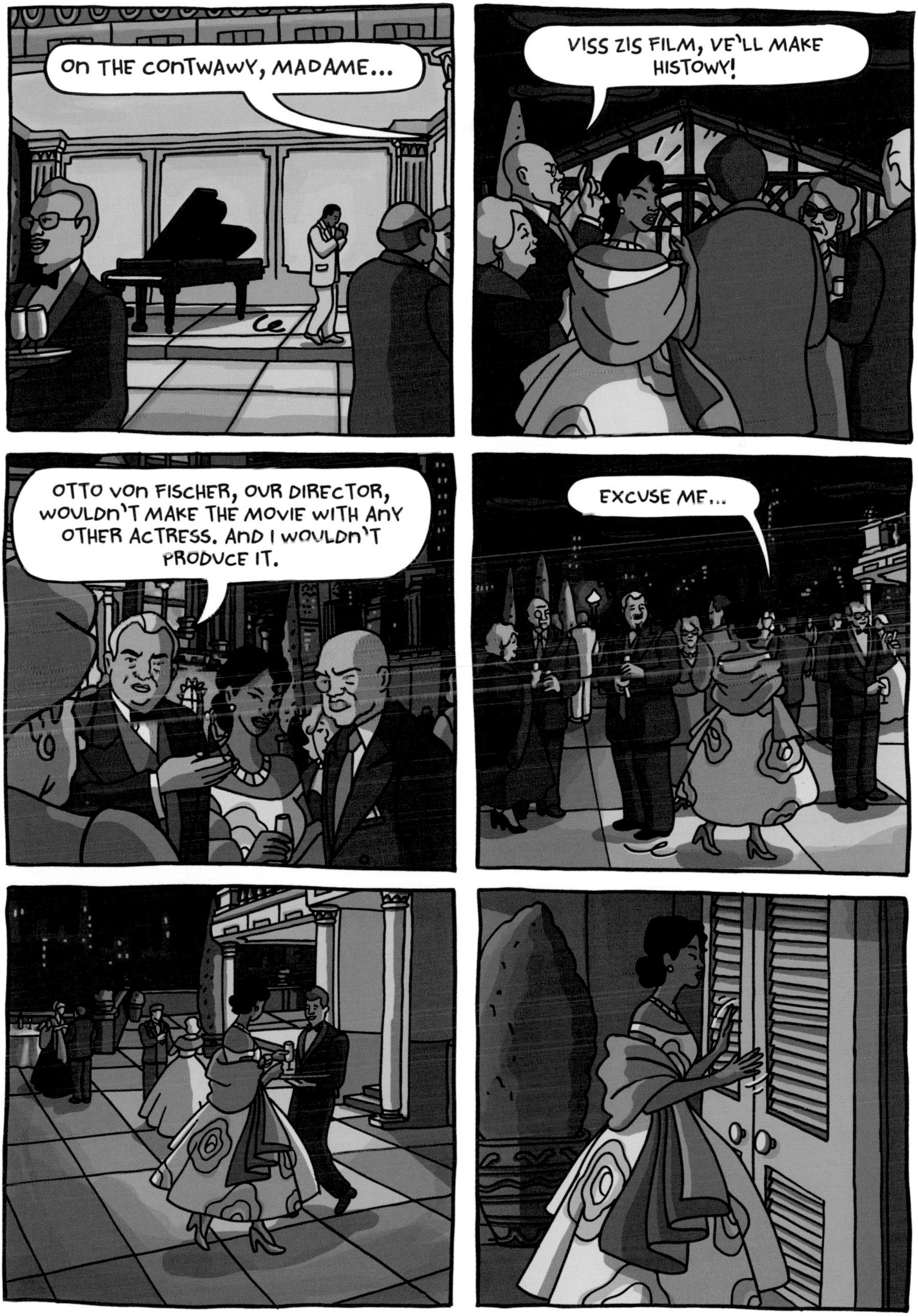
ON THE CONTWAWY, MADAME...
VISS ZIS FILM, VE'LL MAKE HISTOWY!
OTTO VON FISCHER, OUR DIRECTOR, WOULDN'T MAKE THE MOVIE WITH ANY OTHER ACTRESS. AND I WOULDN'T PRODUCE IT.
EXCUSE ME...

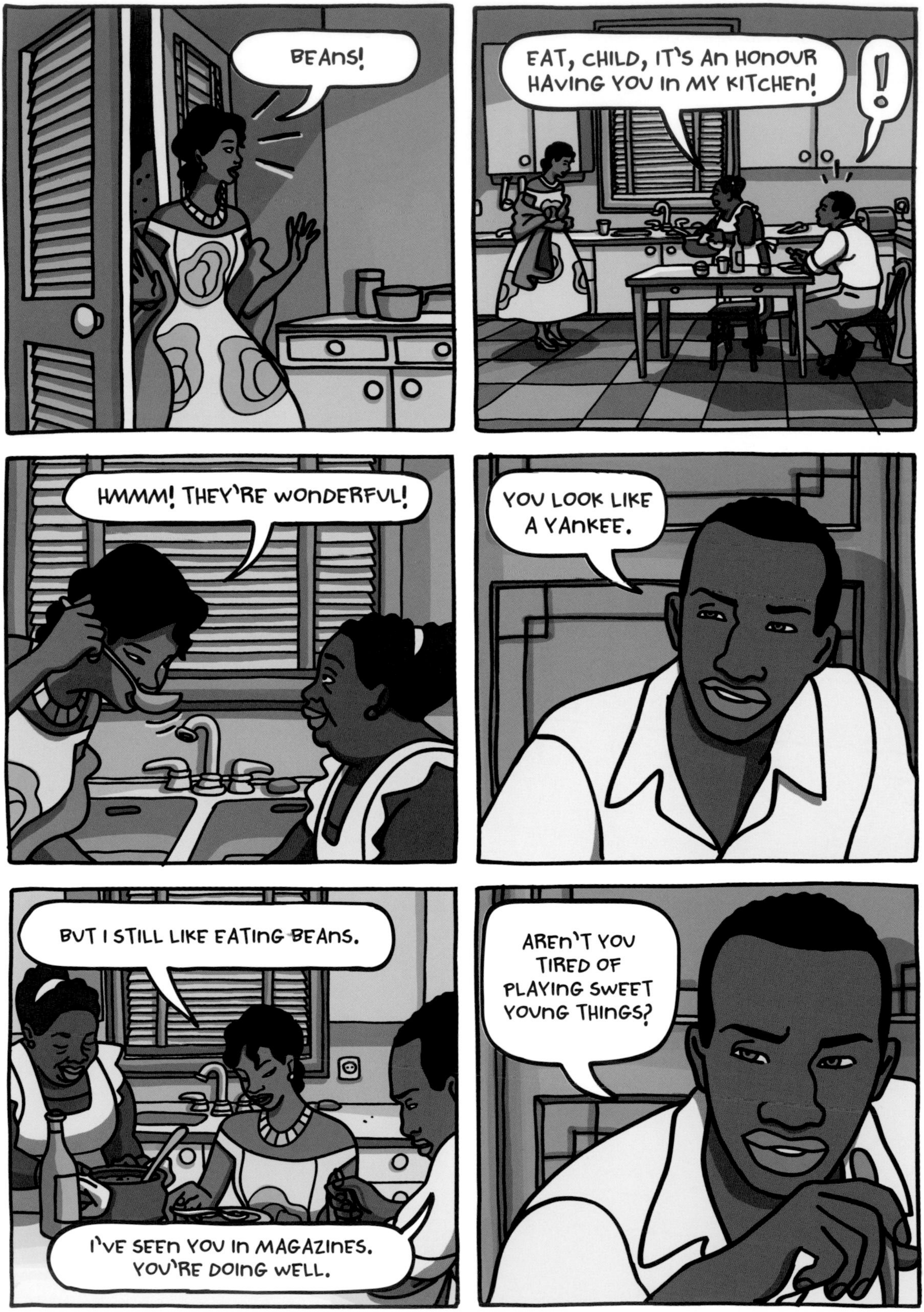
BEANS!
EAT, CHILD, IT'S AN HONOUR HAVING YOU IN MY KITCHEN!
!
HMMM! THEY'RE WONDERFUL!
YOU LOOK LIKE A YANKEE.
BUT I STILL LIKE EATING BEANS.
I'VE SEEN YOU IN MAGAZINES. YOU'RE DOING WELL.
AREN'T YOU TIRED OF PLAYING SWEET YOUNG THINGS?

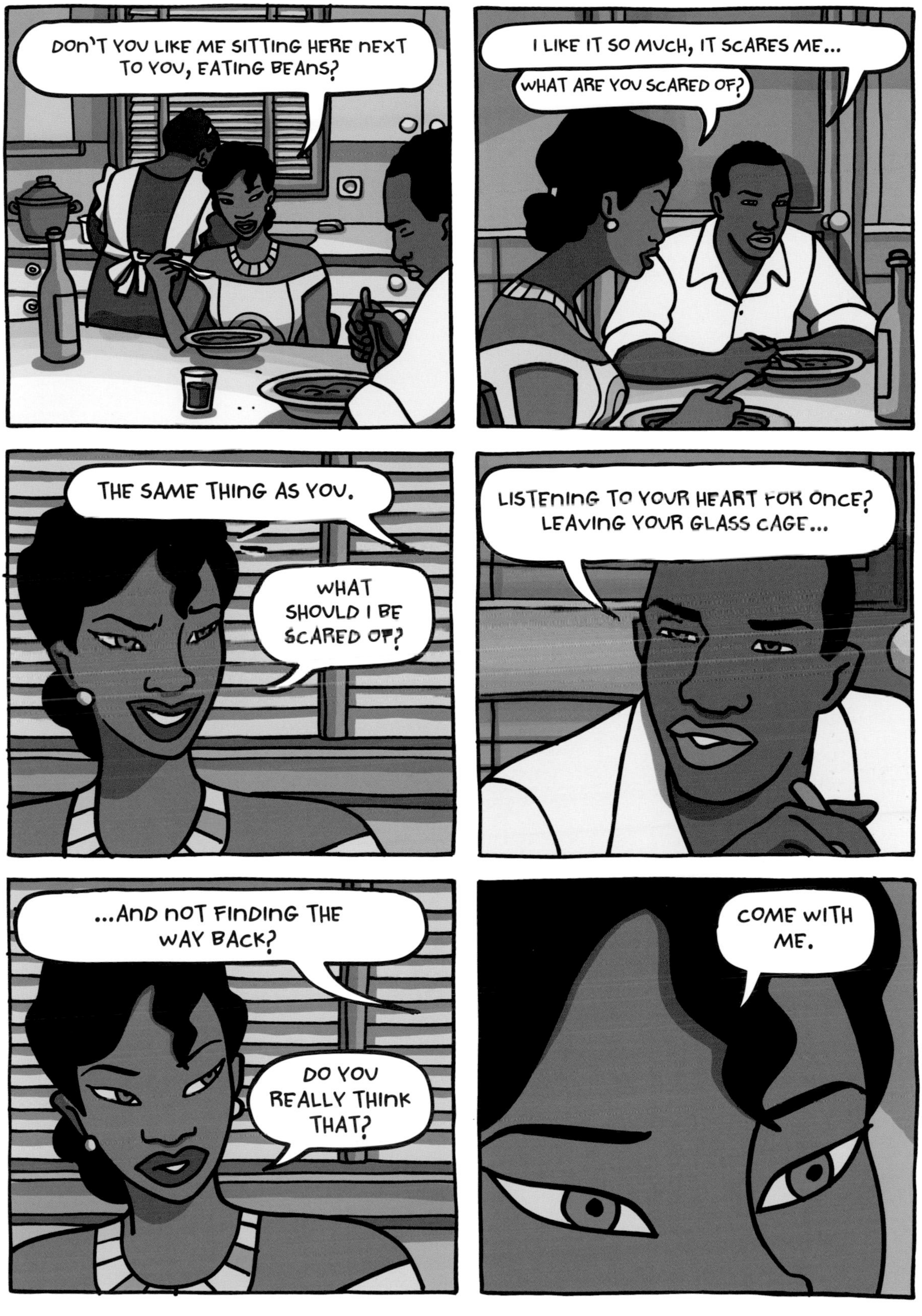
DON'T YOU LIKE ME SITTING HERE NEXT TO YOU, EATING BEANS?
I LIKE IT SO MUCH, IT SCARES ME...
WHAT ARE YOU SCARED OF?
THE SAME THING AS YOU.
WHAT SHOULD I BE SCARED OF?
LISTENING TO YOUR HEART FOR ONCE? LEAVING YOUR GLASS CAGE...
...AND NOT FINDING THE WAY BACK?
DO YOU REALLY THINK THAT?
COME WITH ME.

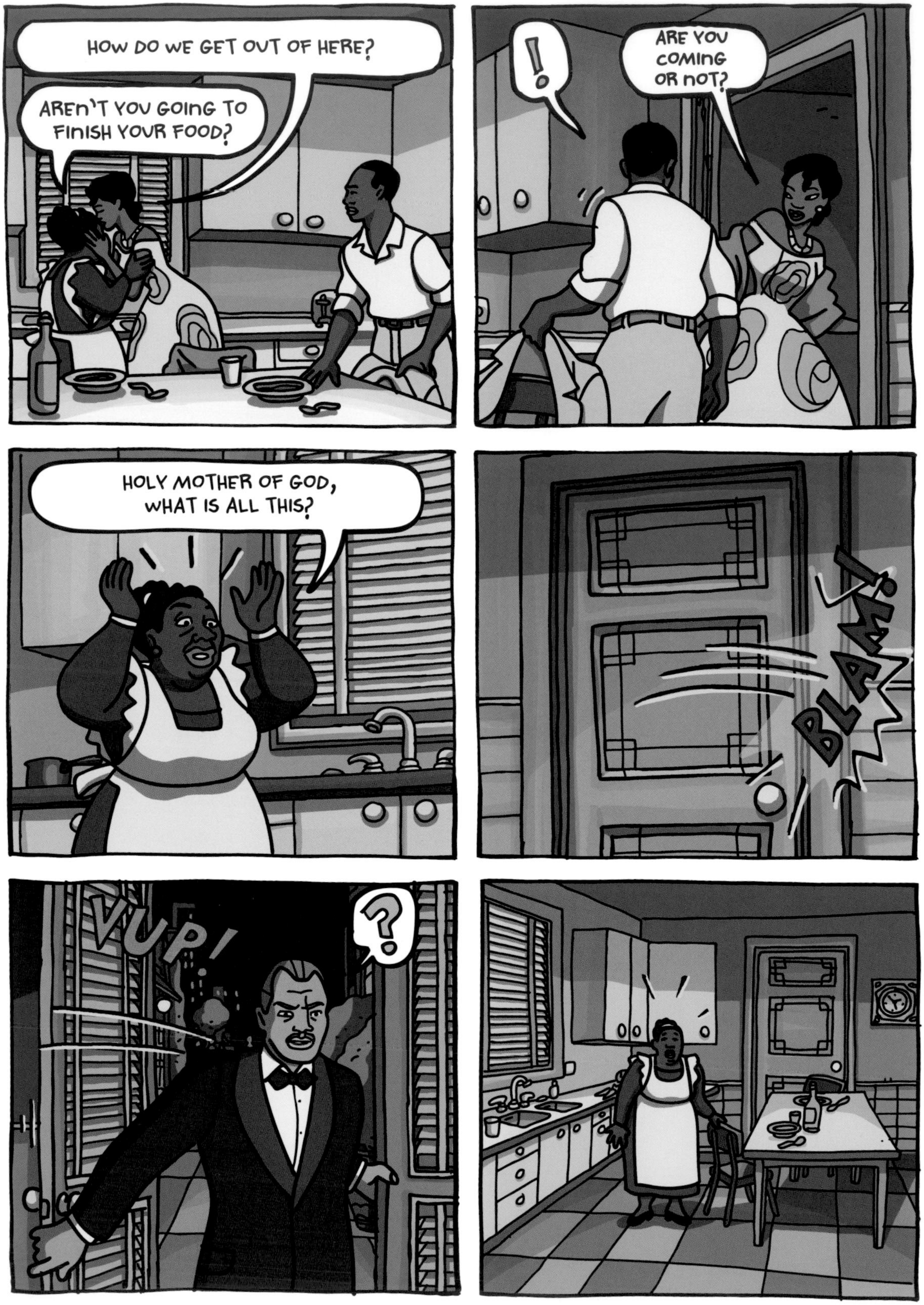
HOW DO WE GET OUT OF HERE?
AREN'T YOU GOING TO FINISH YOUR FOOD?
!
ARE YOU COMING OR NOT?
HOLY MOTHER OF GOD, WHAT IS ALL THIS?
BLAM!
VUP!
?

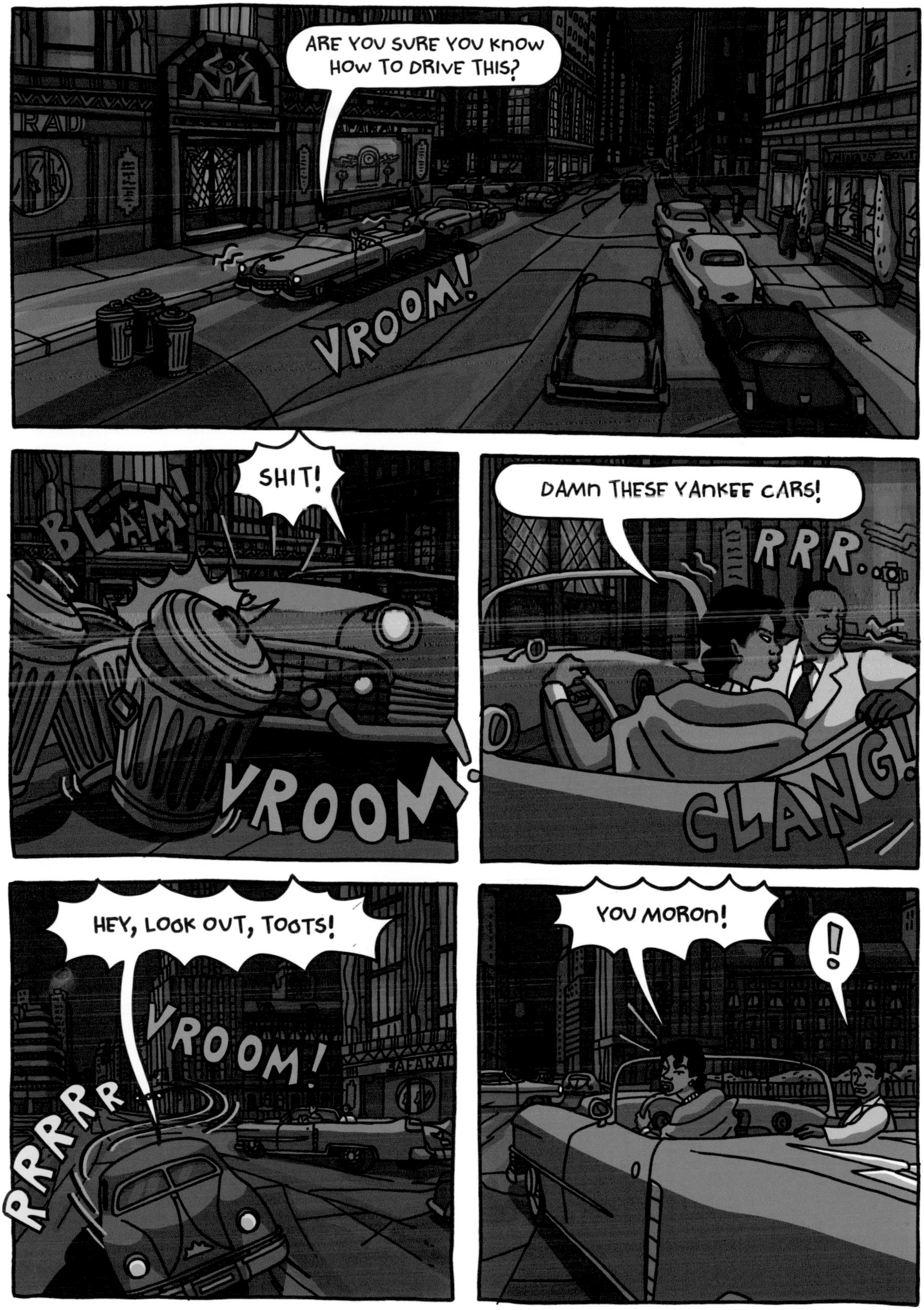
ARE YOU SURE YOU KNOW HOW TO DRIVE THIS?
VROOM!
BLAM!
SHIT!
VROOM!
DAMN THESE YANKEE CARS!
RRR..
CLANG!
HEY, LOOK OUT, TOOTS!
VROOM!
RRRRR..
YOU MORON!
!

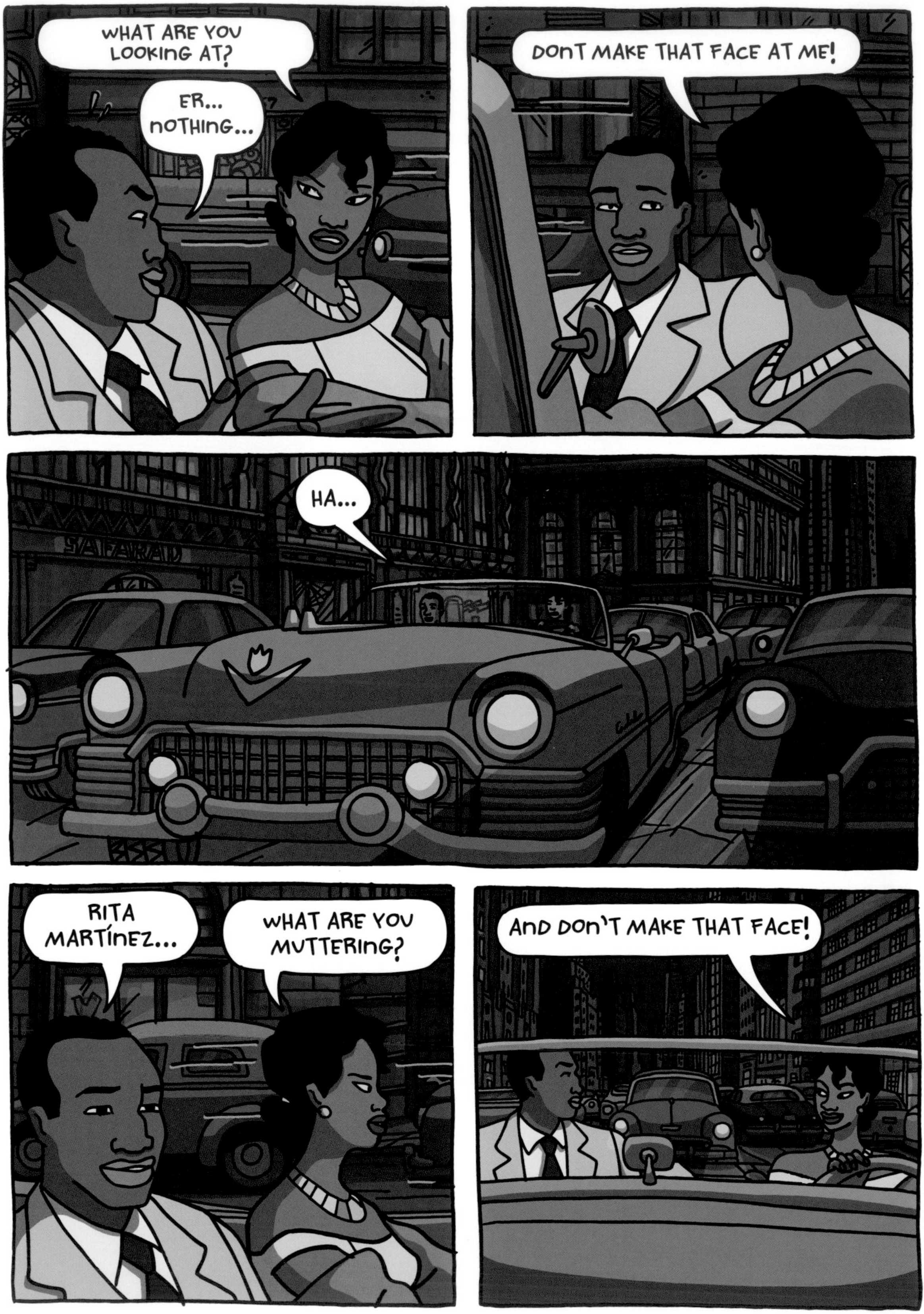
WHAT ARE YOU LOOKING AT?
ER... NOTHING...
DONT MAKE THAT FACE AT ME!
HA...
SAFARAD
RITA MARTÍNEZ...
WHAT ARE YOU MUTTERING?
AND DON'T MAKE THAT FACE!

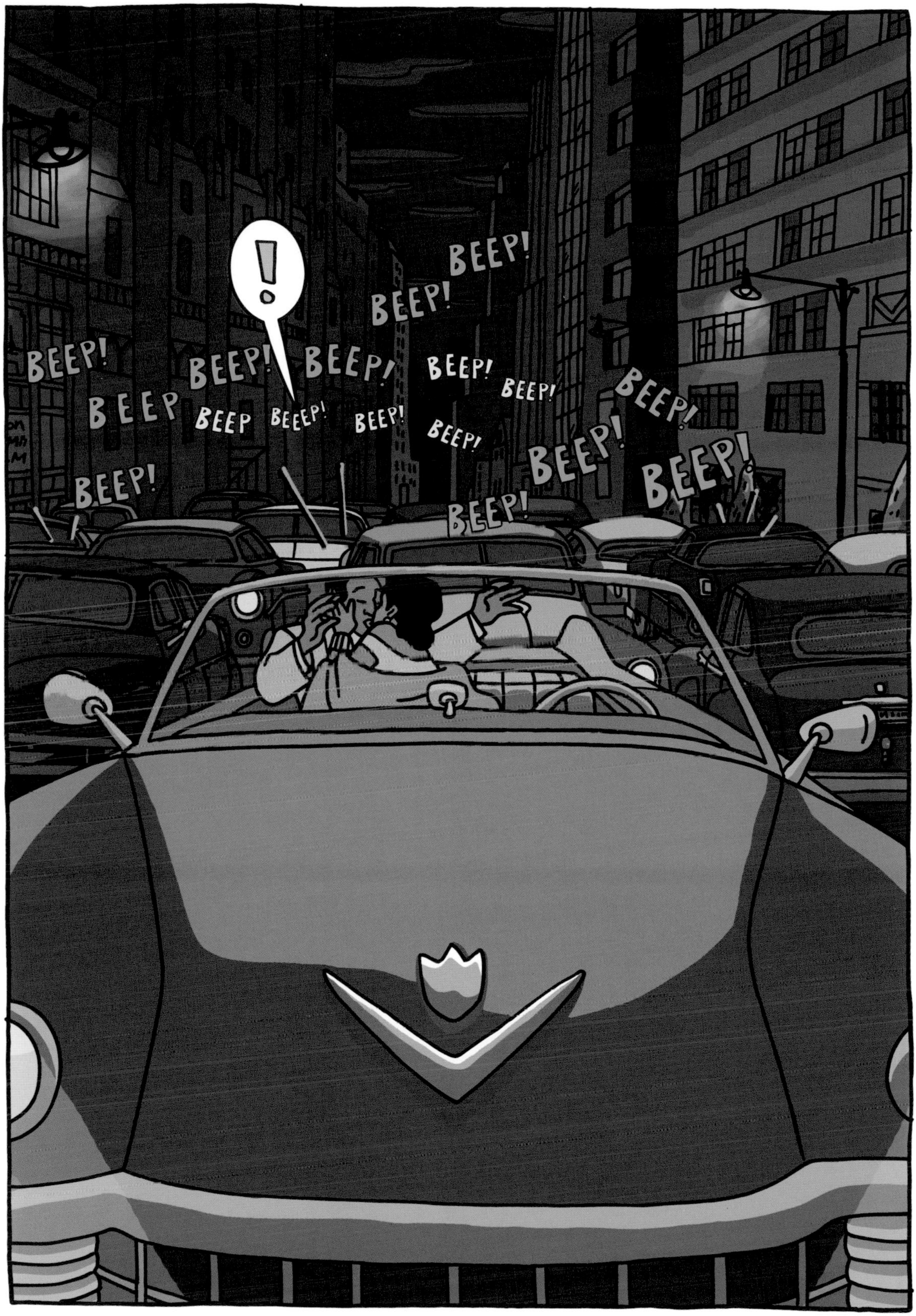

BEEP!
BEEP
BEEP!
BEEP!
BEEP
BEEEP!
!
BEEP!
BEEP!
BEEP!
BEEP!
BEEP!
BEEP!
BEEP!
BEEP!
BEEP!
BEEP!
BEEP!

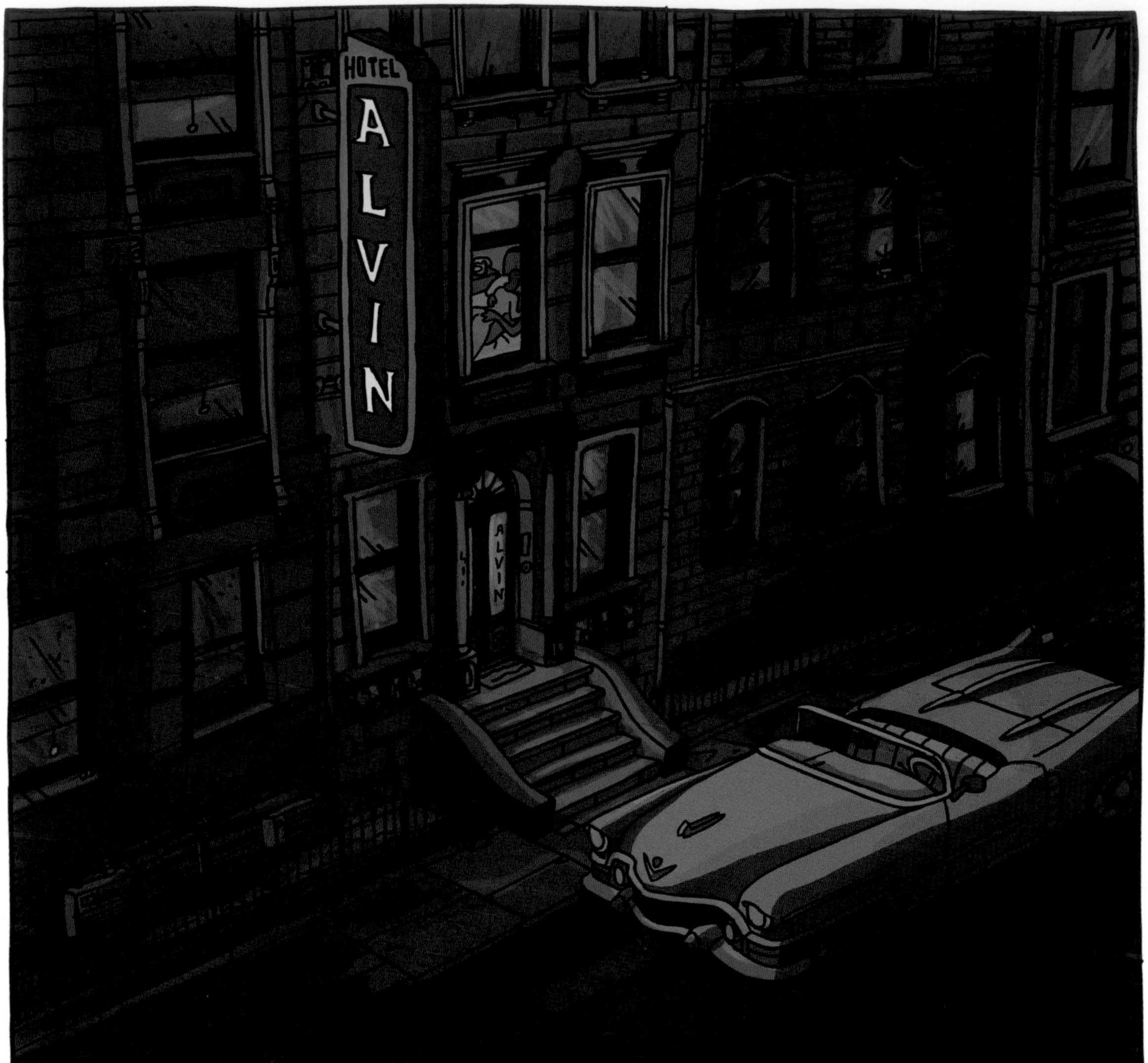
HOTEL
ALVIN
ALVIN

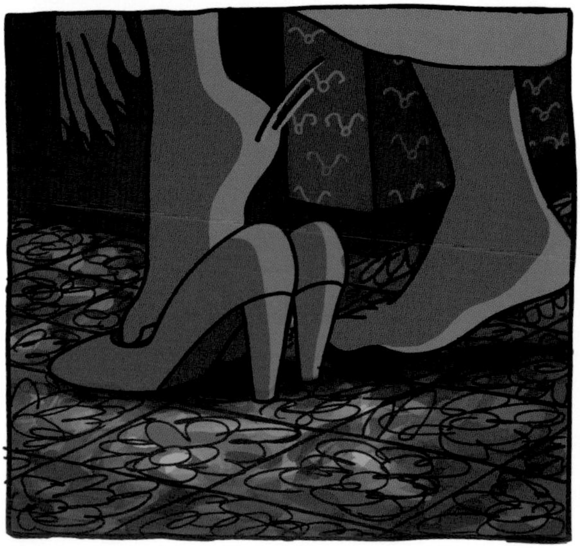

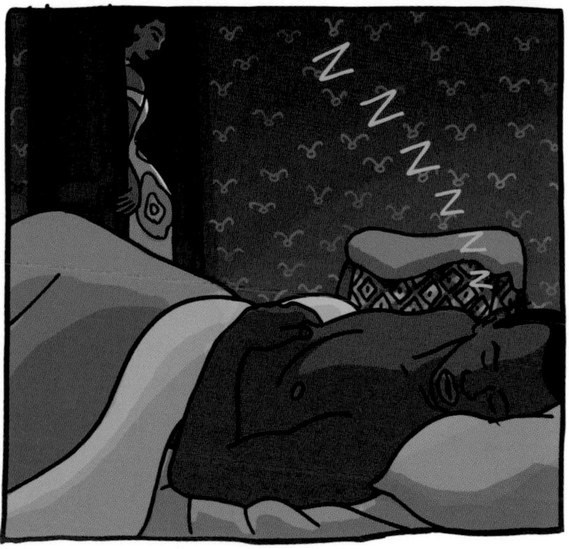
ZZZZZZZ

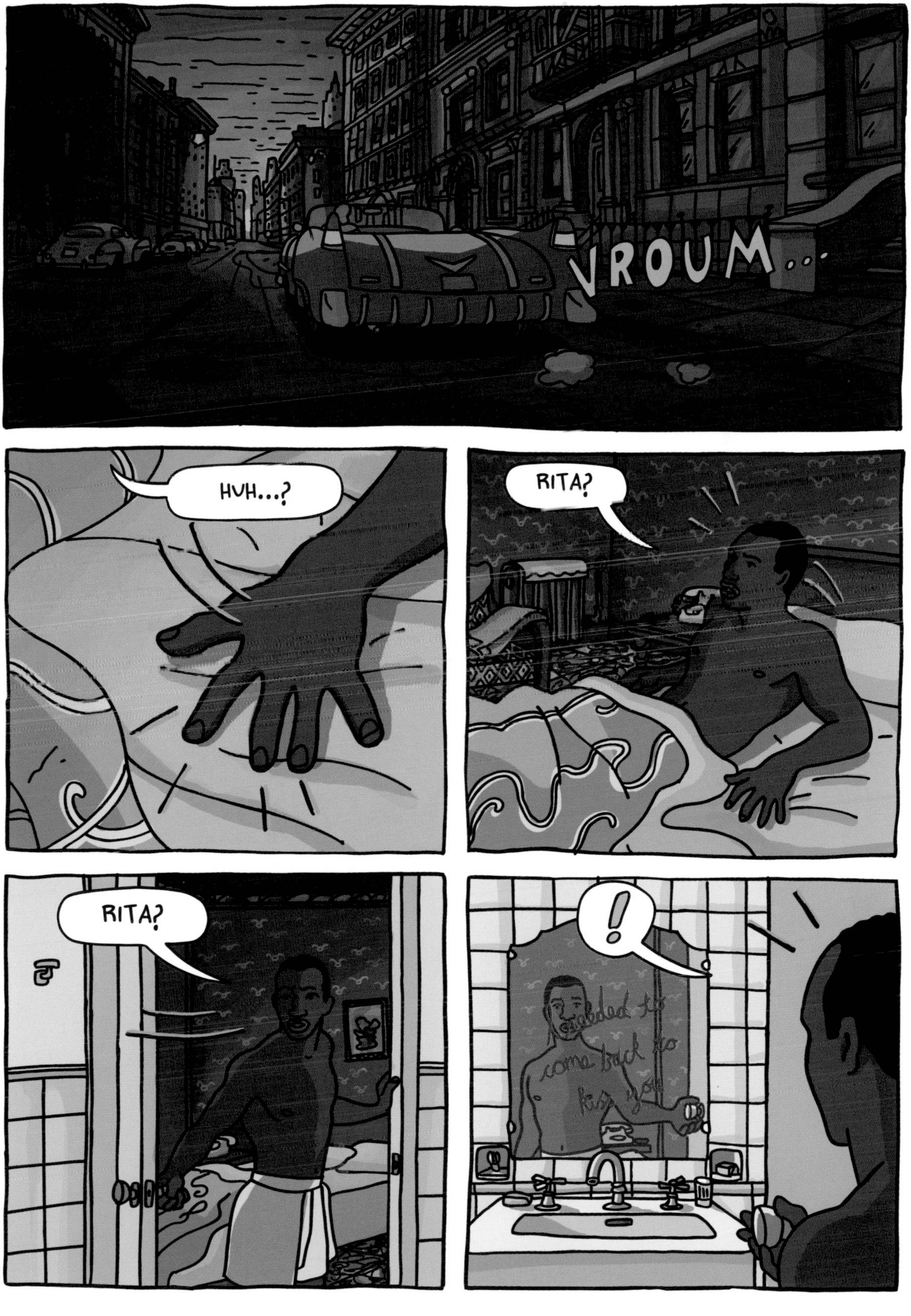
VROUM...
HUH...?
RITA?
RITA?
!
needed to
come back to
kiss you

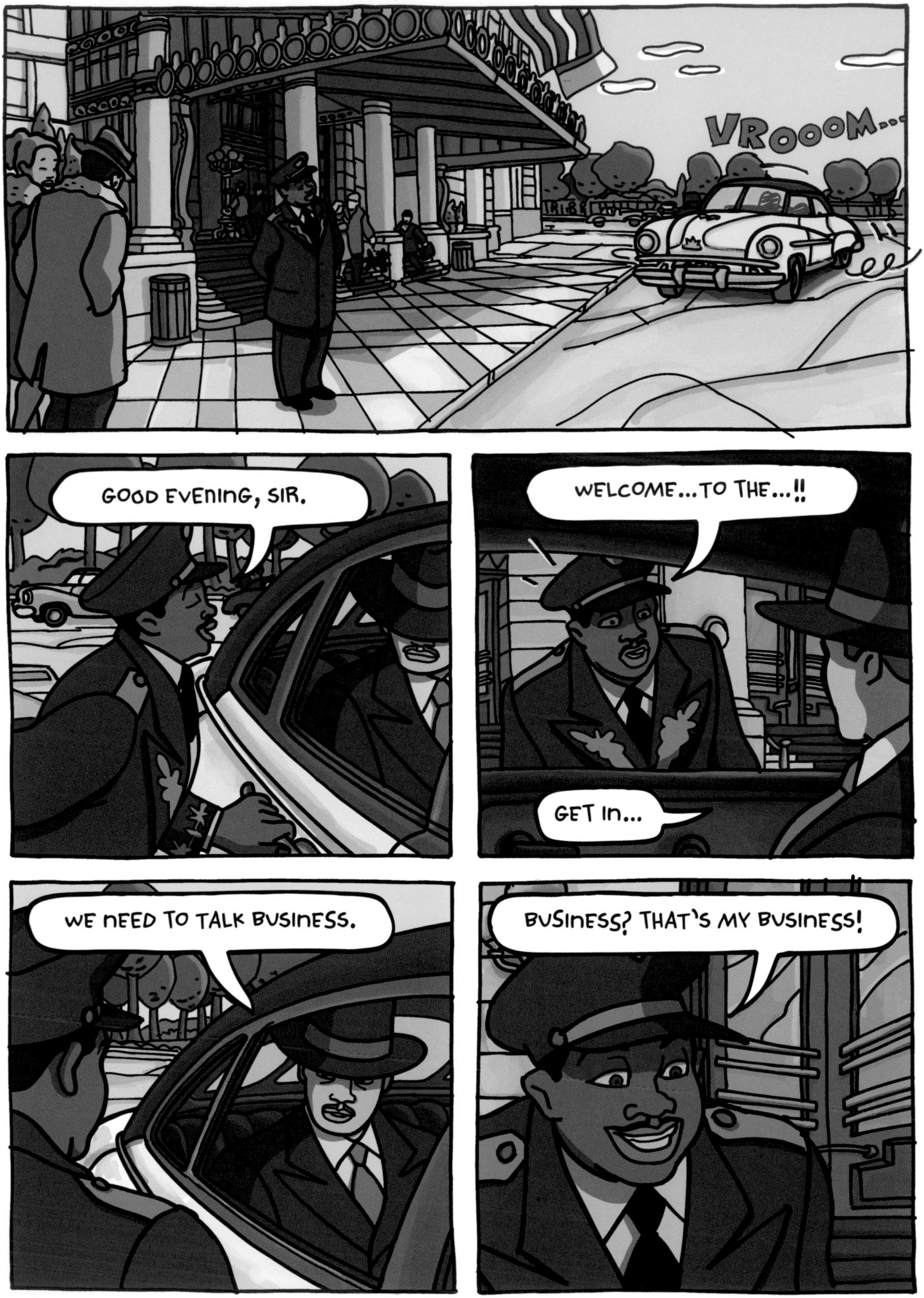
VROOOM...
GOOD EVENING, SIR.
WELCOME...TO THE...!!
GET IN...
WE NEED TO TALK BUSINESS.
BUSINESS? THAT'S MY BUSINESS!

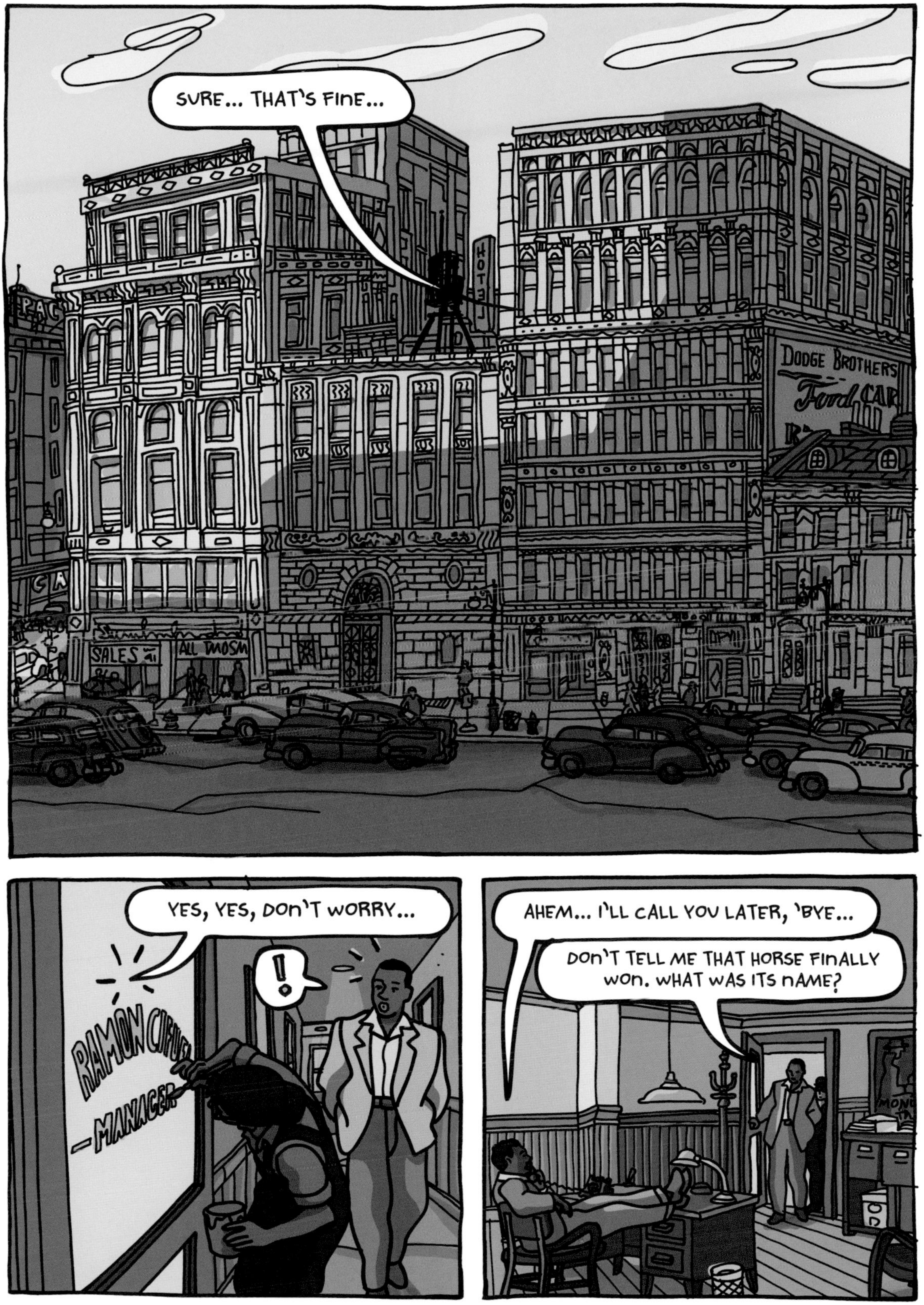
SURE... THAT'S FINE...
HOTEL
DODGE BROTHERS
SALES
YES, YES, DON'T WORRY...
!
— MANAGER
AHEM... I'LL CALL YOU LATER, 'BYE...
DON'T TELL ME THAT HORSE FINALLY WON. WHAT WAS ITS NAME?

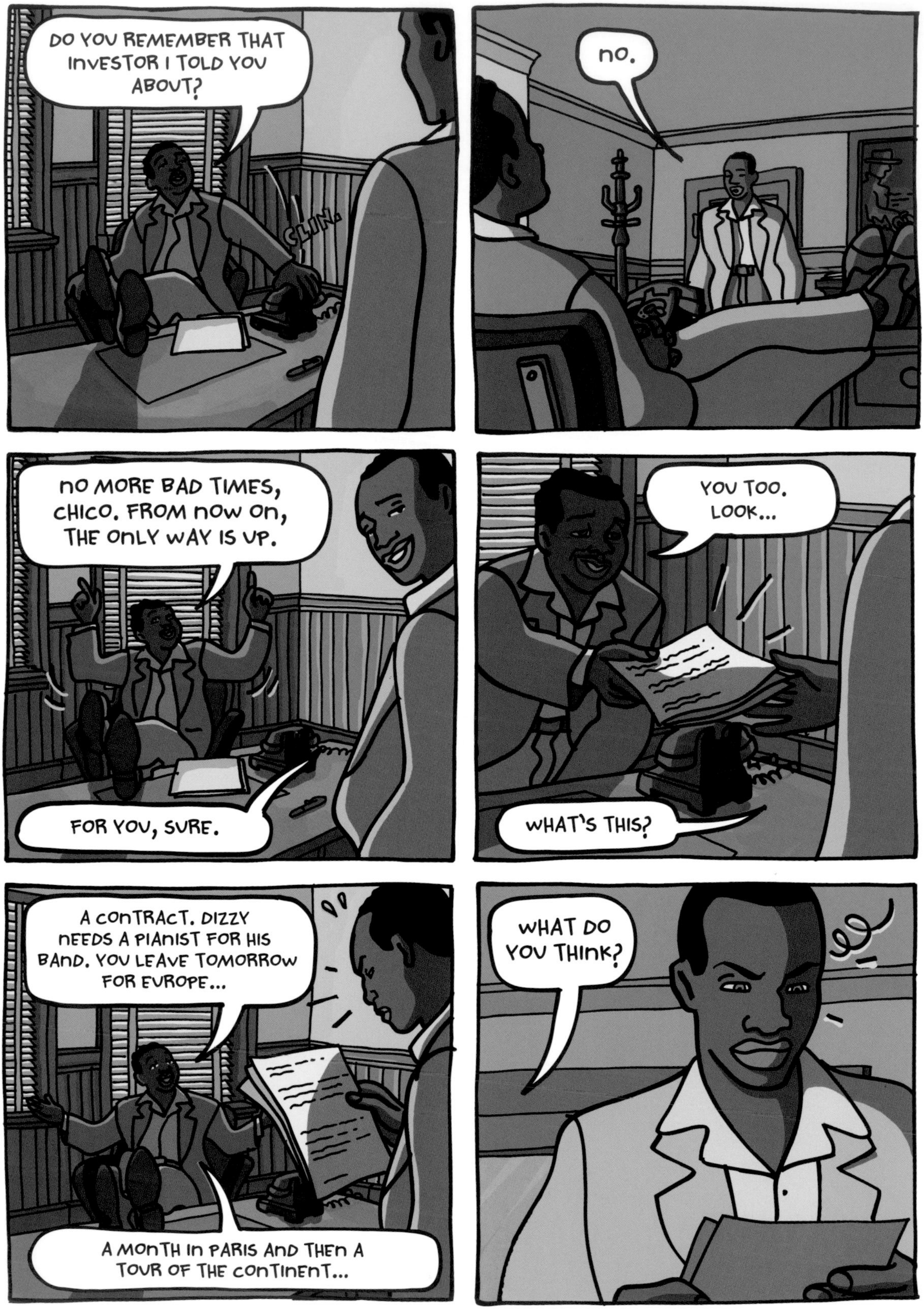
DO YOU REMEMBER THAT INVESTOR I TOLD YOU ABOUT?
CLIN.
NO.
NO MORE BAD TIMES, CHICO. FROM NOW ON, THE ONLY WAY IS UP.
FOR YOU, SURE.
YOU TOO. LOOK...
WHAT'S THIS?
A CONTRACT. DIZZY NEEDS A PIANIST FOR HIS BAND. YOU LEAVE TOMORROW FOR EUROPE...
A MONTH IN PARIS AND THEN A TOUR OF THE CONTINENT...
WHAT DO YOU THINK?

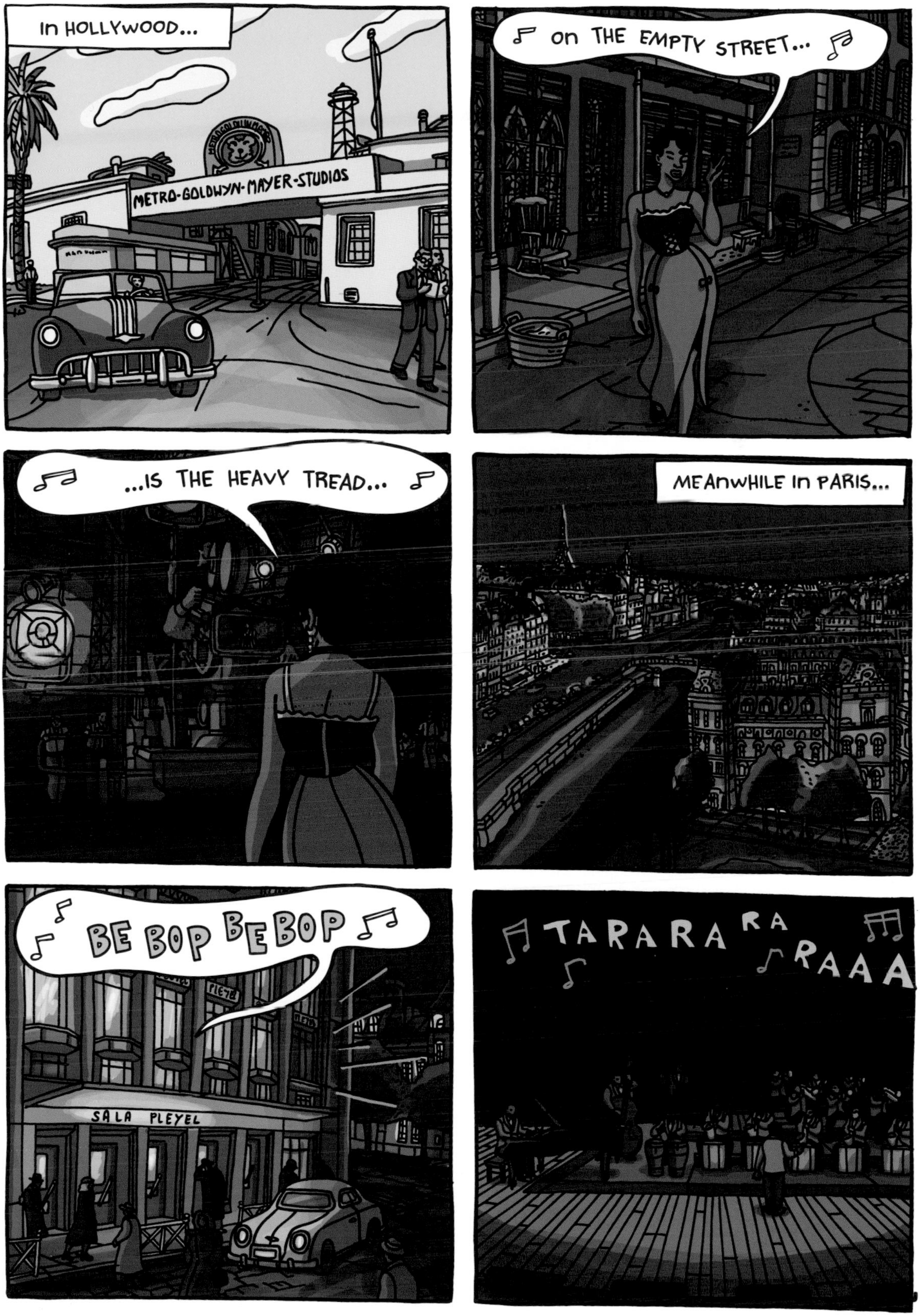
IN HOLLYWOOD...
METRO-GOLDWYN-MAYER-STUDIOS
ON THE EMPTY STREET...
...IS THE HEAVY TREAD...
MEANWHILE IN PARIS...
BE BOP BEBOP
SALA PLEYEL
TARARARA RA RAAA

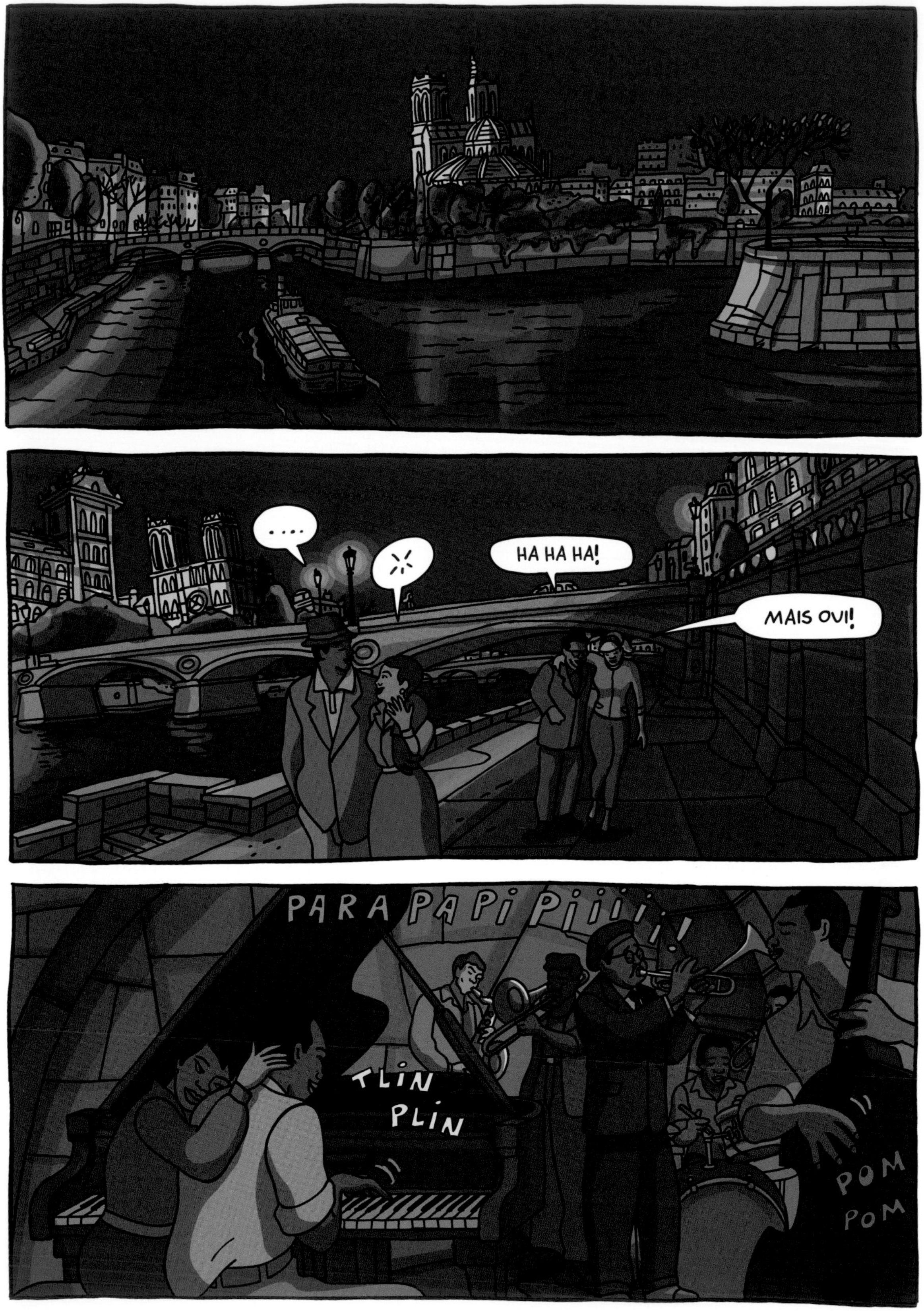
....
HA HA HA!
MAIS OUI!
PARA PA PI PIIIII!
TLIN PLIN
POM POM

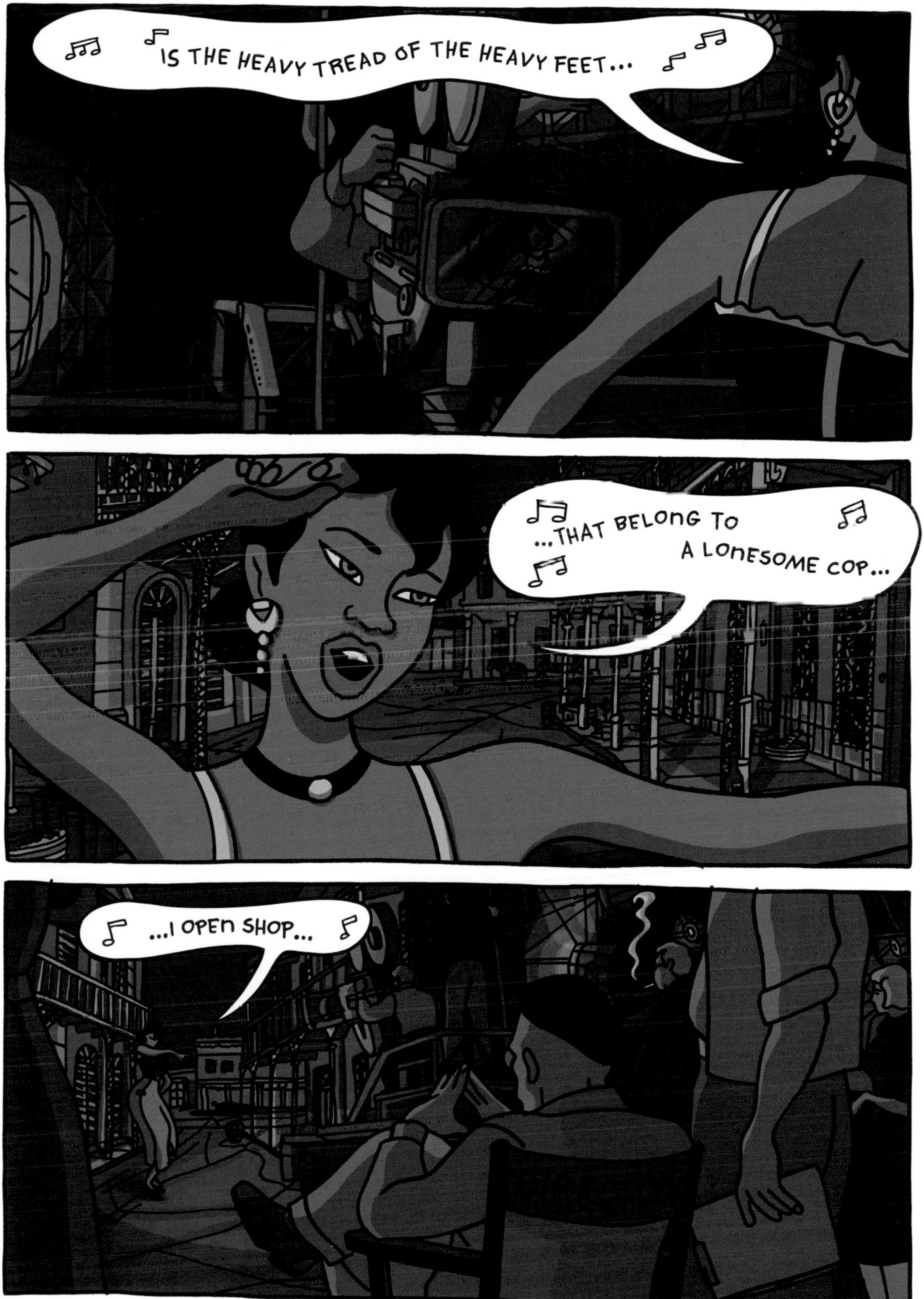
IS THE HEAVY TREAD OF THE HEAVY FEET...
...THAT BELONG TO A LONESOME COP...
...I OPEN SHOP...

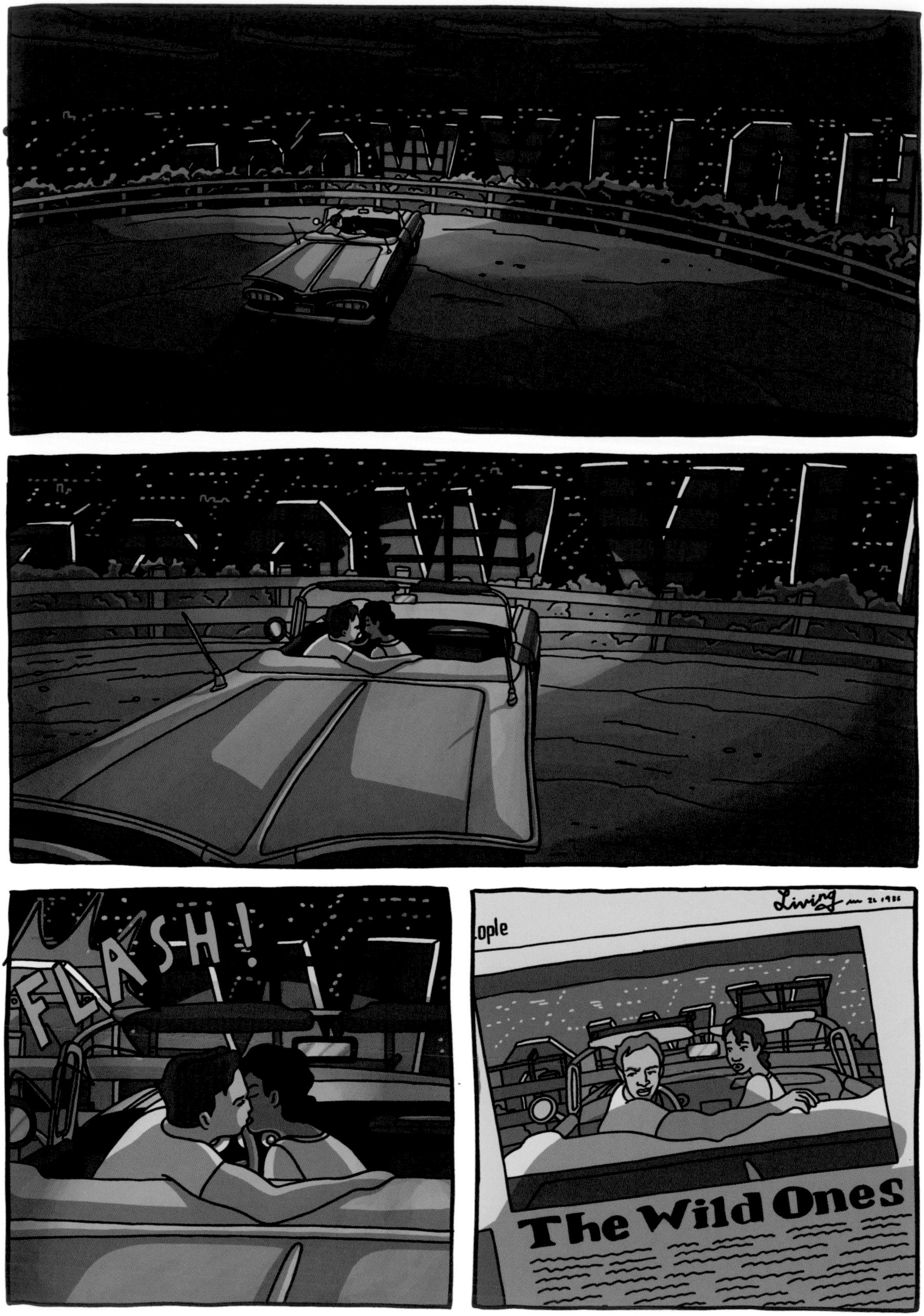
FLASH!
Living
ople
The Wild Ones

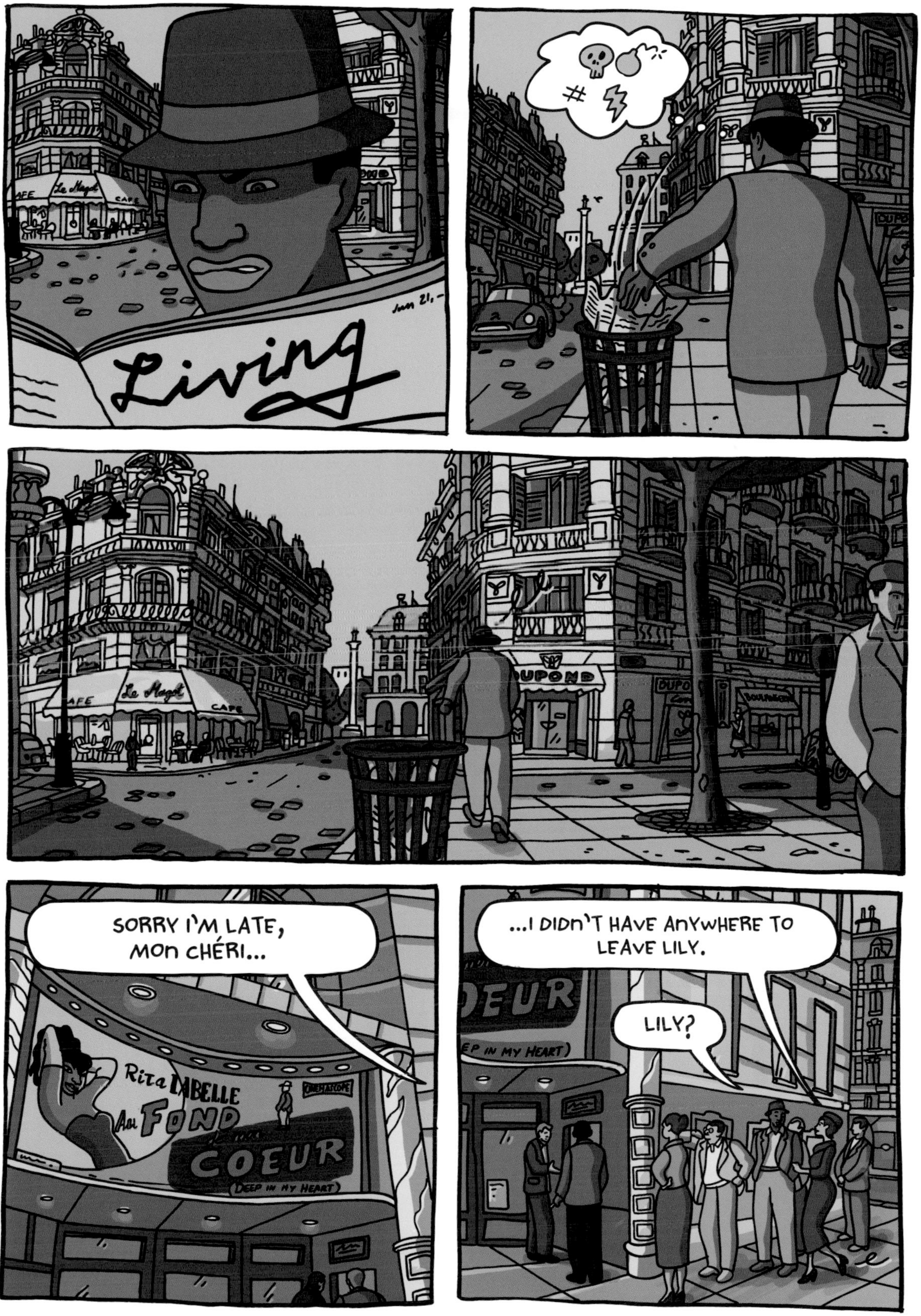
Living
DUPOND
Rita LABELLE
Au FOND
COEUR
(DEEP IN MY HEART)
SORRY I'M LATE, MON CHÉRI...
...I DIDN'T HAVE ANYWHERE TO LEAVE LILY.
LILY?

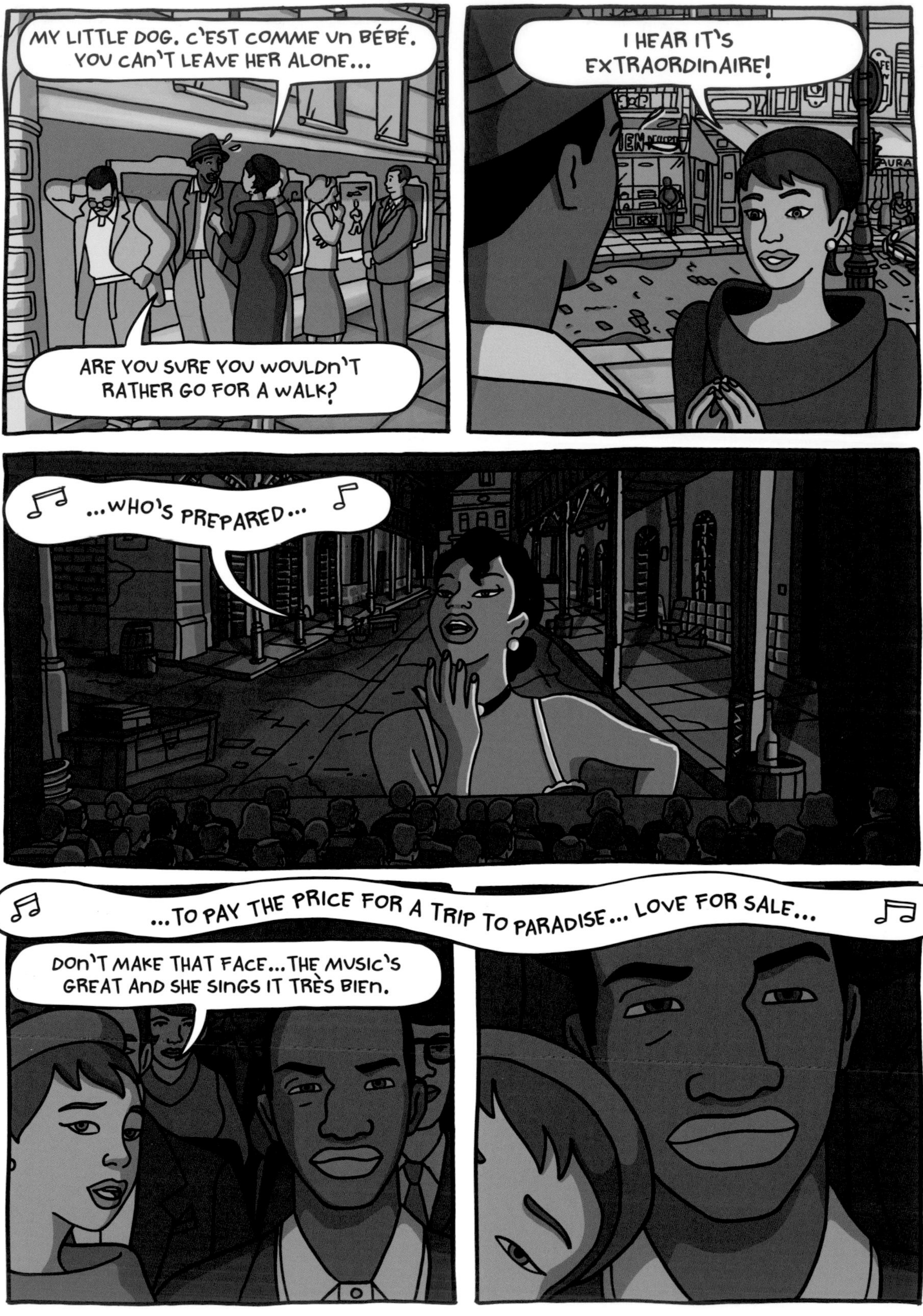
MY LITTLE DOG. C'EST COMME UN BÉBÉ. YOU CAN'T LEAVE HER ALONE...
ARE YOU SURE YOU WOULDN'T RATHER GO FOR A WALK?
I HEAR IT'S EXTRAORDINAIRE!
...WHO'S PREPARED...
...TO PAY THE PRICE FOR A TRIP TO PARADISE... LOVE FOR SALE...
DON'T MAKE THAT FACE... THE MUSIC'S GREAT AND SHE SINGS IT TRÈS BIEN.

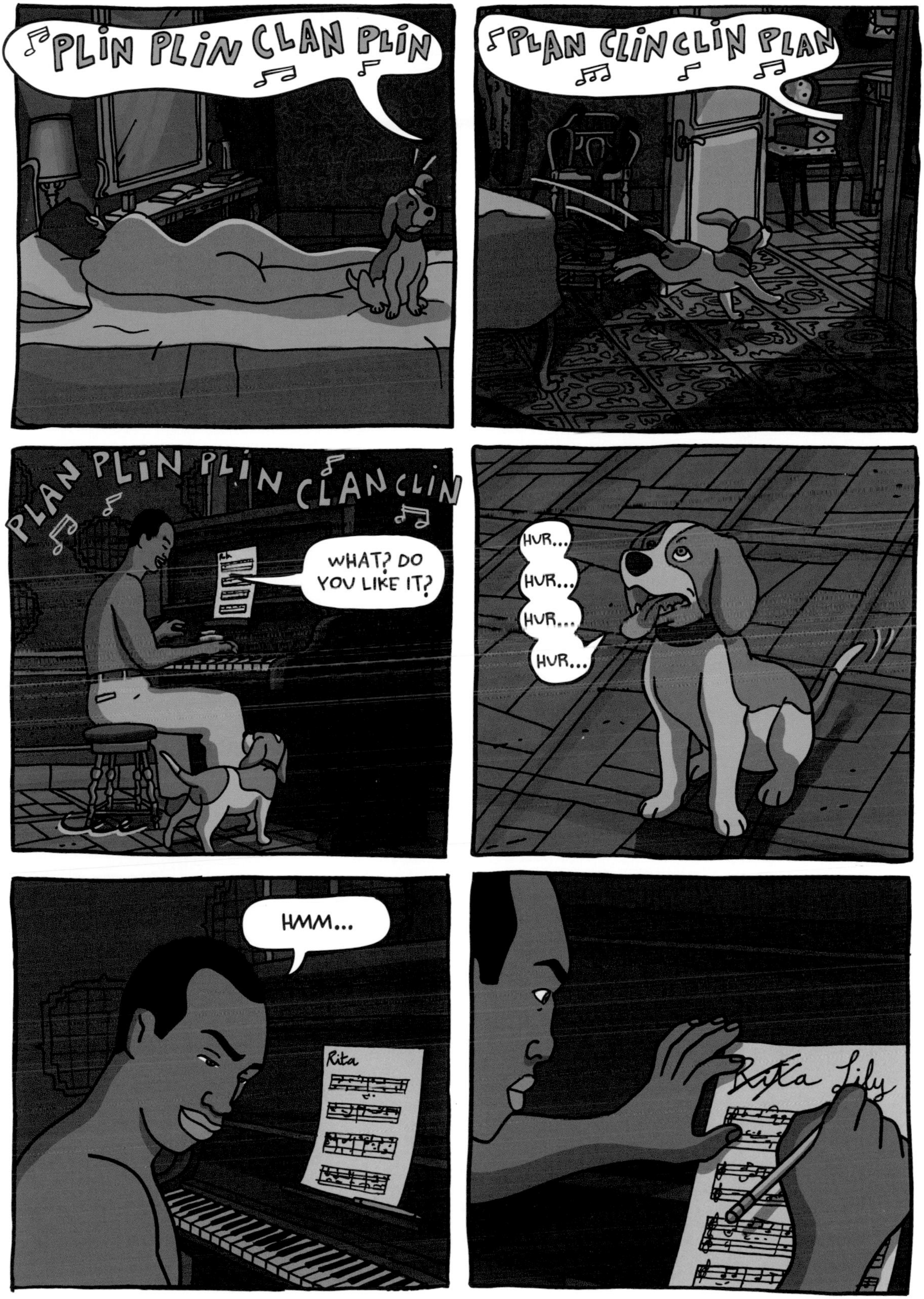
PLIN PLIN CLAN PLIN
PLAN CLIN CLIN PLAN
PLAN PLIN PLIN CLAN CLIN
WHAT? DO YOU LIKE IT?
HUR...
HUR...
HUR...
HUR...
HMM...
Rita
Rita Lily

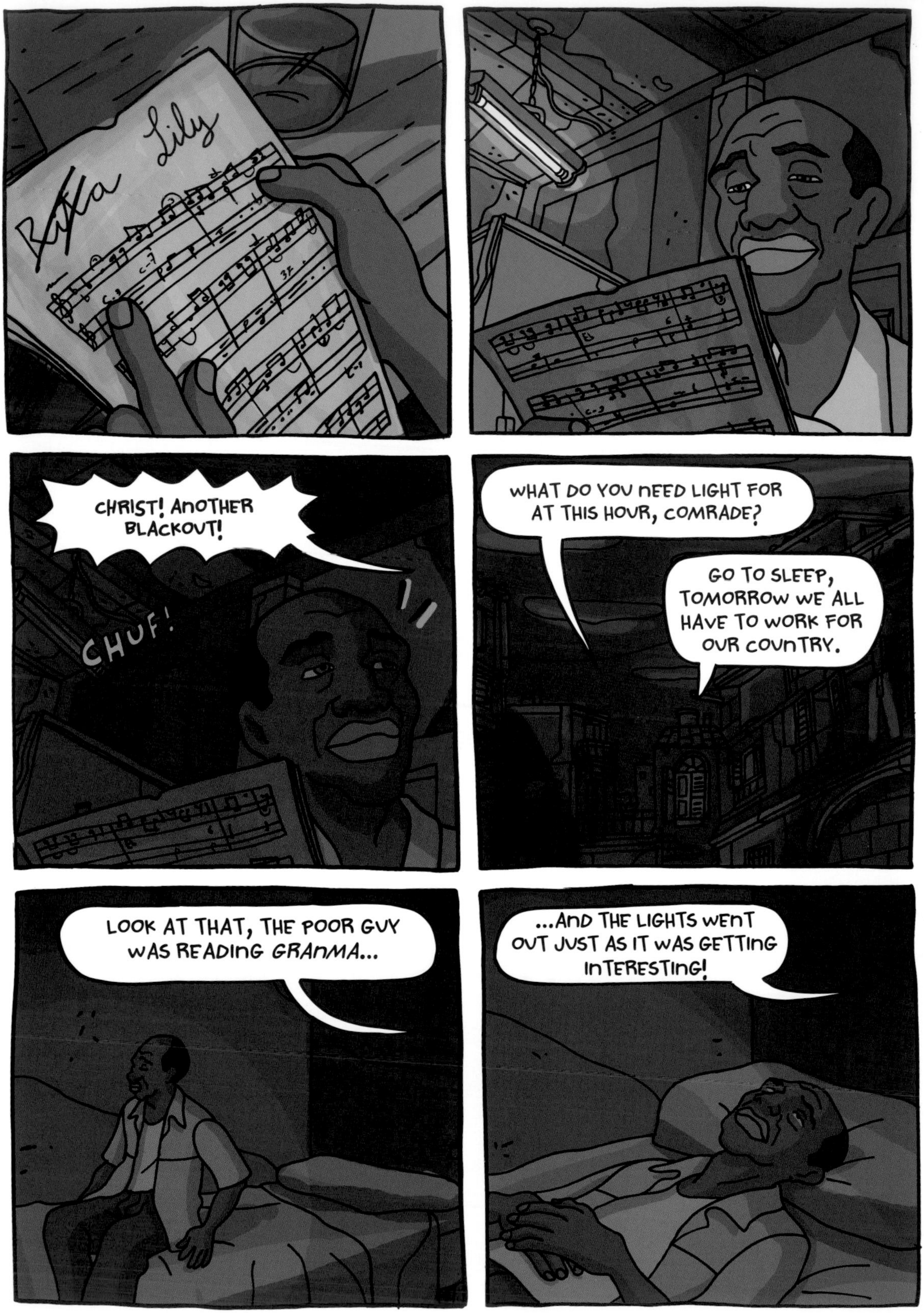
Lily
CHRIST! ANOTHER BLACKOUT!
CHUF!
WHAT DO YOU NEED LIGHT FOR AT THIS HOUR, COMRADE?
GO TO SLEEP, TOMORROW WE ALL HAVE TO WORK FOR OUR COUNTRY.
LOOK AT THAT, THE POOR GUY WAS READING *GRANMA*...
...AND THE LIGHTS WENT OUT JUST AS IT WAS GETTING INTERESTING!

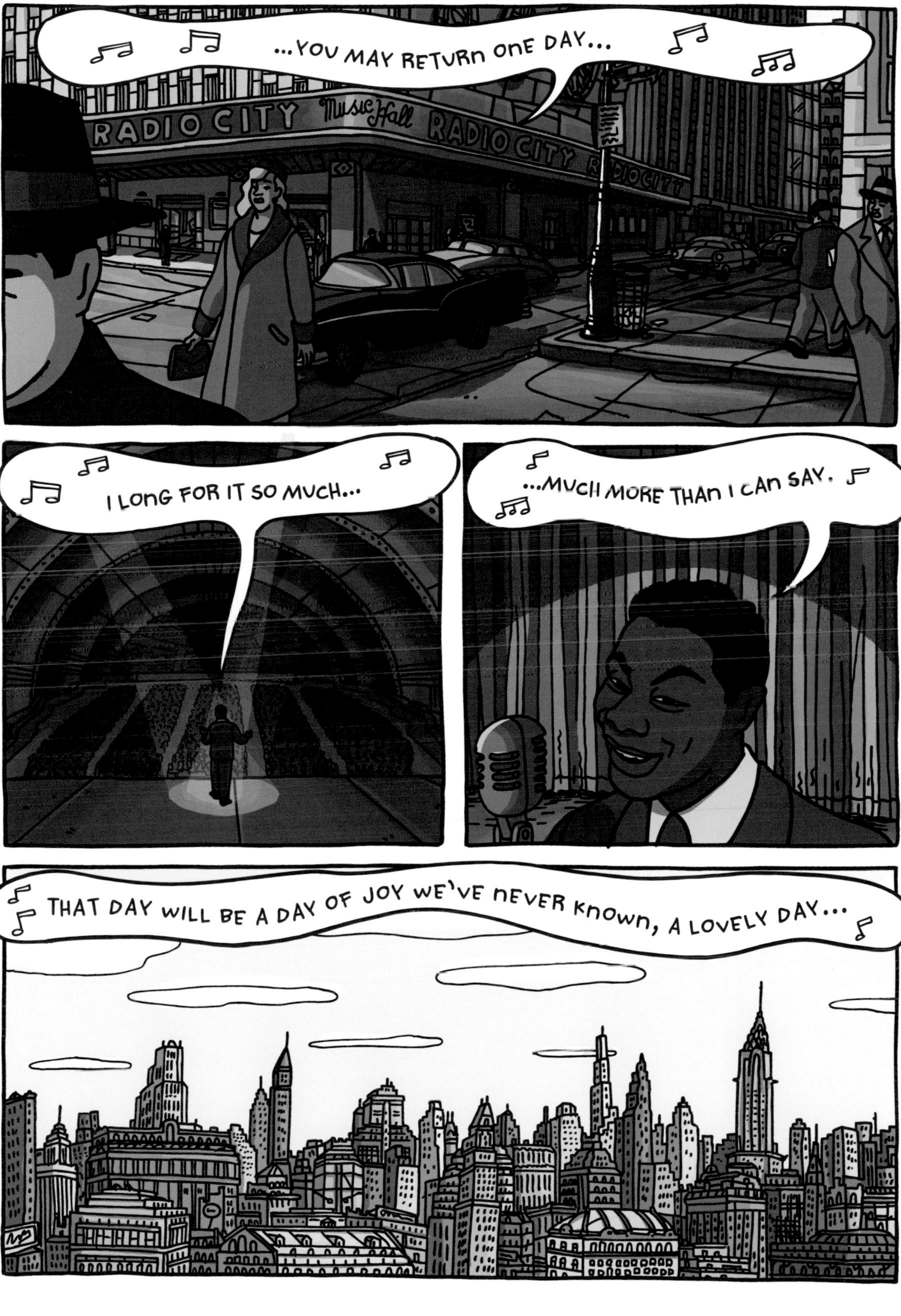
...YOU MAY RETURN ONE DAY...
RADIO CITY
Music Hall
RADIO CITY
RADIO CITY
I LONG FOR IT SO MUCH...
...MUCH MORE THAN I CAN SAY.
THAT DAY WILL BE A DAY OF JOY WE'VE NEVER KNOWN, A LOVELY DAY...

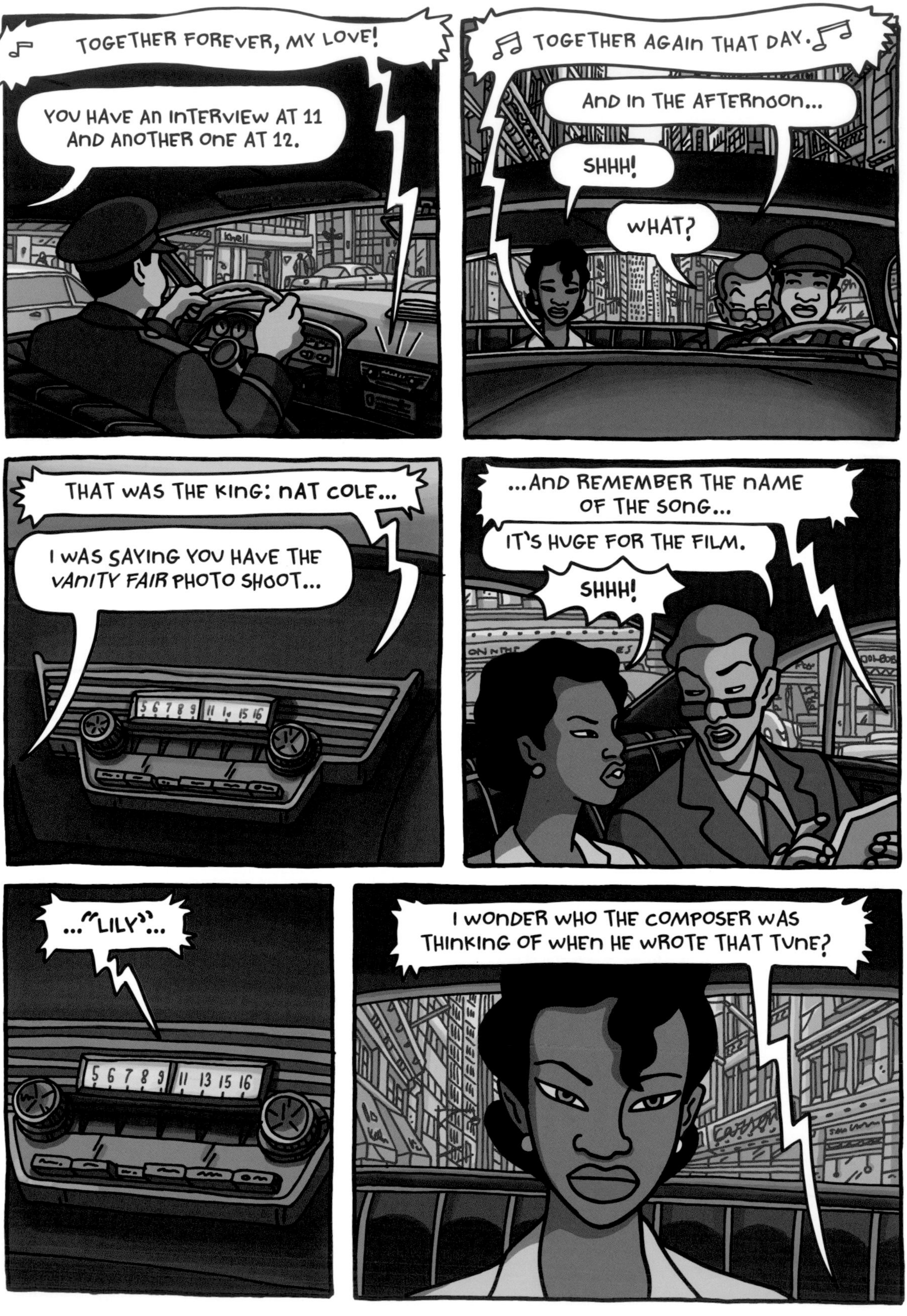
TOGETHER FOREVER, MY LOVE!
YOU HAVE AN INTERVIEW AT 11 AND ANOTHER ONE AT 12.
TOGETHER AGAIN THAT DAY.
AND IN THE AFTERNOON...
SHHH!
WHAT?
THAT WAS THE KING: NAT COLE...
I WAS SAYING YOU HAVE THE *VANITY FAIR* PHOTO SHOOT...
...AND REMEMBER THE NAME OF THE SONG...
IT'S HUGE FOR THE FILM.
SHHH!
..."LILY"...
I WONDER WHO THE COMPOSER WAS THINKING OF WHEN HE WROTE THAT TUNE?

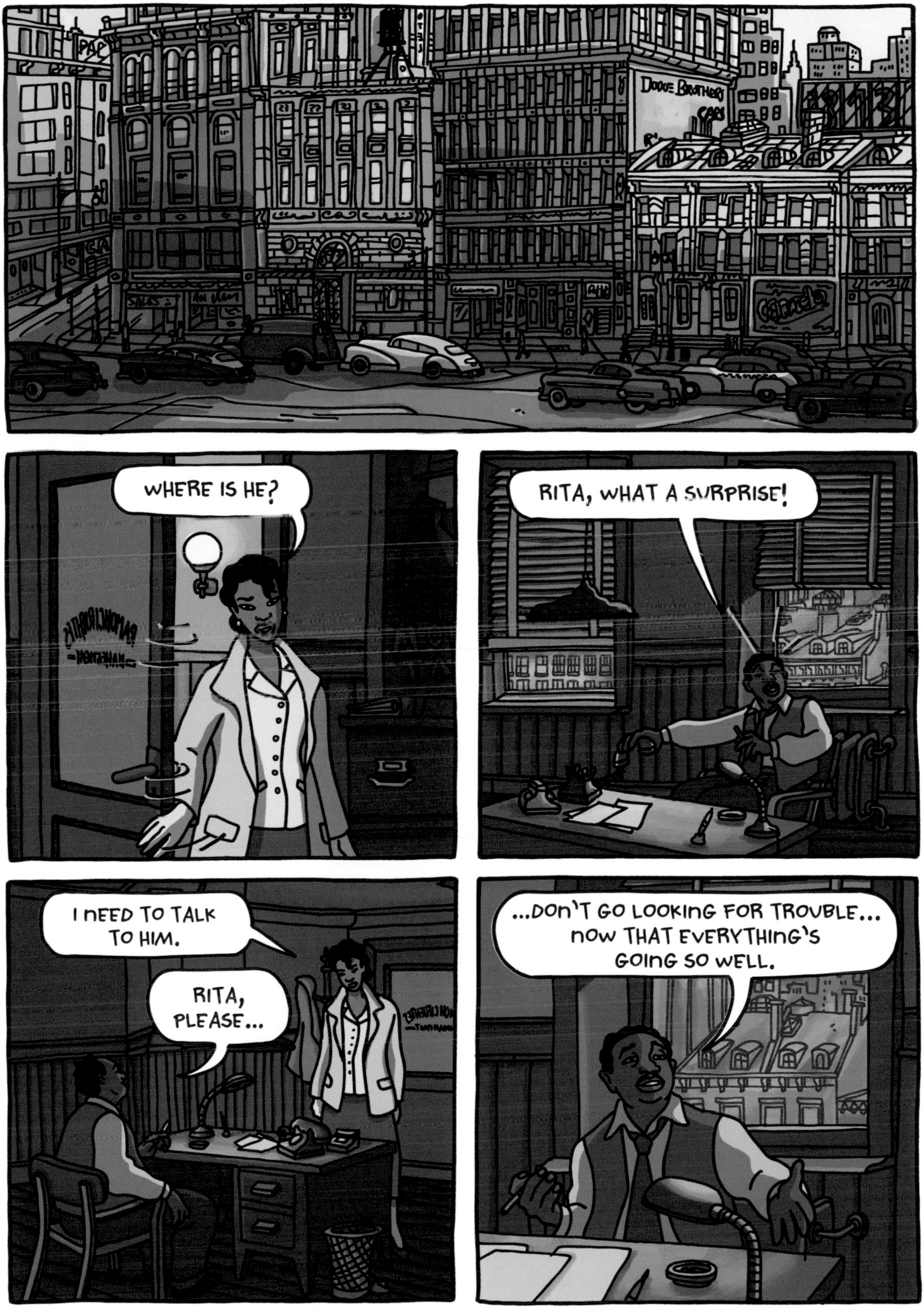

WHERE IS HE?
RITA, WHAT A SURPRISE!
I NEED TO TALK TO HIM.
RITA, PLEASE...
...DON'T GO LOOKING FOR TROUBLE... NOW THAT EVERYTHING'S GOING SO WELL.

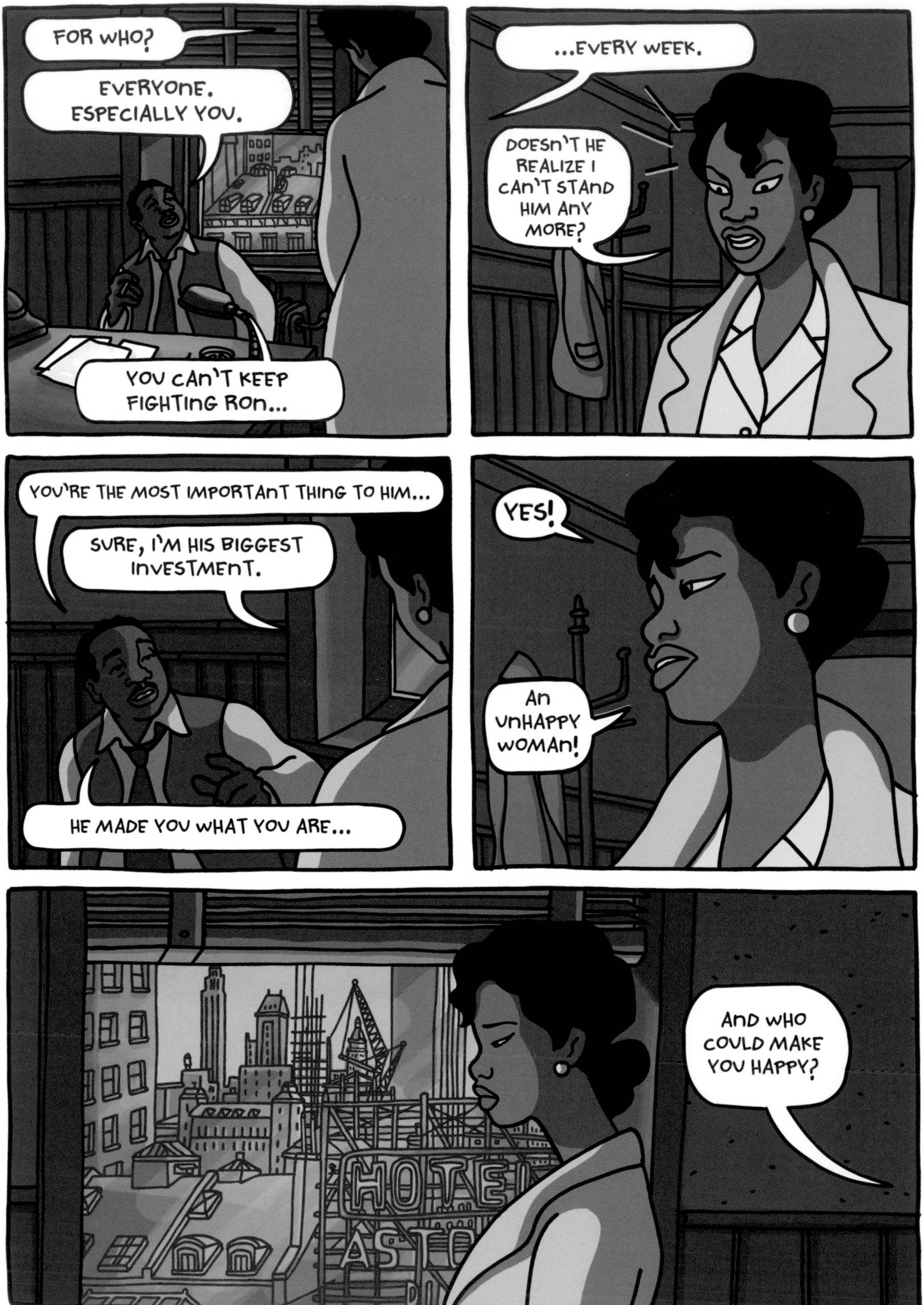
FOR WHO?
EVERYONE. ESPECIALLY YOU.
YOU CAN'T KEEP FIGHTING RON...
...EVERY WEEK.
DOESN'T HE REALIZE I CAN'T STAND HIM ANY MORE?
YOU'RE THE MOST IMPORTANT THING TO HIM...
SURE, I'M HIS BIGGEST INVESTMENT.
HE MADE YOU WHAT YOU ARE...
YES!
AN UNHAPPY WOMAN!
AND WHO COULD MAKE YOU HAPPY?
HOTE
ASTO

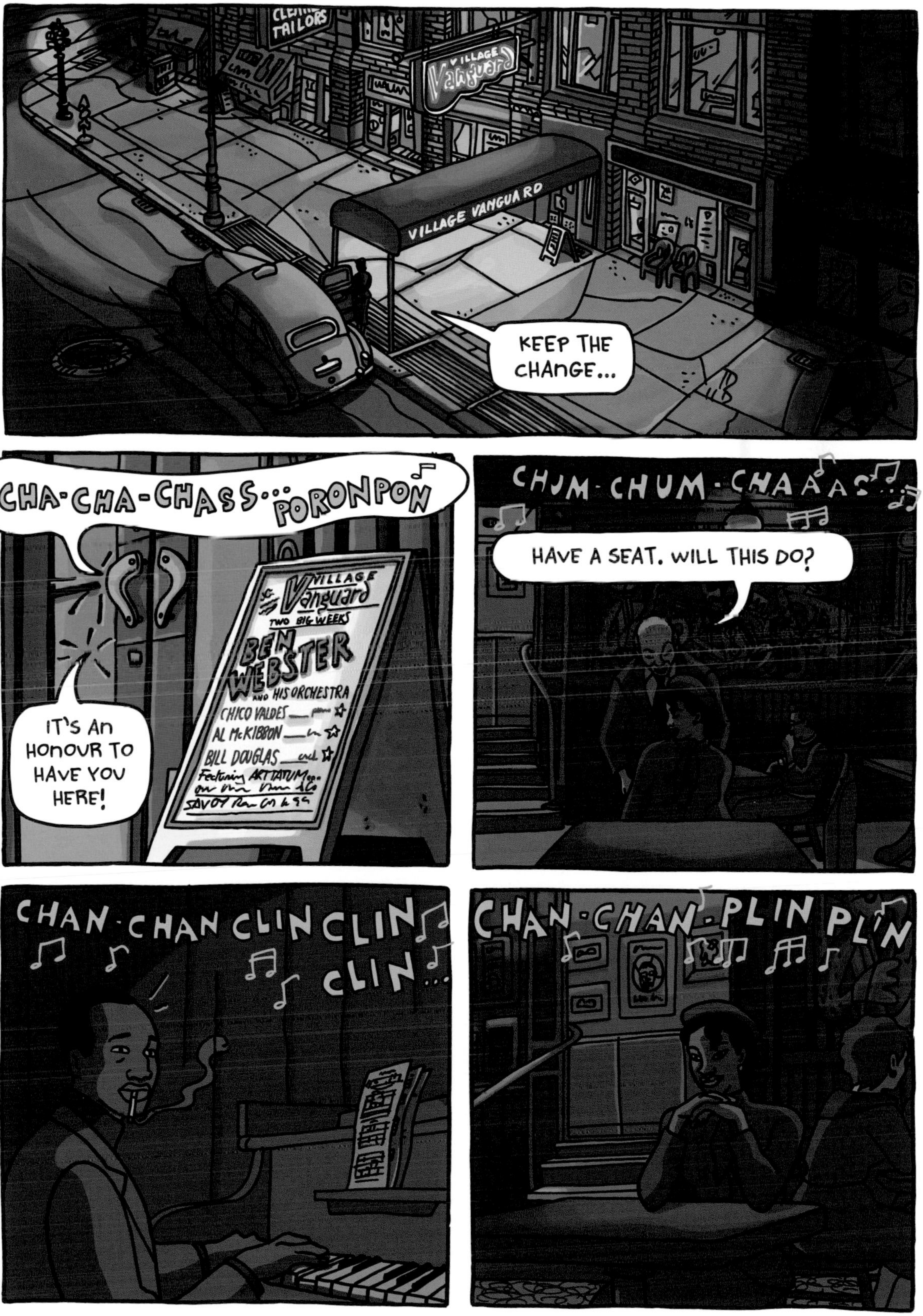
TAILORS
VILLAGE Vanguard
VILLAGE VANGUARD
KEEP THE CHANGE...
CHA-CHA-CHASS... PORONPON
VILLAGE Vanguard
TWO BIG WEEKS
BEN WEBSTER
AND HIS ORCHESTRA
CHICO VALDES
AL McKIBBON
BILL DOUGLAS
Featuring ART TATUM
IT'S AN HONOUR TO HAVE YOU HERE!
CHUM-CHUM-CHAAAS...
HAVE A SEAT. WILL THIS DO?
CHAN-CHAN CLIN CLIN CLIN...
CHAN-CHAN-PLIN PLIN

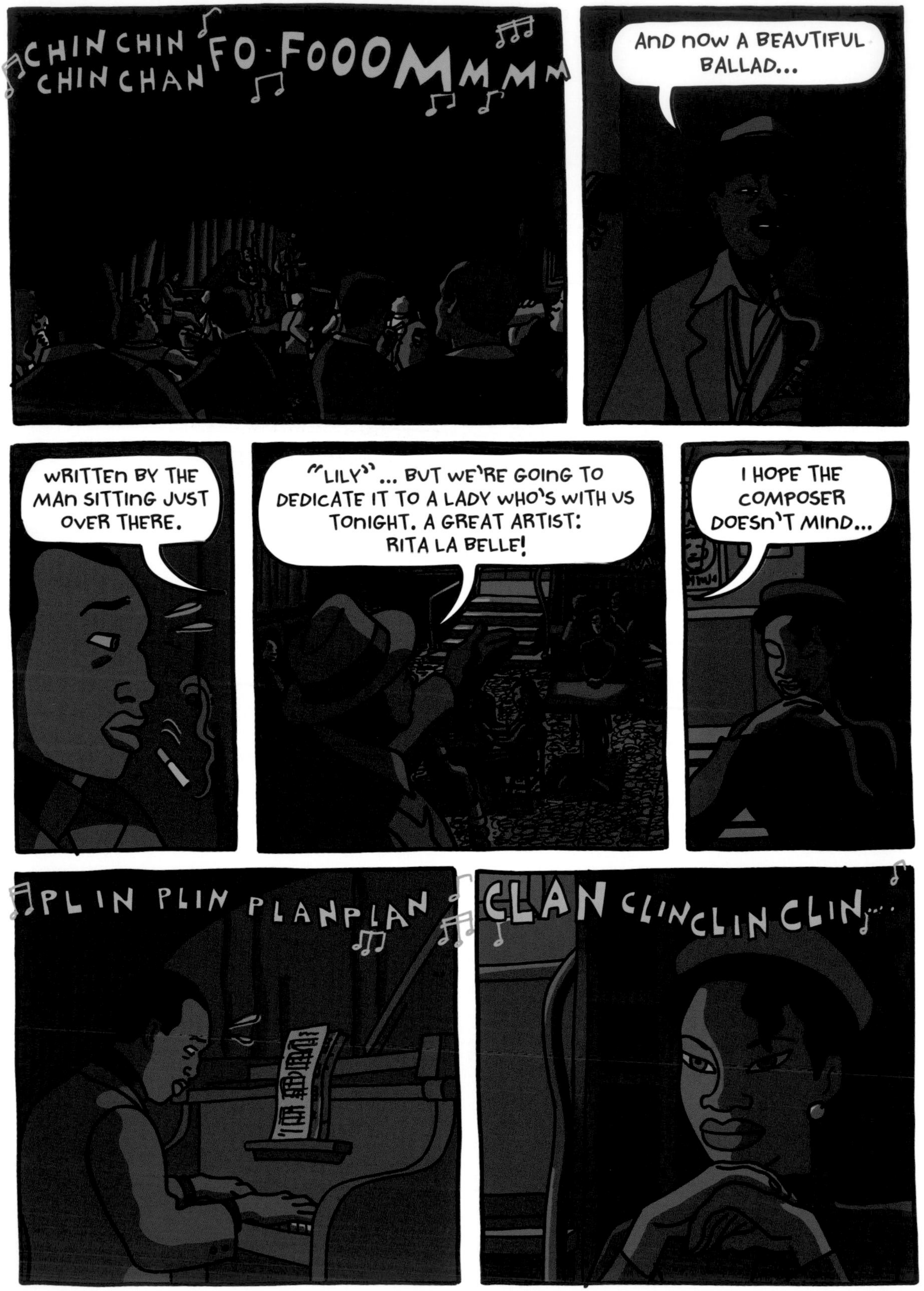
CHIN CHIN CHIN CHAN FO-FOOOMMMM
AND NOW A BEAUTIFUL BALLAD...
WRITTEN BY THE MAN SITTING JUST OVER THERE.
"LILY"... BUT WE'RE GOING TO DEDICATE IT TO A LADY WHO'S WITH US TONIGHT. A GREAT ARTIST: RITA LA BELLE!
I HOPE THE COMPOSER DOESN'T MIND...
PLIN PLIN PLANPLAN
CLAN CLINCLINCLIN...

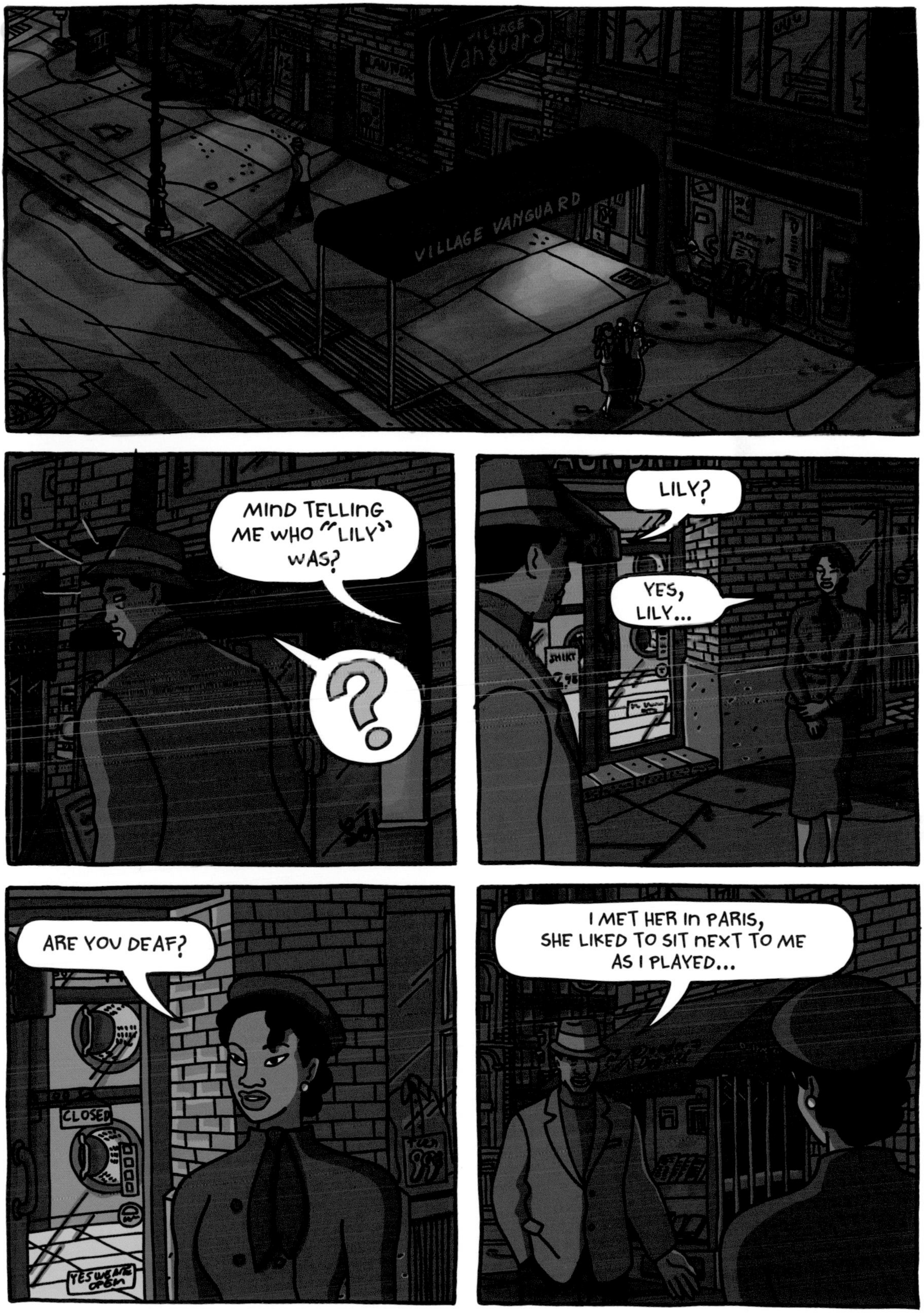
VILLAGE VANGUARD
VILLAGE VANGUARD
MIND TELLING ME WHO "LILY" WAS?
?
LILY?
YES, LILY...
ARE YOU DEAF?
CLOSED
I MET HER IN PARIS, SHE LIKED TO SIT NEXT TO ME AS I PLAYED...

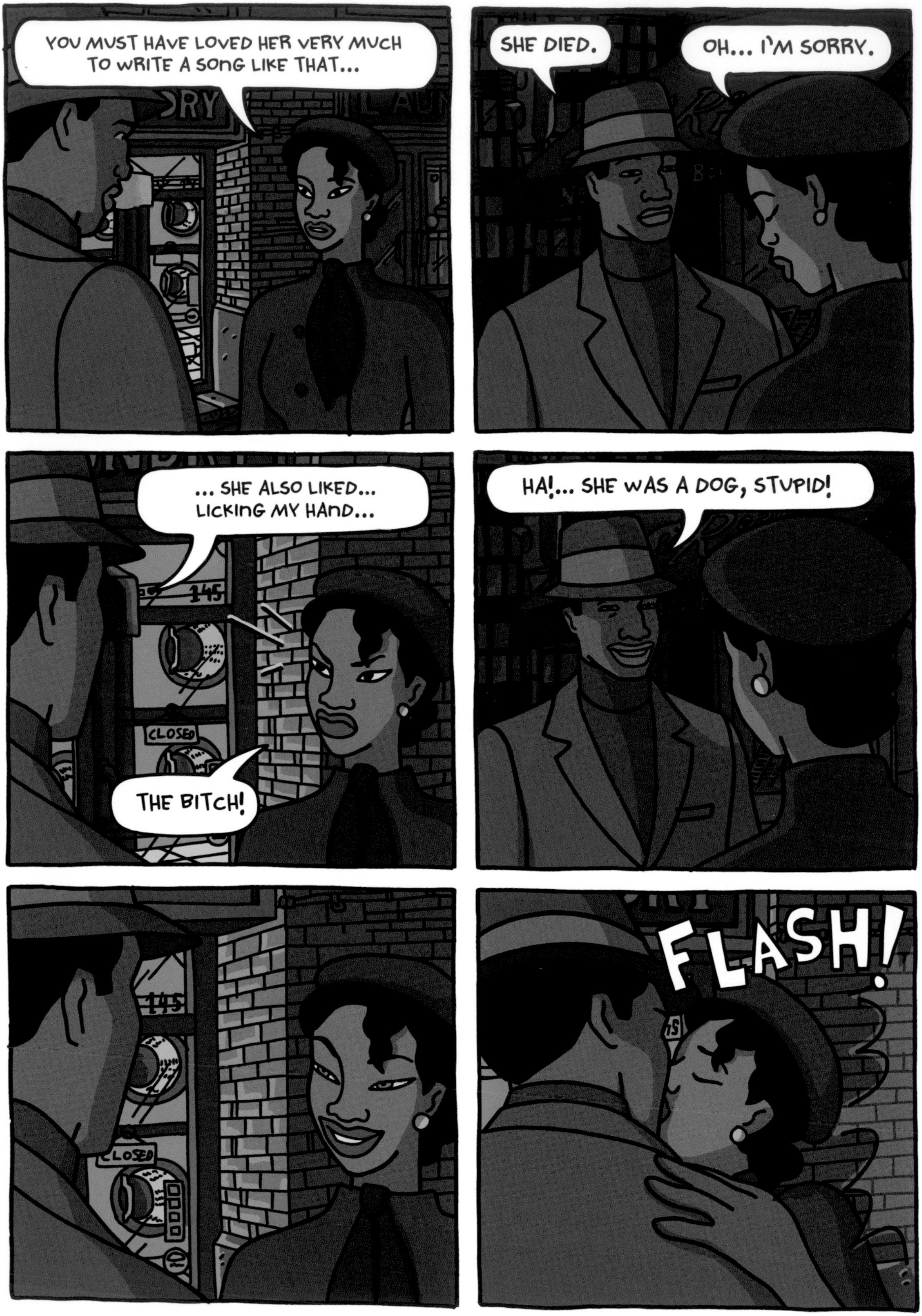
YOU MUST HAVE LOVED HER VERY MUCH TO WRITE A SONG LIKE THAT...
SHE DIED.
OH... I'M SORRY.
... SHE ALSO LIKED... LICKING MY HAND...
THE BITCH!
HA!... SHE WAS A DOG, STUPID!
CLOSED
FLASH!

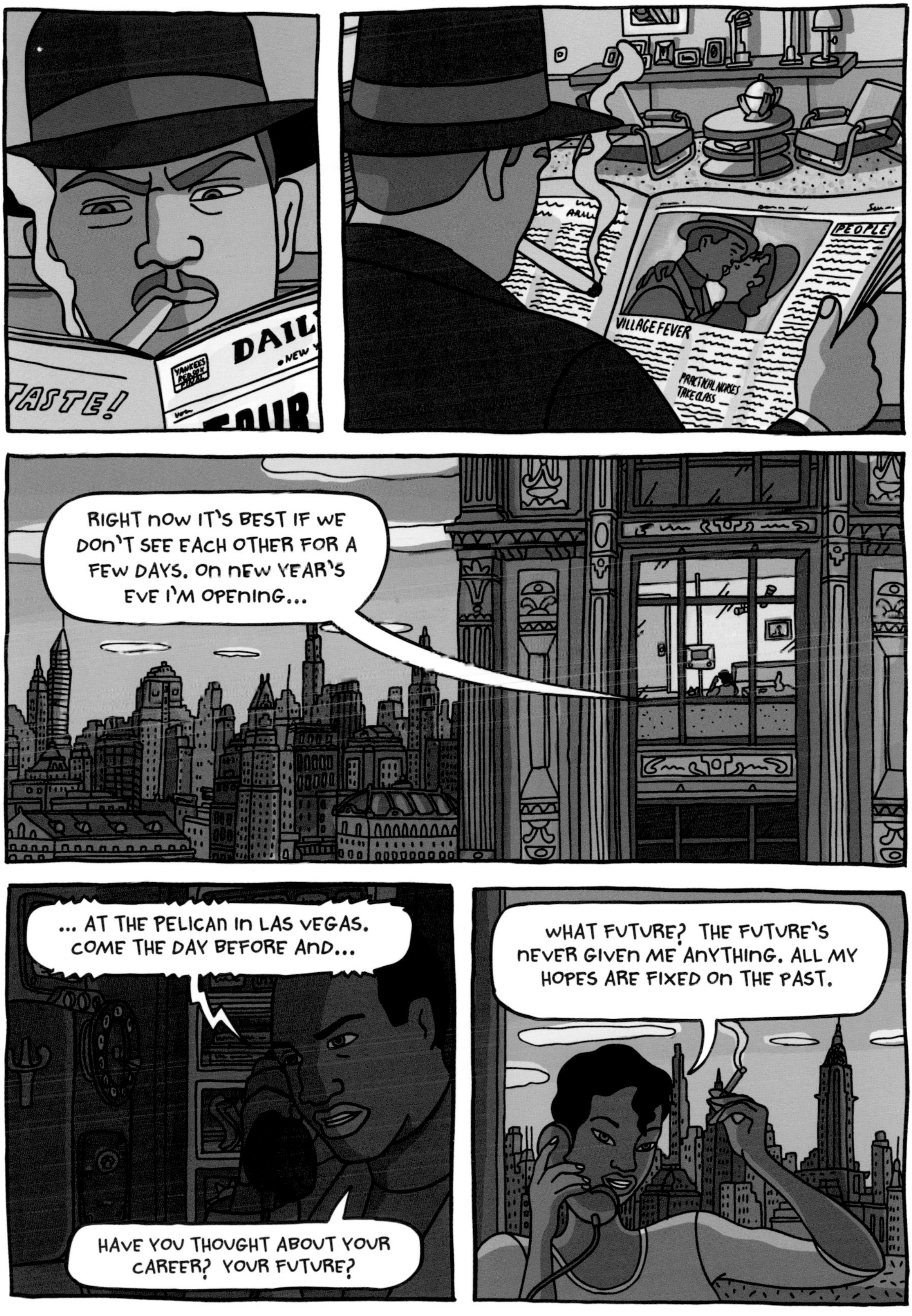
TASTE!
PEOPLE
VILLAGE FEVER
PRACTICAL NURSES TAKE CLASS
RIGHT NOW IT'S BEST IF WE DON'T SEE EACH OTHER FOR A FEW DAYS. ON NEW YEAR'S EVE I'M OPENING...
... AT THE PELICAN IN LAS VEGAS. COME THE DAY BEFORE AND...
HAVE YOU THOUGHT ABOUT YOUR CAREER? YOUR FUTURE?
WHAT FUTURE? THE FUTURE'S NEVER GIVEN ME ANYTHING. ALL MY HOPES ARE FIXED ON THE PAST.

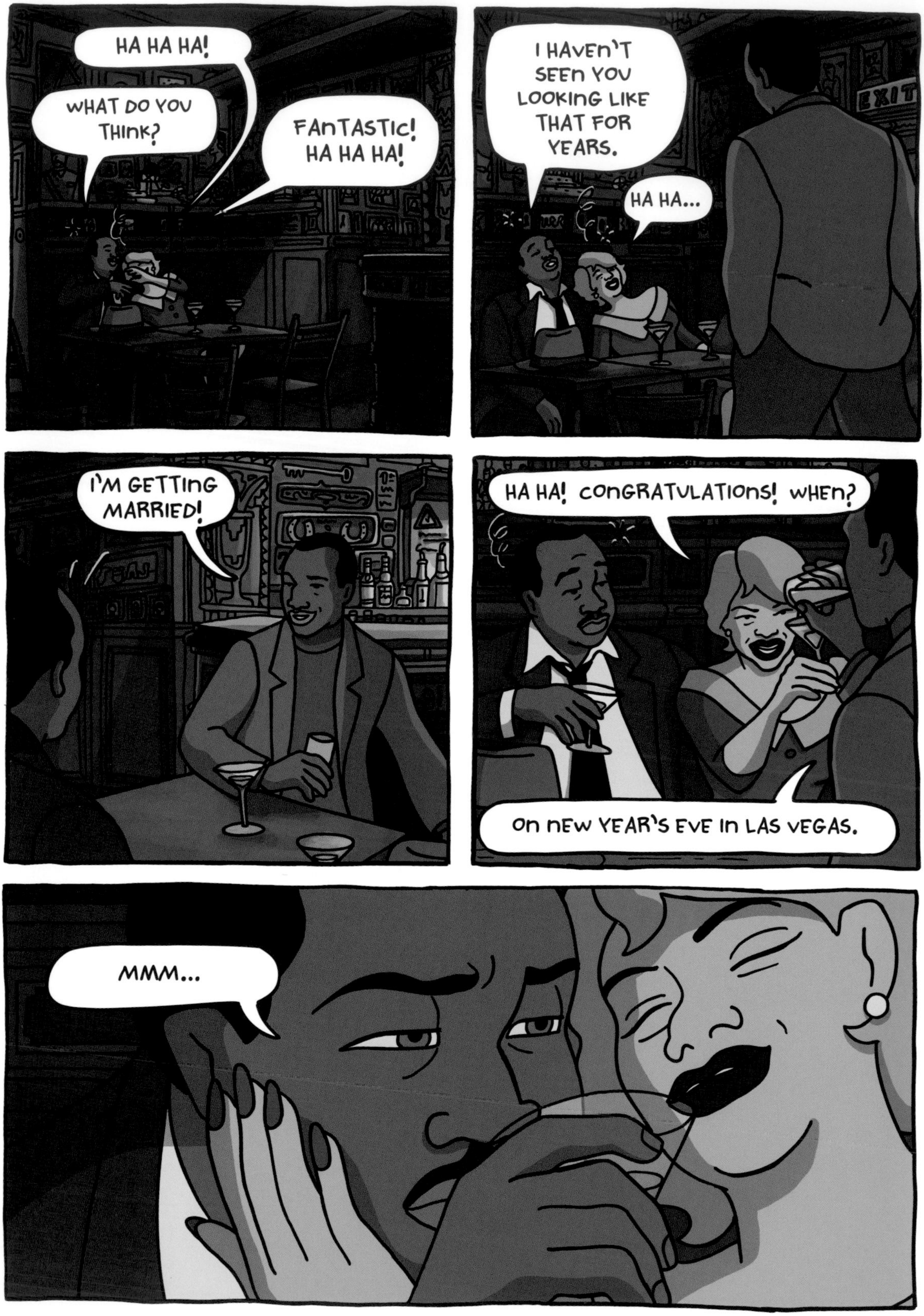
WHAT DO YOU THINK?
HA HA HA!
FANTASTIC! HA HA HA!
I HAVEN'T SEEN YOU LOOKING LIKE THAT FOR YEARS.
HA HA...
I'M GETTING MARRIED!
HA HA! CONGRATULATIONS! WHEN?
ON NEW YEAR'S EVE IN LAS VEGAS.
MMM...

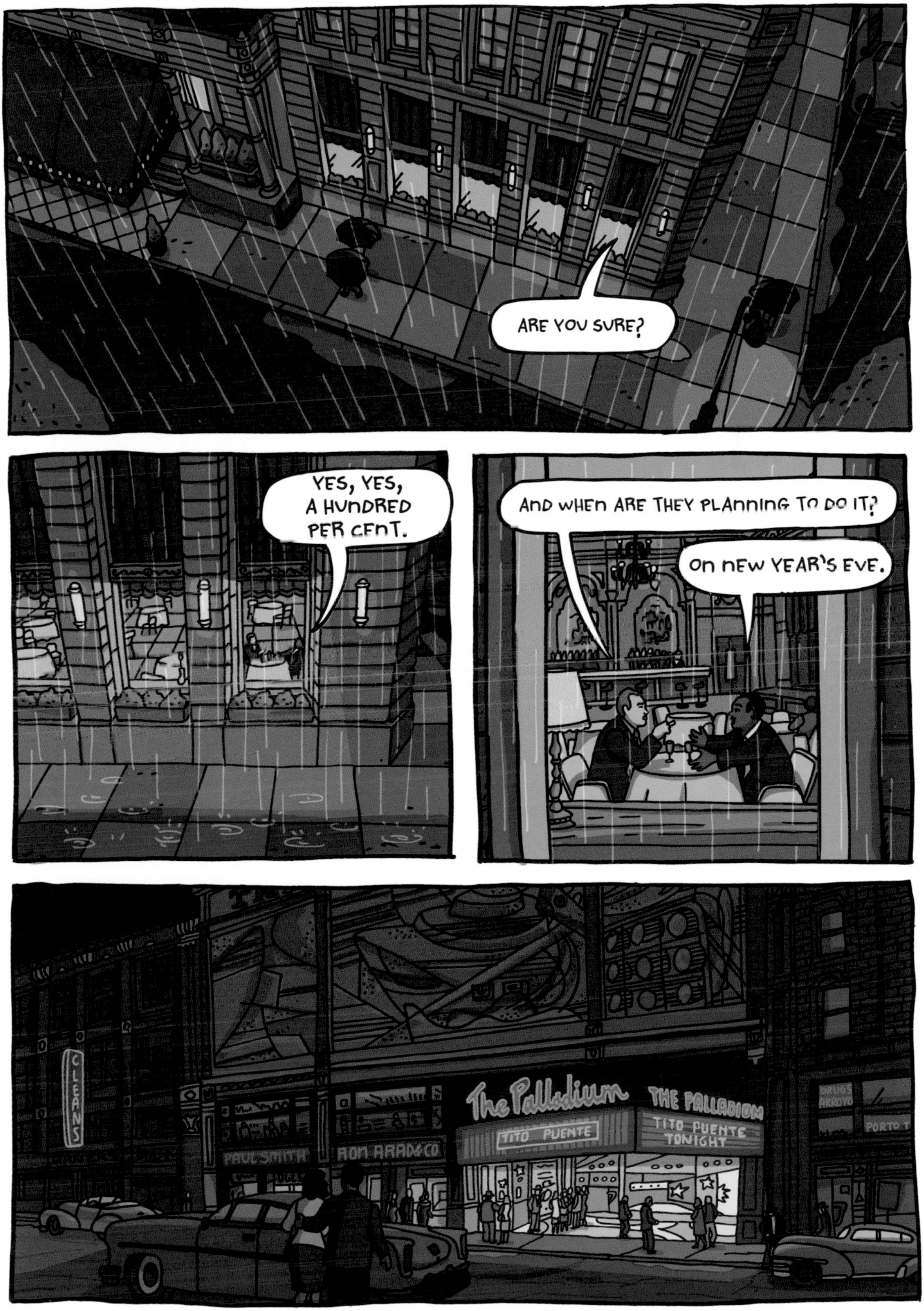
ARE YOU SURE?
YES, YES, A HUNDRED PER CENT.
AND WHEN ARE THEY PLANNING TO DO IT?
ON NEW YEAR'S EVE.
CLEANS
PAUL SMITH
RON ARAD & CO
The Palladium
TITO PUENTE
THE PALLADIUM
TITO PUENTE TONIGHT
DRUGS ARROYO
PORTO

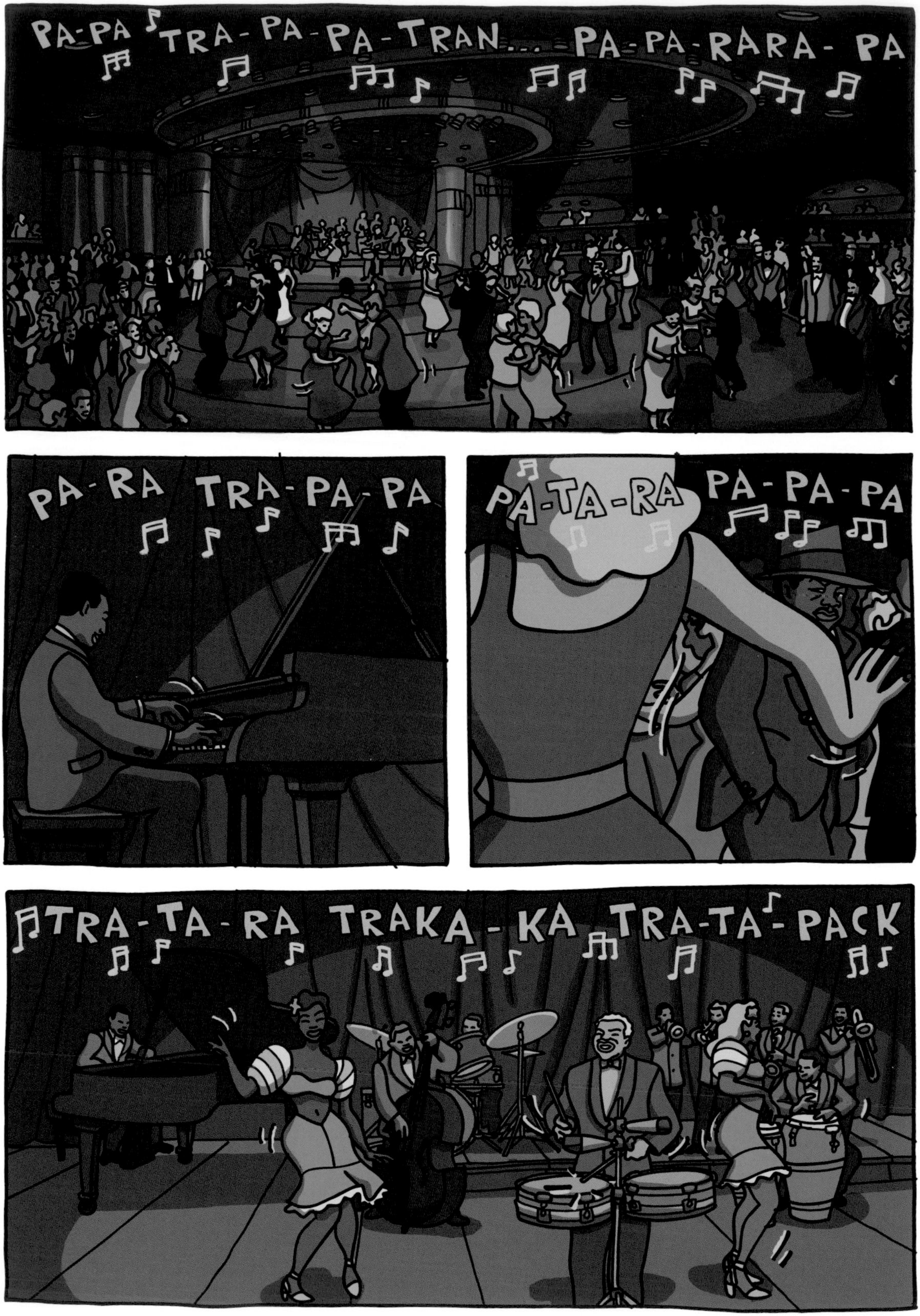
PA-PA TRA-PA-PA-TRAN... PA-PA-RARA-PA
PA-RA TRA-PA-PA
PA-TA-RA PA-PA-PA
TRA-TA-RA TRAKA-KA TRA-TA-PACK

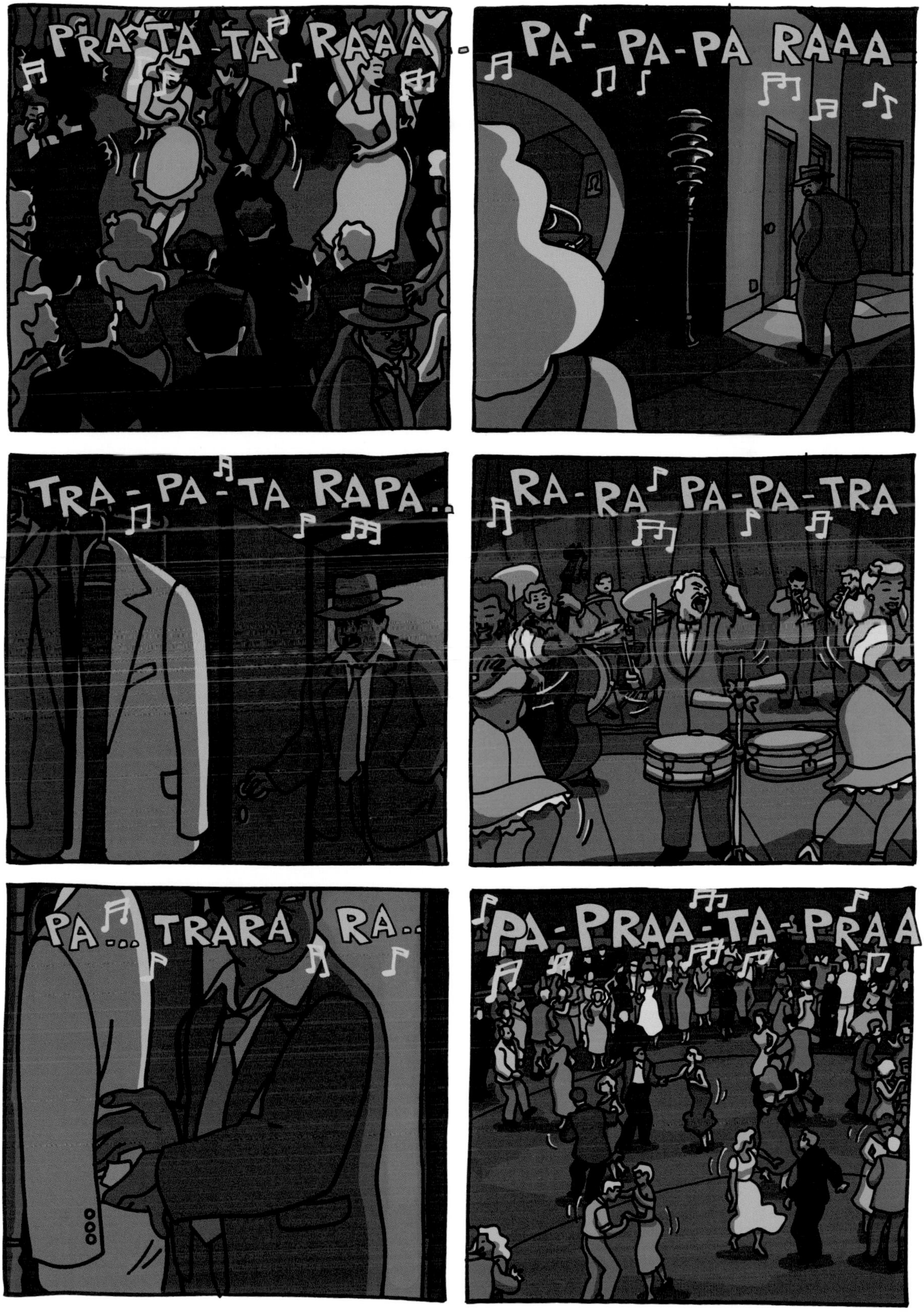
PRA-TA-TA RAAA..
PA-PA-PA RAAA
TRA-PA-TA RAPA..
RA-RA PA-PA-TRA
PA... TRARA RA..
PA-PRAA-TA-PRAA

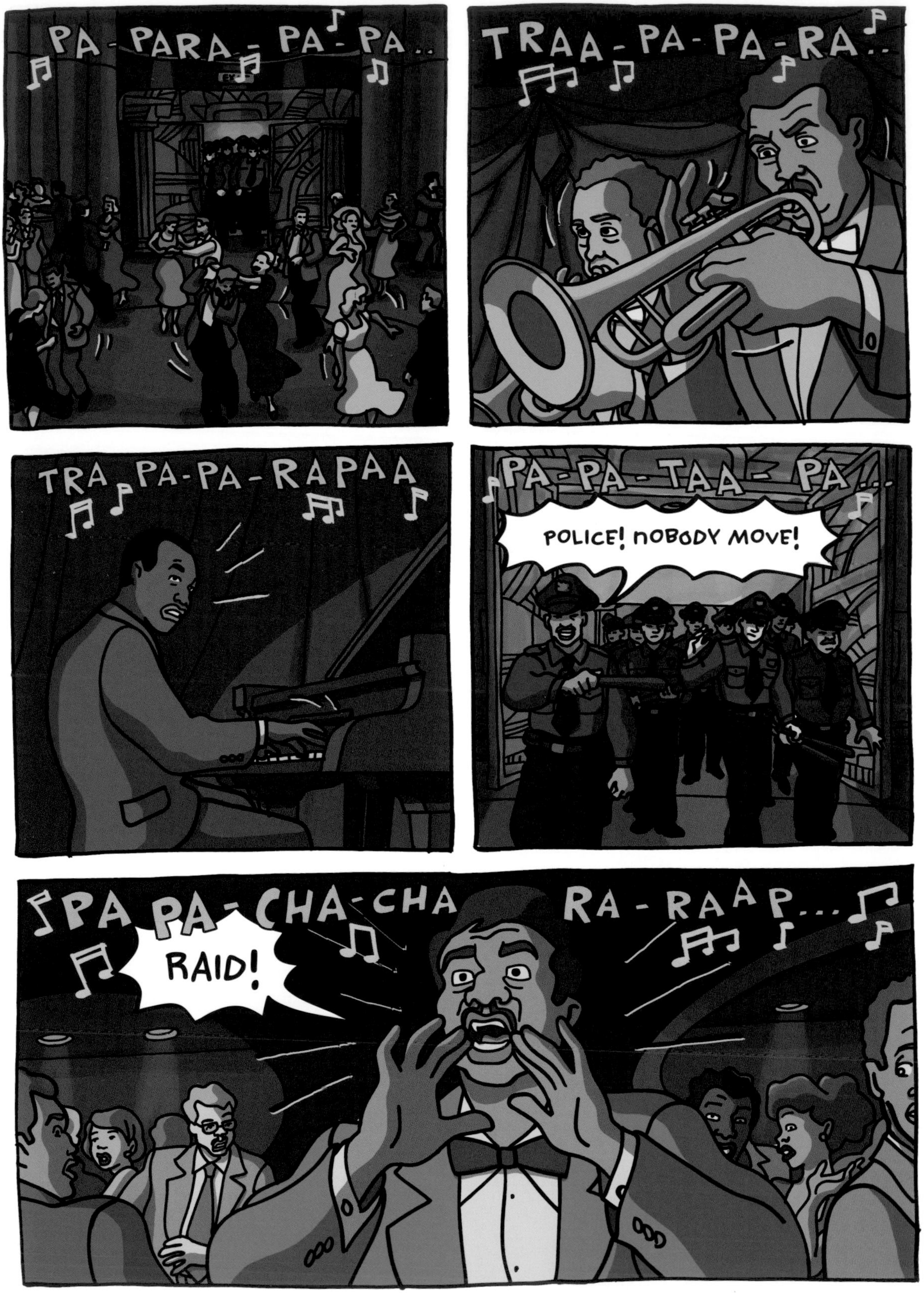
PA-PARA-PA-PA..
TRAA-PA-PA-RA..
TRA-PA-PA-RAPAA
PA-PA-TAA-PA...
POLICE! NOBODY MOVE!
PA PA-CHA-CHA
RAID!
RA-RAAP...

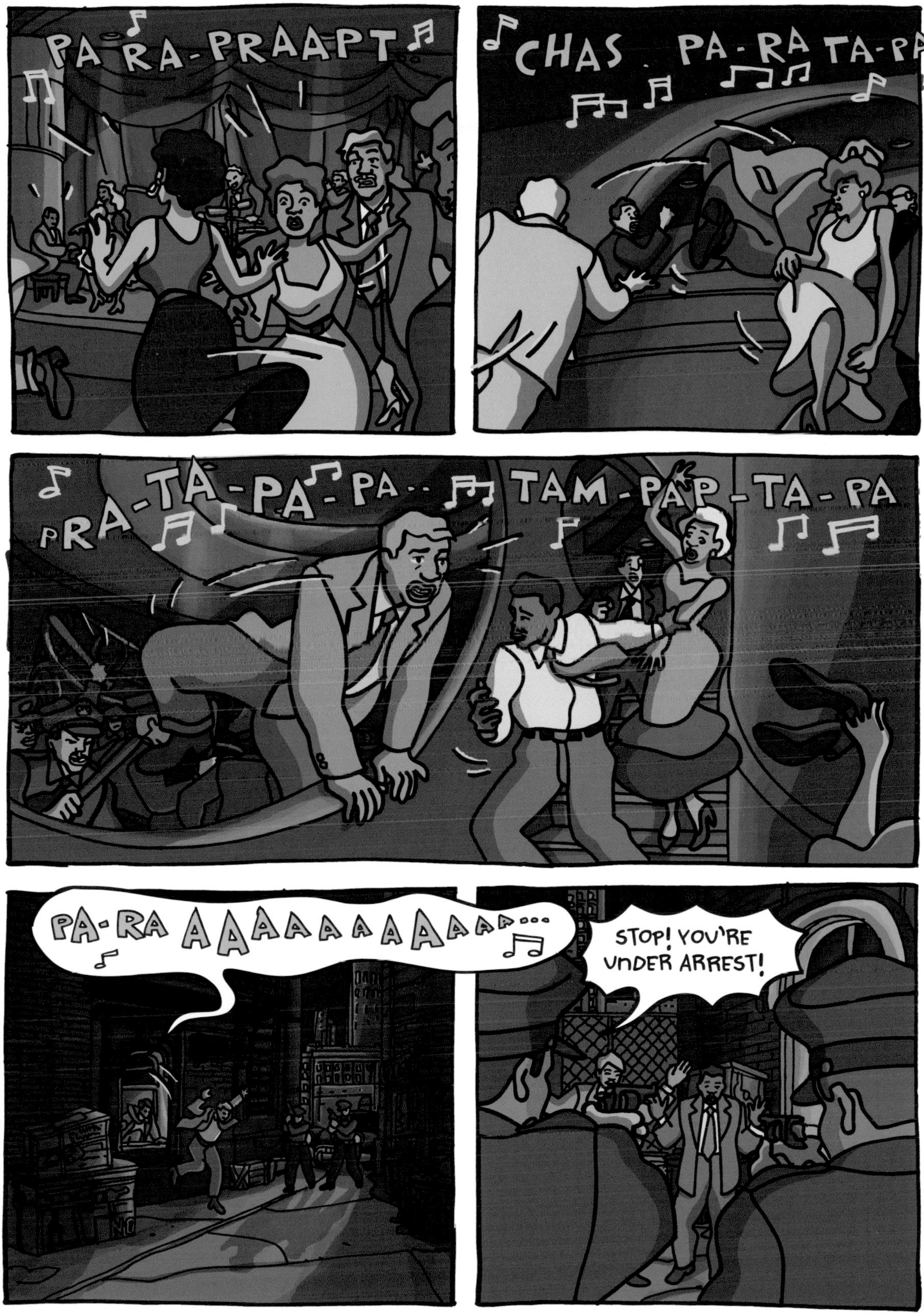
PA RA-PRAAPT
CHAS . PA-RA TA-PA
PRA-TA-PA-PA.. TAM-PAP-TA-PA
PA-RA AAAAAAAAAA...
STOP! YOU'RE UNDER ARREST!

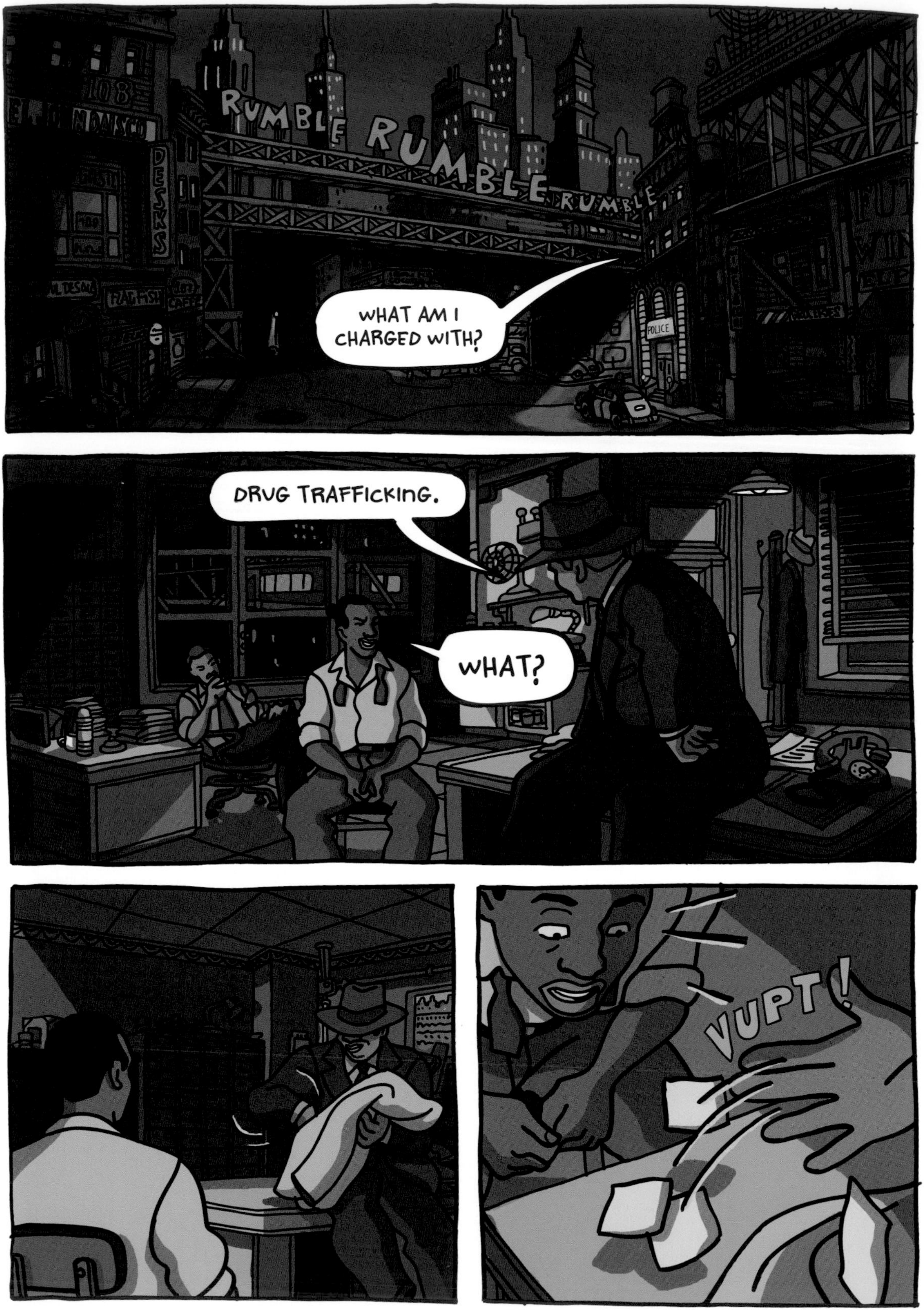
RUMBLE RUMBLE RUMBLE RUMBLE
DESKS
POLICE
WHAT AM I CHARGED WITH?
DRUG TRAFFICKING.
WHAT?
VUPT!

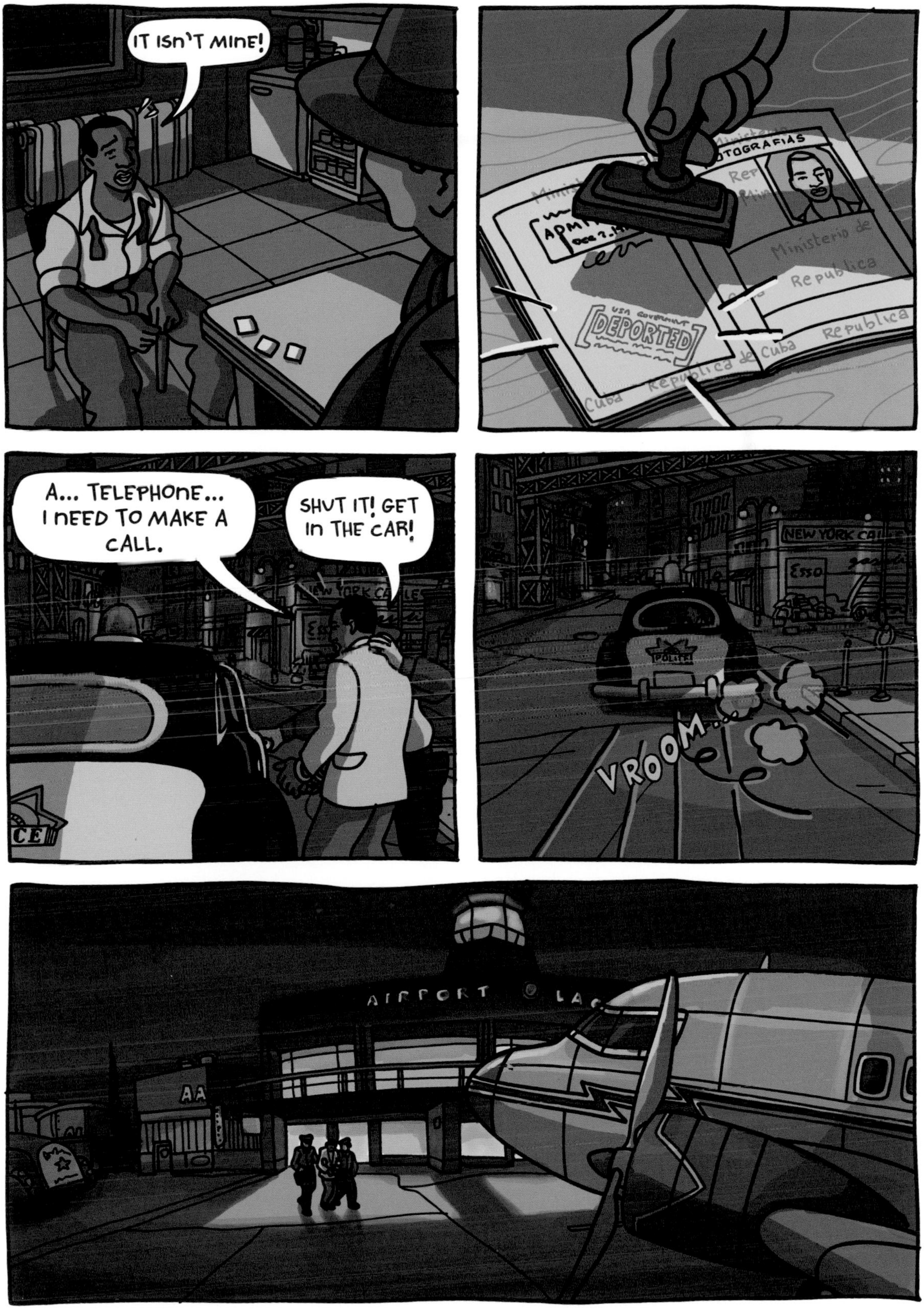
IT ISN'T MINE!
Ministerio de
Republica
USA GOVERNMENT
DEPORTED
Republica de Cuba
Republica
Cuba
A... TELEPHONE... I NEED TO MAKE A CALL.
SHUT IT! GET IN THE CAR!
Esso
VROOM...
AIRPORT
AA

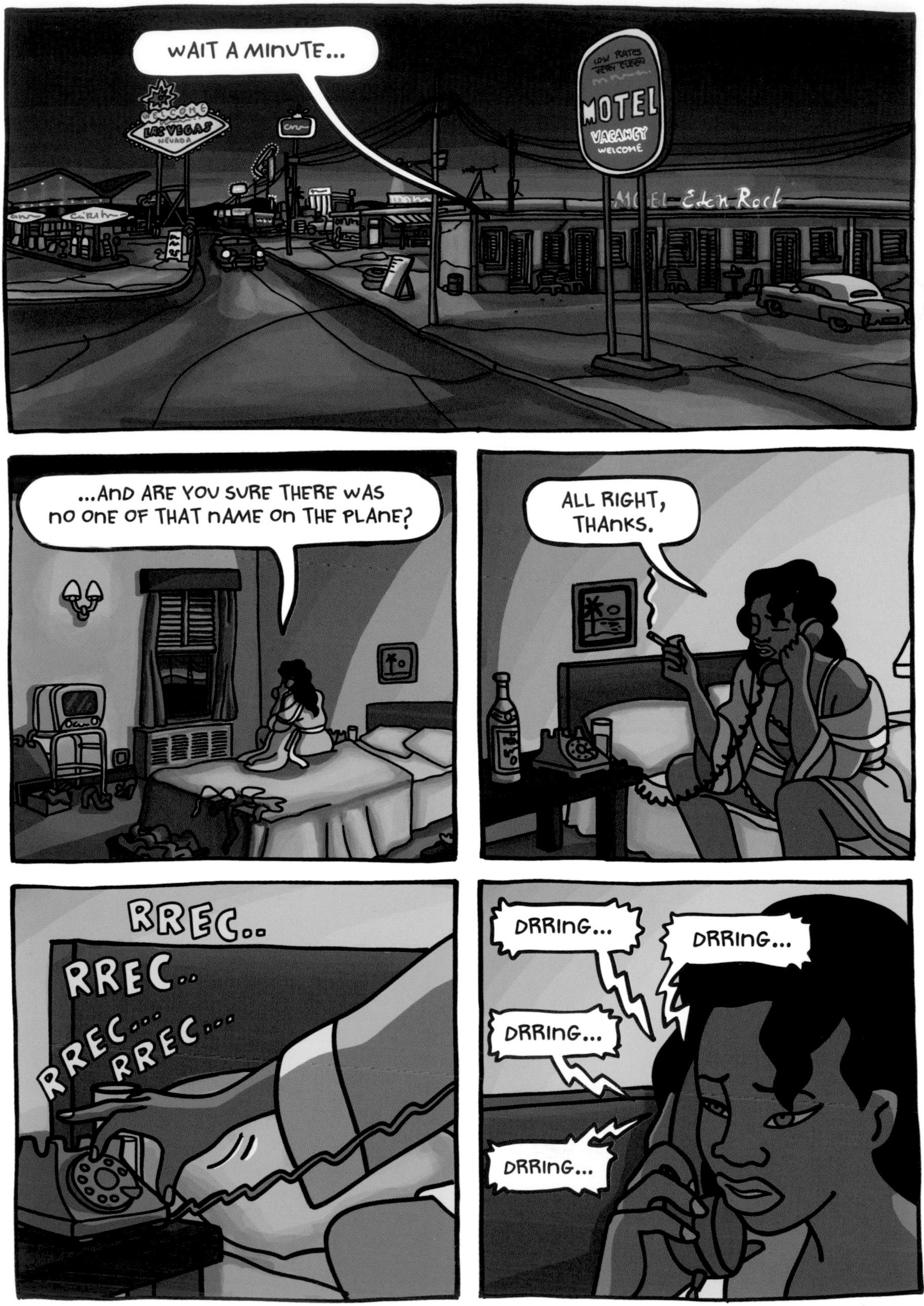

WAIT A MINUTE...
MOTEL
VACANCY
WELCOME
MOTEL Eden Rock
WELCOME LAS VEGAS NEVADA
...AND ARE YOU SURE THERE WAS NO ONE OF THAT NAME ON THE PLANE?
ALL RIGHT, THANKS.
RREC..
RREC..
RREC...
RREC...
DRRING...
DRRING...
DRRING...
DRRING...

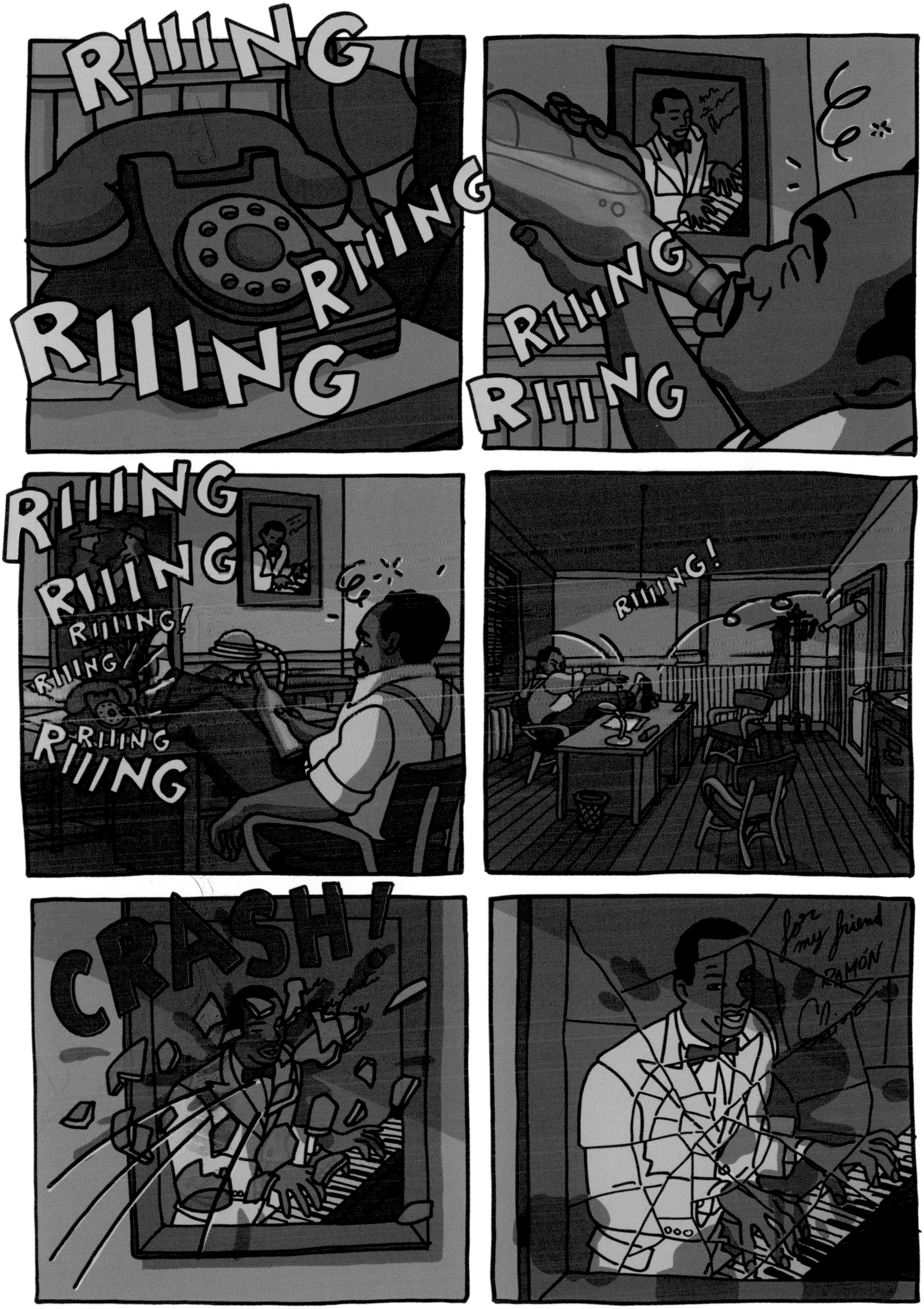
RIIING
RIIING
RIIING
RIIING
RIIING
RIIING
RIIING
RIIING!
RIIING
RIIING
RIIING
RIIING
RIIIING!
CRASH!
for my friend
RAMÓN

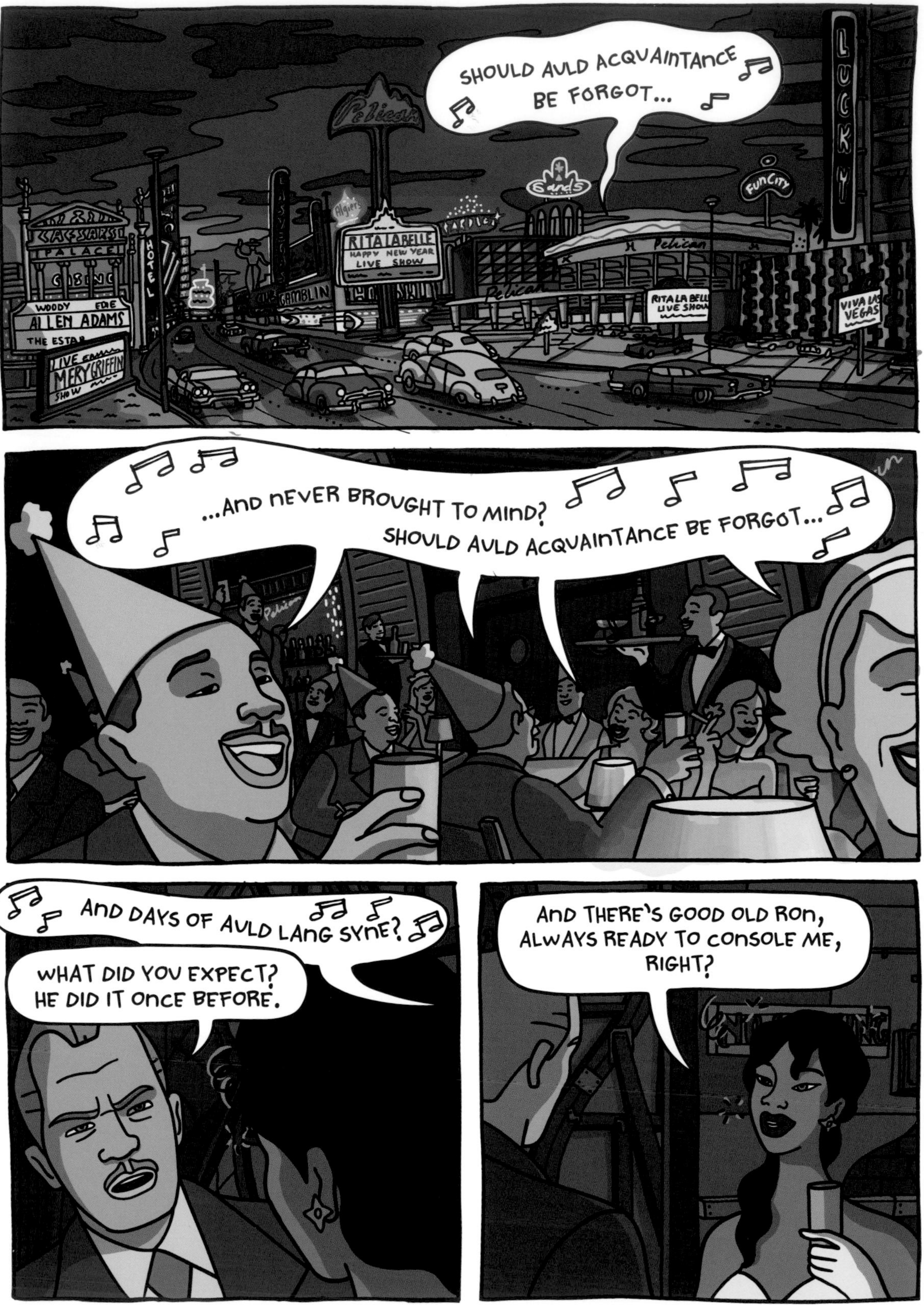

SHOULD AULD ACQUAINTANCE BE FORGOT...
CAESARS PALACE CASINO
WOODY EDIE ALLEN ADAMS
LIVE MERV GRIFFIN SHOW
HOTEL
GAMBLING
RITA LABELLE HAPPY NEW YEAR LIVE SHOW
Pelican
Sands
FUN CITY
LUCKY
RITA LA BELLE LIVE SHOW
VIVA LAS VEGAS
...AND NEVER BROUGHT TO MIND? SHOULD AULD ACQUAINTANCE BE FORGOT...
AND DAYS OF AULD LANG SYNE?
WHAT DID YOU EXPECT? HE DID IT ONCE BEFORE.
AND THERE'S GOOD OLD RON, ALWAYS READY TO CONSOLE ME, RIGHT?

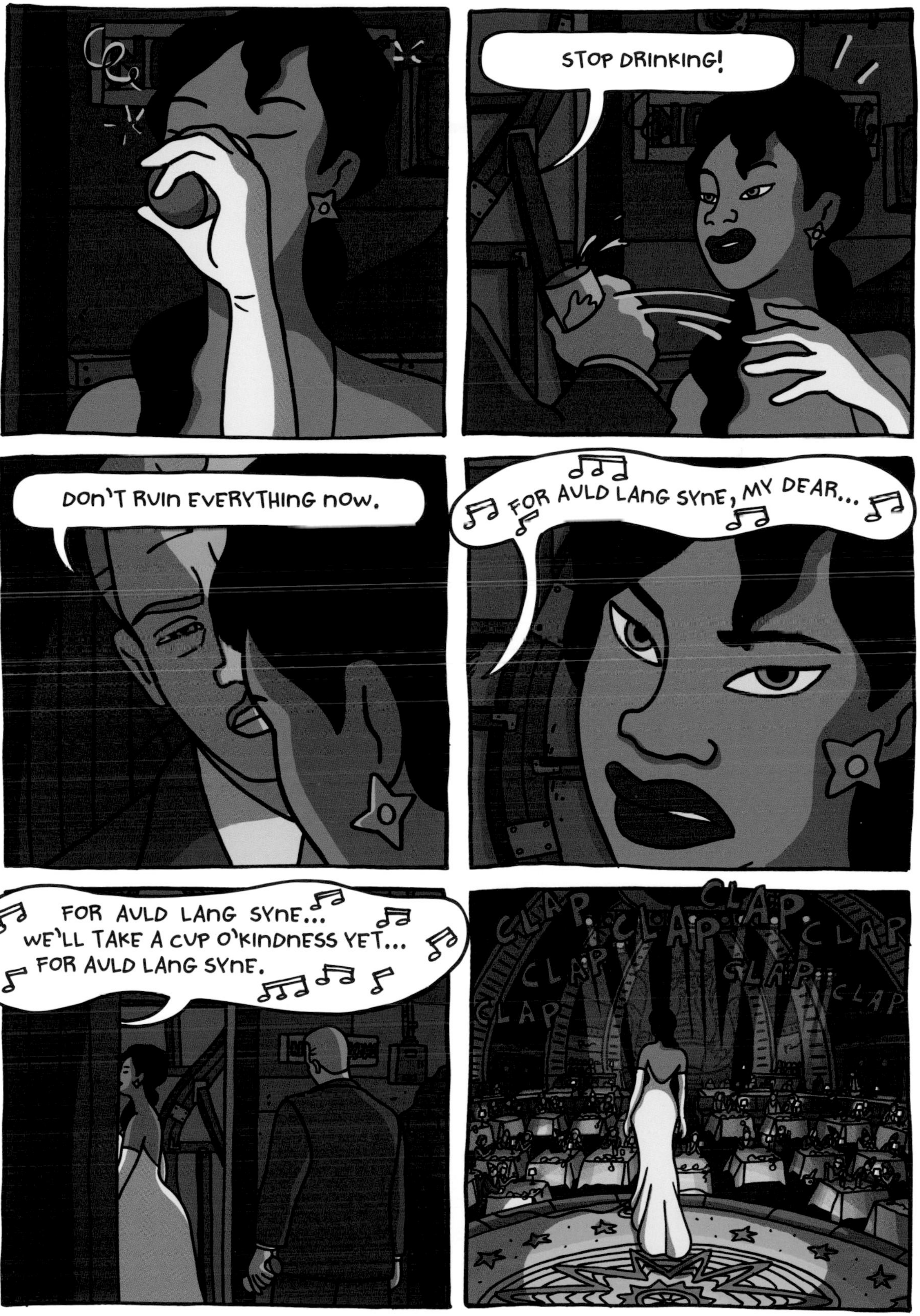
STOP DRINKING!
DON'T RUIN EVERYTHING NOW.
FOR AULD LANG SYNE, MY DEAR...
FOR AULD LANG SYNE... WE'LL TAKE A CUP O'KINDNESS YET... FOR AULD LANG SYNE.
CLAP CLAP CLAP CLAP CLAP CLAP CLAP CLAP CLAP CLAP

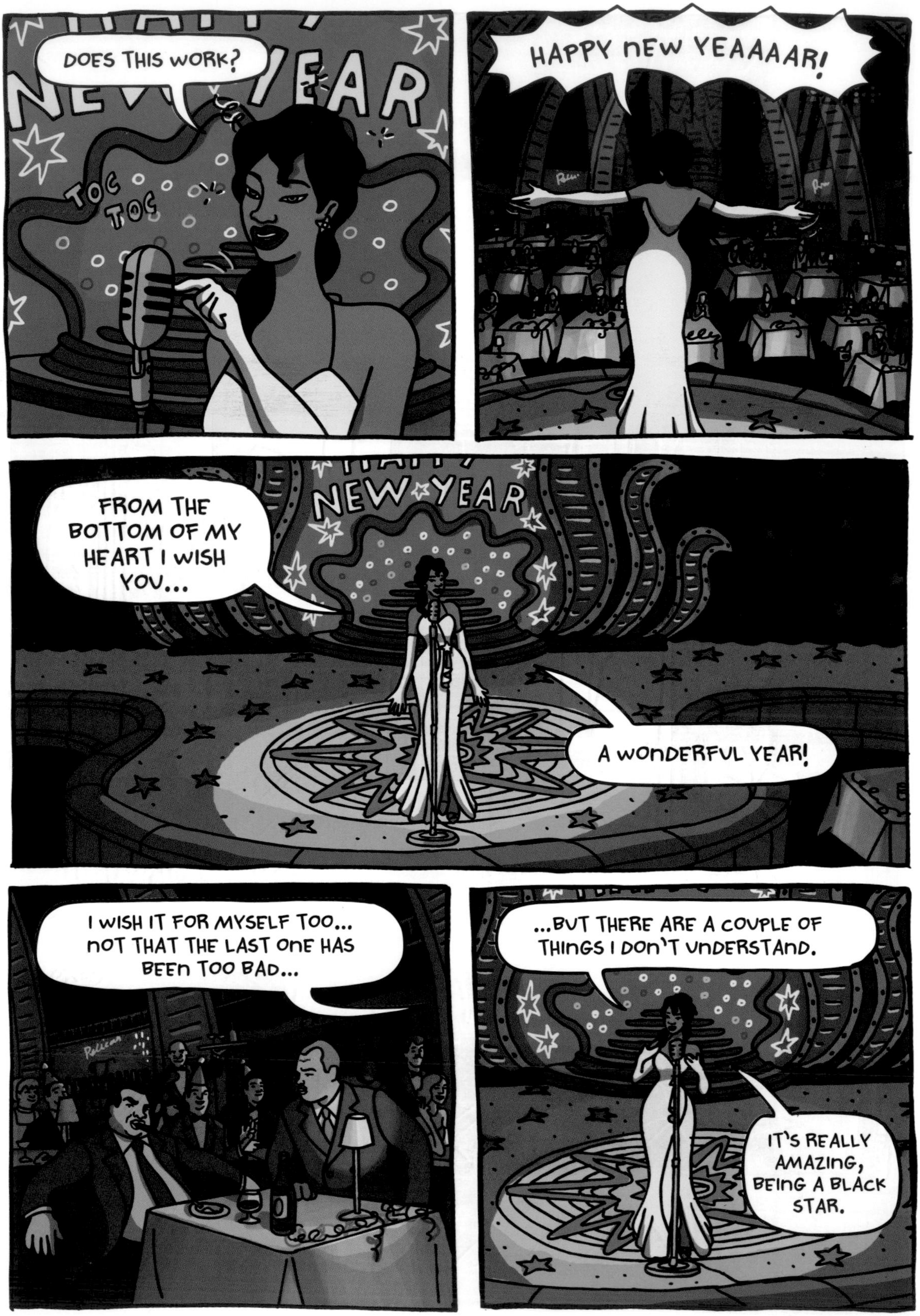
DOES THIS WORK?
TOC TOC
HAPPY NEW YEAAAAR!
HAPPY NEW YEAR
FROM THE BOTTOM OF MY HEART I WISH YOU...
A WONDERFUL YEAR!
I WISH IT FOR MYSELF TOO... NOT THAT THE LAST ONE HAS BEEN TOO BAD...
...BUT THERE ARE A COUPLE OF THINGS I DON'T UNDERSTAND.
IT'S REALLY AMAZING, BEING A BLACK STAR.

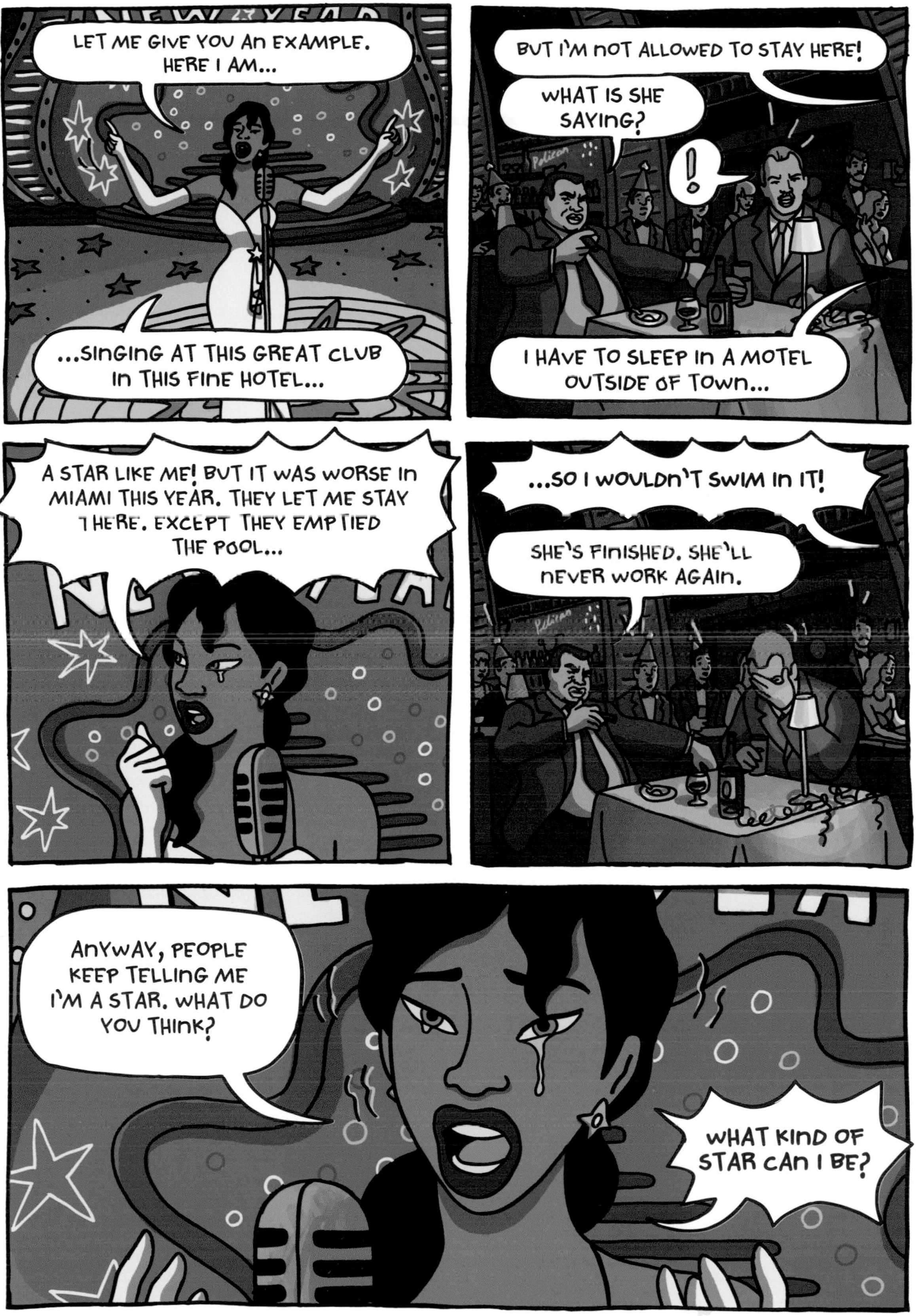
LET ME GIVE YOU AN EXAMPLE. HERE I AM...
...SINGING AT THIS GREAT CLUB IN THIS FINE HOTEL...
BUT I'M NOT ALLOWED TO STAY HERE!
WHAT IS SHE SAYING?
!
I HAVE TO SLEEP IN A MOTEL OUTSIDE OF TOWN...
A STAR LIKE ME! BUT IT WAS WORSE IN MIAMI THIS YEAR. THEY LET ME STAY THERE. EXCEPT THEY EMPTIED THE POOL...
...SO I WOULDN'T SWIM IN IT!
SHE'S FINISHED. SHE'LL NEVER WORK AGAIN.
ANYWAY, PEOPLE KEEP TELLING ME I'M A STAR. WHAT DO YOU THINK?
WHAT KIND OF STAR CAN I BE?

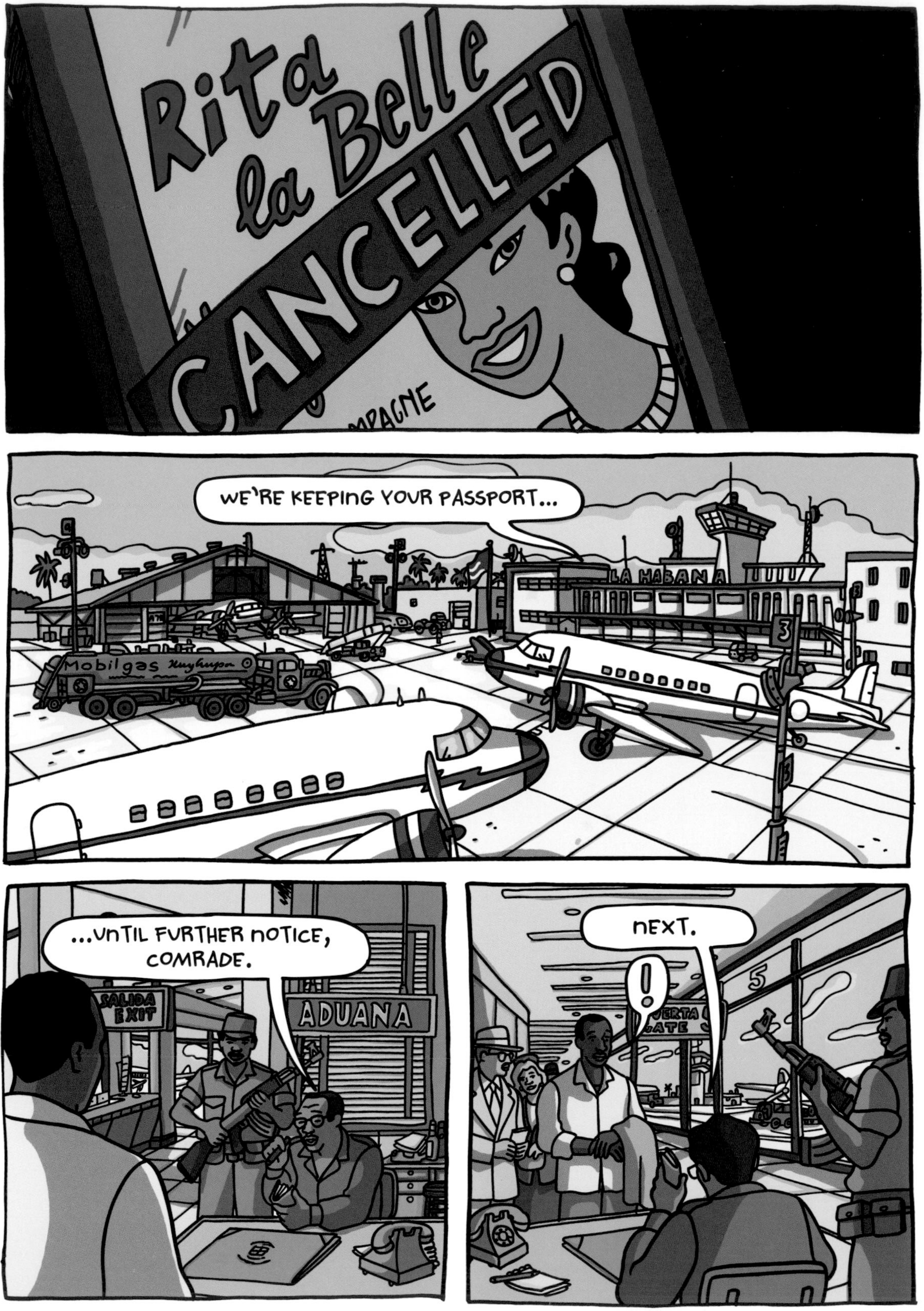
Rita la Belle
CANCELLED
WE'RE KEEPING YOUR PASSPORT...
LA HABANA
Mobilgas
...UNTIL FURTHER NOTICE, COMRADE.
SALIDA EXIT
ADUANA
NEXT.
!

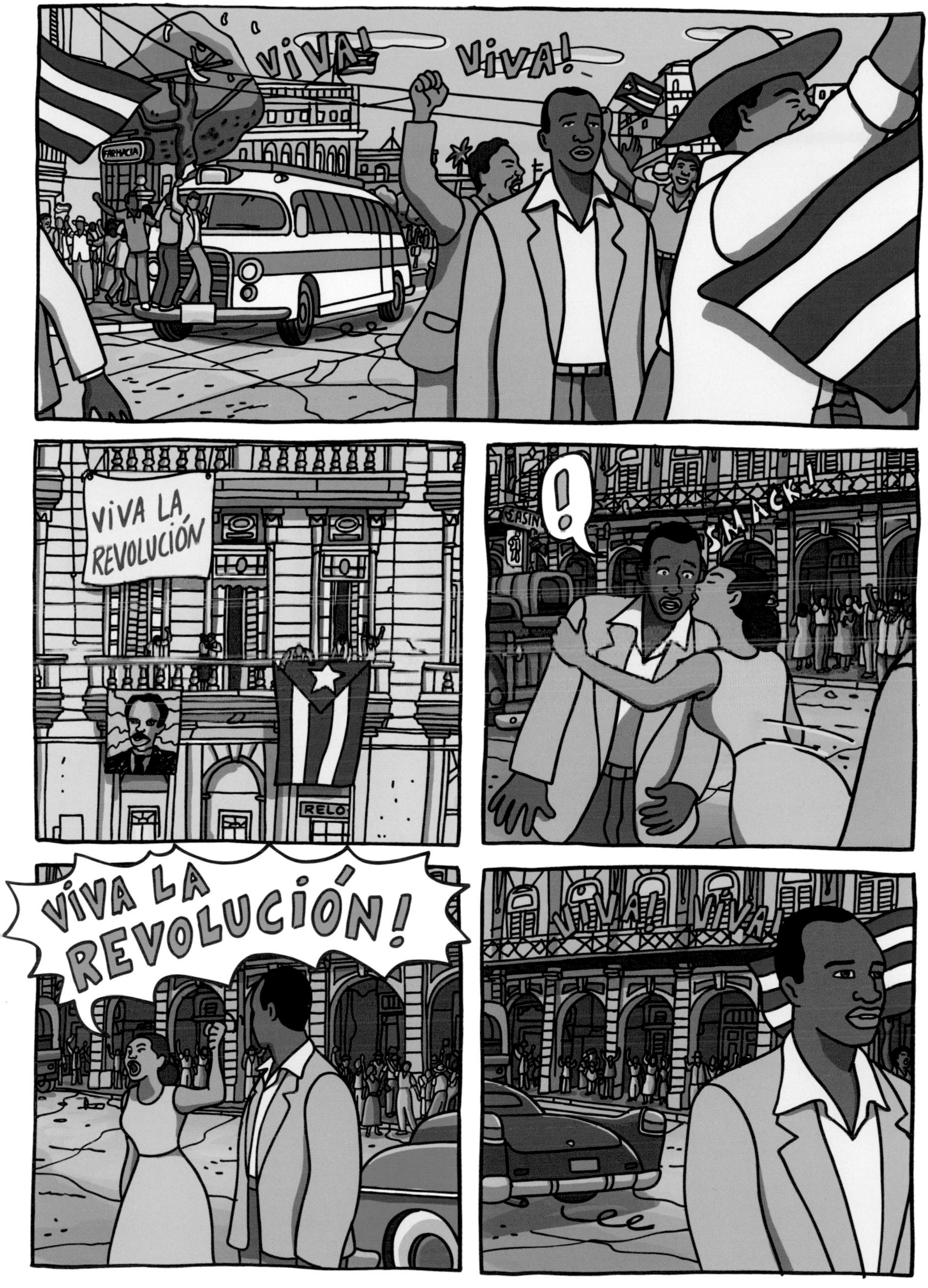
VIVA!
VIVA!
FARMACIA
VIVA LA REVOLUCIÓN
RELO
!
SMACK!
VIVA LA REVOLUCIÓN!
VIVA! VIVA

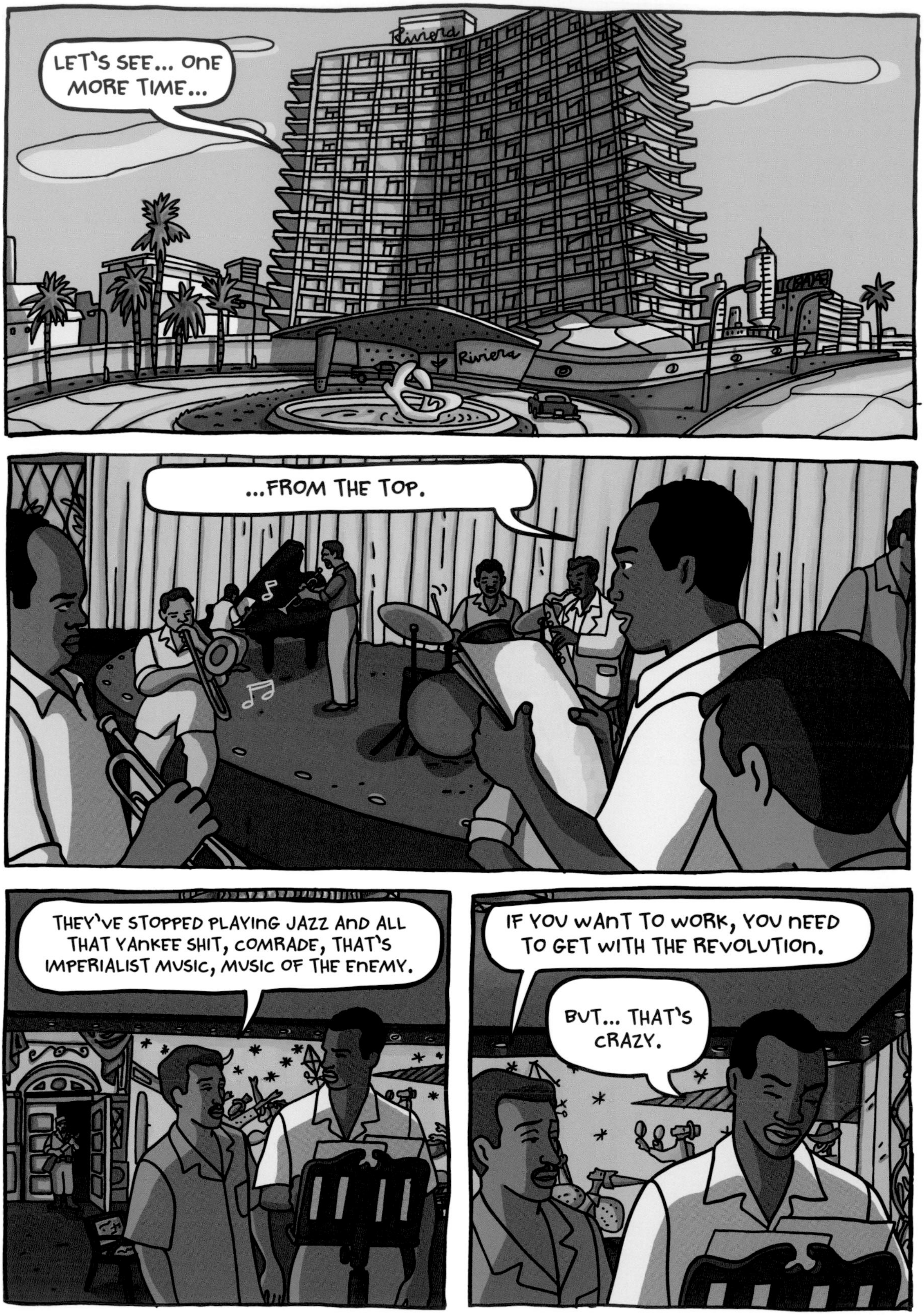

Riviera
LET'S SEE... ONE MORE TIME...
Riviera
...FROM THE TOP.
THEY'VE STOPPED PLAYING JAZZ AND ALL THAT YANKEE SHIT, COMRADE, THAT'S IMPERIALIST MUSIC, MUSIC OF THE ENEMY.
IF YOU WANT TO WORK, YOU NEED TO GET WITH THE REVOLUTION.
BUT... THAT'S CRAZY.

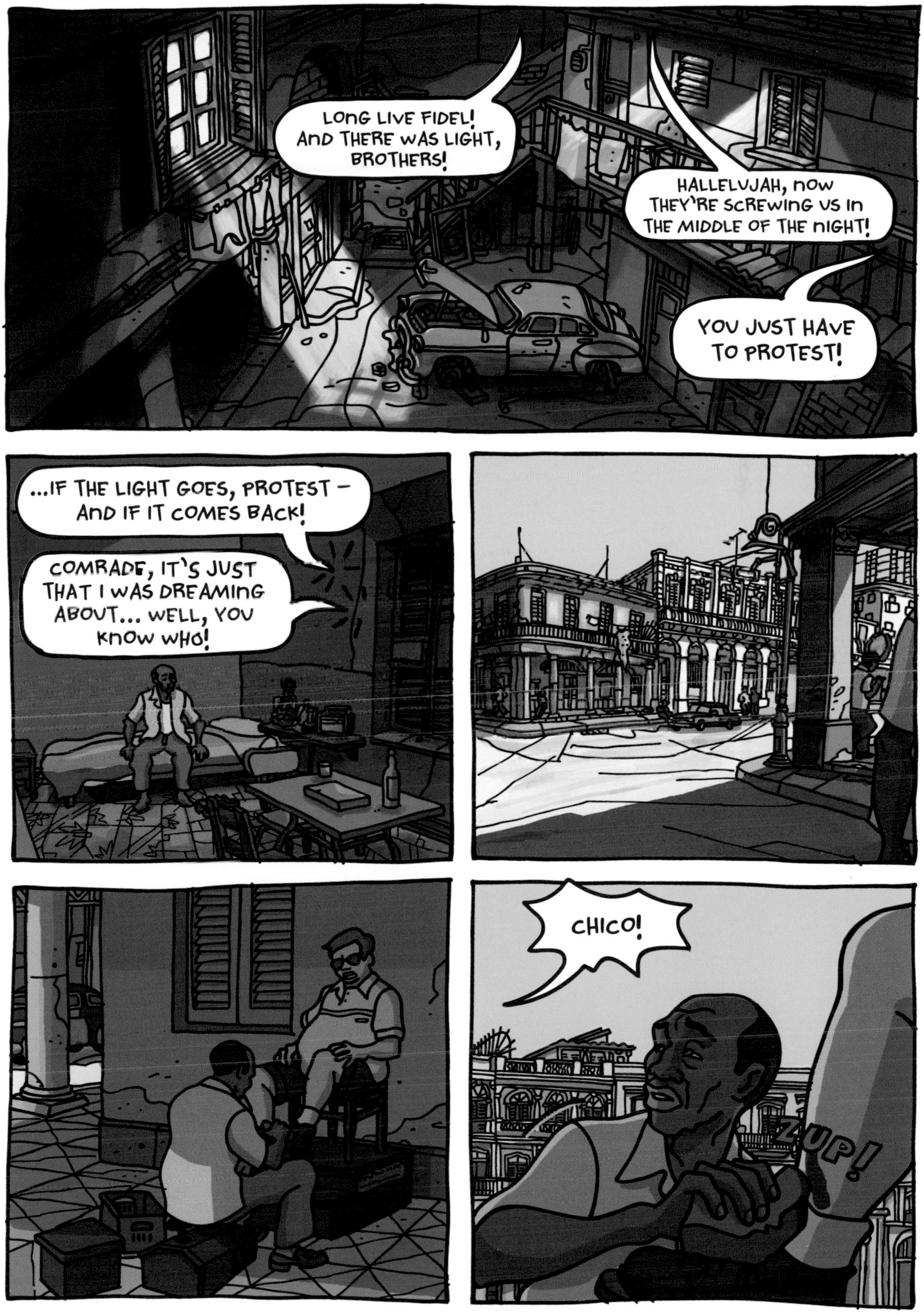
LONG LIVE FIDEL! AND THERE WAS LIGHT, BROTHERS!
HALLELUJAH, NOW THEY'RE SCREWING US IN THE MIDDLE OF THE NIGHT!
YOU JUST HAVE TO PROTEST!
...IF THE LIGHT GOES, PROTEST – AND IF IT COMES BACK!
COMRADE, IT'S JUST THAT I WAS DREAMING ABOUT... WELL, YOU KNOW WHO!
CHICO!
ZUP!

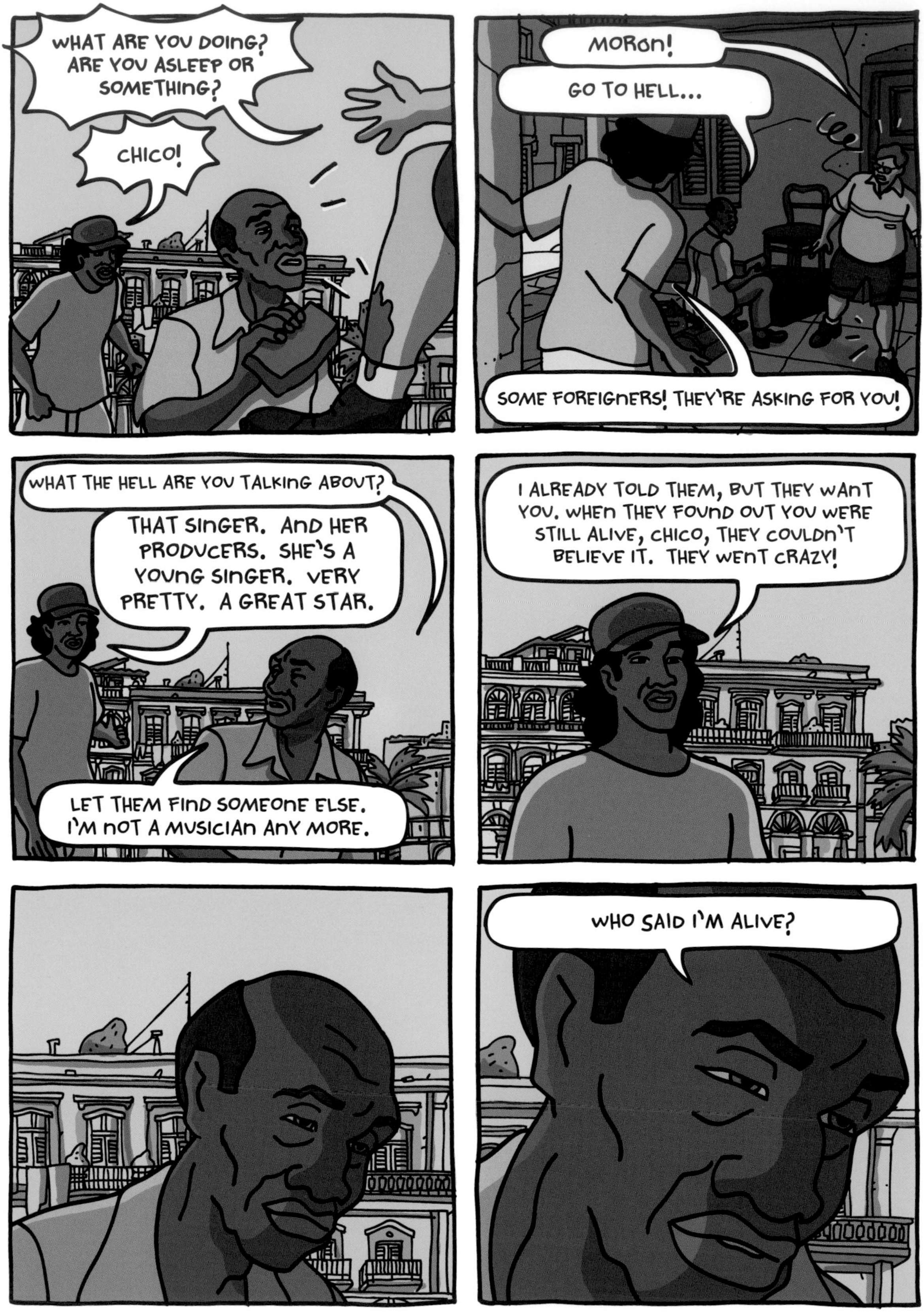
WHAT ARE YOU DOING? ARE YOU ASLEEP OR SOMETHING?
CHICO!
MORON!
GO TO HELL...
SOME FOREIGNERS! THEY'RE ASKING FOR YOU!
WHAT THE HELL ARE YOU TALKING ABOUT?
THAT SINGER. AND HER PRODUCERS. SHE'S A YOUNG SINGER. VERY PRETTY. A GREAT STAR.
LET THEM FIND SOMEONE ELSE. I'M NOT A MUSICIAN ANY MORE.
I ALREADY TOLD THEM, BUT THEY WANT YOU. WHEN THEY FOUND OUT YOU WERE STILL ALIVE, CHICO, THEY COULDN'T BELIEVE IT. THEY WENT CRAZY!
WHO SAID I'M ALIVE?

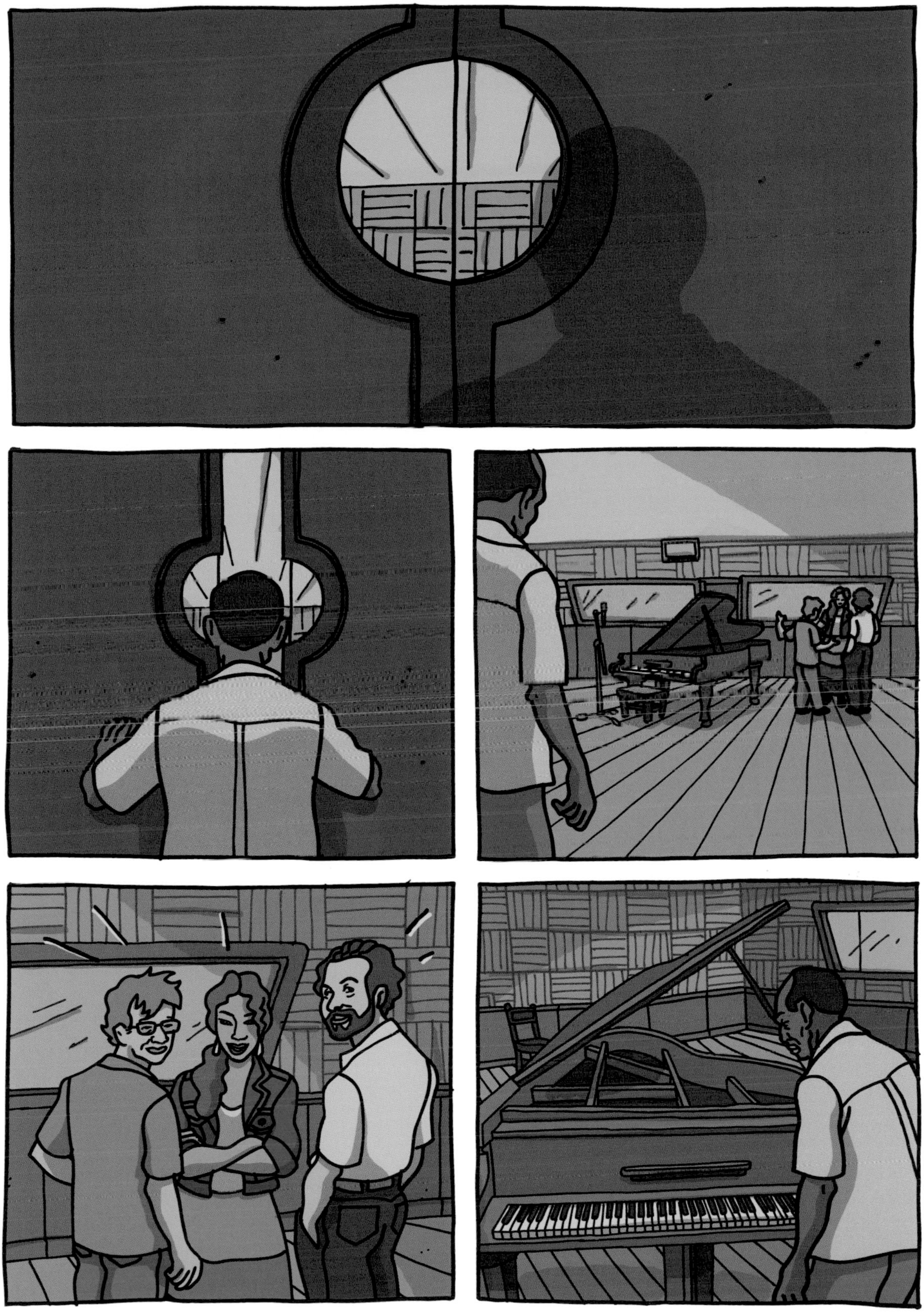

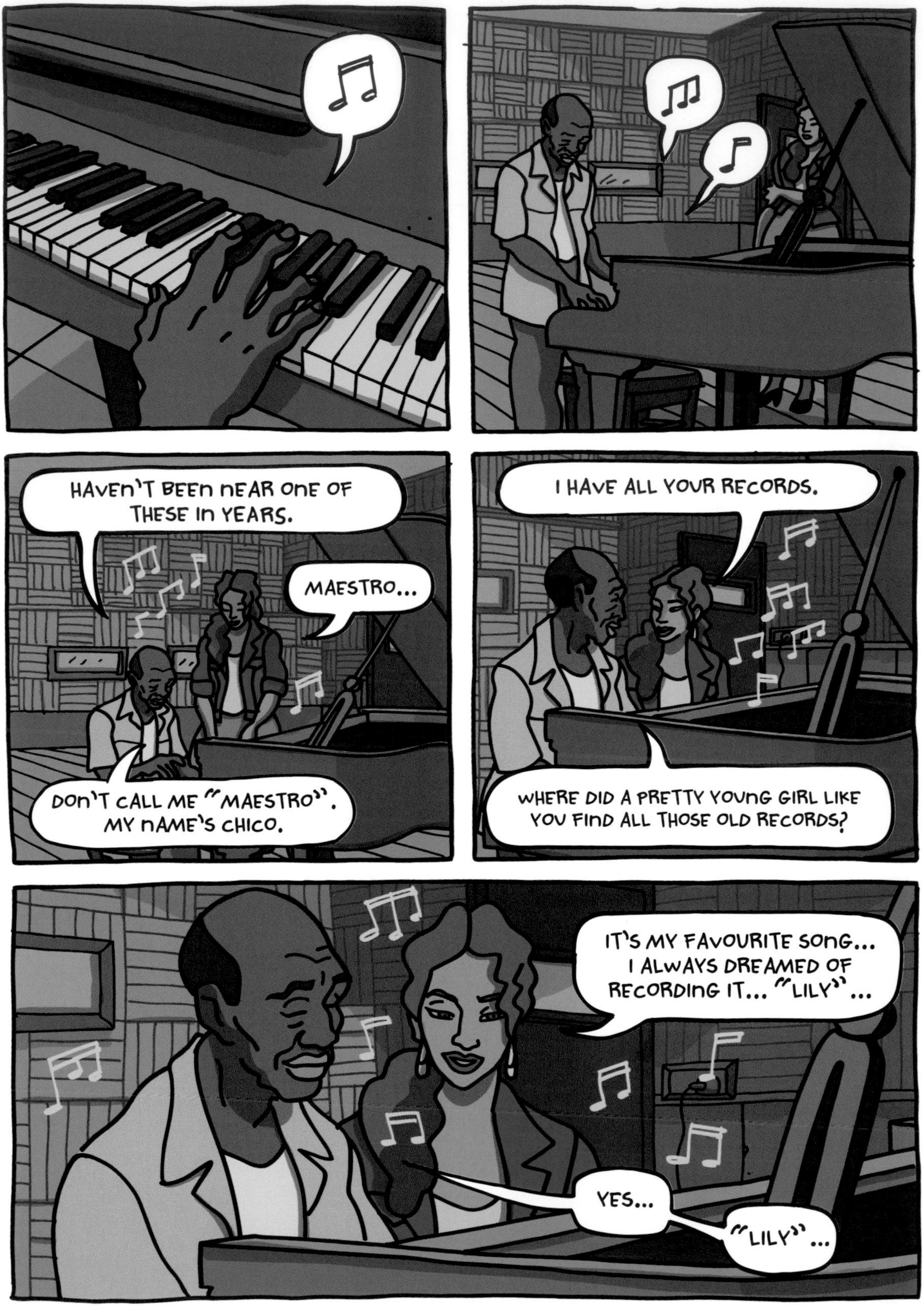
HAVEN'T BEEN NEAR ONE OF THESE IN YEARS.
MAESTRO...
DON'T CALL ME "MAESTRO". MY NAME'S CHICO.
I HAVE ALL YOUR RECORDS.
WHERE DID A PRETTY YOUNG GIRL LIKE YOU FIND ALL THOSE OLD RECORDS?
IT'S MY FAVOURITE SONG... I ALWAYS DREAMED OF RECORDING IT... "LILY"...
YES...
"LILY"...

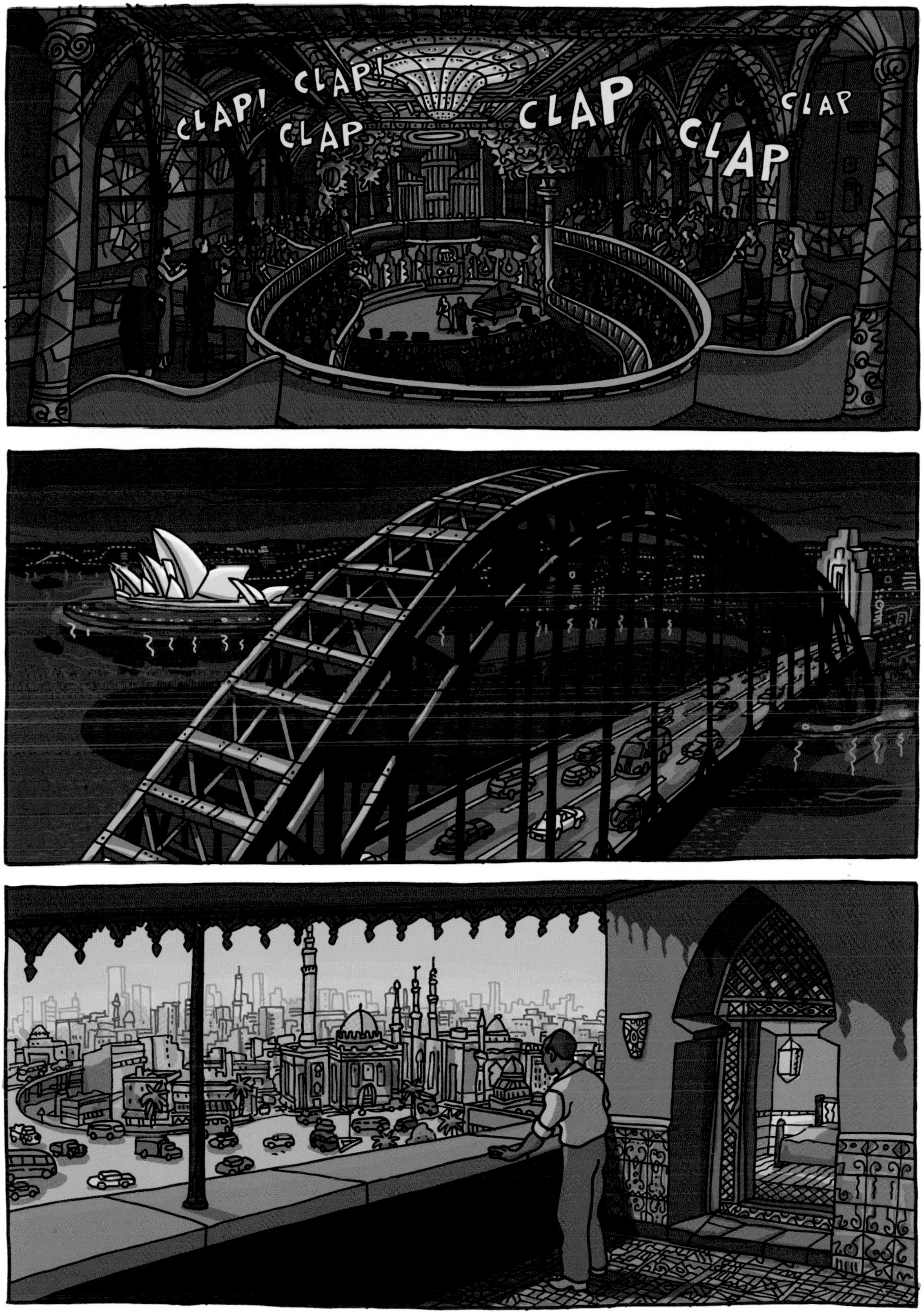
CLAP! CLAP!
CLAP
CLAP
CLAP
CLAP
CLAP

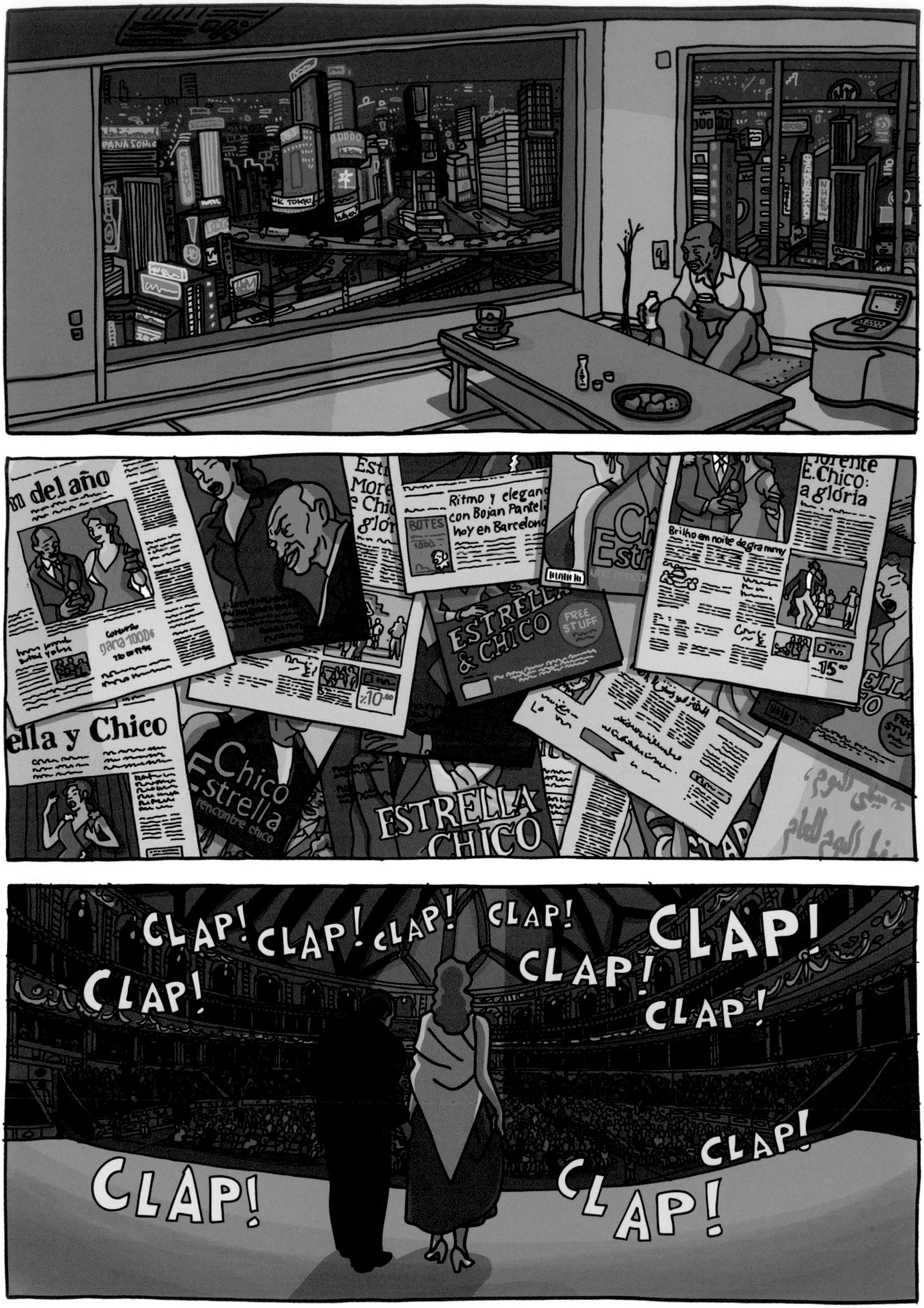
ESTRELLA & CHICO
FREE STUFF
ESTRELLA CHICO
CLAP! CLAP! CLAP! CLAP! CLAP!
CLAP!
CLAP!
CLAP!
CLAP!
CLAP!
CLAP!
CLAP!

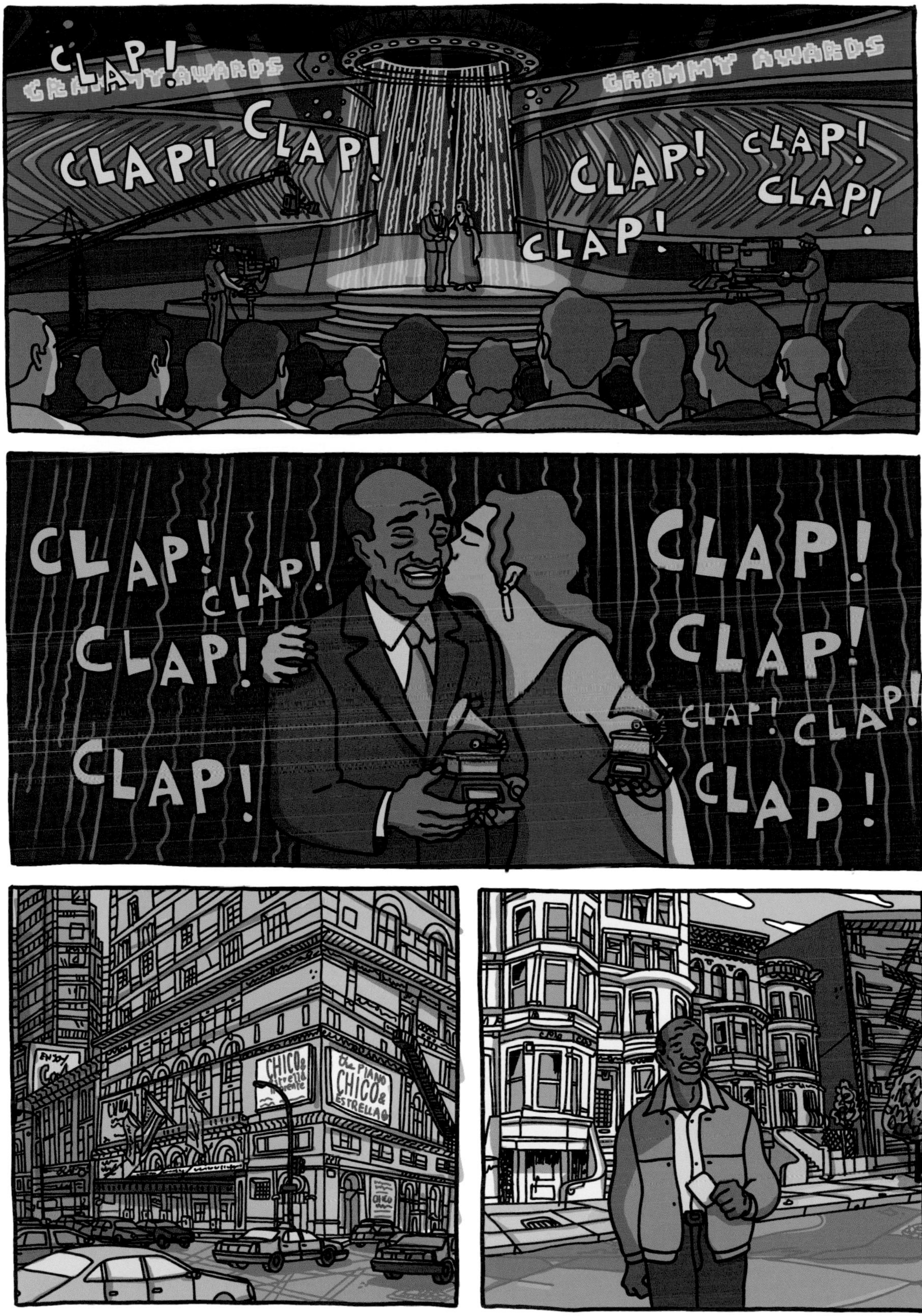
CLAP!
GRAMMY AWARDS
CLAP!
CLAP!
GRAMMY AWARDS
CLAP!
CLAP!
CLAP!
CLAP!
CLAP!
CLAP!
CLAP!
CLAP!
CLAP!
CLAP!
CLAP!
CLAP!
CLAP!
CLAP!
ENJOY
CHICO &
the PIANO
CHICO &
ESTRELLA

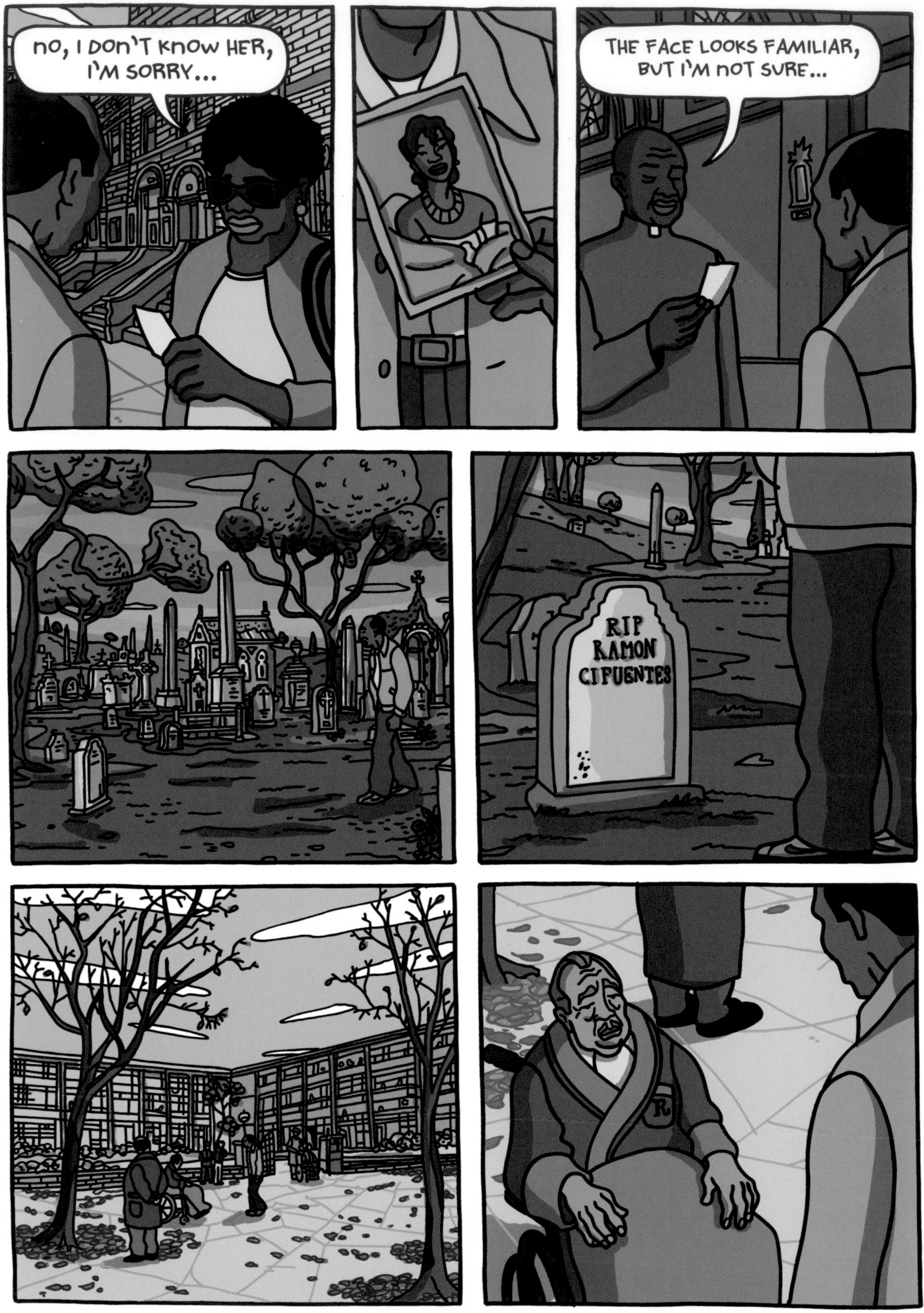
NO, I DON'T KNOW HER, I'M SORRY...
THE FACE LOOKS FAMILIAR, BUT I'M NOT SURE...
RIP RAMON CIFUENTES

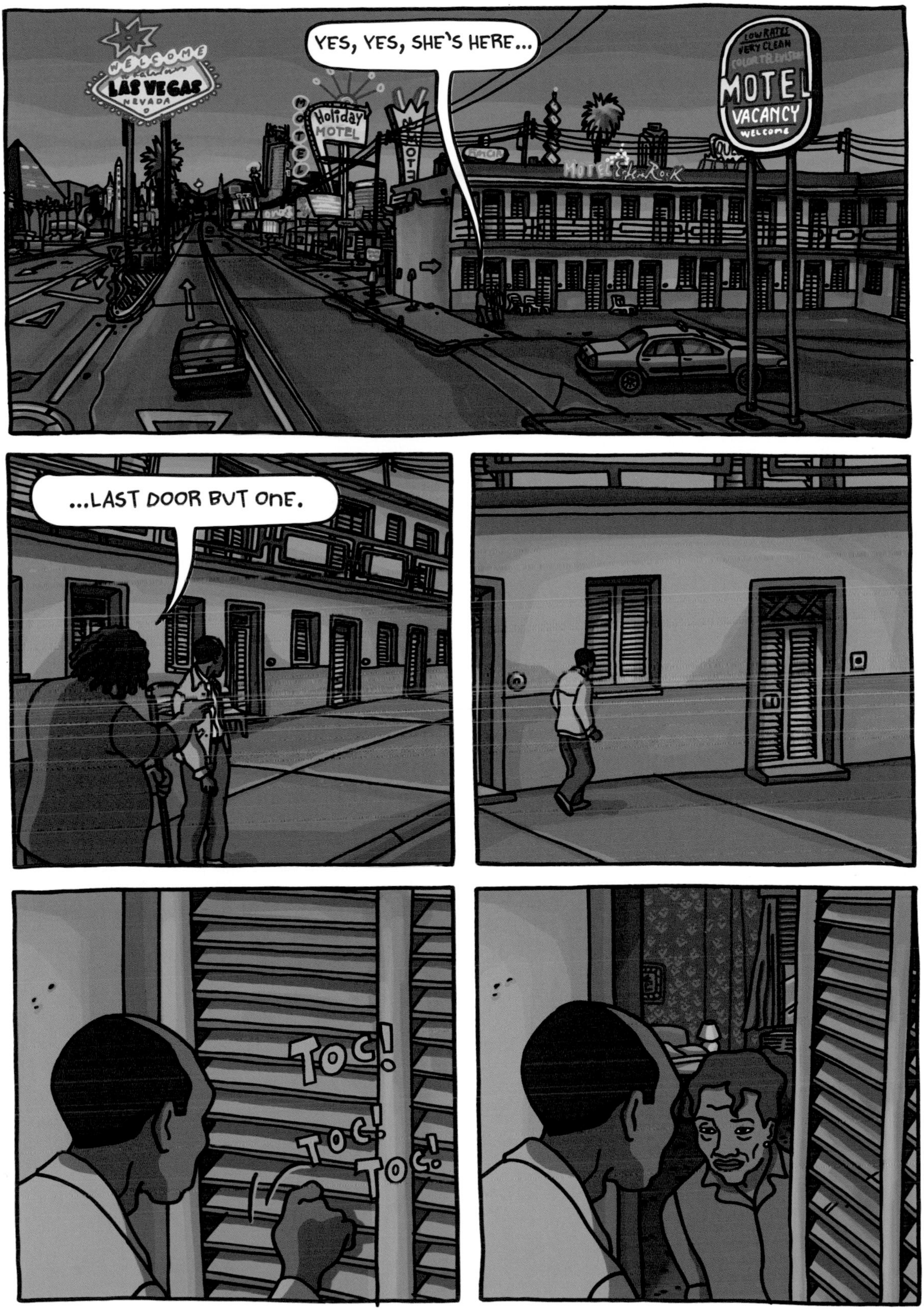
WELCOME
LAS VEGAS
NEVADA
Holiday MOTEL
MOTEL
YES, YES, SHE'S HERE...
LOW RATES
VERY CLEAN
MOTEL
VACANCY
WELCOME
...LAST DOOR BUT ONE.
TOC!
TOC!
TOC!

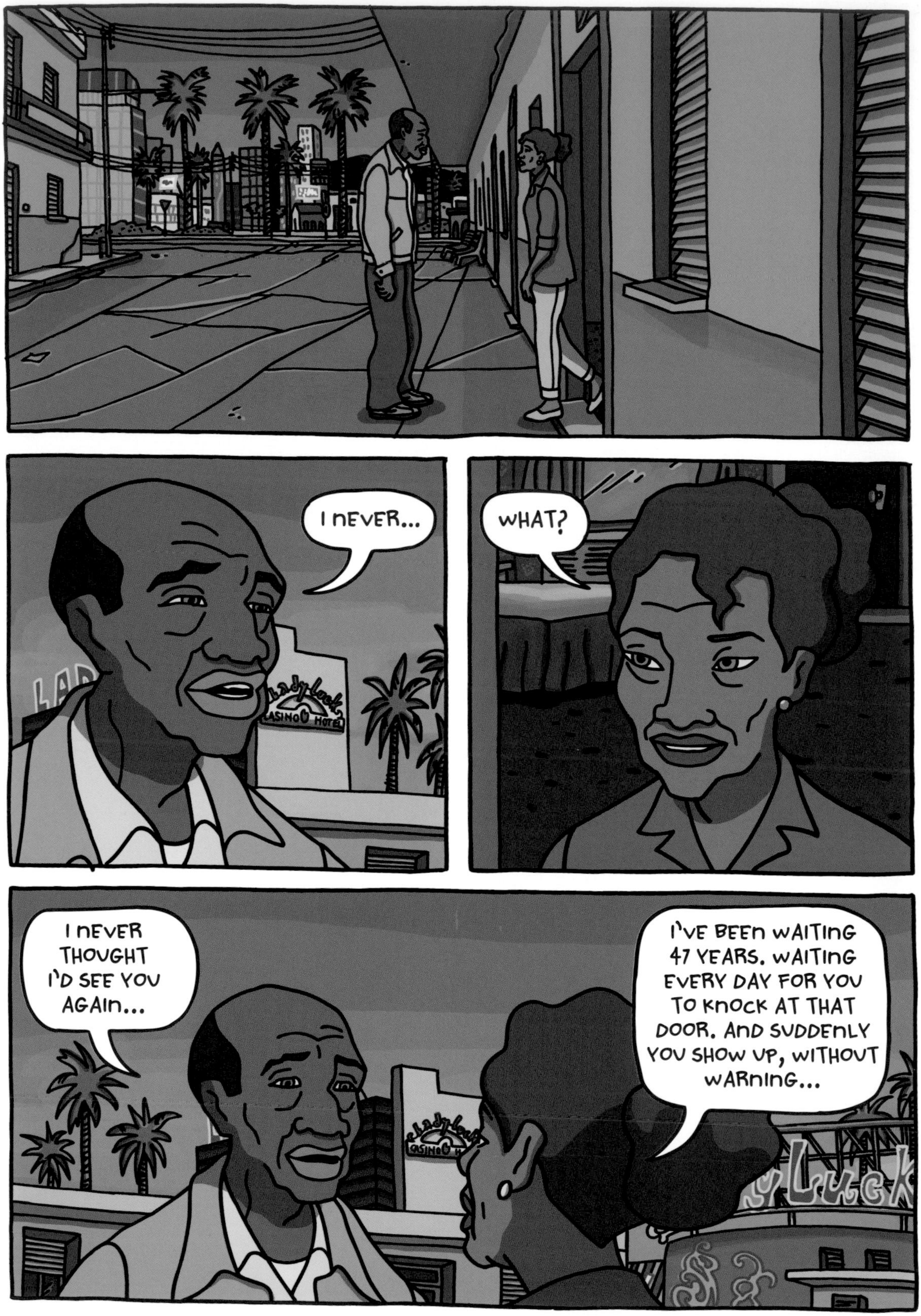
I NEVER...
WHAT?
I NEVER THOUGHT I'D SEE YOU AGAIN...
I'VE BEEN WAITING 47 YEARS. WAITING EVERY DAY FOR YOU TO KNOCK AT THAT DOOR. AND SUDDENLY YOU SHOW UP, WITHOUT WARNING...

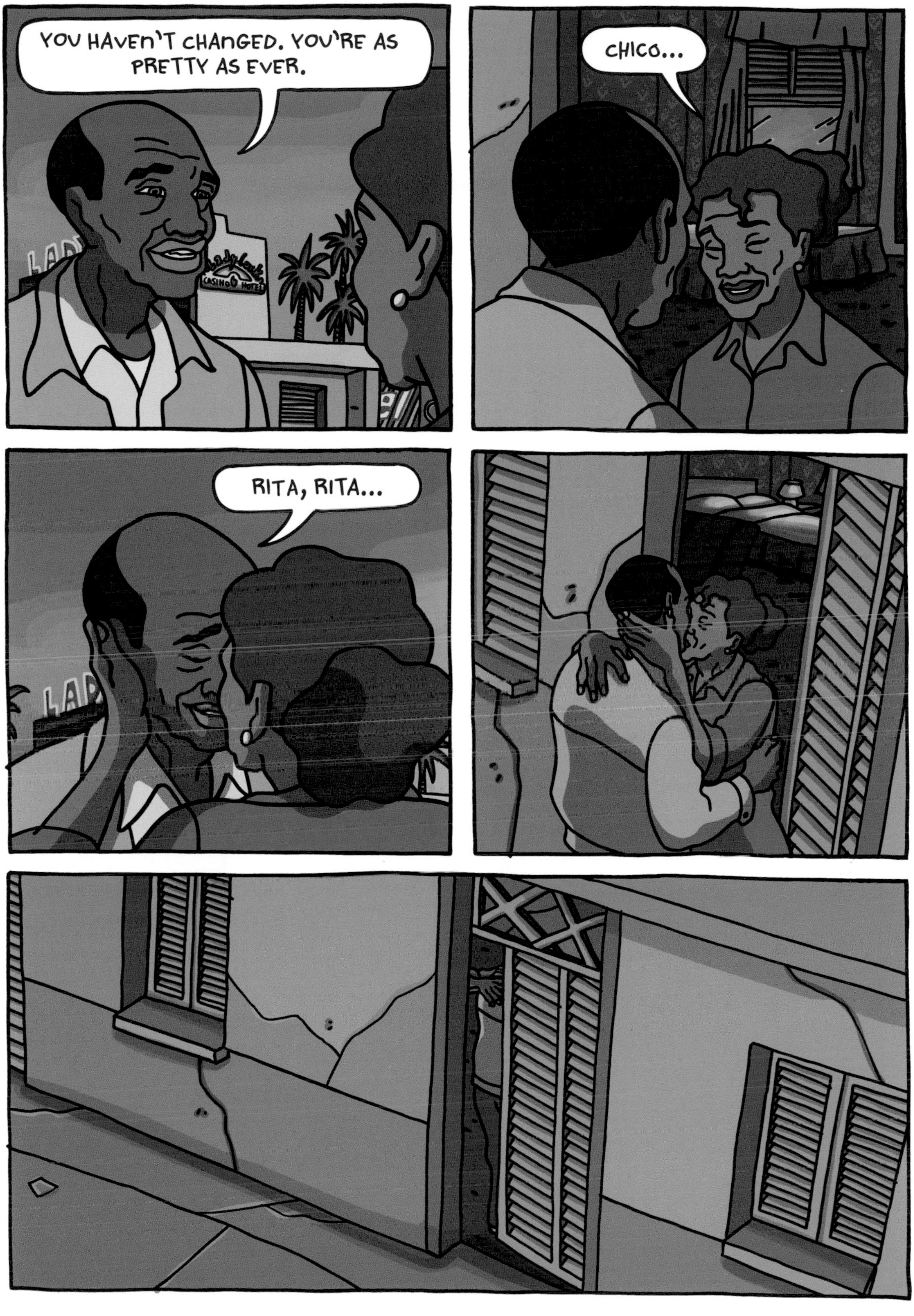
YOU HAVEN'T CHANGED. YOU'RE AS PRETTY AS EVER.
CHICO...
RITA, RITA...

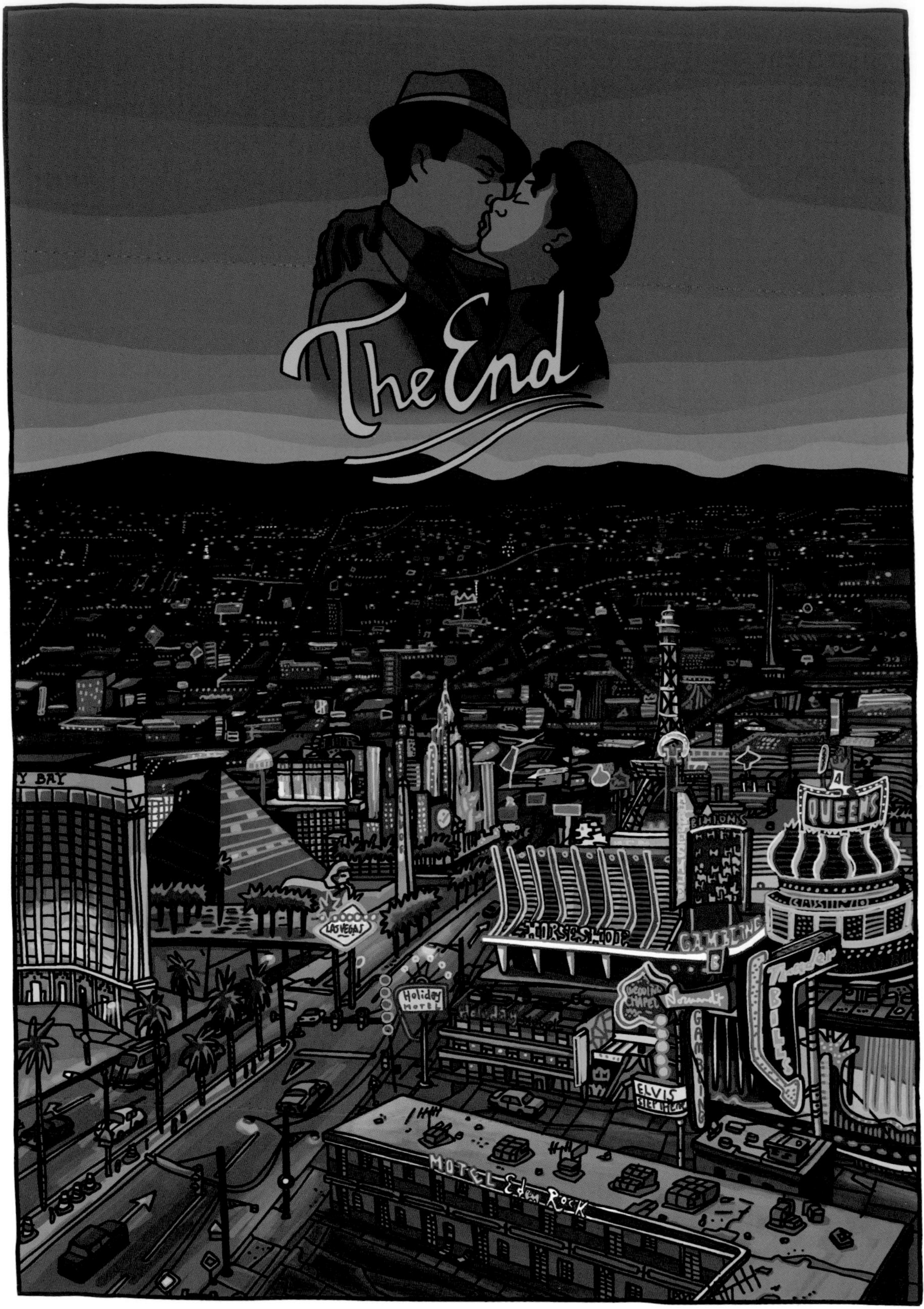
The End
LAS VEGAS
Holiday MOTEL
QUEENS
GAMBLING
ELVIS
MOTEL Eden Rock

Chico & Rita was born out of friendship, my good friendship with Chavi (Javier Mariscal), and my wish to work with him, to do something together.

When I was editing *Calle 54* I thought about who I'd like to design the poster, the album, the graphic look of the film. For me it couldn't be anyone else but Mariscal. So I called him and showed him the first cut of the movie, and he fell in love with it. That was the beginning of our friendship. To the rhythm of Latin jazz and Cuban music. Then came his sleeve designs for the discs issued by Calle 54 Records.

The dream remained: the dream of making a movie together, of seeing Mariscal's colours and lines come to life. One day I saw a music video made in his studio for Compay Segundo. Some of the backgrounds showed Old Havana as drawn by Mariscal. In a flash, the idea was born. We'd make a movie set in Cuba.

And obviously, it had to be a movie about music. The love story of two musicians, a singer and a pianist. It would also be the story of a great many Cuban musicians, from different generations, those who left and those who stayed.

And also the love story of two cities, Havana and New York. The city where Cuban music and jazz fused into something called Afro-Cuban jazz, Cubop, Latin jazz, or whatever you want to call it.

Now you're holding in your hands the book, the comic, graphic novel, whatever. And as was the case with his Garriris chair, here you also have a whole world, straight from the hand and eye of Mariscal, where, in the sunshine of Havana or the cold of New York, Picasso and Tintin dance to the rhythm of his lively pencil.

Fernando Trueba

Acknowledgements

Kiss Me Much (Besame Mucho)
Written by Consuelo Velazquez / English lyrics by Sunny Skylar
©1941 Promotora Hispano Americana De Musica, S.A. /
Peer International Corp., USA
Latin-American Music Pub. Co. Ltd., UK
Used by permission

Be True To Me (Sabor A Mi)
Written by Alvaro Carrillo / English lyrics by Mel Mitchell
©1959 Promotora Hispano Americana De Musica, S.A. /
Peer International Corp., USA
Latin-American Music Pub. Co. Ltd., UK
Used by permission

Love For Sale
Words and music by Cole Porter
©1930 (Renewed) WB MUSIC CORP.
Used by permission